Congress

Congress

A POLITICAL-ECONOMIC HISTORY
OF ROLL CALL VOTING

Keith T. Poole and Howard Rosenthal

OXFORD
UNIVERSITY PRESS

OXFORD
UNIVERSITY PRESS

Oxford   New York
Athens   Auckland   Bangkok   Bogotá   Buenos Aires   Calcutta
Cape Town   Chennai   Dar es Salaam   Delhi   Florence   Hong Kong   Istanbul
Karachi   Kuala Lumpur   Madrid   Melbourne   Mexico City   Mumbai
Nairobi   Paris   São Paulo   Shanghai   Singapore   Taipei   Tokyo   Toronto   Warsaw

and associated companies in
Berlin   Ibadan

Library of Congress Cataloging-in-Publication Data
Poole, Keith T.
Congress : a political-economic history of roll call voting /
Keith T. Poole and Howard Rosenthal.
    p.   cm.
Includes bibliographical references and index.
ISBN 0-19-505577-2; 0-19-514242-X (pbk)
1. United States. Congress—Voting—History   2. Ideology—United
States—History.   3. Pressure groups—United States—History.
I. Rosenthal, Howard, 1939–   .   II. Title.
JK1051 .P66   1997
328.73—dc20   96-395

9 8 7 6 5 4 3 2 1

Printed in the United States of America
on acid-free paper

for WILLIAM H. RIKER

teacher, friend, and colleague,

in memoriam

Preface

This book is dedicated to the memory of William H. Riker. Without Bill, political science would not have become a science in the late twentieth century, and, in particular, the research project discussed in this book would never have been initiated. As our work developed, we benefited from several discussions with Bill; indeed, the material on political realignment, covered in chapter 5, received an earlier, somewhat different treatment, in *Agenda Formation*, the last volume Bill was to edit.

Bill's vision led to the development of the best doctoral program in political science in the world. Twice, in the mid-1960s, he offered Rosenthal the opportunity to join the faculty at Rochester, but living in the arctic was not to be endured, even for the best of intellectual opportunities. Bill's influence was nonetheless transmitted through his magnificent 1962 book, *The Theory of Political Coalitions*. This work directed the early part of Rosenthal's career, sparking a series of essays on coalitions in Fourth Republic France. Coalitions are also important in this book, both through our concern with the relationship between party loyalty and the spatial voting model, and through our discussion of the realignment of the voting space, brought about—in line with Riker's Size Principle—by the overlarge Roosevelt coalition of the second New Deal.

In addition to writing *The Theory of Political Coalitions*, the seminal modern work on coalition behavior, Bill, jointly with Peter Ordeshook, a Rochester Ph.D. and our former colleague, wrote the seminal formal-theory essay on political participation. This work led directly to Rosenthal's lifelong interest in abstention—including his work with Subrata Sen on the "FY" vote in France, and his theoretical work with Thomas Palfrey—and to this book's final chapter, which deals with abstention on congressional roll calls.

Poole did brave the Rochester winters, as a graduate student in the mid-1970s. His thesis supervisor, Richard McKelvey, also a Rochester Ph.D., is perhaps the most outstanding scientist produced by Bill's program. Dick initiated Poole's interest in scaling methods. Dick, following Ordeshook, was lured to tropical Pittsburgh. Dick, Peter, and two other Carnegie Mellon colleagues, Otto Davis and Melvin Hinich, stimulated our quest for scaling methods that could be derived from the behavioral implications of the spatial model of choice. Of particular importance was an after-dinner conversation with Dick and Peter at Dick's house in Pittsburgh in the spring of 1977. Peter described his theory of the "basic space," which Poole realized was the key to linking Philip Converse's theory of constraint with the low-dimensional results that, even then, were coming out of early scaling studies of a variety of forms of voting data. One of these studies was by Lawrence Cahoon—a student of Mel's and Peter's—and his work was what stimulated both Peter and Mel to separately develop the theory that is the foundation of this book.

Dick was also, after his departure for Caltech, responsible for Poole's coming to Carnegie Mellon as a postdoctoral fellow in political economy and then joining the faculty.

Dick's work on the global intransitivity of majority rule, along with earlier work by Kenneth Arrow and Charles Plott, formed part of Bill's deep concern with the instability of political processes. He referred to politics as the "dismal science" because, unlike market institutions, which he saw as always tending toward equilibrium, strategic behavior in political institutions always led to disequilibrium. Bill's pessimistic view on politics versus economics developed not only before markets—via the new interest in speculative bubbles—looked less stable but also before important work by scholars such as Peter Coughlin and Shmuel Nitzan, John Ledyard, Craig Tovey, and McKelvey and Ordeshook themselves restored stability to majority voting models by putting realistic frictions in voting behavior or candidate actions. One such friction, probabilistic voting, is the basis for our empirical model.

This book only partially accords with Bill's pessimistic view. True, for two occasions—both before the Civil War—stable voting patterns break down entirely, and "chaos" results. But, for well over a century, the American political system, at least as seen in congressional roll call voting, has followed a relatively smooth path, smooth enough for the vast bulk of individual voting decisions to be captured via a very simple spatial model. In contrast, in his concern with instability, Bill sought examples of voting cycles in congressional roll calls. His examples, and those also discovered by yet another Rochester student, James Enelow, led to chapter 7 of this book. Our analysis of these examples in terms of the spatial model supports Bill's conclusions about the examples. On the other hand, we, on the basis of other evidence presented in chapter 7, view the examples as the rare exceptions that prove the rule of stable spatial voting. We are sure that, were Bill still with us, he would challenge our results in a way that would lead to new findings.

Acknowledgments

We have many other intellectual debts, particularly to former and present faculty members at Carnegie Mellon, including not only Davis, Hinich, McKelvey, and Ordeshook but also Alberto Alesina, Timothy Groseclose, Dennis Epple, John Londregan, Allan Meltzer, Thomas Palfrey, Thomas Romer, Fallaw Sowell, and Stephen Spear. They were joined, for briefer periods, by visitors and postdoctoral fellows, including David Austen-Smith, Randy Calvert, Peter Coughlin, Alex Cukierman, Lawrence Rothenberg, James Snyder, and Guido Tabellini. All provided valuable discussion, as did our student and collaborator, Nolan McCarty. Epple has suggested several additional experiments we could perform; someday we will get to them. Romer has written four essays with us, applying the results of the spatial analysis to the study of campaign contributions, regulation, economic-interest voting, and shirking. He also was directly responsible for our work on the computerized animation of our results. In addition, he reads the literature. Groseclose, Ordeshook, and Rothenberg read drafts of the book and provided valuable comments. Meltzer, through his Center for the Study of Political Economy, at Carnegie Mellon, provided financial support for the project.

We would also like to thank the two deans, Richard Cyert and Robert Kaplan, who hired us at Carnegie. Both were strong supporters of our careers. Both sought to make a business school an important center for basic social science, as well as an MBA mill.

We also received useful comments on parts of the book from our West Coast colleagues Rod Kiewiet, John Ferejohn, Morgan Kousser, Mathew McCubbins, Gary Cox, Gary Jacobson, Tom Gilligan, John Petrocik, Keith Krehbiel, and Barry Weingast; and from our European colleagues Erik Berglöf, Mathias Dewatripont, and Gerard Roland. Lance Davis, Claudia Goldin, and Gary Libecap pushed us to make our work relevant to economic historians. Gil Rosenthal, Jean-Laurent Rosenthal, Margherita Rosenthal, and Paula Scott contributed comments. Kathleen Much, of the Center for Advanced Study in the Behavioral Sciences, did an outstanding job of editing the manuscript.

The work of Kenneth Martis, of the Department of Geology and Geography at the University of West Virginia, has been extremely important to us. In his atlases, Martis has painstakingly assembled the data on congressional-district boundaries for all of American history. This work has led to the creation of the maps in our VOTEVIEW program, which allows one to see the geographic distribution of the vote on any roll call. Of equal importance, he has also definitively researched the political-party affiliation of members of Congress. His work is far superior to the codings that were done in a WPA project in the 1930s and that are contained in the data distributed by the Interuniversity Consortium for Political and Social Research (ICPSR). The Martis codings are used throughout this book and in VOTEVIEW.

We also need to thank those who helped us get the job done. Dave Seaman and Bill Whitson, of the Purdue University Computing Center, brought our work to supercomputing. Seaman tutored us in Cyber FORTRAN and provided the basic programming insights that led to an efficient program. Carol Goldburg helped us track down errors in the ICPSR data. Ezra Angrist did much of the coding of the congressional-district maps. We are especially grateful to two very talented undergraduate assistants: Douglas Skiba at Carnegie Mellon, who produced the basic PC animation program, ANIMATE, which he then used to provide the initial development of VOTEVIEW, and Boris Shor at Princeton, who produced VOTEVIEW for Windows.

Many administrators and secretaries were of assistance. We would just like to thank a few especially competent individuals. Joy Lee, a secretary like none before or after, worked at Carnegie in the mid-1980s. Larry Yuter and Tom Bielak, of the Graduate School of Industrial Administration (GSIA) computing group, kept our software and hardware humming. When we were no longer at the same university, Diane Price and Sandy Schmidt at Princeton had much to do with facilitating our collaboration.

In 1989–90, Rosenthal was a visiting professor of economics at MIT with a very reduced teaching load. It was then that we began writing this book. James Alt, Morris Fiorina, Paul Joskow, Kenneth Shepsle, Jean Tirole, and other participants in the Harvard-MIT political economy program were supportive colleagues during that year. Over the period 1991–93, five months in residence as a fellow at the International

Centre for Economic Research in Turin, Italy, provided additional valuable time for research. Two leaves of absence, in 1991–92 and 1995, were spent as a fellow at the Center for Advanced Study in the Behavioral Sciences and as a Brussels region fellow at the European Center for Applied Research in Economics at the Free University of Brussels, respectively. We thank these organizations, as well as Carnegie Mellon University and Princeton University, for support.

In 1992 and again in 1995, Poole spent two quarters at Caltech, where much work on this book was accomplished in a very intellectually stimulating and enjoyable environment. We thank Division Heads David Grether and John Ledyard and the amateur radio club of Caltech, W6UE, for their support.

Organization of the Book

In what we believe to be a Rikerian approach, this book is not a "history" in a conventional sense. Chapters 1 and 2 provide an essential overview and a basic model for what follows. Chapters 3, 4, and 5 are closest to a conventional history in that they provide a summary of the structure of congressional voting and discuss political realignment in American history; they are important background for subsequent chapters. The remaining chapters may all be read independently because, with one exception, they use historical data to investigate distinct theoretical questions. Chapter 6 compares ideological models of roll call voting to those based on constituencies' economic interests. Chapter 7 analyzes strategic voting; chapter 9 deals with how congressional committees affect the policy process; and chapter 10 deals with the rational-choice theory of turnout. Chapter 8, which deals with interest groups and political polarization, is the only chapter in the book that does not use data from the entire history of roll call voting. But it does develop a methodology that will allow many historical sources, such as newspaper editorials, to be incorporated in the framework we have used to analyze congressional behavior.

We should note that chapters 1 and 2 are entirely new. Chapter 2 attempts to explain scaling to a wide audience. Chapters 3, 4, and 5 draw heavily on essays by Poole and Rosenthal (1991a, 1991c, 1993a, and 1994b) but also contain a substantial amount of new material, including previously unpublished results in Poole and Rosenthal (1987b). Appendix B draws on Poole (1988); Poole, Sowell, and Spear (1992); and previously unpublished work in Poole and Spear (1992). Chapter 6 is a synthesis of our own work on economic models of voting, contained in Poole and Rosenthal (1985a, 1991b, 1993b, and 1994a); Poole and Romer (1993); and Romer and Rosenthal (1985); as well as a substantial amount of new material. Chapters 7, 8, 9, and 10 are entirely new.

In addition to our work on Congress, other scholars have begun to apply our methods to other voting bodies (DeBrock and Hendricks, 1996; Myagkov and Kiewiet, 1996; Rothenberg, 1994). Our scaled legislator positions have already been used in published work by Macdonald and Rabinowitz (1987); Cox and McCubbins (1993); Kiewiet and McCubbins (1991); Romer and Weingast (1991); and Rothenberg (1994).

We hope this book will have an audience among readers with general interests in the social sciences, including economics, history, and political science. Consequently, we have written this book for readers without technical training. We have included explanatory boxes for most of the mathematical and statistical concepts we use. The hard technical work is reserved for the appendices. The book should certainly be accessible to anyone who has completed even an introductory course in statistics.

Data and Programs

NOMINATE Programs

The W-NOMINATE program is available from our World Wide Web site at http://voteview.polsci.uh.edu. We will support W-NOMINATE and answer questions directed to kpoole@uh.edu. The D-NOMINATE program was written for the Cyber 205 Computer at the John Von Neumann Supercomputer Center at Princeton University; a copy of the source code is also available on the World Wide Web site. We do not support this program.

Data

The D-NOMINATE coordinates for members of the first 99 Congresses were developed with the support of the National Science Foundation. These, plus the spliced coordinates for the 100th Congress, are available on the World Wide Web site. W-NOMINATE coordinates for the first 104 Congresses are also available from the site. Coordinates for roll calls are available in the *.INF files on the site.

In the course of our research, we reformatted the ICPSR roll call codebooks and roll call voting data records in ASCII. These files (*.DTL and *.RCL) for the House of Representatives are available from the ICPSR as study number 9822, "U.S. Congressional Roll Coll Voting Records, 1789–1987: Reformatted Data."

VOTEVIEW and ANIMATE

The spatial maps and maps of the United States that are shown in this book are from the output of VOTEVIEW, a program we have developed wholly with internal funds provided by Carnegie Mellon and Princeton. ANIMATE is an animation of our dynamic model, which shows how legislator coordinates change throughout 200 years of history. It has interactive features for users. ANIMATE runs under DOS with EGA color graphics.

One version of VOTEVIEW also runs under DOS with EGA graphics. Another version, which requires at least a 486-33 machine with 8MB of memory, runs under Windows. It has many more features than VOTEVIEW for DOS. Questions about either program, suggestions for improvement, and bug reports can be sent to kp2a@andrew.cmu.edu. We intend to make future improvements only in the Windows version. Either version of VOTEVIEW provides access, through the *.INF files, to the D-NOMINATE coordinates.

Order forms and prices for either version of VOTEVIEW and ANIMATE can be obtained either from the World Wide Web site or by writing to Richard Schaeffer, financial officer, GSIA, Carnegie Mellon University (CMU), Pittsburgh, PA 15213. Proceeds from sales are used solely to defray costs of reproduction and of improvements in the program.

Contents

1 Introduction: The Liberal/Conservative Structure   3
2 The Spatial Model and Congressional Voting   11
3 The Spatial Model: Accuracy and Dimensionality   27
4 The Spatial Model: Stability, Replacement, and Polarization   58
5 Party Realignment in Congress   86
6 Issues, Constituency Interests, and the Basic Space   115
7 Sophisticated Voting and Agenda Manipulation   146
8 Roll Call Voting and Interest-Group Ratings   165
9 Committees and Roll Calls   184
10 Abstention from Roll Call Voting   210
11 The Unidimensional Congress   227
Appendix A: The NOMINATE Method of Estimating Spatial Models of Voting   233
Appendix B: The Dimensionality of Spatial Voting   252
Appendix C: Roll Call Coding Categories   259
Notes   263
References   281
Index   291

Congress

1
Introduction: The Liberal/Conservative Structure

Roll Call Voting and the Liberal/Conservative Continuum

"All politics are local," said Tip O'Neill, Speaker of the House from 1977 to 1987. If only because the Congress of the United States must amalgamate the diverse preferences of constituencies,[1] the task of finding a simple structure to explain how members of Congress vote when the roll is called might well be a hopeless one. Perhaps only detailed accounts of action on particular bills can fully capture the legislative process. But any science of politics must seek to find simple structures that organize this apparent complexity. We have developed a parsimonious model that accounts for the vast majority of the millions of individual roll call decisions during the 200 years of roll call voting in the House of Representatives and the Senate.

Aggregating the local loyalties of members of Congress into legislation is a matter of solving an institutional labyrinth replete with committees, subcommittees, and conference committees.[2] The outcomes reflect not only the preferences of the legislators themselves, but the pressures and appeals of countless staff members, lobbyists, and constituents. Moreover, activity in Congress will be responsive to the veto power of the president. One might expect chaotic rather than orderly behavior.[3]

When, on the other hand, local concerns give way to a disciplined two-party system, day-to-day roll call voting is devoid of interest. A stylized description of Great Britain, for example, would indicate that national elections create a parliamentary majority. Until the next elections, the winning party proposes legislation. The legislation is routinely approved by all members of the majority and opposed by all members of the minority.[4]

Such a model obviously doesn't work on our shores. President Reagan was able to enact his economic program in 1981, including a large tax cut and cuts in domestic spending, in spite of a divided government, with the Democrats being in the majority in the House of Representatives. Defections of "boll weevil" Democrats from the South eroded the majority.

It is tempting to resuscitate a model of pure party conflict by arguing that, at least for the last 50 years, the United States has really had a three-party system, with the Democrats split into northern and southern factions. In the three-party model, majorities would be formed by shifting alliances between two of the three parties. But this model doesn't work cleanly either. When the 1964 Civil Rights Act was passed, northern and southern Democrats took opposite sides. But, the Republican party also

3

split, with its more conservative members joining the southern Democrats. Similarly, throughout the 1830s and 1840s, slavery roll calls cut across parties, dividing North from South, rather than Whigs from Democrats.

More generally, roll calls typically split one or both of the parties. Why are there splits? Perhaps it is because American legislators are parochial—"all politics are local"—and because they are overwhelmingly responsive to the needs of their constituents and not responsive to national interests.[5] If so, for many issues, we would need an issue-specific economic model that specifies and measures constituency interests.[6] When a roll call involves a strong element of *geographic* distribution of resources, our simple structure may in fact fail to account for voting behavior. More typically, as we shall show in chapter 6, roll call voting is accounted for by the structure, and little is gained by attempting to enrich this accounting by introducing measures of the economic interests of constituencies.

Searching for the impact of specific economic interests may be, more fundamentally, fruitless because the legislative process is dynamic, with a vast set of issues being considered as time progresses. In a dynamic setting, rational actors may find it in their interest to coalesce and logroll (trade votes).

The linkage of commercial issues was nicely captured by Representative Hewitt (D-NY) during the debate on the Interstate Commerce Act in 1884:

> Men of business in New York despair of wise legislation upon these great commercial questions from this House. They have seen this House resist the resumption of specie payments. They have seen this House thrust the silver bill down the reluctant throats of an unwilling community; and now they behold this House and this side of it forcing reactionary measures upon the commerce of the country which will paralyze the business of the port which is the throat of the commerce of this country.[7]

In other words, Hewitt saw railroad-freight regulation as linked to previous votes on the gold standard and on a direct subsidy to the silver interests in Nevada. Each vote can thus reflect coalition behavior, as well as the apparent substance of the vote. "Anticommercial" interests are likely to stick together on a large set of bills. When such coalitions are stable, a parsimonious model that uses a simple structure may encapsulate the coalitions and give a better account of voting patterns than do attempts to deal with the substance of the roll call in isolation. In fact, we find that a model of flexible coalitions is typically far superior to models in the literature that use economic interests.

What simple structure permits flexible coalitions? Briefly, one in which legislators can be described by a continuum of positions. Although the continuum is an abstraction, it is convenient to use the word *ideology* as a shorthand code for these positions. Henceforth in this book, we use *ideology* as a shorthand in the sense intended by Converse (1964) in his seminal essay on belief systems. That is, voting is along ideological lines when positions are predictable across a wide set of issues. Someone who favors higher minimum wages is also likely to favor lower defense spending, affirmative action programs, higher capital-gains taxes, and so on. We can think of the continuum of ideological positions as ranging from the Left to the Right, or from very liberal to moderate to very conservative.

In contemporary America, this continuum is a perceived reality, a part of the common knowledge not only of the players on K Street and the Beltway but also of many ordinary citizens. Consider these six senators: Edward Kennedy (D-MA), Robert Byrd (D-WV), Sam Nunn (D-GA), Alphonse D'Amato (R-NY), Strom Thurmond (R-SC), and Jesse Helms (R-NC). American politics buffs would generally agree that the order given for these six is their appropriate liberal/conservative ordering. Our method of estimating the continuum allows us to provide interval-level measurements of positions, not only for the contemporary period but also for all Congresses, beginning with the first, which convened in 1789.[8] Moreover, we will show that this structure is a predominant feature of nearly all roll call voting.

We can represent most roll calls as splits along the continuum—everyone to one side of a critical point will vote one way and everyone to the other side will vote the opposite way. Which side wins depends on where the critical point is located. If it is to the left of the median of legislator locations, the conservatives get a majority. Conversely, if it is to the right, the liberals win. As the critical point shifts, coalitions shift. Coalitions are therefore flexible but they must conform to splits along the continuum.

The fact that most roll calls are splits implies that we can represent most votes as mappings of the issues onto the continuum—examples would be the level of the minimum wage; the extent to which assault weapons should be banned; and whether prayer, silent or vocal, should be permitted in schools. Consequently, nearly everything becomes a straight liberal/conservative issue.

Nonetheless, several caveats should be noted:

1. *The simple ideological structure of Congress does not lead to a predictive model for specific issues.* True, in the short term, one can predict votes with accuracy. For example, in Poole and Rosenthal (1991a), we show how the final vote on the confirmation of Robert Bork as a Supreme Court justice could have been forecast from the early announcements of members of the Senate Judiciary Committee. Indeed, divisive voting on Supreme Court nominations, when it occurs, fits very nicely into the structure. But to obtain medium- and long-term forecasts, one would need to model how issues *map* onto the structure. This book will not help one to understand why, sometime before Bork was rejected, a perhaps equally conservative nominee, Antonin Scalia, was confirmed by a 99-to-0 vote. The book's basic message is more limited: If issues do come to a vote, a mapping will tend to occur and make votes consistent with the structure.

2. *Just one continuum of positions may not be enough.* We may need two or more sets of positions to describe roll call voting behavior. Each underlying continuum is termed a dimension. For most of American history, the structure is indeed one-dimensional; at times a second dimension is an essential part of the picture. A second continuum was most important during two periods when the race issue was central to American politics. The first time was during the debate over slavery in the 1830s and 1840s. (By the 1850s the slavery issue had become so intense that at first, roll call voting patterns were chaotic rather than structured; later, patterns were restructured, with the slavery issue becoming the primary dimension.) The second occasion was the civil-rights controversy of the 1940s, 1950s, and 1960s. From the late 1970s onward, roll call voting again became largely a matter of positioning on a single, liberal/conservative dimension.

In addition to the substantive issue of race, party loyalty—ranging from strong loyalty to one party in the two-party system to strong loyalty to the other—could provide a basis for a second continuum of positions. Indeed, legislators might be viewed, on every vote, as trading off the implementation of their liberal/conservative preferences against the need to be loyal to their party coalition. In 1989, for example, Senate majority leader George Mitchell was able to defeat President Bush's proposed capital-gains tax cut by transforming a vote on an economic issue into a crucial test of party loyalty.

Undoubtedly, party loyalty is involved in our finding that a slightly better accounting of roll call votes is gained by using two dimensions, even in periods when the race issue is largely inactive. One's loyalty to the party, however, is hardly totally independent of one's liberal/conservative position. Indeed, for most of American history, parties have defined clusters on the first dimension—which, at some risk of oversimplification, basically represents conflict over economic redistribution. Nonetheless, the clusters are just clusters rather than permanently jelled voting blocs. Some degree of intraparty diversity has always been tolerated in Congress. In the contemporary Congress, there will be some issues, such as the 1981 tax bill, on which moderate Democrats vote with Republicans; and there will be others, such as the 1991 civil-rights bill, where moderate Republicans vote with Democrats. On those occasions when whips and leaders enforce party discipline, the roll call split will occur at the point on the first dimension that most clearly divides Democrats from Republicans.

3. *Our method for finding the dimensions is blind both to the party affiliation of the legislator and to the substance of the roll call vote.* The simple structure we find is an abstraction. The fact that a simple abstraction accounts for the data suggests that, although there is some flexibility involved in forming coalitions, coalition formation is constrained. Parties are obviously an important constraining influence.[9] We observe not only clustering of legislators by party but also clustering of roll calls by the vote's substance. Although these clusters enable us to interpret the results, the basic finding is that a simple abstract model accounts for the data.

4. *Voting may appear as splits along a continuum even on bills that represent packages dealing with a multitude of policy areas.* On these bills, substantial vote trading or vote buying may have taken place. For example, President Reagan obtained the defection of the "boll weevils" in exchange for subsidies to Louisiana sugar producers that ought to have been anathema to the free-market credo of his administration. Yet when all the deals are done, roll call voting respects the continuum. If votes are in fact bought on an issue, the buyers will seek legislators with a low price. These should be legislators who are indifferent, or nearly indifferent, on the issue—that is, legislators who would be close to the point that would separate Yea voters from Nays if there were no vote buying.[10] So vote buying is more likely to move the separating point than to create a chaotic pattern of voting. Similarly, even on issues in which a specific constituency interest could cause a legislator to deviate from his usual voting patterns, the legislator must be sure that the deviation is correctly perceived by constituents. Otherwise, the legislator's reputation may be better served by voting with people that the legislator usually votes with.

5. *Voting may not appear as splits along the continuum if legislators are behaving strategically with respect to the agenda represented by a sequence of amendments to a bill.* For example, conservatives might act strategically by voting with the liberals and against the moderates. Suppose a bill looked too liberal to be likely to win passage, and that an attempt was made to moderate the bill by introducing a "saving" amendment. If the amendment were passed, it, rather than the original bill, would be

voted on against the status quo. Conservatives who would like to see the status quo preserved might cast a strategic vote *against* the amendment, even though they would prefer a more moderate bill to a very liberal one. But, as we explain in the next chapter, as long as legislators know each other's preferences and the agenda, both ends voting against the middle and other deviant voting patterns should not occur. In our example, the reason is that the liberals will not be fooled by the tactics of the conservatives. They, too, will act strategically and vote *for* the amendment, even though they truly prefer the original bill. Thus even when legislators act strategically, the roll call will still engender a split along the continuum.

6. *The structure will not be perfect.* As in almost any social-science endeavor, allowances must be made for errors. We allow for errors via a probabilistic model of voting. Legislators who are very close to the critical point on a roll call are almost as likely to vote Yea as they are to vote Nay, whereas legislators who are very far from the critical point are highly predictable. Thus, on a roll call that was close to a 50–50 vote in the Senate, we would be very surprised if Kennedy voted on the conservative side or Helms on the liberal side. Overall, the structure will be useful only if we can find critical points on each roll call that yield very few errors.

When we seek the critical point on each roll call, however, we do not aim to minimize the number of legislators incorrectly classified—those on the liberal side of the point who vote conservative, and vice versa. Rather, roughly speaking, we pick the point to minimize errors which are weighted by distance from the point. This seems natural; a vote by Ernest Hollings (D-SC) to support the Bork nomination was a less serious error than a Kennedy vote to confirm would have been. When we estimate positions of the legislators and the critical points (or cutting lines if there are two dimensions), we, in fact, find that voting errors are overwhelmingly concentrated among legislators whose positions are close to the point. This pattern of errors would not hold if, in contrast, both ends frequently voted against the middle, because extremists were either voting together for strategic reasons or simply expressing their distaste for the winning motion. This pattern of errors is an important element of support for our model of simple structure.

The Dynamics of the Structure of Roll Call Voting

Finding a liberal/conservative structure of roll call voting at any moment in time would be interesting, but our effort is more ambitious. We study the dynamics of the structure. Exploring dynamics will allow us to examine many interesting questions, including:

- Is the voting continuum stable? In the professional jargon of political science, do major "realignments" occur at critical times in American history—the collapse of Federalism and the advent of Jacksonian democracy; the Civil War; the 1890s; the Great Depression? In contrast to some earlier literature, we find remarkable stability since the Civil War, with the only perturbation being the emergence of the civil-rights continuum in the 1940s.
- Are individual senators and representatives stable in their positions on the continuum? Again, we find remarkable and increasing stability. At least in this cen-

tury, the relative order on the continuum barely changes. Members of Congress come to Washington with a staked-out position on the continuum, and then, largely "die with their ideological boots on." In particular, they do not alter their behavior and "shirk" just before they retire.

• Is the range of political conflict, the length of the continuum, changing? We find a gradual condensing of the continuum in the past century, a diminishing of conflict. During this same period, the amount of *intra*party diversity has remained roughly constant. The shortening of the continuum is due almost entirely to a reduction in the separation of the two parties. Since the mid-1970s, this long-term trend has reversed, and the parties have polarized. Their differences, albeit still slight in comparison to the situation at the turn of the century, have widened dramatically.

A Look at the Rest of the Book

The second chapter of this book presents the details of our dynamic model of the structure of roll call voting and discusses how we estimated the model. The rest of the book is concerned with substantive insights drawn from the estimation results.

In chapter 3, we first discuss the overall fit of the model—we find that a two-dimensional model, with a simple linear time trend in legislator positions, is the best fit to the roll call record. We then turn to a discussion of the issue content of the two dimensions over time. We end the chapter with a discussion of a variety of sets of supporting evidence for our finding of low dimensionality.

This finding of low dimensionality initially generated widespread disbelief. In 1985, our working paper, "The Unidimensional Congress," provoked both our political-science colleagues, many of whom have studied the intricate inner workings of the Hill, and our economics colleagues, many of whom have been struck by the complex web of economic interests that seek to influence legislation. Indeed, Van Doren (1990) has argued that roll call voting is only a small part of the congressional process, and that most issues are screened out without reaching the floor. Snyder (1992b) has formalized this argument in a model of committee gatekeeping. Koford (1989, 1991, 1994) presented a series of methodological arguments against the finding of low dimensionality. Our discussion of low dimensionality in chapter 3 replies to these arguments.[11]

In chapter 4, we discuss the stability of our estimated coordinates. We find that after the Civil War, legislators are very stable in their estimated coordinates. Spatial movement in our dynamic model was never extensive in relation to the span of the space, and it declined steadily after the Civil War, except for some slight upturns during the realignment of the 1890s and during the late 1930s. We find that changes in congressional voting patterns occur almost entirely through the process of replacement of retiring or defeated legislators. During the New Deal, these replacements among the northern Democrats had the effect of moving the Democratic party sharply to the Left. In effect, legislators elected during the early stages of the New Deal were willing to have the federal government become much more active in managing the economy. This was also true, to some extent, of Republicans who became more liberal from roughly the onset of the Depression until the middle of the Nixon presidency. The liberal trend among Republicans was countered, beginning with the second New Deal, by a conservative trend among southern Democrats. The result was a reduction in the polarization of the two parties. In the past two decades, however, new Republican cohorts have been increasingly conservative and southern Democrats increasingly liberal, leading to an increase in polarization.

In chapter 5, we cover political realignment by examining two episodes, both in the antebellum era, when the model breaks down entirely; and two other episodes, both involving race, when a second continuum must be brought into play. These episodes all center on major changes in the party system: the collapse of the Federalists; the collapse of the Whigs; and the split, in the mid-twentieth century, between northern and southern Democrats. We also indicate why we do not regard 1896 and 1932, two dates that are commonly thought of as denoting realignments, as dates that correspond to realignments in the structure of roll call voting.

Our discussion of issues continues in chapter 6. We argue that the presence of spatial voting is not inconsistent with voting on the basis of economic interests. Economic interests, although difficult to measure, arguably have an important influence. Even so, we show, through several case studies, that members of Congress often express these interests strategically by logrolling—that is, trading votes across issues. This logrolling can be implicit or explicit, but the essential point is that various interests are packaged. This packaging tends to produce only a few dimensions of voting. We examine five issues in detail: the interstate-commerce legislation of the 1870s and 1880s; the minimum wage; food stamps; occupational safety; and strip mining.

We also show in chapter 6 that economic interests cannot be viewed as those of a representative, or pivotal, voter in each constituency. Our simple analysis demonstrates that, even if economic interests were perfectly measured, pivotal-voter models would fail as models of congressional voting.

Although chapter 6 argues that simple models of voting on economic interests are poor alternatives to the spatial model of voting, the chapter indicates that economic interests can enter into the process that maps issues into a low-dimensional spatial model. As a result, the mapping between quantitative issues and the space can shift in time. We illustrate this point by examining minimum-wage legislation, and legislation on inspection of firms by the Occupational Safety and Health Administration (OSHA).

In chapter 7, we study amendment voting and agendas. We examine the rare episodes of strategic voting that have been noted in the literature and study the performance of our model in these cases.

Chapter 8 ties our analysis of roll call voting to the ratings of members of Congress that are published by interest groups such as the Americans for Democratic Action (ADA), the Chamber of Commerce of the United States (CCUS), and the National Farmers Organization (NFO). We treat the interest groups as voters and use their "votes" to place the House and Senate in a common framework. The results confirm our earlier analysis. But the analysis also reveals a substantive message: The interest groups turn out to be more polarized than the legislators. Liberal and conservative groups are pulling at both ends, contributing to the polarization of politicians.

In chapter 9, we explore the representativeness of congressional committees. Our major finding is that, particularly before 1947, committees are seen as representative of the full chamber. Few committees are dominated by extreme conservatives or extreme liberals. But the evidence also shows that committees are likely to be information specialists in their oversight areas and to have common interests in these areas. Committee members vote together more often than would be expected from their party positions and liberal/conservative positions.

Chapter 10 looks at turnout. In recent years, abstention, particularly after paired and announced votes are considered, is not an important aspect of voting in Congress. Historically, however, participation rates were far lower. The global increase in turnout rates reflects better transportation and better health. At all times, abstention has also reflected preferences and strategy. Indifferent voters near the critical dividing points on roll calls tend to abstain. In the modern House, voters on the majority side of a roll call tend to be more silent than those on the minority side.

Finding a simple structure that accounts for roll call voting is, from a scientific viewpoint, merely a beginning. Future research will need to ask what produces a stable structure and how specific issues map into the structure. We conclude, therefore, in chapter 11, with a summary directed at focusing future research on roll call voting and tying the analysis of roll call voting to the study of the larger legislative process. This final chapter also contains an epilogue which brings our analysis up-to-date.

2

The Spatial Model and Congressional Voting

The Constraint Hypothesis

Congress both considers a wide variety of substantive issues and represents the diverse constituencies of 435 congressional districts and 50 states. If we succeed in accounting for individual roll call decisions with a parsimonious model, it follows that considerable constraint operates across issues.[1]

The presence of constraint is evident in the everyday language used to discuss politics. Expressions such as "liberal," "moderate," and "conservative" are part of the common language used to denote the political orientation of a member of Congress; such labels are useful because they furnish a rough guide to the positions a politician is likely to take on a wide variety of issues. A contemporary liberal, for example, is likely to support an increase in the minimum wage; oppose a reduction in the capital-gains tax; oppose the use of military force abroad; oppose further funds for Star Wars; support mandatory affirmative action programs; and support federal funding of health care and day care programs. Indeed, just knowing that a politician opposes increasing the minimum wage is enough information to predict, with a fair degree of reliability, the politician's views on many seemingly unrelated issues.

To illustrate how constraint relates to roll call voting, consider some well-known members of the 101st Senate. Practitioners and observers of American politics will readily agree that John Kerry (D-MA) is an extreme liberal; Albert Gore (D-TN) is a liberal near the center of his party; Sam Nunn (D-GA) is a moderate; Robert Dole (R-KS) is a conservative near the center of his party; and Jesse Helms (R-NC) is an extreme conservative. In other words, we can line up these gentlemen, from left to right, as below.

Liberal   Kerry   Gore   Nunn   Dole   Helms   **Conservative**

If roll call voting is constrained to satisfy a single liberal/conservative dimension, we ought to observe only the following voting patterns:

Unanimous agreement
Kerry against everyone else
Kerry and Gore against Nunn, Dole, and Helms
Kerry, Gore, and Nunn against Dole and Helms
Helms against everyone else

11

Other possible patterns are ruled out. For example, Kerry and Helms cannot combine against the middle. No one in Washington expects to see this happen, except in very unusual circumstances. The cartoon reproduced as figure 2.1 is amusing because it depicts a rare agreement. To see if roll call voting fits the expected pattern, we can look at every roll call to see if one of the allowable voting patterns holds. For example, of the five senators cited above, only Kerry supported the Leahy amendment on September 26, 1989, which would have cut funding for the B-2 bomber; only Kerry and Gore opposed the Robb amendment, on July 20, 1989, giving the president authority to pursue funding for non-Communist forces in Cambodia; only Dole and Helms voted to confirm John Tower as secretary of defense on March 9, 1989; and everyone else rejected Helms's May 2, 1989, amendment to remove funding for the commission established for Martin Luther King, Jr., day. Of course, all five voted together on noncontroversial measures, such as confirming James Baker as secretary of state. Omitting the uninteresting unanimous vote, we can then simultaneously order these roll calls and the senators as follows:

Kerry   *B-2 bomber*   Gore   *Cambodia*   Nunn   *Tower*   Dole   *MLK, Jr.*   Helms

The basic implication of the constraint hypothesis is that all issues tend to be mapped onto a fixed ordering, or placement, of legislators.[2] This fixed ordering can be thought of as the underlying, "basic" or "predictive," dimension.[3]

In this book, we represent the positions of legislators not just by a simple ordering but by an interval scale, like the Fahrenheit temperature scale. Thus each legislator has a position that can be described by a number. The number represents the legislator's ideal point—his preferred level of conservatism that he would like to see in any issue that is voted on. Moreover, the legislator's preferences along the dimension are (for methodological reasons that we discuss in appendix A) assumed to be single-peaked and symmetric, as illustrated by figure 2.2. *Single-peaked* means

Figure 2.1. An extreme liberal, John Kerry (D-MA), and an extreme conservative, Jesse Helms (R-NC), have a rare agreement. Copyright 1989, Boston Globe; distributed by Los Angeles Times Syndicate. Reprinted by permission.

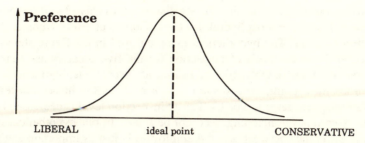

Figure 2.2. Single-peaked preference on the underlying dimension. The ideal point represents the point of highest preference. Positions more liberal or more conservative than the ideal point are less preferred.

that as the policy moves further away from the ideal point in either direction—either more liberal or more conservative—the legislator is worse off. *Symmetric* means that the legislator is indifferent between two policies that are equidistant from the ideal point.

To order an issue along the underlying dimension as well, we need a mapping between policy outcomes and the underlying dimension. To take an example drawn from the actual roll call votes that we analyze in chapter 6, consider legislation specifying which firms will be subject to inspection by the Occupational Safety and Health Administration (OSHA). Firms with more than a legislated number of employees will be subject to inspection; smaller firms will be exempt. Presumably, the liberal pole (here defined as maximum government intervention in the market, with all firms being inspected) of the mapping is anchored by zero employees—all firms are inspected—whereas the conservative end (no inspections) is anchored by firms with an unlimited number of employees. Figure 2.3 shows a mapping and the hypothetical preferences of the five senators cited.

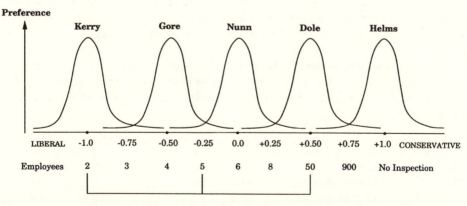

Figure 2.3. Five senators and the mapping of the OSHA inspection issue. All five have single-peaked preferences. The more conservative senators desire higher firm-size limits on inspection. The midpoint between the mapped position of two policies determines voting behavior. Senators with ideal points to the left of the midpoint vote for the lower inspection level; those to the right vote for the higher level.

We have created figure 2.3 so that the legislators are evenly placed on the underlying dimension. Kerry, the most liberal, is at −1; Gore is at −0.5; Nunn at 0; Dole at +0.5; and Helms at +1. The hypothetical mapping used in the figure shows that the most preferred firm-size levels of inspection for the five senators are Kerry, 2 employees; Gore, 4; Nunn, 6; Dole, 50; and Helms, no inspections. For inspection levels higher than his ideal point, each senator is worse off as the inspection level is increased. Similarly, a senator is worse off as an inspection level is decreased below his ideal point. Note that the mapping need not be linear. In our hypothetical mapping, the firm-size difference between 2 and 4 employees is just as important as the difference between 6 and 50.

In this book, we assume that for every roll call vote, legislators vote as if they were voting *sincerely* on a mapping of the Yea and Nay outcomes. That is, a legislator votes for the alternative that is closer to his ideal point.[4] There is a simple rule for deciding which is closer. Just average the mapped positions of the Yea and Nay outcomes. The average is the roll call midpoint. The midpoint represents the critical point discussed previously. If the Yea outcome is to the left of the midpoint, the Yea voters are all the legislators with ideal points to the left of the midpoint. The other legislators vote Nay.

To illustrate, suppose a committee reported a bill that permitted inspection of firms with at least 50 employees, Dole's ideal point; and suppose Kerry proposed his ideal point, 2 employees, as an amendment. The mapped position of the bill is 0.5; of the amendment, −1. The midpoint is $(0.5 +(−1))/2 =−0.25$, so only Kerry and Gore support the amendment. (See figure 2.3.)

If the status quo were no inspection, Helms would be expected to oppose any departure from the status quo, but all the other senators might support some form of an inspection program. If the inspection bill were voted on with an "open" rule (where all amendments are freely entertained), the outcome would be expected to be Nunn's ideal point of 6; 6 will beat any other level in a pairwise vote.[5]

If, on the other hand, someone could force a take it-or-leave-it, "closed" vote on a proposal against the status quo, an inspection level lower than a firm size of 6 could be passed.[6] From figure 2.3, we see that, since Nunn prefers Gore's ideal point of 4 employees to no inspection, if Gore could force a take-it-or-leave-it vote, an inspection level of 4 employees would win by a 3–2 vote, with Kerry, Gore, and Nunn prevailing over Dole and Helms. The mapping midpoint of 4 versus no inspection is +0.25.

For the constraint hypothesis to hold, one must be able to map most issues onto the underlying dimension. Thus, if we consider the minimum-wage rate, the capital-gains tax rate, and OSHA as issues, the mapped ideal points might be similar to the following diagram:

		Kerry	Gore	Nunn	Dole	Helms
Mapped	⌈ OSHA	2	4	6	50	No inspection
Ideal	⎨ Minimum wage	$8	$6	$5	$4	$0
Points	⌊ Capital-gains tax	60%	33%	20%	10%	0%

Of course, not all issues are as readily quantified as OSHA inspections, the minimum wage, and the capital-gains tax. For example, the Cambodia funding issue from 1989 might involve a combination of policies. Which of the contending factions should receive support? Should they receive just humanitarian aid or military aid as well? What types of weapons should be delivered? Indeed, our quantitative examples must be similarly qualified. Minimum-wage bills, for example, also specify which occupations are covered, whether teenagers are covered, and so on. Even for issues with complex alternatives, however, we maintain the constraint hypothesis: The roll call alternatives map onto the underlying dimension.

Why Constraint May Operate in the Presence of Strategic Behavior

It would be naive, however, to expect that members of Congress will always vote sincerely. One possibility is that they logroll; that is, members trade votes over issues. Even if preferences all mapped onto a single dimension, vote trading might result in voting patterns that contradicted a unidimensional model.

If we voted on the minimum wage and a capital-gains tax, for example, sincere voting, with an open agenda, would lead to Nunn's ideal point of a $5 minimum wage and a 20 percent tax rate. But what if Helms cared a great deal about the capital-gains tax and very little about the minimum wage, whereas Kerry cared a great deal about the minimum wage and little about taxes? Then Helms might agree to support a $6 minimum wage in return for Kerry's supporting a 10% capital-gains tax. The minimum-wage bill would be passed with the votes of Kerry, Gore, and Helms, and the tax bill would pass with the votes of Kerry, Dole, and Helms.[7] Although a Kerry-Helms trade is possible, such a trade would be highly unexpected and therefore highly publicized. Even if the trade were beneficial to constituents, the constituents might not process the relatively complex information correctly. If constituents are mainly sensitive to consistent voting patterns along the predictive dimension, Kerry and Helms may find such trades ill-advised.

More likely trades simply involve changing the mapping. What if the Democratic leadership promised Nunn that a committee would act favorably on another matter of interest to Nunn, if he would oppose any lowering of the capital-gains tax from a status quo rate of 28 percent? Then Nunn would vote with Kerry and Gore on the issue (rather than with Dole and Helms), but this strategic vote would still be consistent with a unidimensional voting pattern.

Moreover, if legislators, perhaps as a result of being concerned about establishing a reputation for consistency, seek to sustain a pattern of unidimensional voting, vote trading may allow observations of roll call votes to appear as if they were preferences mapped onto an underlying dimension even when true preferences have a far more complex pattern. Consider the following hypothetical scrambling of the original preferences:

Issue with Ideal Points	Kerry	Gore	Nunn	Dole	Helms
OSHA	6	4	2	50	No inspection
Minimum wage	$4	$6	$8	$0	$5
Capital-gains tax	0%	33%	20%	10%	60%

Say the status quo on OSHA was firms with 50 employees. Then with an open agenda, 6 employees would prevail. Kerry, Gore, and Nunn would prevail over Helms and Dole under sincere voting. If $3.35 were the status quo on the minimum wage, $5 would prevail, with only Dole and Kerry being opposed. If the capital-gains tax were 28 percent, 20 percent would prevail, with Gore and Helms in the minority.

Say, too, that Helms cared nearly exclusively about capital gains, Nunn about the minimum wage, and Dole about OSHA inspections. The three senators make a trade: They agree to enact, for each issue, the ideal point of the senator who cares. Kerry and Gore continue to vote sincerely. So the outcomes are 50 employees on OSHA, an $8 minimum wage, and a 60 percent capital-gains tax. The parties to the deal—Nunn, Dole, and Helms—would oppose any attempts by Kerry or Gore to have tighter OSHA enforcement. Only Kerry would vote against a proposal to move the minimum wage from $3.35 to $8, and only Kerry and Gore would oppose the attempt to raise the capital-gains tax. So any votes would still be consistent with a mapping onto an underlying dimension in which the ordering of legislators was Kerry-Gore-Nunn-Dole-Helms. In sum, logrolling does not necessarily render the notion of constraint inoperative and may in fact contribute to a strengthening of the operation of constraint. Logrolling is one form of *strategic* voting. In seeking to further their own interests or those of their constituents, strategic voters may not vote for the closer of the two alternatives on a roll call. Strategic behavior may also occur when voting on a bill is preceded by voting on one or more amendments. Strategic voting on amendments, however, does not necessarily invalidate the model's hypothesis that all votes can be treated as sincere votes. We illustrate this point with House action on the Common Situs Picketing Bill in 1977.[8]

Common Situs was a pro-labor bill which would allow a single union to shut down an entire construction site or other business operation. As it appeared likely that the strongly pro-labor bill reported out of committee would fail, Representative Ronald Sarasin introduced a "saving" amendment. The Sarasin amendment was designed to temper provisions of the bill, making it more appealing to moderates. That is, denoting the mapped location of the bill as B, the amendment as A, and the status quo as Q, the true liberal-conservative ordering of the outcomes was B-A-Q. Since A is closer than B to Q, A might succeed even if B were to fail.

House rules forced, first, a vote to determine a winner between the committee bill and the amendment. The winner of that vote would face the status quo in a final vote. *Suppose sincere voting were to result in the amendment being passed in the initial vote.* Then liberal voters to the left of (B +A)/2, the A-versus-B midpoint, would have voted first against the amendment and then for the amended bill; those more moderate voters between (B +A)/2 and (A +Q)/2 would have voted for the amendment and for the amended bill; and the most conservative voters, those to the right of (A +Q)/2, would have voted for the amendment but against the amended bill.

With such an agenda, however, sincere voting clearly doesn't make sense. Suppose on the final vote, A would defeat Q but B would lose to Q; then if A wins the initial vote, the final outcome is A, whereas if B wins, the final outcome is Q. Consequently, strategic (sophisticated) voters view the initial vote as one involving A and Q. Conservative voters, then, should vote against the amendment, because the status quo would be more likely to prevail if the final vote pitted it against the more extreme committee bill. So they should vote Nay on the initial vote and Nay on the final vote. Similarly, liberals should support the amendment if they believe the committee bill is doomed to failure; so they should vote Yea on both votes. Moderates can be of two types. The more liberal type likes the amended bill best, the committee bill second best, and the status quo least. People of this bent clearly should vote Yea on both votes. The less liberal type also likes the amended bill best but places the status quo second. This type should vote Yea on the initial vote on the amendment (A) versus the committee bill (B), and Yea on a final vote between the amended bill and the status quo. On the vote between the bill and the amendment, then, we should expect to see liberals and all moderates—that is, all legislators to the left of (A + Q)/2—voting Yea and all legislators to their right voting Nay. On the final vote, between the amended bill and the status quo, we should also expect to see sincere voting with a midpoint of (A + Q)/2.

Whether voters are sincere or strategic, we thus expect to see both votes split perfectly on the underlying dimension. The difference is that on the initial vote, with sincere voting, the bill appears in its true location as the liberal outcome (B), whereas with strategic voting, the bill appears as its strategic equivalent, the conservative outcome (Q). (The amendment [A] exhibits, in either sincere or strategic voting, its true location on both votes; the status quo [Q] exhibits its true location on the final vote.)

The actual roll call voting patterns on the Common Situs Picketing Bill will, even when voting is strategic, provide useful information about the legislator locations because we will observe liberal/conservative splits. A strategic vote means only that we have to do some reinterpretation of alternatives. On the initial vote, the legislators, instead of voting sincerely on A versus B, are voting strategically. But voting strategically means acting as if one is voting sincerely on A versus Q. This insight allows us to learn the true location of A.[9] If the amendment passes, both the initial and the final vote would be votes of A versus Q; so we would expect an identical vote in support of A on both votes.

Consequently, neither logrolling nor strategic voting on agendas necessarily invalidates our use of the simple spatial model. We consider logrolling in chapter 6, and amendment voting, including the Common Situs Bill votes, in chapter 7.

Multidimensionality

Our examples of roll call voting, whether sincere, logrolled, or strategic votes over agendas, have all assumed a single underlying dimension. Political discourse often distinguishes between economic and social conservatives. An economic conservative is generally thought of as believing that government should not intervene in private economic transactions with redistributive taxation; in-kind transfer programs; and regulation of wages, working conditions, and externalities such as air and water pollution. On the other hand, social conservatives believe that government should intervene to regulate personal behavior in matters of freedom of speech and association; sexual and reproductive behavior; gambling; consumption of drugs and alcohol; and (in earlier times) enslavement or segregation of nonwhites.

Of course, economic and social conservatism might be highly correlated. True libertarians, those who want to minimize all forms of government regulation, may be hard to find outside the Economics Department of the University of Chicago. On the other hand, economic liberals who are social conservatives, such as some blue-collar

Roman Catholics, may be more numerous. Thus, more than one underlying dimension may be required to describe voting behavior.

When there are in fact two dimensions, we still model individual legislator preferences as declining with distance from an ideal point. Because preferences in the model are a function of (Euclidean) distance, political scientists refer to our analysis as a *spatial model*. The unidimensional concept of symmetric preference is generalized to include the concept of circular indifference contours. For any circle centered on his ideal point, the legislator is indifferent concerning policies whose mappings are points on the circle. The larger the circle, the greater the distance from the ideal point, and so the less desirable is any policy that is mapped onto the circle.

A set of indifference contours is illustrated, for our hypothetical five-person Senate, in figure 2.4. Abstractly, the space can be thought of as having a horizontal dimension and a vertical dimension. In the figure, the OSHA firm-inspection level is assumed to be a horizontal-dimension issue. Its earlier mapping is preserved. Appropriating funds for enforcement of the Voting Rights Act is mapped as an issue on the vertical dimension.[10] Other issues may be neither strictly horizontal nor strictly vertical. We illustrate this in the figure by having penalties for nonregistrants for the military draft mapped as an issue at an angle of 45° to the horizontal axis.

The concept of the midpoint in one dimension generalizes to a cutting line in two dimensions. The cutting line is the perpendicular bisector of the line joining the two alternatives, and separates the Yea and Nay voters. Figure 2.5 shows a cutting line for a vote between punishments of 6 months and 10 years. The three-dimensional analogs

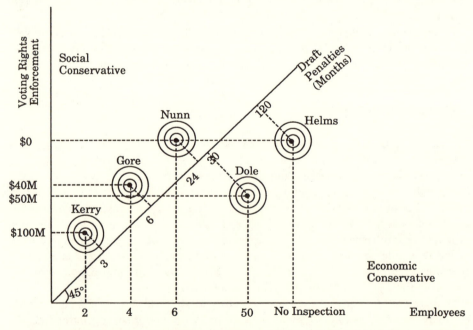

Figure 2.4. Two-dimensional indifference contours and the mapping of three issues in the basic space. Lines from each senator show ideal points on the issues. The circular indifference contours indicate that preference is decreasing in distance from the ideal point.

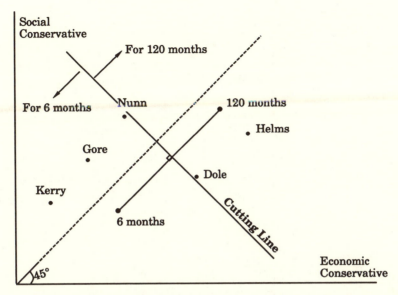

Figure 2.5. Cutting line on a roll call for punishment for draft evasion. The outcomes are on a line parallel to the 45° line. The cutting line is the perpendicular bisector of the line joining the outcomes. Positions on the draft issue combine aspects of economic conservatism and social conservatism.

of circular indifference contours and cutting lines are spherical indifference surfaces and separating planes.

Just how many dimensions are needed to describe the structure of roll call voting is an empirical question. The analysis we present shows a structure that is largely unidimensional, with a second dimension having a smaller, although sometimes important, influence. As we show in chapter 3, virtually no substantive concern is served by going beyond two dimensions.

As with one dimension, a pattern of voting constrained to a low-dimensional mapping can be consistent with strategic behavior. To see this, we can recall the Common Situs Picketing Bill example. In this scenario, a moderate saving amendment (A) defeats a more liberal committee bill (B) on an initial vote and then is matched against the status quo (Q). With a single dimension, only four strict preference orderings are possible: B > A > Q (B is preferred to A, which is preferred to Q); A > B > Q; A > Q > B; and Q > A > B. But, unless the three options are on a line in two dimensions, two dimensions will produce the other two possibilities, B > Q > A and Q > B > A. This is shown in figure 2.6. Although the saving amendment is closer to Q than B is, it is off the line joining B and Q. The three cutting lines mark off six regions of the space that correspond to the six types of legislator preferences. Below each type, we give (assuming A wins the initial vote) first its sincere voting pattern and then its strategic pattern. If, in a final vote, Q loses to A but beats B, in strategic voting, the initial B-versus-A vote is again really an A-versus-Q vote. Even in strategic voting, voters are split by a cutting line. This split provides information about the true locations of the A and Q outcomes.

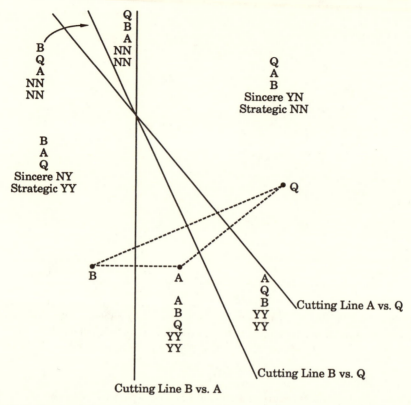

Figure 2.6. Sincere and strategic voting in two dimensions. With three alternatives, there are six types of strict preferences in two dimensions. The three cutting lines between the three pairs of alternatives determine six wedges or pie slices. Each slice corresponds to one of the preference types. If the status quo (Q) defeats the bill (B) in the final vote but loses to the amended bill, legislators who have the preferences QAB and BAQ vote differently on the initial vote between A and B if they are strategic than if they are sincere.

Even with two dimensions, however, about 15 percent of the individual votes fail to fit a simple spatial structure. This is illustrated in figure 2.7, which shows votes on the Panama Canal Treaty and on the National Science Foundation (NSF) budget. The ideal points of northern Democrats are marked by D tokens; of southern Democrats, by S; and of Republicans, by R. Some locations are so close that there is overlapping, but a particular letter always overlaps the same letter. The top panels show all the senator locations and the cutting line. The bottom panels show that there are some errors—Yea voters on the Nay side of the cutting line, and vice versa. Nevertheless, the errors tend to be close to the cutting line.

A probabilistic model accounts for this pattern. The closer a legislator is to an alternative, the more likely he is to vote for it. At one extreme, if one alternative is at the legislator's ideal point and the other alternative is very far from it, he has a probability close to one of voting for the closer alternative. At the other extreme, if the alterna-

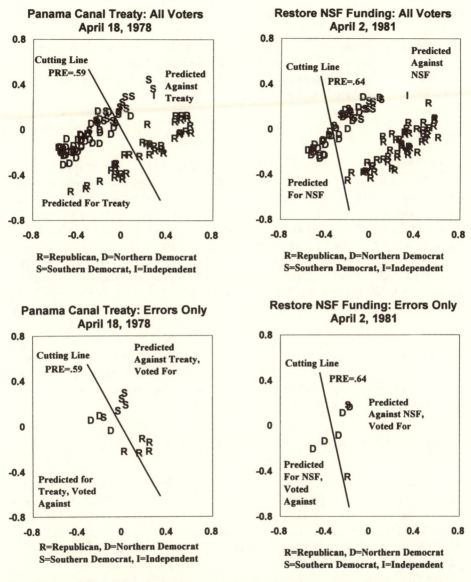

Figure 2.7. Ideal points, cutting lines, and errors on two roll calls. Each token corresponds to a senator's ideal point. Errors are concentrated near the cutting lines. The ideal points and cutting lines are the estimates of the D-NOMINATE model, with a linear trend in legislator positions. (The "Independent" is Harry Byrd, Jr. [VA].)

tives are equidistant from him, the legislator acts as if he based his decision on a coin toss. Since legislators close to the cutting line are close to equidistant from the two alternatives, their actual votes are more likely to be errors than are the votes of legislators with ideal points far from the cutting line.

Estimation

Our discussion has concerned a set of examples in which all the spatial locations were known. But our task is to recover the locations of some 11,000 legislators and 70,000 roll calls from the 11,000,000 recorded individual decisions of Congresses stretching from 1789 to 1985.[11] How do we do this?

Minimizing Classification Errors in One Dimension

If we had but a single dimension with errorless voting, we could easily recover the order of the legislators and the roll call midpoints. We could use a brute-force technique whereby we tried all possible orderings until we found the right one. But even for a single House, where there are 435 men and women who can be voting on more than 1,000 items, brute force will abuse even the mightiest of computers. Fortunately, a simple iterative procedure works quite well and, in practice, needs only a few steps to converge to an ordering that minimizes classification error. This technique resembles arranging a deck of cards by first sorting the cards by suit and then sorting by order within the suit. To illustrate, say we started with the following highly erroneous ordering of the previously cited senators,

Nunn   Helms   Gore   Kerry   Dole

and we observed only that the splits were Kerry against the others on the B-2; Kerry and Gore against the other three on Cambodia; Dole and Helms against the other three on Tower; and Helms against the others on MLK, Jr. The (nonunique) placement of roll call midpoints below minimizes classification errors:

Cambodia
Nunn   Helms   Tower   Gore   B-2   Kerry   Dole
MLK, Jr.

Note that this placement of the roll call midpoints minimizes classification errors only if the the substantively liberal outcome on each issue is supported by senators placed at the right end of the order. Thus Kerry and Dole are both predicted to oppose further funds for the B-2 bomber. The placements of the roll calls lead to five classification errors. Dole is incorrectly classified on B-2, Cambodia, and Tower; and Nunn is incorrect on Tower and MLK, Jr.

After this first step, the next step is to see if, holding the midpoints fixed, we can move the senators, one by one, and reduce the classification errors. The following rearrangement eliminates all but two errors, Dole on MLK, Jr. and Nunn on Cambodia:

Cambodia
Helms   Dole   Tower   Nunn   Gore   B-2   Kerry
MLK, Jr.

But after this step, we can hold the legislators constant and rearrange the midpoints and eliminate all the errors:

Helms   MLK, Jr.   Dole   Tower   Nunn   Cambodia   Gore   B-2   Kerry

This order is correct; it is just the mirror image of the commonsense order assumed in the example given earlier. Our recovery example was deliberately chosen to emphasize that what is at the left and right is just a convention. An ordering and its mirror image both contain the same information.[12]

Of course, actual data will contain errors, but we could nonetheless apply the classification-error-minimization procedure to the data. Doing so offers an important advantage. The sorting process is, in statisticians' lingo, a robust way of finding out where the senators and cutting lines are located. Thus, the recovery based on optimal classification isn't likely to be sensitive to the process generating the errors; that is, to whatever causes roll call voting to be a less than perfect fit to the spatial model.

Unfortunately, optimal classification also has a couple of disadvantages. First, it gives us no information about the locations of the alternatives. Only the midpoint is relevant to the classification. Any pair of outcomes that have the same midpoint make the same classification predictions. So we can't work back from classifications to identify roll call outcomes. Second, classification is impractical in a setting of more than one dimension.

NOMINATE

Because of these disadvantages, we developed an alternative procedure, which we have named NOMINATE; this stands for *NOMINА1 Three-step Estimation*. This procedure can be used with relative ease in multidimensional settings. It involves a specific probabilistic model, which allows us to use the pattern of errors to recover the outcome coordinates. Think first of Yea and Nay outcomes that are very close to each other. In this case, most legislators will be nearly indifferent and will be voting with probabilities close to 0.5. Then consider a second roll call with the same cutting line, but with Yea and Nay outcomes that are very far apart. In this case, preferences will be sharper and more probabilities will be close to 1 or 0. Fewer errors should occur.

It is evident, paradoxically, that we need errors to recover the roll call outcomes. We oversimplified earlier when we said we could recover the outcome locations in the case of errorless strategic voting. In fact, we could recover only the cutting lines.[13] Without errors, the midpoint in one dimension or the cutting line in two dimensions or the separating hyperplane in higher dimensions is nicely tied down and identified by the basic liberal/conservative split on a roll call in one dimension, or, more generally, by the split of the Euclidean space into Yea and Nay camps. In contrast, the Yea and Nay locations are revealed only by the pattern of errors.

The use of errors to identify outcome locations has two potentially severe problems. First, our model includes a signal-to-noise ratio. This parameter measures how strong the spatial component of the voting decision is in relation to whatever generates errors. We assume the signal-to-noise ratio is constant across all of American history. (Attempts at relaxing that assumption did not make important improvements in our ability to account for the data.) Although some roll calls are almost certainly noisier than others, the data do not provide enough information to identify both the noise level and how far the outcomes are from the cutting line. Thus our outcome estimates will be much "noisier" than our estimates of legislator positions or cutting lines. We do have simulation evidence (discussed in appendix A) that shows that our recovery of legislator positions and cutting lines is quite robust and can sort out the mix of signal-to-noise ratios across roll calls. (Variations in noise across legislators are a smaller problem. A legislator is analogous to a roll call midpoint. Unless the legislator's voting pattern is extremely noisy, his position will be pinned down by his overall pattern of voting, even when there is little or no error.)[14]

Second, to recover the outcome coordinates, we need to assume a specific form of preferences, not just the ordinal assumption that preference is decreasing in distance. Basically, preference decreases, as shown in figures 2.2 and 2.3. (The mathematical specification appears in appendix A.) Not all specifications that decrease in distance will do the trick. When preferences are quadratic in distance—a form that often facilitates theoretical modeling—the outcomes cannot be recovered, even when errors are present. The form assumed in NOMINATE is exponential, or bell-shaped, utility (see figure 2.2). This form is perhaps a politically realistic one in that voter preferences are not very sensitive to small departures from the ideal point, shift sharply for intermediate changes in outcome locations, but then show little distinction between outcomes that are very far from the ideal point.

The procedure we use to recover the space works in an alternating fashion, directly analogous to our illustration of ordinal sorting. We start with an initial configuration of legislators and a signal-to-noise ratio. We then sequentially process the roll calls, estimating the outcome coordinates. We then reestimate the signal-to-noise ratio, keeping all spatial coordinates fixed. And then we sequentially process the legislators, keeping the roll call coordinates and the signal-to-noise ratio fixed. As we move the parameters of the model, we don't try to minimize classification errors. Instead, we try to maximize the probabilities the model assigns to the observed votes. That is, if a senator voted Yea on a roll call, we would like the corresponding ideal point to be as close as possible to the Yea outcome and as far as possible from the Nay outcome. Of course, we have to trade off the senator's probabilities on this particular roll call against her probabilities on all the other roll calls. We continue the described iterations until we find that the locations have stabilized. A global iteration of the model is a passage through the roll calls, the signal-to-noise ratio, and legislator steps. Stability occurs after a sequence of three or four of the global iterations.

The results of the estimation are likely to be quite accurate with respect to legislators' ideal points and roll call cutpoints or cutting lines. A typical legislator in American history cast 900 votes during his career (and many more in the modern period)—900 is a rough but reliable indication of the effective number of observations used to estimate the legislator locations. The roll call cutpoints and cutting lines are also pinned down sharply, particularly in the modern House, where the effective number of observations is close to 435 on most roll calls. Less accurate estimates pertain to earlier periods, particularly to the first several Senates where there were as few as 26 senators.

As mentioned above, our estimates of roll call outcomes are much less reliable than the estimates of legislator locations or roll call cuts. Consequently, this book contains no discussion of the outcomes for individual roll calls. The average location of sets of outcomes, such as all winning outcomes in a House, will, by an appeal to the law of large numbers, be quite accurately estimated.[15] A discussion of winning outcomes is contained in chapter 4.

Legislators' Positions over Time

With respect to legislators, we need to ask not only what a legislator's position is at any point in time, but how her position changes over time. A strong hypothesis is that the legislator has a constant position over time. Rather than adapt to changing constituent preferences, congressmen enter a house and stay put until they die with their ideological boots on. If this hypothesis is maintained, we can then, using the fact that periods of service overlap, place all the legislators in a house of Congress in a common space for all of American history. In fact, we can estimate a common space as long as there is a sufficient degree of constraint on how legislators are allowed to move. We impose such a constraint by limiting their movement to polynomial functions of time. The simplest function assumes that legislators maintain constant positions throughout their congressional careers. The next simplest is a linear trend, which allows a legislator to become, in one dimension, either more conservative or more liberal during his career. With linear trends, legislators can thus never do ideological flip-flops; switching back and forth is possible only with quadratic and higher polynomials. Empirically, however, we find that essentially all movement is captured by a simple linear movement, as illustrated in figure 2.8. Our dynamic procedure is named D-NOMINATE.

Estimating the dynamic model is very similar to estimating a static model. The only real difference is that, when a legislator's position is estimated, the coefficients of the time polynomial, as well as the constant, must be estimated. Of course, our dynamic estimation for all of congressional history used a very large data base that could only

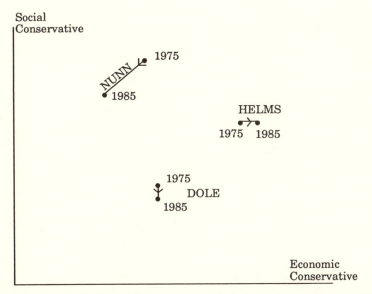

Figure 2.8. Linear movement of senators. In the linear-trend model, senators' ideal points move on lines throughout their careers. Some senators, such as Nunn, move more than other senators, such as Dole. Typically, they move very little, relative to the space, as illustrated by the figure.

be manipulated with a supercomputer. Estimating a two-dimensional model with a linear trend for the House of Representatives required about three hours of CPU time on a Cyber 205 supercomputer.

Summary of the Model and Estimation Methods

The technically inclined reader will find the details of our model and the estimation procedure in appendix A. To summarize: First, we have adopted a simple spatial model with probabilistic voting. Second, assuming this model is a correct model of actual behavior, we have developed a method for recovering the positions of legislator and roll call outcomes solely from observed individual roll call decisions; that is, the method is blind to any external information, such as political parties, about the legislators and the roll calls. The direct linkage of the recovery method to the spatial model is our innovation to modern methods of roll call analysis introduced by MacRae (1958, 1970). Third, the recovery of legislator positions and roll call cutting lines is likely to be very accurate even if the technical assumptions of our procedure are violated. And fourth, the recovery of roll call outcomes may be very sensitive to the technical assumptions.

In the remainder of this book, we employ D-NOMINATE to estimate dynamic models of roll call voting. To estimate static models for a single Congress, we used W-NOMINATE, an improved version of NOMINATE. Having established the methodological basis for the remainder of the book, we can now proceed to a discussion of the results of the analysis.

3
The Spatial Model: Accuracy and Dimensionality

In this chapter, we investigate the performance of low-dimensional spatial models and discuss the substantive meaning of the dimensions. With respect to performance, we show that a simple spatial model adequately accounts for the roll call data. Our preferred model has only two dimensions; it limits temporal change in the positions of individual legislators to simple linear functions of time. In fact, this very simple model improves only marginally, albeit significantly, on an even simpler model that is one-dimensional, with legislators being constrained to a fixed position throughout their congressional careers. These basic results are presented in the first section of this chapter, which gives the overall fit of the various spatial models that we estimated.

In the second section, we address the issue content of the first and second dimensions; the first dimension almost always picks up the fundamental economic issues that separate the two major political parties of the time, while the second dimension divides the parties internally over regional issues (usually race). In the third section, we offer supporting evidence for our basic finding of low dimensionality; this section also confronts the controversy this finding has created in the relevant literature.

Overall Fit of the Spatial Models

We applied the D-NOMINATE algorithm to all roll call votes cast in the House and the Senate from 1789 to 1985 (the first 98 Congresses and the first session of the 99th).[1] All roll calls with at least 2.5 percent minority voting were included (97 – 3 and closer votes if 100 Senators voted). For a given Congress, every legislator who cast at least 25 votes was included.[2] Applying these criteria, 9,759 members of the House and 1,714 senators were included in the analysis. For the House, 32,953 roll calls were analyzed, and the total number of individual decisions was 8,110,702. For the Senate, there were 37,281 roll calls and 2,317,915 decisions.

One-, two-, and three-dimensional spatial models were estimated, and time polynomials up to degree 3 (cubic) were estimated for the legislators. A two-dimensional model with a linear time trend (like the one shown in figure 2.8) for the legislators accounts for about 85 percent of the individual decisions. Adding dimensions and higher-order time trends did not appreciably increase the fit of the model.

A straightforward method to measure the fit of the model is simply to count, across all roll calls, the percentage of correct classifications.[3] The classification results for the two-century history of both houses of Congress are shown in table 3.1. The table reports classifications for all roll calls in the estimation and for close roll calls, in which the minority got over 40 percent of the vote cast. With a two-dimensional model, classification is better than 80 percent for close votes, as well as for all votes.

A reasonable fit is obtained from a one-dimensional model in which each legislator's position is constant throughout his or her career. On the other hand, there is considerable improvement—about three percentage points—from adding a second dimension. Allowing for a linear trend in legislator positions adds another percentage point. That we get a smaller boost in the percentages from the time trend than from the dimensions is expected (see the box on adding parameters to the model).

Introducing more parameters to a dynamic spatial model—through extra dimensions or higher-order polynomials—does not appreciably add to our understanding of

Table 3.1 Classification Percentages, Proportional Reduction in Errors, and Geometric Mean Probabilities (1789–1985)

	House			Senate		
	Number of Dimensions			Number of Dimensions		
Degree of Polynomial	1	2	3	1	2	3
Classification Percentage: All Scaled Votes						
Constant	82.7[a]	84.4	84.9	80.0	83.6	84.1
Linear	83.0	85.2	—[c]	81.3	84.5	85.5
Quadratic	83.1	85.3	—	81.5	84.8	85.9
Cubic	83.2	85.4	—	81.6	85.0	86.1
Classification Percentage: Votes with at Least 40 Percent Minority						
Constant	80.5[b]	82.9	83.7	78.9	82.7	83.4
Linear	80.9	83.8	—	79.4	83.6	84.8
Quadratic	81.0	83.9	—	79.7	83.8	85.1
Cubic	81.1	84.1	—	79.8	84.0	85.3
Aggregate Proportional Reduction in Error (*APRE*): All Scaled Votes						
Constant	.479	.531	.546	.435	.512	.530
Linear	.489	.553	—	.448	.543	.571
Quadratic	.494	.559	—	.453	.549	.583
Cubic	.494	.562	—	.456	.553	.589
Geometric Mean Probability: All Scaled Votes						
Constant	.678	.696	.707	.660	.692	.700
Linear	.682	.709	—	.666	.704	.716
Quadratic	.684	.712	—	.668	.708	.721
Cubic	.684	.714	—	.670	.708	.725

a. The percentage of correct classifications is for all roll calls that were included in the scalings—i.e., those with at least 2.5 percent or better on the minority side.

b. The percentage of correct classifications is for all roll calls with at least 40 percent or better on the minority side.

c. Higher polynomial models for 3 dimensions were not estimated because of computer-time considerations.

Adding Parameters to the Model

When legislator positions are allowed to have a time trend, we add parameters to the model. We add only one parameter per legislator for each dimension. If, for example, we add a time trend to the one-dimensional, constant-position model for the House, we would add 9,759 parameters if we had a time trend for every representative included in our analysis of the first 99 Congresses; but as we have time trends only for members voting at least 25 times in at least 3 Congresses, we in fact add only 4,185 parameters. When a dimension is added to a model, the number of roll call parameters added equals twice the number of roll calls (32,955), because each roll call is represented by Yea and Nay points in the space. In addition, legislator parameters are added. (The number of parameters added for a legislator equals the degree of the time polynomial for the legislator [see appendix A].) For example, adding a second dimension to the one-dimensional, constant-position model means $2 \times 32,955 + 9,759 = 75,669$ parameters.

More generally, since roll calls outnumber legislators by more than 5 to 1, we add about 10 times as many parameters in adding a dimension as we do in adding another polynomial term in legislator positions. It is thus not surprising that our classification shows more improvement when we increase the dimensionality of the space than when we increase the order of the time polynomial.

---

the political process. That is, the additional dimensions have no obvious interpretations, nor does the complexity inherent in higher-order polynomials. Moreover, adding extra parameters results in only a very marginal increase in our ability to account for voting decisions. For example, consider adding parameters to the two-dimensional linear model in the Senate. Allowing for a quadratic term in the time polynomial improves classification only by 0.3 percent, at a cost of 1,456 additional parameters (2 dimensions $\times$ 728 senators serving in 4 or more Congresses). Allowing for a third dimension improves classification by only 1.0 percent at a cost of 77,479 more parameters (two more per roll call and one or two additional parameters per legislator). Allowing for both generates an improvement of only 1.1 percent.

Another way to evaluate the fit of the models is to focus on the proportional reduction in error, or the *PRE,* of the models.[4] A *PRE* measure allows us to see how much the D-NOMINATE model improves on a suitable benchmark model. In other words, does D-NOMINATE make substantially fewer classification errors than the benchmark? Our benchmark number of errors is the minority vote—that is, the minimum number of the Yea votes and the Nay votes. In technical lingo, the majority-minority split on a roll call is known as the "marginals."

Why is the minority vote an attractive benchmark? Suppose the actual vote was 65 Yeas to 35 Nays. Without any information from the spatial model, one could always predict on the basis of the marginals. In the example, one would correctly classify 65 of the votes by predicting that everyone would vote Yea. There would be 35 classification errors from this prediction. Clearly, if there is useful information on the legislator positions and the roll call outcomes estimated by D-NOMINATE, classification should result in fewer than these 35 benchmark errors. When the minority vote is the benchmark, the *PRE* is equal to the minority vote minus the number of D-NOMINATE classification errors, with the difference being divided by the minority vote. That is:

$$PRE = \frac{\text{Minority Vote} - \text{D-NOMINATE Classification Errors}}{\text{Minority Vote}}$$

This measure is 1 if there are no classification errors and zero if the spatial-model errors equal the minority vote. In the example, if D-NOMINATE also leads to 35 errors, the *PRE* is 0. Suppose, alternatively, that the first dimension classifies 75 legislators correctly, and that adding the second dimension results in 88 legislators being correctly classified—that is, the first dimension has reduced the 35 benchmark errors to 25; and adding the second dimension has reduced the errors to 12. The *PRE* would equal $(35 - 25)/35$, or .286, for one dimension; and $(35 - 12)/35$, or .657, for two dimensions. In this book, we will frequently use the *PRE* measure to analyze individual roll call votes because it controls for the margin of the roll call and facilitates comparisons of votes. (Note that the *PRE* can be negative if the spatial model makes more errors than the marginals.) We denote the *PRE* for the one-dimensional linear model as *PRE1,* and we use *PRE2* for the two-dimensional linear model.

Groups of roll calls may be evaluated by focusing on the aggregate proportional reduction in error (*APRE*). Specifically, we sum all roll calls, indexed by j, $j = 1, 2, \ldots,$ n, with n denoting the number of roll calls in the group being aggregated.

$$APRE = \frac{\sum_{j=1}^{n} \{\text{Minority Vote} - \text{D-NOMINATE Classification Errors}\}_j}{\sum_{j=1}^{n} \text{Minority Vote}_j}$$

APRE1 and *APRE2* are defined analogously to *PRE1* and *PRE2*. Table 3.1 shows the *APRE* for the various spatial models.[5]

In addition to computing classification percentages, the model may be evaluated by an alternative method that gives more weight to errors that are far from the cutting line than to errors close to the cutting line—for example, a vote by Edward Kennedy (D-MA) to confirm Judge Robert Bork as a Supreme Court justice would be a more serious error than a similar decision by Sam Nunn (D-GA). Such a measure is the geometric mean probability (GMP) of the actual choices (see the box on GMPs).

Summary GMPs for the various estimations are presented in table 3.1. The pattern matches that found for the classification percentages—little is gained by going beyond two dimensions or a linear trend.[6]

Figure 3.1 plots the percentage correctly classified for the one- and two-dimensional dynamic models for every Congress. The striking point about figure 3.1 is how closely the Senate and House track each other over time. The correlations between the Senate and House classifications are .74 for the one-dimensional dynamic model and .69 for the two-dimensional dynamic model. The spatial model breaks down during two periods. The first, from 1815 to 1825 (the period of the 14th through the 19th

---

Geometric Mean Probability

The *likelihood* of an observed choice is simply the probability the model assigns to that choice. Thus, if a legislator who actually voted Yea was predicted to vote Yea, with a probability of 0.9, by the D-NOMINATE two-dimensional linear model, the likelihood of the choice for that model would be 0.9. Since all choices are assumed to be independent, the likelihood of all the choices for all the legislators is just the product of all the likelihoods.

The *log-likelihood* is the natural logarithm of the likelihood. As examples, the natural logarithm of 0.9 is -0.105; of 0.5, -0.693; and of 0.1, -2.303. The log-likelihood for all the choices for all the legislators is just the sum of all the log-likelihoods for the choices.

The *geometric mean probability is the exponential (or anti-log) of the average log-likelihood*—that is:

$$\text{GMP} = \exp\,[\text{log-likelihood of all observed choices}/N],$$

where N is the total number of choices.

Since the GMP is a probability, its maximum value is 1.0. This would occur if the model assigned a probability of 1.0 to every observed choice. The minimum value is 0.0, which occurs if the model assigned a probability of 0.0 to every observed choice.

As a measure of fit, the GMP penalizes models that assign very low probabilities to observed choices. For example, compare a model that assigned a probability of 0.5 to every observed choice to one that assigned a probability of 0.9 to half the choices and 0.1 to the other half. The average probability assigned by both models is 0.5. But the geometric mean probability for the latter model is 0.3 $[\exp(((\ln(0.9)+\ln(0.1))/2) = \exp((-0.105-2.303)/2) = 0.3]$.

Congresses) is marked by the collapse of the Federalist party and the Era of Good Feelings when the United States had, in effect, a one-party government. The era perhaps reached its peak with the elections of 1820, when only a single electoral vote was cast against President Monroe's reelection, and when the Jeffersonian Republicans won more than 85 percent of the seats in the House of Representatives. The second period was in the early 1850s (during the 32nd and 33rd Congresses), when the conflict over slavery led to the collapse of the Whig party. Later in this chapter, we offer evidence that allowing for more dimensions in these breakdown periods does not improve the model—that is, either the spatial model fits with one or two dimensions, or there is "chaos" in the voting.

Another way of measuring how well our dynamic spatial model fits the roll call data is to look at the residuals—that is, the distribution of the errors (involving those legislators whose roll call votes are not predicted correctly). As discussed in chapter 2, the errors should be close to the cutting line. In our model, the probability of voting either Yea or Nay is ½ for a legislator whose ideal point is on the cutting line. Legislators far from the cutting line will have either very high or very low probabilities of

House

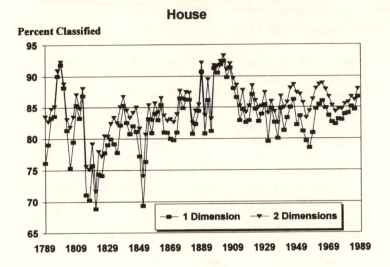

Senate

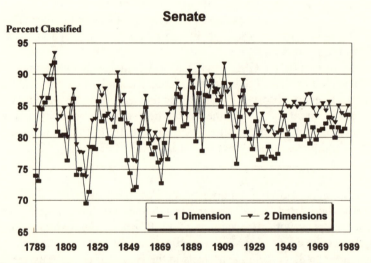

Figure 3.1. Classification in the dynamic spatial model. These graphs show the percentage correctly classified for all roll call voting decisions in each Congress. Each symbol corresponds to a Congress. The one-dimensional model usually classifies almost as well as the two-dimensional model. The patterns for the House and Senate are very similar. The model shown is the dynamic model with a linear trend in legislator positions. (In all the time-series graphs in this book, each plotted point refers to a Congress or a two-year period. The year that corresponds to each Congress is the year following congressional elections. Many early Congresses did not have their first votes until December of that year and had their last votes in March of the year used to designate the next Congress.)

voting Yea (see the box on the GMP). Consequently, if our model is correct, the errors should drop off sharply as distance from the cutting line increases. Figure 3.2 shows the distribution of errors for our preferred two-dimensional dynamic model, along with the theoretical distribution of errors.[7] The graphs for the Senate are very similar to those shown for the House.

Figure 3.2 shows the percentage of the total choices that were errors as a function of the legislator's distance from the cutting line. (Recall that, as the cutting line is distinct for each roll call, each legislator's distance from the cutting line will vary with the roll call.) The distances are grouped in intervals of 0.1 units of the space. Since the space is 2 units in diameter, the maximum distance of a legislator from the cutting line is 2 units, but most of the distances are less than 0.5 units. For example, the "All" graph in figure 3.2 is based on all of the individual roll call vote choices included in our dynamic two-dimensional model for the first 99 Houses.[8] The estimated legislator ideal point was within 0.1 unit of the estimated roll call cutting line for 2,039,460 actual choices. But, for a more distant interval of 0.1, that where the legislator ideal point was 0.5 to 0.6 units from the cutting line (corresponding to ".6" in the figure), there were only 572,307 actual choices. Note that the error rate decreases sharply with distance from the cutting line. The error rate for the 0 to 0.1 interval is 34.8 percent. In sharp contrast, the error rate for the 0.5 to 0.6 interval is a mere 4.4 percent.

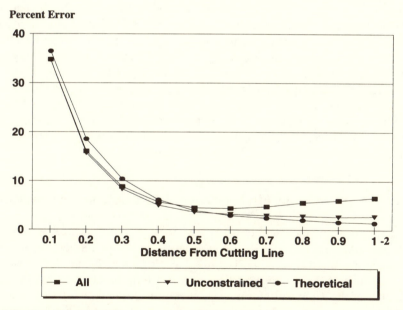

Figure 3.2. Classification errors, by legislator's distance from the cutting line in the House of Representatives (1789–1985). The error rate falls sharply as legislators become more distant from the cutting line. The "0.1" refers to all instances where a legislator's ideal point was 0.1 units or less from the cutting line on a roll call. The "All" line includes all roll call votes; the "Unconstrained" line has all roll call votes where the D-NOMINATE cutting-line estimate was unconstrained.

Figure 3.2 also shows the theoretical error distribution and the actual error distribution for just those roll calls that were "unconstrained." As we explain in appendix A, the estimated policy locations for very lopsided roll calls—for example, 95–5—often had to be constrained. That is, if the estimated cutting line fell outside the legislators' locations, so that a unanimous vote was predicted, we constrained the cutting line to be at the edge of the space.[9] When these constrained roll calls are included in the error calculations, the error distributions turn slightly upward after 0.6 units away from the cutting line. Until this point, the actual distribution of errors corresponds to the theoretical distribution very closely. Removing the constrained roll calls continues the correspondence beyond 0.6 units.

The reason for the very small upward turn is that on some near-unanimous votes (for example, 95–5), members may engage in "protest" voting while knowing that their protest (for example, voting against funding for the State Department) will have no effect on the outcome.

As we pointed out above, either the spatial model fits with one or two dimensions, or there is chaos in voting. Chaos is rare, as the information in table 3.1 and in figures 3.1 and 3.2 has disclosed. Quite the contrary: The important regularity we have found is that 84 percent of all individual decisions can be accounted for by a two-dimensional model, in which individual legislators have ideal points that are fixed throughout their tenures in office. Put differently, the PRE measure shows that the spatial model explains over half the decisions not explained by the minority-vote benchmark. This regularity is an important pattern, but the pattern does not arise from a well-specified theoretical model that would fix the dimensionality of the space.

It is clear that what is not explained by a low-dimensional model with stable individual positions is not explained by a higher-dimensional, more dynamically flexible model. We can allow for substantial readjustment in legislator positions by estimating each Congress separately. Later in this chapter, we show that separate estimates for various Congresses disclose little improvement over the two-dimensional linear fit, even with as many as 15 dimensions. The unexplained votes thus reflect either responses to specific constituency interests on particular issues, special-interest lobbying, and logrolls, or other forms of strategic behavior.

The Issue Content of the First and Second Dimensions: An Overview

What is the substantive content of the space? To begin with, consider what the space would look like in a classical British two-party system with a very high degree of party discipline in roll call voting. The space would be largely one-dimensional, with the ideal points of the members of the Left party forming one tight cluster, and the ideal points of the Right party forming another tight cluster. The roll call cutting lines would all be vertical or nearly vertical and tightly clustered, equidistant from the two party clusters. The tight clusters would in fact be single points or lines except for the fact that occasionally discipline breaks down and free votes are allowed.

In many figures in this book, the American political parties also present distinct clusters, even though the parties are not as disciplined as they are in Great Britain. Indeed, throughout most of American history, we found that numerous roll calls in nearly every Congress had cutting lines through the space that perfectly, or nearly perfectly, divided the two parties. These would be the cutting lines for party-line votes. We show below that these cutting lines typically define votes that fall on the first dimension.

The political parties, either through the discipline of powerful leaders or through successful trades, function as effective logrollers. Parties thus help to map complex issues (to bundle diverse economic interests) into a low-dimensional space. The first dimension represents conflict over the role of government in the economy. The historical exceptions to this statement are 1817–35, during the Era of Good Feelings, and 1853–76, before and after the Civil War. When party is coterminous with the first dimension, the second dimension allows party members to be differentiated with respect to a second set of issues. For example, in the 1840s, the first dimension was largely concerned with internal improvements and the second, with slavery (which was a sectional economic issue [Fogel and Engerman, 1974], as well as a moral issue [Fogel, 1989]).

To indicate the issue content of the two dimensions more systematically, we discuss, in the next section, the history of the spatial positions of legislators from the major political parties. We then discuss the issue content of the first and second dimensions.

Spatial Maps of the Party Systems

The United States has had three periods with distinct two-party systems. The first, the Jeffersonian Republican/Federalist party system, ended with the Era of Good Feelings. The second, the Democratic/Whig system, was organized after the Era of Good Feelings and lasted until the early 1850s. The third, the Democratic/Republican system, was organized by the late 1850s and continues today, although we will frequently refer to this system as having been perturbed into a three-party system (northern Democrats, southern Democrats, Republicans) by civil-rights issues that arose in the mid-twentieth century. Figures 3.3 and 3.4 show two-dimensional spatial maps for representative Senates and Houses in each of the three two-party systems and in the three-party perturbation. As we note below, the first dimension almost always divides the two major political parties, whereas the second dimension picks up divisions within the parties.

We noted in chapter 2 that votes that involve only the first dimension will have vertical cutting lines—that is, cutting lines at an angle of 90° to the horizontal axis of the space. In contrast, purely second-dimension votes will have angles of 0° (or, equivalently, 180°). Votes that mix the two dimensions, such as our draft-evasion punishment example in figure 2.5, will have angles that vary from 0° to 180°. Consequently, just as we can summarize the information about the distribution of legislators' ideal points in a scatter plot (the top plots, of figures 3.3 and 3.4, for each of the Senates and Houses covered), we can summarize the information about the distribution of roll calls in a bar graph (a histogram) of cutting-line angles (the bottom plots of figures 3.3 and 3.4).

On the bar graphs, we have indicated where the party-line votes fell. For these plots, we defined a party-line vote as one where at least 65 percent of one party opposed at least 65 percent of the second party.[10] Since the first dimension always divides the political parties during stable periods, the cutting-line angle of a party-line vote will be

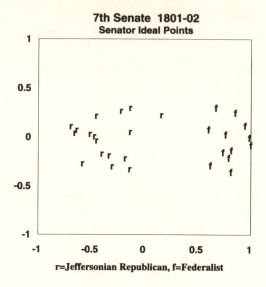

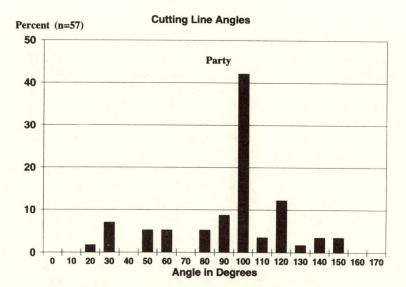

Figure 3.3. Ideal-point and cutting-line angle estimates for selected Senates. In the top panel for each Senate, each lowercase letter represents a legislator. The bottom panel shows the distribution of cutting-line angles. The values shown by the bars sum to 100 percent. The label "Party" shows where the party-line votes were concentrated. Where relevant, "N vs S" and "Conservative Coalition" show, respectively, the concentrations of votes that were regional

close to 90°. We exclude constrained roll calls because they almost always are constrained at the left or right edge of the first dimension and therefore have an angle of 90°. Including them would exaggerate the number of party-line cutting angles.

The Federalist period. By the 3rd Congress, the factions associated with Jefferson and Hamilton began to solidify into the Jeffersonian Republican and Federalist par-

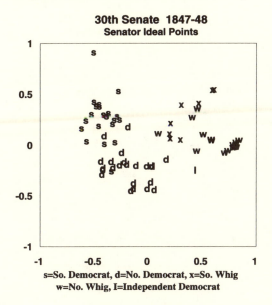

30th Senate 1847-48
Senator Ideal Points

s=So. Democrat, d=No. Democrat, x=So. Whig
w=No. Whig, I=Independent Democrat

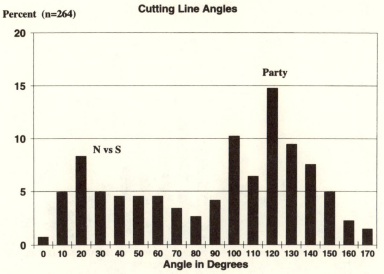

Percent (n=264)   **Cutting Line Angles**

Angle in Degrees

North-South splits and votes that pitted Republicans and southern Democrats against northern Democrats. Votes in the 80 bar are those with cutting lines between 80° and 90°. These votes and those in the 90 bar represent vertical cutting lines or first-dimension votes. Those in the 0 and 170 bars represent second-dimension votes. The graphs show that pure second-dimension votes are very rare.

ties, respectively. This division initially occurred because of the sharp disagreements over foreign policy regarding the French Revolution and its aftermath and Hamilton's economic program of excise taxes, tariffs, a national bank, and the payment of the Revolutionary War debt of the States and the Continental Congress. Figure 3.4 covers the 5th House (1797–98), during which the infamous Alien and Sedition Acts were passed; and figure 3.3 covers the 7th Senate (1801–2), during which Jefferson served

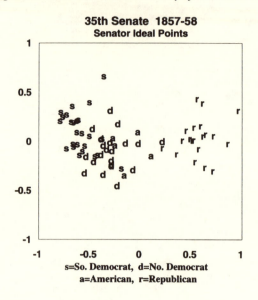

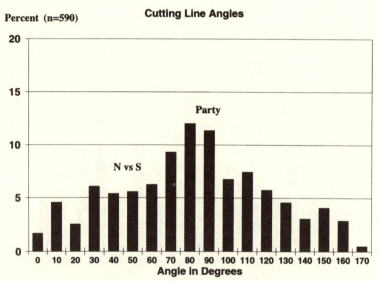

Figure 3.3. *(continued)*

his first term. The gap between the Republicans and Federalists, and the grouping of the cutting-line angles around 90°, are typical of a well-organized political-party system.

The Era of Good Feelings. The War of 1812 produced a deep regional split in the United States. New England and the coastal areas of the middle states opposed declaring war on Britain. The South and West largely supported the war.[11] Opposition in New England was so pronounced that the British did not blockade the coast above New London, Connecticut. The War of 1812 destroyed the Federalist party and led to a period of one-party rule from 1815 to 1824. This became known as the Era of Good

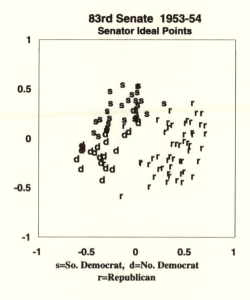

83rd Senate 1953-54
Senator Ideal Points

s=So. Democrat, d=No. Democrat
r=Republican

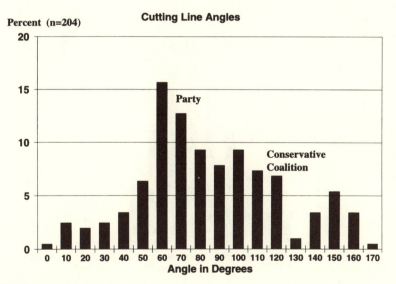

Cutting Line Angles

Percent (n=204)

Angle in Degrees

Figure 3.3. *(continued)*

Feelings after President Monroe toured New England in 1817 in large part to bring about greater national harmony.

The effect of this period on congressional voting was dramatic. Figure 3.1 shows that roll call voting through the period fit the spatial model very poorly. With the collapse of the Federalist party, the first dimension becomes a regional dimension pitting the northeastern Jeffersonians of various hues against the southern and western Jeffersonians. As we discuss in chapter 5, the first dimension largely accounts for the voting on the Missouri Compromise of 1820, which occurred largely along sectional lines. The poor fit would have been even worse were it not for such sectional votes.

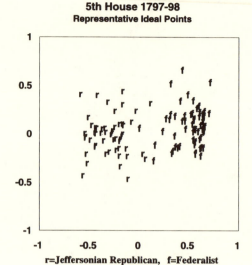

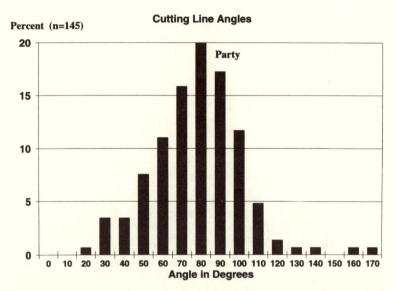

Figure 3.4. Ideal-point and cutting-line angle estimates for selected Houses. See the caption for figure 3.3 for details.

The Whig/Democratic period. During the 1830s and 1840s, the first dimension reverted to a party dimension and the second dimension picked up the conflict between the North and the South over slavery. This can be seen clearly in the spatial maps of the 30th Senate (1847–48) and the 27th House (1841–42). The s token denotes the southern Democrats, and x denotes the southern Whigs.[12] The clear separation of the southern and northern Democrats and of the southern and northern Whigs is evident. On the cutting-line angle plots, we have indicated the cutting-line angle of the North-versus-South votes (shown as "N vs S" in figures 3.3 and 3.4).[13] Note that the cutting-

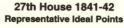

27th House 1841-42
Representative Ideal Points

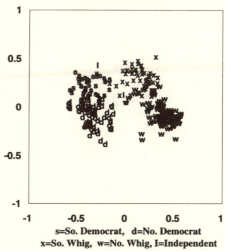

s=So. Democrat, d=No. Democrat
x=So. Whig, w=No. Whig, I=Independent

Cutting Line Angles

Percent (n=849)

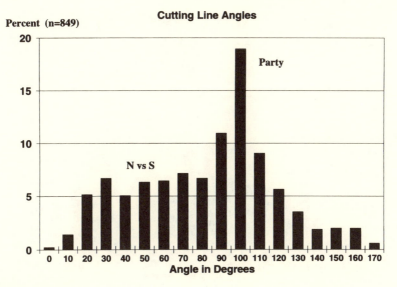

Figure 3.4. *(continued)*

line angle for political party is now tilted toward approximately 110°. As is evident from an examination of the legislator configurations, the first dimension is primarily the party, but it also has a slight regional component in it in that the southern and northern Whigs are slightly separated along it.

The Civil War era. The realignment of the 1850s wiped out the Whig party. It was replaced by the Republican party in the North. The Democratic party was predominant in the South. Consequently, the first dimension, until roughly the 1870s, is concerned mainly with issues related to slavery, the Civil War, and Reconstruction. For the 35th

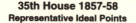

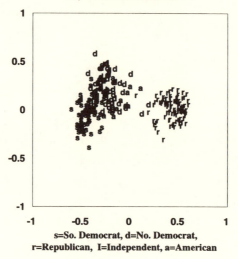

s=So. Democrat, d=No. Democrat,
r=Republican, I=Independent, a=American

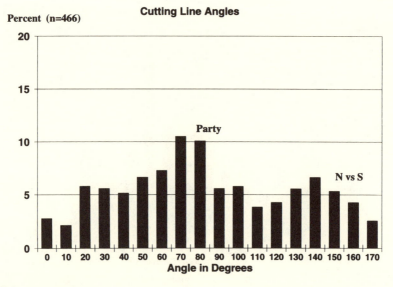

Figure 3.4. *(continued)*

Congress (1857–58), the southern Democrats are found to be to the left of the northern Democrats on this new first dimension. There is still some North-versus-South
component in the new second dimension, but it is weak. Indeed, as is evident from the
legislator configurations, a 90°cutting line separates the bulk of the southern Democrats from their northern colleagues. But since there were no southern Republicans, all
the North-versus-South votes split the Democratic party.

From Reconstruction to the New Deal. In the late nineteenth century, the second dimension weakly separates the western and southern states from the northeastern

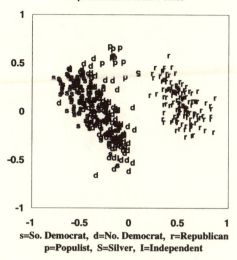

53rd House 1893-94
Representative Ideal Points

s=So. Democrat, d=No. Democrat, r=Republican
p=Populist, S=Silver, I=Independent

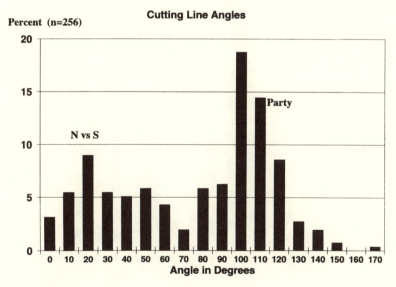

Cutting Line Angles

Percent (n=256)

Figure 3.4. (*continued*)

states. This effect was stronger in the House than in the Senate. For example, figure 3.4 shows the 53rd House (1893–94), which came just before the realignment of the 1890s.[14] The d tokens in the southeast quadrant are from the northeastern states. The North-versus-South votes during this period were really a case of the South plus the West against the Northeast—the regional lineup on bimetalism that we discuss in chapter 5. The second dimension in this period thus involved an agrarian-industrial, or urban-rural, contrast. Representatives from the largest cities were at the bottom of the plot on the second dimension.[15]

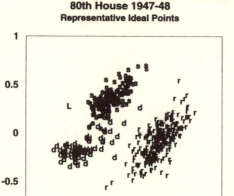

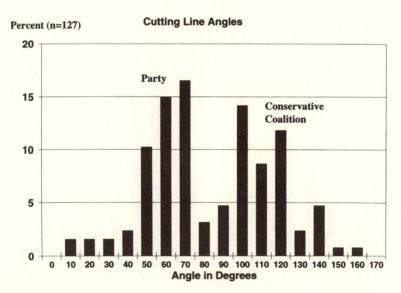

Figure 3.4. *(continued)*

The three-party system of the mid-twentieth century. The period from the late New Deal until the mid-1970s saw the development of the only genuine three-political-party system in American history. The southern and northern Democrats may have joined together to organize the House and Senate, but as the plots of the 83rd Senate (1953–54) and the 80th House (1947–48) show, they were widely separated on the second dimension. This dimension picked up the conflict over civil rights. The approximate inclination of 45°for the two parties reflects the high degree of conservative-coalition voting (southern Democrats and Republicans versus northern Democrats) that occurred throughout this period on a wide variety of non-race-related matters.

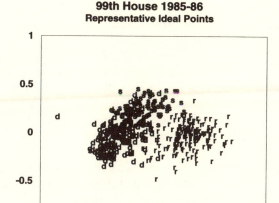

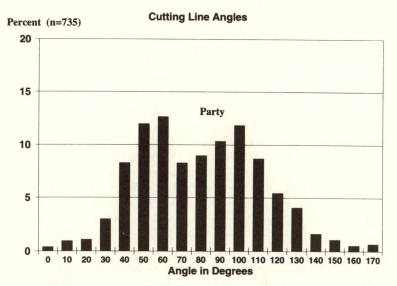

Figure 3.4. *(continued)*

In the three-party-system period, it is useful to think of a major-party loyalty dimension as defined by the axis through the space that captures party-line votes. This dimension can be thought of as ranging from strong loyalty to the Democrats to weak loyalty to either party and to strong loyalty to the Republicans. (In other periods, when party cutting lines are vertical, the horizontal dimension can be thought of as both a party-loyalty dimension and an economic dimension.) An axis perpendicular to the party-loyalty dimension would then express a liberal/conservative dimension that is independent of party loyalty. Votes with cutting lines that are on neither the party-loyalty axis nor the independent liberal/conservative axis represent votes in which legislators make a trade-off—instead of voting on their liberal/conservative positions, they maintain some loyalty to their parties. Almost all votes reflect, to some degree, this type of trade-off.

The contemporary Congress: a return to unidimensional politics. Finally, figure 3.4 shows the spatial map for the 99th House. Note that the separation between northern and southern Democrats has decreased. This process has continued through the 101st Congress, to such an extent that the second dimension has all but disappeared. Indeed, the modern Congress is truly unidimensional. (See McCarty et al. [1996] for evidence through the 104th Congress.)

In sum, one way of interpreting the dynamics of the space is that the horizontal axis usually picks up the conflict between, roughly speaking, rich and poor (or, more accurately, rich and less rich). Other issues (slavery, civil rights, currency inflation) crosscut this basic conflict. If (to anticipate chapter 5) one of these other issues becomes too intense, dimensional alignments break down and a reorganization of the party system results.

The First Dimension Captures Party Loyalty

Except for very brief periods, the first dimension divides the two major political parties (as noted previously). This dimension can be thought of as ranging from strong loyalty to one party (the Jeffersonian Republicans or the Democrats) to weak loyalty to either party and to strong loyalty to the second, opposing party (Federalists, Whigs, or Republicans). The second dimension differentiates the members by region within each party.

In figure 3.5, we show the *APRE* for party-line votes in the House and the Senate for the first 100 Congresses. We use a more stringent definition of party-line voting than we used in figures 3.3 and 3.4 in order to isolate the effect of political party as much as possible. We define a party-line vote as one where 90 percent of the majority party votes against 90 percent of the minority party. We graph *APRE1* and the gain in *APRE* from adding the second dimension (*APRE2* − *APRE1*). We show only those Houses and Senates in which there were at least five party-line roll calls.[16]

In the House the patterns are very clear. The second dimension plays no role in party-line voting until after the 80th Congress. As we will discuss in chapter 5, the striking pattern in the *APRE* plots of the House is due to the emergence of a three-party system in the late 1930s—northern Democrats, southern Democrats, Republicans—brought about by race. Almost by definition, to get 90 percent of Democrats to vote the same way on a roll call meant that southerners and northerners were in agreement. Since the second dimension of the space throughout this period separated northerners from southerners, a party-line vote fell along both dimensions. After the passage of the civil-rights laws in the 1960s, this division in the Democratic party slowly faded in the mid-to-late 1970s so that party-line voting returned to a more normal pattern.

The pattern of party-line voting in the Senate is essentially the same as in the House (and for the same reasons). The exception is the period from the 69th Senate through the 74th (1925–36), when the second dimension also plays an important role. During

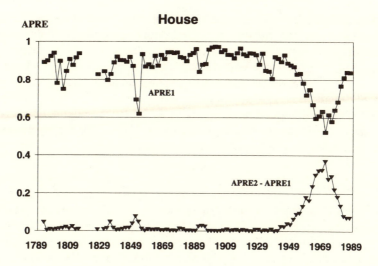

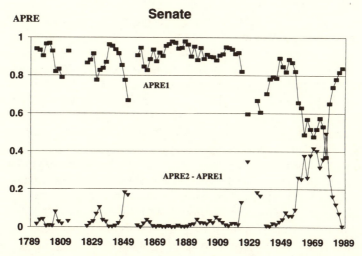

Figure 3.5. Aggregate proportionate reduction in error (*APRE*) on party-line votes (1789–1988). Party-line votes are ones for which at least 90 percent of the majority party opposes 90 percent of the minority party. *APRE1* refers to the first dimension, and *APRE2 − APRE1*, to the additional reduction in errors brought about by the second dimension. The *APRE1* graph shows that party-line votes always fit the spatial model very well, except for three periods: the time of the collapse, around 1852, of the Democratic/Whig system; the period of the three-party post–World War II system; and, only in the Senate, the Progressive Republican era in the 1920s. In contrast to the "chaos" around 1852, party-line voting in the three-party period is still a good fit for the spatial model, but two dimensions are required. The Senate during the Progressive era is an intermediate case.

this period, a small group of midwestern Republican senators voted with the Democrats to such an extent that they were located among the Democrats along the first dimension but above the Democrats on the second dimension. These included the two prominent Progressives: George Norris of Nebraska and Robert M. La Follette, Jr., of Wisconsin (La Follette, Sr., had bolted the Republican party and run for president as a third-party candidate in 1924).[17] Consequently, a party-line vote fell along both dimensions, with a cutting-line angle of about −45°. By the middle of the New Deal, most of these Republicans were replaced by Democrats, and party-line voting returned to a more normal pattern along the first dimension.[18]

The Content of the Second Dimension

Relatively few issues have consistently sparked a second dimension in spatial terms. We coded all the roll calls for all 100 Houses and Senates on a wide variety of issues: slavery; presidential impeachment; the national bank; voting rights; disputed elections; price controls; and so on.[19] (Appendix C shows the specific issue codes we used to categorize the roll calls.)[20] To isolate strongly second-dimensional votes, we listed all issue areas in which there were at least 10 roll calls with a gain in the *APRE* of at least 0.2 from adding the second dimension (*APRE2* − *APRE1*). These are shown, for the House, in table 3.2 and, for the Senate, in table 3.3 (issue areas for which *APRE1* is less than 0.2 are indicated in italics).

Before the formation of the Democrat-Whig party system in the mid-1830s,[21] the public-works issue is the one most often picked up by the second dimension. After 1837 (the first year of the 25th Congress), slavery and the disposition of public lands dominate until the fateful 32nd Congress and the Compromise of 1850, after which slavery becomes a first-dimension issue (see chapter 5). From the Civil War until the realignment of the 1890s (see chapter 5), the predominant second-dimension issue is bimetallism (U.S. currency; banking and finance). After the turn of the century, there is no consistent pattern on the second dimension in either the House or the Senate until after World War II, when civil-rights issues split the Democratic party and created the three-party system we discussed above in connection with figure 3.5.

There are more second-dimension issues in the Senate than in the House, which is consistent with the finding (in table 3.1) that the second dimension is, overall, more important in the Senate than in the House. For example, in the linear model, classifications are improved by 3.8 percent in moving from a one-dimensional model to a two-dimensional model for the Senate but by only 2.9 percent in the House. The increase in the second-dimension issues in the Senate dates from the late nineteenth century. For the period preceding the 52nd Congress (1891–93), the number of entries in the House table exactly equals that in the Senate table. Some of the increase in the Senate may reflect the absence there of closed rules and an agenda that is correspondingly more open than in the House. On the other hand, a very large number of entries in the Senate concern civil rights and voting rights during the time of the three-party system, with 11 entries in these categories, as against only one in the House. This almost certainly reflects the fact that the Senate was the body in which southern legislators, using the filibuster, sought to block legislation that occasioned much less debate in the House, where it enjoyed broad majority support. Thus, on the whole, race-related matters—slavery in the nineteenth century and civil rights in the twentieth—

Table 3.2 Second-Dimension Issues in the House

Congress	No. of Votes	APRE1	APRE2	APRE2 − APRE1	Issue
2	17	.394	.643	.249	Ratio of representatives to population
9	*13*	*−.006*	*.260*	*.266*	*Slavery*
14	*18*	*.130*	*.349*	*.219*	*Tariffs*
16	10	.430	.647	.217	Tariffs
17	*15*	*.063*	*.395*	*.332*	*Public works*
18	*10*	*.167*	*.691*	*.524*	*Public works*
19	13	.326	.578	.252	Public works
20	39	.363	.588	.225	Public works
22	18	.237	.511	.273	Military pensions/ veterans benefits
23	41	.213	.579	.367	Public works
24	*23*	*.072*	*.587*	*.515*	*Public works*
25	39	.495	.731	.237	Slavery
	30	.309	.595	.286	Public works
26	27	.490	.695	.205	Slavery
27	*20*	*.022*	*.335*	*.313*	*Election of House officers*
28	44	.433	.719	.286	Slavery
30	29	.324	.793	.469	Slavery
31	26	.357	.678	.320	Slavery
32	111	.215	.439	.225	Public lands
	14	.279	.495	.216	Slavery
33	*65*	*.164*	*.370*	*.206*	*Public lands*
	75	.238	.524	.286	Public works
39	*20*	*.156*	*.368*	*.211*	*Banking and finance*
41	49	.225	.445	.220	Public lands
43	*14*	*.026*	*.248*	*.222*	*Congressional pay and benefits*
	30	*.156*	*.376*	*.220*	*U.S. currency*
44	18	.440	.682	.242	U.S. currency
45	15	.368	.672	.304	U.S. currency
52	29	.375	.638	.262	U.S. currency
53	41	.372	.742	.370	U.S. currency
62	*10*	*−.016*	*.365*	*.381*	*Immigration/naturalization*
66	*18*	*−.024*	*.437*	*.461*	*Temperance and liquor*
69	11	.222	.480	.259	Agriculture
81	10	.484	.692	.208	Union regulation/ Davis-Bacon
82	11	.429	.633	.204	Price controls
89	22	.527	.757	.230	Civil rights/ desegregation/busing
91	*12*	*.171*	*.409*	*.238*	*Agriculture*
92	16	.314	.557	.244	Agriculture
93	*32*	*.136*	*.459*	*.322*	*Agriculture*
96	*20*	*.141*	*.359*	*.218*	*Public works*
97	14	.109	.380	.271	Public works

Note: This table shows only those Congresses with an issue area in which there were at least 10 roll calls with a gain in *APRE* of at least 0.2 from adding the second dimension. Issue areas for which *APRE1* is less than 0.2 are indicated in italics.

Table 3.3 Second-Dimension Issues in the Senate

Congress	No. of Votes	APRE1	APRE2	APRE2 −APRE1	Issue
1	27	.286	.641	.355	Banking and finance
2	20	.313	.656	.344	Ratio of representatives to population
14	12	.397	.675	.278	Military pensions/veterans' benefits
17	*18*	*.045*	*.270*	*.225*	*Public lands*
18	57	.375	.580	.205	Tariffs
18	*13*	*.097*	*.531*	*.434*	*Public works*
19	18	.394	.643	.249	Public works
20	16	.235	.562	.327	Public lands
	20	.410	.686	.276	Public works
23	14	.222	.676	.454	Public works
24	*42*	*.119*	*.415*	*.296*	*Public works*
30	14	.265	.475	.210	Impeachments and investigations
	12	.331	.799	.468	Slavery
31	*49*	*.181*	*.437*	*.256*	*Public lands*
	77	.379	.774	.395	Slavery
	12	*−.068*	*.233*	*.301*	*Treaties*
32	29	.235	.454	.219	Public lands
33	73	.220	.432	.213	Public lands
40	*11*	*.073*	*.318*	*.245*	*Public lands*
	11	*.055*	*.411*	*.356*	*Public works*
41	*12*	*.163*	*.378*	*.215*	*Supreme court*
	19	*.056*	*.375*	*.319*	*U.S. currency*
43	*20*	*.083*	*.576*	*.493*	*Banking and finance*
	30	*.190*	*.453*	*.263*	*Public works*
	46	*.055*	*.712*	*.657*	*U.S. currency*
45	11	.256	.604	.348	Banking and finance
	37	*.180*	*.639*	*.459*	*U.S. currency*
47	10	.251	.536	.285	Public lands
52	17	.290	.804	.515	Banking and finance
	16	.328	.856	.527	U.S. currency
	10	*.078*	*.278*	*.200*	*Judiciary*
53	49	.157	.765	.609	*Banking and finance*
	52	*.180*	*.758*	*.578*	*U.S. currency*
62	14	.218	.491	.273	Agriculture
	21	.205	.522	.317	Tariffs
63	18	.228	.526	.298	Judiciary
	27	.280	.549	.269	Interstate commerce/antitrust
65	*41*	*.128*	*.569*	*.441*	*Tax rates*
	16	.301	.533	.232	Banking and finance
	27	*.028*	*.274*	*.246*	*Temperance and liquor*
	116	*.172*	*.445*	*.273*	*World War I*
66	*11*	*.133*	*.464*	*.330*	*Interstate commerce/antitrust*
71	*10*	*.120*	*.536*	*.416*	*Tax rates*
	33	.297	.501	.204	Agriculture
73	12	.215	.508	.293	Tax rates
	17	.365	.619	.254	Banking and finance
	14	.504	.711	.206	Tariffs
	10	*.152*	*.388*	*.236*	*Public works*
74	*11*	*.126*	*.378*	*.252*	*Military pensions/veterans' benefits*

Table 3.3 *(continued)*

Congress	No. of Votes	APRE1	APRE2	APRE2 −APRE1	Issue
77	*14*	*.152*	*.421*	*.269*	*Agriculture*
81	*10*	*.128*	*.583*	*.455*	*Civil rights/desegregation/busing*
86	16	.306	.579	.273	Civil rights/desegregation/busing
87	10	.221	.687	.466	Civil rights/desegregation/busing
	24	.381	.614	.233	Education
88	13	.282	.520	.239	Tax rates
	59	*.158*	*.779*	*.621*	*Civil rights/desegregation/busing*
	10	.429	.717	.289	Impeachments and investigations
	25	.255	.661	.407	Education
	13	.340	.616	.275	Campaign contributions/ ethics/lobbying
	16	.226	.776	.551	Workplace conditions/8-hour day
	13	*.066*	*.789*	*.723*	*Judiciary*
90	23	.380	.682	.303	Civil rights/desegregation/busing
	10	.369	.578	.208	Campaign contributions/ ethics/lobbying
	13	.314	.514	.200	Interstate commerce/antitrust
	17	.305	.617	.312	Housing/housing programs/ rent control
91	16	.485	.770	.285	Civil rights/desegregation/busing
	18	.392	.627	.235	Education
92	44	.395	.612	.217	Tax rates
	47	.402	.713	.311	Civil rights/desegregation/busing
	38	.376	.657	.280	Education
	27	.460	.764	.304	Campaign contributions/ ethics/lobbying
	20	.562	.785	.223	Judiciary
94	21	.555	.771	.216	Civil rights/desegregation/busing
	28	.543	.861	.318	Disputed elections to congress
	22	.521	.740	.219	Voting rights
96	15	.473	.692	.219	Civil rights/desegregation/busing
97	19	.399	.675	.276	Civil rights/desegregation/busing
98	12	.219	.475	.256	Debt ceilings

Note: This table shows only Congresses with an issue area in which there were at least 10 roll calls with a gain in *APRE* of at least 0.2 from adding the second dimension. Issue areas for which *APRE1* is less than 0.2 are indicated in italics.

predominate among the issues where the second dimension results in a big gain in the *APRE*. This observation supports our view that a one-dimensional model typically provides a good fit to the data, with a second dimension being needed in periods when race issues are distinct from economic ones.[22]

The Dimensionality of Congressional Voting

Since low dimensionality is an important and, to many, an unexpected, empirical result, we will discuss a variety of sets of supporting evidence for it, including two sets of quite technical evidence. In appendix B, we ask whether the true dimensionality of roll call voting can be determined. The answer is a *qualified* yes. We offer evidence that it is extremely unlikely that there are more than three—and, in most Congresses, no more than two—dimensions of voting. Also in appendix B, we compare our ability to classify with a one-dimensional model with what might be expected if legislators and roll calls were distributed within a multidimensional sphere and if there were perfect voting in this higher-dimensional space. We show that our empirical results are very unlikely to have been generated by "perfect" voting in a high-dimensional (that is, more than two) voting space.

In this section, we discuss four sets of less technical evidence. First, restricting ourselves to three Houses, we show the increments in the percentage classified correctly when W-NOMINATE is estimated with as many as 15 dimensions. Second, we evaluate the classification ability of the second dimension from the dynamic, two-dimensional model, with linear-trend estimation, and compare this to the first dimension. Third, we show that the results of W-NOMINATE are reasonably stable when the algorithm is applied to subsets of roll calls that have been defined by substantive content. Fourth, since dimensionality may depend on the agenda, we compare the model's performance with measures of the diversity of the agenda.

What Happens When a High-Dimensional Model Is Estimated?

To check the dimensionality of our dynamic models, we selected three Houses and estimated the constant or *static* model (to distinguish it from our various dynamic estimations on multiple Congresses) up to 15 dimensions. We chose the 32nd House (1851–52), the 85th House (1957–58), and the 97th House (1981–82) for our high-dimensional analyses. The 32nd is one of the worst-fitting Houses in two dimensions and thus a good candidate to exhibit high dimensionality. The 85th House represents the post–World War II civil-rights era, when the two-dimensional linear model clearly dominates the one-dimensional linear model.[23] The 97th House is included because it appears that roll call voting became nearly unidimensional by the 1980s.

Figure 3.6 displays the classification gains for the second through the fifteenth dimensions for each of the three Houses. The classification percentage for the first dimension was 70.3 for the 32nd House, 79.0 for the 85th, and 84.6 for the 97th. The lines in the figure indicate how much the corresponding dimension adds to the total of correctly classified. Note that the lines do not drop off smoothly because, as we explained in chapter 2, W-NOMINATE is maximizing log-likelihood, not classification.

The 97th House is, at most, two-dimensional, with the second dimension being very weak. After two dimensions, the added classification gains are minuscule, for there is a clear pattern of noise fitting beyond two dimensions. Even though, in contrast to the 97th, the 85th House is strongly two-dimensional, there is little evidence of classification gains from the addition of dimensions. The 32nd does show evidence of gains for up to four dimensions, but even four dimensions account for only 80 percent of the decisions, and ten, for only 85 percent.

The results for the 32nd House carry over to our other period of "spatial collapse," the Era of Good Feelings. Classification on the first dimension is 70 percent for the 17th House and reaches only 80 percent in four dimensions and 88 in ten. These results show that either voting is accounted for by a low-dimensional spatial model, or it is, in effect, spatially chaotic. There appears to be no middle ground. In other words, there is never a period in American history in which, if we do not obtain a good fit

Increase in Classification Percentage

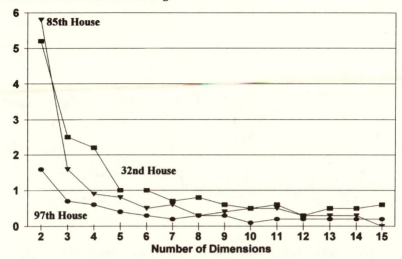

Figure 3.6. Classification gains from adding dimensions for three Houses. The lines plot the increase that occurs in the classification percentage as dimensions are added. The 97th House (1981–82) shows a strong one-dimensional result, to which additional dimensions add very little. The 85th House (1957–58) was elected during the period of the three-party system and shows a substantial gain from adding a second dimension. The "chaotic" 32nd House (1851–52) shows gains but the overall level of classification remains low. Additional dimensions are largely fitting "noise" in the data. The results are from W-NOMINATE.

with a one- or two-dimensional model, we can obtain a good fit with a three- or four-dimensional model.

The Relative Importance of the Second Dimension

Although the evidence presented above suggests a marginal role for (at most) a second dimension—and a weak one at that—it is important to evaluate the second dimension by other than its marginal impact. Specifically, Koford (1989, 1991) argues that a one-dimensional model will provide a good fit even when spaces have higher levels of dimensionality. For example, in a truly two-dimensional space, one dimension will have some success at classifying any vote that is not strictly orthogonal to the dimension. As a result, the marginal increases in fit, on the order of 3 percent, may understate the importance of the second dimension.

The natural question, then, is, How well does the second dimension do in classifying by itself? To study this problem, we took the second-dimension legislator coordinates from our preferred model—two dimensions with a linear trend—and, for each roll call, found a cutpoint that minimized classification errors. We used the minimum number of errors to compute classification percentages. We made the same computation for the first dimension.

The results of these computations for the House are shown in figure 3.7. The average percentage classification for the first 100 Houses, using the first dimension, is 84.3 percent; but the second dimension accounts for only 70.8 percent. The 70.8 per-

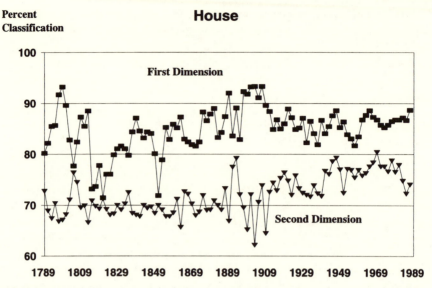

Figure 3.7. Classification on the first and second dimension. These graphs show the results when roll calls are placed to minimize classification errors, while keeping the D-NOMINATE legislator coordinates fixed. The first-dimension coordinates almost always classify at a rate of 80 percent or better. The second dimension barely betters the benchmark model of the percentage vote on the winning side.

cent is particularly unimpressive if we consider that predicting by the marginals would lead to a 66.7 percent classification. If the two dimensions were indeed of equal importance, then in some Congresses, dimension two might do better than dimension one. But in all 100 Houses, the first dimension did best (although the difference between the two was slim in the 17th House). The Senate results are a tad weaker—83.8 percent for dimension one versus 73.6 percent for two. The marginals here led to a 66.1 percent classification. In addition, dimension two does better in Senates 2, 17, and 18. But the second dimension is clearly a second fiddle.

Our overwhelming results that show that the first dimension dwarfs the second and higher dimensions convinced even Koford (1991), who admitted that his first analysis was incorrect. At the same time, however, he claimed that we would find gains from higher dimensionality if we, unparsimoniously, allowed a variation in the salience the legislators place on the dimensions. That is, legislators, in addition to having ideal points, would also be assigned weights on each dimension. Their squared distances to roll call alternatives would then be computed as a weighted sum of the dimensions.[24] But we were also able to show (Poole and Rosenthal, 1994b) that allowing for variable salience would not result in a high-dimensional model that yielded important gains in classification over a low-dimensional, constant-salience model.

Do Different Issues Give Different Scales?

In contrast to our emphasis on low dimensionality, Clausen (1973) has argued that there are five "dimensions" to congressional voting, represented by the issue areas of government management, social welfare, agriculture, civil liberties, and foreign and defense policy. We have coded every House and Senate roll call, from 1789 to 1988, according to these five categories; for completeness, we added a sixth category, termed "miscellaneous" (see appendix C). If the issues are really distinct dimensions, we ought to get sharp differences in legislator coordinates when the issues are scaled separately.

To conduct this experiment with separate scalings, we chose the 95th House because it had the largest number of roll call votes (1,540). There were 714 government-management votes; 286 social-welfare votes; 311 foreign-and-defense-policy votes; and, to have enough votes for scaling, 229 in a residual set that combined agriculture, civil liberties, and miscellaneous issues. We then ran one- and two-dimensional (static) W-NOMINATE procedures on each of these four clusters of votes. Because it is difficult to directly compare coordinates from two-dimensional scalings, we based our comparisons on correlations between all unique pairwise distances among legislators. (If there are N legislators, there are $N(N - 1)/2$ unique pairs of legislators.)

Correlations between the management, welfare, and residual categories for one-dimensional scalings are, as shown in table 3.4, all high, around 0.9. Correlations between the foreign-and-defense-policy category and the other three categories were somewhat lower, in the 0.7 to 0.8 range.[25] As a whole, the results hardly suggest that each of these clusterings of substantive issues generates a separate spatial dimension.

When the same subsets of votes are scaled separately in two dimensions, the correlations between categories are somewhat lower than they are in one dimension (see table 3.4). This result is not surprising: The 95th House had nearly unidimensional voting. From the D-NOMINATE unidimensional scaling with a linear trend that was applied to the whole data set, we find one-dimensional correct classifications for 83 percent of the votes in each of the four categories. With two dimensions, the percentage of correct classifications increases only to 84 percent for social welfare and for foreign and defense policy, and to 85 percent for the other two categories.[26]

Moving from one dimension to two doubles the number of estimated parameters, with only slight increases occurring in classification ability. In breaking down the roll calls into four categories and estimating each separately, the number of legislator parameters is effectively quadrupled. With a further doubling of all parameters—in moving from one dimension to two—one is likely to be fitting idiosyncratic noise in the data. The fit to the noise weakens the underlying strong correlations between leg-

Table 3.4 Interpoint Distance Correlations, the Clausen Category Scalings, 95th House

Clausen Category	Correlations			
	(1)	(2)	(3)	(4)
(1) Government management	1.0	.914[a]	.796	.908
(2) Social welfare	.883[b]	1.0	.765	.881
(3) Foreign and defense policy	.770	.654	1.0	.724
(4) Miscellaneous policy, civil liberties, and agriculture	.832	.746	.613	1.0

[a]Numbers above diagonal are correlations from one-dimensional scalings.

[b]Numbers below diagonal are correlations from two-dimensional scalings.

islator positions. We also note that the spirit of Clausen's work suggests that each category should be scaled in only one dimension. In summary, our breakdown of the 95th House by use of Clausen categories indicates that the categories represent highly related, not distinct, dimensions.

The Agenda and Dimensionality

Macdonald and Rabinowitz (1987) argue that American political conflict is basically one-dimensional within the time span of any one Congress, but that the dimension of conflict evolves slowly. One basis for the Macdonald-Rabinowitz argument would be that short-term coalition arrangements enforce a logroll across issues that generates voting patterns consistent with a unidimensional spatial model. Another potential consideration is that short-run unidimensionality may reflect the fact that, in any two-year period, Congress must place some restrictions on the issues that can be given time for consideration.

An explanation related to that of Macdonald and Rabinowitz is a selection-bias argument that was originally made by Van Doren (1990) and developed, in the context of a simple formal model, by Snyder (1992b). Van Doren's basic idea is that only a small fraction of the potential issues ever get voted on, either because they are supported by only a small fraction of the membership or because, even if there is widespread support, an issue is screened from roll call voting by committees. Snyder formalized the role of committees in a simple model where committees had gatekeeping power.[27] If there were more voting, the story goes, there would be more dimensions uncovered by scaling techniques.

The selection-bias story is logically correct but empirically irrelevant. One important observation is that our low-dimensionality result applies not only to the House, but also to the Senate, where gatekeeping is less prevalent. Another is that certain legislation, particularly in regard to appropriations, must be considered annually and cannot be screened. Indeed, a very diverse set of issues gets voted on, even in a relatively small portion of the time that Congress is in session. Consider the three-month period between January 10, 1967, and April 10, 1967, during the 90th Congress, one of the textbook Congresses that inspired the new institutionalism's emphasis on committee jurisdictions and rules (Shepsle and Weingast, 1994), including gatekeeping powers. How winnowed were the issues? During this period, contested votes (over 2.5 percent on the minority side) in the House of Representatives were taken on the following issues:

1. The seating of Adam Clayton Powell, Jr.
2. The debt ceiling
3. Foreign travel by members of the Agriculture Committee
4. The Vietnam War
5. Emergency food assistance to India
6. The interest-equalization tax
7. The establishment of a National Holiday Commission
8. Appropriations for the Trust Territory of the Pacific Islands
9. Appropriations for various cabinet-level departments
10. The Alliance for Progress

11. The size of the staff for the Committee on Science and Astronautics
12. Funds for the House Un-American Activities Committee
13. The copyright law

Winnowing may have occurred, but the range of substantive issues voted on remains vast. If one were to consider the entire length of the 90th House, a much wider variety of issues would appear. Clearly, the breadth of issues is sufficient to manifest high dimensionality.

To make our observation for the 90th House more systematic, at least in a crude way, we computed, for each of the 100 Houses and Senates, the Herfindahl concentration index[28] for the six Clausen categories. The lower the degree of concentration, the more diverse the agenda. The observation that the index is related to trend (the correlation [R] is -0.46 for the House and -0.53 for the Senate) suggests that the congressional agenda has become more diverse as government has expanded. The index is significantly correlated with the geometric mean probabilities from the two-dimensional, linear-trend model, but in a counterhypothesis direction for the House ($R = -0.310$). The results for the Senate are quite weak ($R = 0.145$), but in the correct direction. For the House, as the roll call set becomes more diverse, the model fits better. The House result is undoubtedly a spurious one. The worst-fitting years occur early in the time series, but the agenda has become more diverse over time. Indeed, diversity of the agenda, at least as measured by this index, is not significantly related to the ability (the difference in geometric mean probabilities) of the two-dimensional model to improve over the one-dimensional linear model ($R = -0.062$ for the House and -0.049 for the Senate, respectively).

One reason for these generally negative results for the diversity hypothesis is that the index has exhibited little variation. For Congresses 40 to 100, the index averaged 0.347, with a standard deviation of 0.061, in the House and averaged 0.361, with a standard deviation of 0.166, in the Senate. In the last 120 years, Congress has had a full and wide-ranging agenda, so low-dimensional voting did not occur simply because votes were restricted to a narrow topical area.

In a nutshell, the roll call voting agenda of Congress is always a cornucopia of diverse issues, even if many issues are screened from the agenda. This diversity notwithstanding, to the extent that spatial models are useful in describing the roll call voting data, only low-dimensional models are needed.

Summary

Congressional roll call voting, throughout most of American history, has had a simple structure. A two-dimensional spatial model that allows for a linear time trend accounts for most of the roll call voting. The primary dimension is concerned with political party, whereas the second dimension picks up issues that split the two major parties. Race has indeed been the most important issue dividing the political parties internally.

We now turn to an examination of the temporal stability of individual legislator positions; the changes in position that are brought about by the replacement of legislators; and the polarization of the parties within each of the political-party systems.

4

The Spatial Model: Stability, Replacement, and Polarization

This chapter takes a broad look at policy changes in American history, with policy measured by both the location of groups of legislators and the locations of winning roll call outcomes in the voting space. Policy changes can occur either because legislators' preferences change or because there is a change in the institutional structure that aggregates preferences to produce policies. In this chapter, we concentrate on changes in preferences and on how changes in majority control of either house translate into changes in policy outcomes.

In the first section of the chapter, we look at changes in the mean positions of the major political parties in the three major party systems: the Federalist/Republican system; the Whig/Democratic; and the Republican/Democratic. We find that there were some important changes in the positions of the parties, but much more modest changes in the mean positions of either House. Nonetheless, as a result of the "tyranny of the majority," slight changes in mean position, when accompanied by a shift in majority control, can lead to substantial changes in policy. The policy changes are discussed in the second section. We find that the swings in policy during the nineteenth century and the early twentieth century were much greater than those later in the twentieth century. Although the New Deal initiated a large policy shift comparable to those of the nineteenth century, since the end of World War II, policy swings have dampened considerably. This chapter seeks to identify the origin of these changes.

Indeed, the preferences expressed in a legislature can change because individual legislators change their own preferences, as measured by their spatial position. We show in the third section that our estimates of legislator coordinates remain very stable from Congress to Congress, with the correlations almost always exceeding 0.95. Given this stability in legislator coordinates, changes in preferences must occur almost entirely through the process of replacing retiring or defeated legislators. Therefore, in the fourth section, we consider replacement in Congress, including a detailed analysis of replacement since Reconstruction. In particular, we note that, beginning in 1936, successive waves of northern and southern Democratic replacements in Congress had the effect of shifting the northern Democratic wing to the Left on the first dimension and shifting the southern Democratic wing to the center on the first dimension and sharply upward on the second dimension. The Republican party remained fairly stable, although, through the 1960s, it drifted to the Left in both the House and Senate and subsequently has moved back to the right again.

Finally, we investigate the polarization of preferences. We develop measures of the dispersion of political parties around their respective party mean positions, and of the degree of separation of the two major parties within each stable period. These measures allow us to compare various party systems over time. We find that the most polarized period in congressional voting was from the post-Reconstruction period through the end of World War I. In contrast, the post–World War II period has been the least polarized of the major party systems, largely because of the North-South split within the Democratic party.

The History of Party Positions in the Basic Space

The overall first-dimension mean positions since Reconstruction for the House and the Senate are one of the two series shown in figure 4.1. The same information for the Federalist/Jeffersonian Republican period and the Whig/Democratic period is shown for the House in figure 4.2.

There is very little variation in these overall means. The shifts are due largely to shifts in the party balance in either house. For example, the mean has a generally liberal tendency in figure 4.2, reflecting the Jeffersonians' gradual rise to dominance. Similarly, figure 4.1 shows Congress becoming more conservative during the realignment to the Republicans of the mass electorate in the 1890s. The change is especially evident in the Senate, which had been stacked (Stewart and Weingast, 1992) with senators from pro-Republican western states. This is followed by a liberal shift during the Progressive era; a conservative shift during the period of Republican dominance that followed World War I; a liberal shift begun by the Great Depression; and a conservative swing of the pendulum again in the 1940s. The House shows a long period of stability during the years of Democratic control that began in 1954. The same stability is broken for the Senate by the Republican swing in the 1980 elections.

We can discuss changes in the mean—with small exceptions like the conservative swing in the Senate in 1980—for both houses in the same breath because these changes reflect more the fundamental issues that politicians had to confront (such as the Great Depression), than the differences in the institutional structure of the two houses. That the power of the Speaker has varied in the history of the House (Cooper and Brady, 1981), or that the use of closed rules has varied, or that cloture rules were indeed changed in the Senate seem not to count for very much. During the post-Reconstruction period (after 1879), the first-dimension chamber means correlate at 0.75; and they correlate at 0.85 during the twentieth century. Many of the differences in the series have to do with differences in the party ratios in the two chambers, due, in turn, either to differences in apportionment and the mode of election; to staggered six-year terms in the Senate; or to random shifts in votes, such as the election in which the Republicans won control of the Senate in 1980 by capturing several states with very small margins. Indeed, a simple regression, with the Senate first-dimension mean as the dependent variable and the House first-dimension mean and the difference between the Republican chamber proportions as independent variables, produces an R^2 of 0.87 for the post-Reconstruction period. For the twentieth century, the R^2 is 0.95.

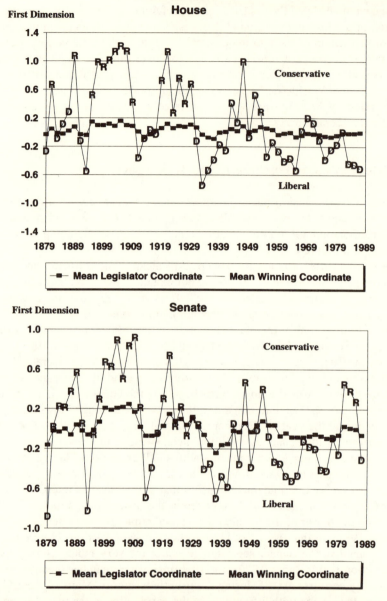

Figure 4.1. Chamber means for legislators and winning outcomes on roll calls, post-Reconstruction (1879–1988). The legislator series is quite stable, reflecting a competitive two-party system. The winning outcomes are more volatile, largely reflecting changes in control within a chamber. Outcomes in both houses become very liberal after the Great Depression, but only the Senate swings to the right after 1980, when the Republicans take the Senate but the Democrats retain the House. The results are for the first dimension, from the D-NOMINATE model, with a linear trend. The letters "D" and "R" indicate which party controlled each house.

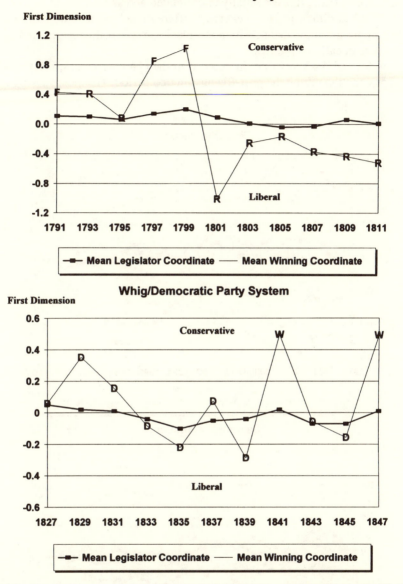

Figure 4.2. Chamber means for legislators and winning outcomes on House roll calls in the first two-party systems. The legislator series is quite stable, reflecting a competitive two-party system. The winning outcomes are more volatile, largely reflecting changes in control within a chamber. Outcomes become more liberal with the ascendancy of the Jeffersonians in 1801. There is less volatility in the Whig/Democratic period, but the most conservative outcomes do occur in the two Houses controlled by the Whigs (in 1841 and 1847). The results are for the first dimension, from the D-NOMINATE model, with a linear trend. The letters indicate which party controlled the House.

In contrast, the second dimension mean exhibits little overall variation. In the post-Reconstruction period, it is essentially uncorrelated across Houses (0.09). This is because the second dimension has generally differentiated parties internally on a second, less important, dimension, which is linked to race. It thus is less indicative of central issues in national politics.[1]

Figures 4.3 and 4.4 show that, in contrast to the chamber means, party means exhibit more variation during the post-Reconstruction period. The most striking features

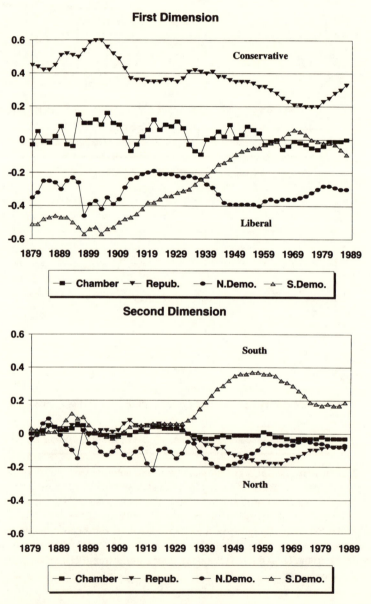

Figure 4.3. Mean legislator coordinates, by party, House of Representatives, post-Reconstruction (1879–1988).

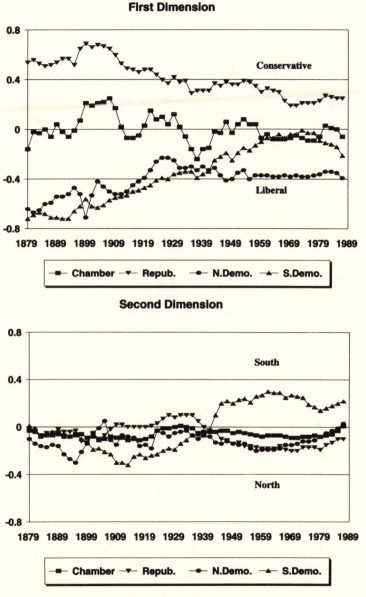

Figure 4.4. Mean legislator coordinates, by party, Senate, post-Reconstruction (1879–1988).

on the first dimension are the 70-year rightward drift of the southern Democrats in both chambers and the narrowing of the gap between the Democrats and the Republicans by the 1950s. These changes are largely common to the party delegations in both chambers. The correlation is 0.91 for Republicans and 0.86 for Democrats. Both of these correlations are higher than the entire chamber correlation (0.82), which is consistent with our claim that cross-chamber differences are largely matters of differences in party ratios.

In the nineteenth century, the southern Democrats are to the Left of their northern counterparts on the first dimension. Beginning at the turn of the twentieth century, both northern and southern Democrats drift toward the center, until the 1920s, when the northern Democrats begin moving back to the Left. The northern Democrats generally move leftward through the New Deal, with the effect being more pronounced in the House. The southern Democrats cross over the northern Democrats in the early 1940s and continue to move steadily to the Right until the mid-to-late 1960s. After the passage of the Civil Rights Act of 1964 and the Voting Rights Act of 1965, the southern Democrats begin to move slowly back to the Left again but are still considerably to the Right of their northern counterparts at the end of our time series in 1988.

The House Republicans drift slowly to the Left until the early 1970s, dramatically narrowing the gap between themselves and the Democrats. Beginning in the 1970s, they begin to move back to the Right. The pattern for the Senate Republicans is basically the same as that for their House counterparts, but the leftward movement was not as pronounced until the mid-1950s, and the move back to the Right, at the end of the series, is also not as pronounced as that of the House. The strong rightward drift of House Republicans and the less pronounced move of Senate Republicans are consistent with House Republicans, led by Newt Gingrich and defined by the "Contract with America," being the more radical advocates of policy change in the mid-1990s.

The two chambers differ somewhat in their patterns of change on the second dimension. Largely because there is little variation over time in the position of Democrats, the Democrat cross-chamber correlation is 0.00! Similarly, the correlation for northern Democrats is 0.10.

In contrast, the cross-chamber second dimension correlation for southern Democrats is 0.88. This reflects the fact that, in both houses, the southern Democrats separate from northern Democrats and move upward in a "socially" conservative direction after the introduction of civil-rights issues in the second New Deal. The Republicans respond to the same issues by moving downward in a "northern" or "socially liberal" direction. The biggest separation of the parties on the second dimension occurs during the mid-1960s during the voting on the civil-rights bills. After the New Deal, the second dimension captures the race or civil-rights issue.

Before the New Deal, there is an important difference between the chambers that relates to the Republican inter-chamber correlation on the second dimension being only 0.78. In 1925, the second-dimension mean in the House was higher for the Republicans than for the Democrats. The reverse was true in the Senate. Recall our discussion of party-line voting in chapter 3—specifically, the results displayed in figure 3.5. The second dimension was needed from the 69th Senate through the 74th (1925–36) to fully account for party-line voting because a small group of midwestern Republican senators voted with the Democrats to such an extent that they were located just above the Democrats—among them on the first dimension but above them on the second. The midwestern Republicans cause the Republicans' mean on the second dimension to be greater than the mean of the Democrats in the 1925 Senate. The Republicans' mean crosses over the Democrats' mean only in 1940.[2] Thereafter, the Republicans' second-dimension mean is less than the mean of the Democrats.

The pattern of sharp differences in overall party means, including important regional differences within parties, holds also for the two earlier party systems, which are shown in figures 4.5 and 4.6. In both cases, we have broken down the parties into northern and southern wings to aid in the interpretation of the dimensions.

Figure 4.5 shows the development of the Federalist/Jeffersonian Republican system for the 1789–1811 period (congresses 1–12), for the House of Representatives. Although the authors of the Constitution opposed political parties (Hofstadter, 1969,

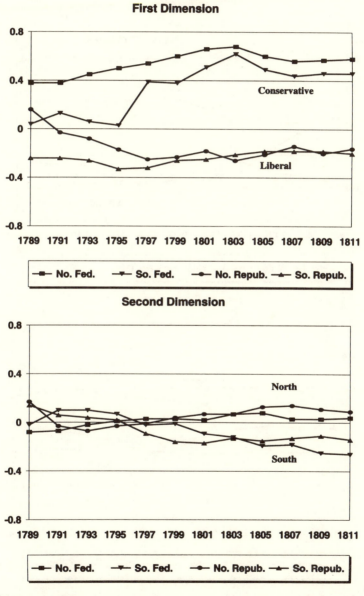

Figure 4.5. Mean legislator coordinates, by party and region, House of Representatives, Federalist/Jeffersonian party system (1789–1812). As the party system becomes organized, party differentiates on the first dimension and region on the second.

pp. 40–73), by the second Congress, two voting blocs emerged—one being identified with the policies of Alexander Hamilton and the other with Thomas Jefferson's policies. These became the Federalist and Republican parties.[3]

Figure 4.5 clearly shows the evolution of a political-party system. By the 5th House (which was elected in 1796), the Federalists and the Republicans are distinctly sepa-

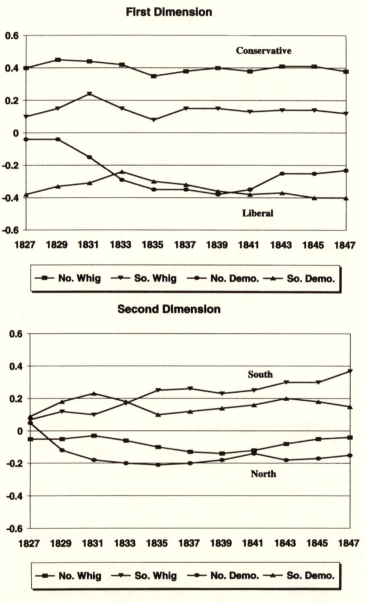

Figure 4.6. Mean legislator coordinates by party and region, House of Representatives, Whig-Democratic system (1827–48). Party differentiates on the first dimension. As the conflict over slavery builds, regions become differentiated on the second dimension.

rated on the first dimension, with no meaningful North-South effects occurring. The emergence of party polarization on the first dimension does not affect the stability of the chamber mean, as shown in figure 4.2. A coherent two-party pattern on the second dimension does not emerge until the 7th Congress (which was elected in 1800). After 1800, the second dimension, though minor in importance, is clearly a North-South dimension, which arises as slavery takes a more important place on the agenda (see chapter 5).

Figure 4.6 shows the Whig/Democratic party system for the 1827–48 period.[4] It begins with the elections of 1826 because the presidential election of 1824 split the Jeffersonian Republicans into blocs that aligned themselves with the presidential candidates, Jackson, Clay, and Crawford.[5] It ends with the elections of 1846 because the Congress elected in 1848 wrote the Compromise of 1850, which destabilized the Whig/Democratic party system (see chapter 5).

Once again, we see the emergence of a coherent two-party system. Before the election of Andrew Jackson in 1828, the two wings of the Democratic party are quite distinct on the first dimension, with no coherent structure at all on the second dimension. By 1833 the two wings of the Democratic party are indistinguishable on the first dimension; the southern Whigs are the more moderate wing of the Whig party. The second dimension clearly evolves into a North-South dimension, with the separation occurring as early as 1829.

Party Polarization and Policy Swings

We have observed that during the periods of the three two-party systems in American history, the parties have been polarized on at least the first of the two dimensions of the basic space. At the same time, the means of the two dimensions are quite stable. In contrast to our finding of stability, shifts in the means could have occurred in the following way. Moderates, when elected, would have long tenures in office and be a fixed point in our dynamic estimation. Electoral swings would put large numbers of extreme liberals in office one year and replace them with extreme conservatives two years later. But, the data tell us that very large swings of this form rarely happen in American politics. If extreme liberals enter Congress, they are typically offset by the entry of extreme conservatives.

This result is not surprising. Because the parties need to win office to enjoy the spoils and to make policy, competitive forces should lead them to be reasonably balanced. At the same time, they could represent polarized rather than convergent positions, both out of a need to appeal to partisans or to satisfy their own ideology[6] and out of incentives to polarize that are inherent in the American system of checks and balances.[7]

Suppose the two parties were very disciplined and at loggerheads on every issue. In this case, every roll call vote would be along party lines, and every member within each party would vote identically. Then every member within each party would have the same coordinate, so just two points would represent all the legislators—all the members of one party at one point; all the members of the second party at another point. Such a system would be a perfectly polarized one.

In this perfectly polarized system, the majority party would win every vote; and every vote would be a "perfect" one in that a simple spatial model, with two locations for the corresponding members of the two parties, would fit the voting perfectly. One party would vote Yea, the other Nay, and there would be no voting errors. Moreover, the disciplined, majority party would exercise agenda control and propose its ideal point on every roll call. The outcome would always be the majority party's ideal point. Thus any shift in party control would lead to a large swing in policy. In the Senate, shifting from a 51R–49D ratio to a 49R–51D ratio would change the mean coordinate only slightly, but policy would shift dramatically.

In such a system, a graph of policy-outcome means over time would look like a perfect square wave, with the swings corresponding to whichever party had majority control. Unfortunately, measuring these swings accurately is very difficult. As we explained in chapter 2, even though the cutting line (or point in one dimension) is always identified, we need some error to be present to identify the Yea and Nay outcome locations. If a roll call vote fits our model perfectly—that is, everyone on the Yea side of the cutting line votes Yea, and everyone on the Nay side of the cutting line votes Nay—then any pair of points equidistant from and on opposite sides of the cutting line is consistent with the perfect vote. Unfortunately (or fortunately) for us, as we have documented in this chapter and in chapter 3, our model fits the roll call data so well that, on many roll calls, there are not enough errors to clearly identify the Yea/Nay outcome locations.

Nevertheless, we can at least get a rough idea of the extent of policy swings by selecting the subset of roll calls with at least one outcome inside the space spanned by the legislators and by using the mean of the winning coordinate of this subset as a measure of policy swings over time.[8] This will not be a perfect measure, but it will at least identify the periods of dramatic change.[9] Of course, our measure is an imperfect measure of policy because many roll calls are directed at position-taking by legislators rather than at actual legislation and because many provisions passed by one house either are not passed by the other house, deleted by a conference committee or subject to sustained vetoes by the president.

Figure 4.1 shows the policy swings on the first dimension for the House and the Senate for the post-Reconstruction, Democratic/Republican party system; and figure 4.2 shows the House swings for the other two periods we analyzed above. In both figures, policy swings are much more volatile than changes in the chamber means.

With the end of Reconstruction and the revival of the Democratic party, policy swings become quite large through World War II. There is a large, prolonged conservative swing during the period of Republican dominance that runs from the election of 1896 to that of 1912. There is also a prolonged conservative swing in the House in the 1920s. It is dampened in the Senate because of the group of midwestern Republicans (discussed earlier) who were voting with the Democrats on many issues. The Great Depression induced a liberal swing. It occurred earlier in the House, because the Democrats gained control of the House in the 1930 elections and of the Senate in 1932.

After World War II, the splitting of the Democratic party into northern and southern wings had the effect of considerably dampening swings in both chambers. There is some volatility induced by Republican control in the 80th Congress (1947–48) and in the 83rd (1953–54). Policies between 1954 and 1980 were generally liberal, especially during the period of the Great Society and during the Watergate period of the Nixon presidency. Policies were less liberal when Democratic congressional majorities faced a weak president (Johnson in his last two years and Carter) or a strong Republican (Nixon in his first term and Reagan in his first two years). The sharp swing in the Senate that occurred when the Republicans gained control of it in 1981 may be a harbinger of future changes now that Republicans control both chambers. As the southern Democratic party fades and the two parties become more homogeneous, polarization is bound to increase, and policy swings like those in the nineteenth and early twentieth centuries are likely to return.

Figure 4.2 shows that the victory of the Jeffersonians in the elections of 1800 had a dramatic effect on policy. This comports well with historical accounts of the bitterness of the landmark 1800 elections (Hofstadter, 1969). Subsequent to the 1800 elections, policy moderated dramatically.

Recall that figure 4.6 shows that in its early period, the Whig/Democratic party system was not well structured, and we see the same lack of structure in figure 4.2. The two wings of the Democratic party did not coalesce until 1833, and it was only then that policy swung to the Left of the chamber mean. The two large peaks in 1841 and 1847 correspond to the only Whig majorities during this period.

Our observations about the sources of policy swings are summarized in the regressions reported in table 4.1. In the first column shown for either chamber, we regressed the mean winning policy coordinate on the indicator variables for party control of the House, the Senate, and the presidency and for the Republican party's seat share in both houses. In the second column, we eliminated all variables not significant in the first column. (Because the policy process can be expected to exhibit persistence over time, we corrected for first-order autocorrelation.) The observations are given for the 54 Congresses elected from 1879 to 1985.

Each chamber is quite responsive to its internal partisan balance. A shift in partisan control shifts the mean winning coordinate about 0.4 to 0.5 units, or roughly one-quarter of the span of the space. A 1 percent increase in the Republicans' seat share moves policy rightward about 0.02 units. In table 4.1, all internal chamber effects are highly significant.

In contrast, neither chamber seems very responsive to its external environment. Although we pointed to shifts under Johnson, Nixon, Carter, and Reagan, there is no systematic evidence that Congress simply responds to the partisan identity of the president. Similarly, in one chamber, there is no accommodation to partisan control of the other chamber, although there is weak evidence that the House shows some accommodation to the seat shares in the Senate.

We have obtained a strong positive result: Winning outcomes are highly responsive to the balance of partisan forces within each house of Congress.[10] On the other hand, a negative result is that each house of Congress adopts its winning outcomes in a way that ignores the institutional structure of the legislative process. The overall absence of significant accommodation may indicate that most accommodation takes place in conference. Since conference reports are typically approved by overwhelming majorities, they tend to be constrained roll calls that are excluded from our analysis of winning coordinates. This finding would be consistent with the view that the bulk of roll call voting is concerned with position-taking rather than policy-making. Future research should investigate whether these results would hold when the computation of mean winning policy coordinates is restricted to policy-relevant votes.

Table 4.1 Policy Shifts in the House (1879–1985): Regressions with the Mean Winning Policy Coordinate, First Dimension, as the Dependent Variable

| | Coefficient | | | | |
| | House | | Senate | | |
Variable	(1)	(2)	(1)	(2)	Variable Definition
C	−1.324***	−1.243***	−1.213***	−1.162***	Intercept term
	(0.268)[a]	(0.255)	(0.232)	(0.202)	
HDUM	0.567)***	0.486***	−0.015		Party controlling House
	(0.141)	(0.117)	(0.124)		(0 = Democratic,
					1 = Repubican)
SDUM	−0.131		0.378***	0.389***	Party controlling Senate
	(0.136)		(0.119)	(0.099)	(0 = Democratic,
					1 = Republican)
PRESDUM	−0.038		0.072		Party controlling presidency
	(0.094)		(0.082)		(0 = Democratic,
					1 = Republican)
HREP	1.680**	1.852***	0.636		Republican party's share
	(0.594)	(0.557)	(0.534)		of House seats
SREP	1.317*	0.854	1.546**	2.105***	Republican party's share
	(0.757)	(0.590)	(0.634)	(0.490)	of Senate seats
ρ	0.354**	0.370**	0.304*	0.257*	First-order autocorrelation
	(0.151)	(0.145)	(0.144)	(0.137)	
Adjusted R^2	0.797	0.800	0.763	0.767	
Standard error of regression	0.245	0.243	0.216	0.214	
Durbin-Watson	1.874	1.853	1.944	1.986	
F statistic	34.361	52.063	28.426	56.955	
Mean dependent variable	0.157	0.157	0.012	0.012	
Number of observations	54	54	54	54	

a. Standard errors are in parentheses.
* Statistically significant with one-tail p value < 0.05.
** Statistically significant with one-tail p value < 0.01.
*** Statistically significant with one-tail p value < 0.001.

Spatial Stability

We have seen that, to whatever extent roll call voting can be captured by a spatial model, a low-dimensional model—say, a one-and-a-half-dimensional one—suffices. Our estimates of the model have disclosed that although the overall chamber means are relatively stable, there is considerable internal change within parties. Moreover, changes in party control induce dramatic changes in policy, as measured by mean winning coordinates.

Of course, it is meaningful to speak of changes in policy only if the dimension itself is stable. In this section, therefore, we address two issues: Is the major, first dimension stable, and are individual positions stable? If the answers to these two questions are both yes, we have to conclude that changes in the preferences expressed in the legislature occur through the replacement of legislators, a topic investigated in the next section. Replacement, particularly through its effect on party control, then induces the policy changes we saw in the previous section.

The Stability of the Major Dimension

Given the pace of events, it would be possible for the major dimension to show rapid legislator shifts. In our dynamic model, very rapid shifts are precluded by our imposition of the restriction that individual movement can be only linear over time. Although the absence of substantial gains in fit from using higher-order polynomial models (see table 3.1) constitutes evidence that legislators do not shift back and forth in the space, we thought it important to evaluate stability in a manner that allows for the maximum possible adjustment.[11]

To perform this evaluation, we did separate estimates of coordinates for each House and Senate (W-NOMINATE coordinates) of Congresses 1 to 100. This procedure finds the best one-dimensional fit for each Congress and allows for the maximum Congress-to-Congress adjustment of individual positions. Because there is no constraint that ties the estimates together, we cannot compare individual coordinates directly, but we can compute the correlations between the coordinates for members common to two Houses or two Senates. Rather than deal with a sparse 100-by-100 correlation matrix, we focus on the correlations of the first 96 Congresses with each of the succeeding four Congresses.[12] This choice allows us to look at stability for as far forward as one decade.

We averaged these correlations across the first 96 Congresses and for four periods of history. For both houses of Congress, the separate scalings are remarkably similar, especially since the end of the Civil War, as seen in the upper portion of table 4.2.[13] After 1861, a senator could count on a stable alignment, relative to his colleagues, over an entire six-year term. (A $t+1$ correlation refers to the correlation of coordinates of members common to one Congress and the succeeding Congress.)

In the lower portion of table 4.2, we display the individual pairwise correlations only for situations where either the correlation of $t+1$ was less than 0.8, or a later correlation was less than 0.5—that is, we show periods of instability. Consistent with the preceding discussion and the discussion of overall fit in chapter 3, the low correlations are overwhelmingly concentrated in pairs where at least one Congress preceded the end of the Civil War.

It is also noteworthy that a preponderance of the low correlations fall, for both houses, in the Era of Good Feelings (pairs where at least one Congress falls in Congresses 14–18); and, for the Senate, in the period around 1850. These cases are not spatial flip-flops, where two solid major dimensions bear little relation to one another, but simply cases of a bad fit, where there is not a strong first dimension in a Congress. (The only geometric mean probabilities below 0.6 for the House static scalings occur in Congresses 14, 15, 17, and 32; for the Senate static scalings, Congresses 32 and 33 were the only ones below 0.6.)

Table 4.2 Correlations of Legislator Coordinates from Static, Biennial Scalings

Averages for Years	Senate				House				Number of Congresses
	$t+1$[a]	$t+2$	$t+3$	$t+4$	$t+1$	$t+2$	$t+3$	$t+4$	
1789–1860	.77	.77	.69	.55	.87	.81	.75	.70	36
1861–1900	.94	.91	.91	.91	.96	.95	.93	.95	20
1901–1944	.90	.85	.81	.78	.94	.93	.92	.91	22
1945–1980	.94	.92	.90	.87	.96	.94	.93	.91	18
1789–1980	.87	.85	.80	.74	.92	.89	.86	.84	96
Individual Congress[b]									
1 (1789)	.62	.71	.59	—[c]					
2 (1791)	.27	.35	—	—	.88	.84	.68	.38	
3 (1793)	.84	.75	.50	.01					
8 (1803)					.75	.78	.86	.79	
9 (1805)	.77	.93	.86	.83					
11 (1809)	.76	.73	.85	—					
13 (1813)	.93	.94	.64	.15	.93	.45	.30	.18	
14 (1815)	.70	.34	.13	.73	.18	.02	.07	.49	
15 (1817)	.30	.51	.46	.44	.88	.46	.55	.46	
16 (1819)	.10	.26	.57	.42	.60	.73	.78	.88	
17 (1821)	.22	.30	.05	.40	.59	.62	.74	.78	
18 (1823)	.26	.56	.51	.63	.62	.72	.79	.64	
20 (1827)					.94	.90	.55	.39	
21 (1829)					.94	.64	.46	.66	
22 (1831)	.77	.77	.85	.59	.73	.60	.78	.83	
27 (1841)	.95	.98	.93	.39					
30 (1847)	.62	.90	.69	.51					
31 (1849)	.26	.71	.89	.82					
32 (1851)	.65	.60	.62	.63	.76	.69	.63	.63	
36 (1859)					.90	.90	.59	.49	
37 (1861)					.96	.93	.42	.80	
72 (1931)	.90	.89	.60	.41					
73 (1933)	.90	.81	.70	.42					
74 (1935)	.78	.63	.40	.55					
77 (1941)	.74	.70	.79	.82					
84 (1955)	.97	.88	.89	.50					
87 (1961)	.78	.92	.85	.87					

[a] The notation $t+k$, $k = 1, 2, 3, 4$, refers to the correlation of legislator coordinates for legislators serving in Congress t, given in the left-hand column, with their coordinates in Congress $t+k$. Correlation is computed only for those legislators serving in both Congresses.

[b] The first year of service for the Congress follows. Results are shown only for those Congresses for which either the $t+1$ correlation was less than 0.8, or where any $t+k$ correlation, $k = 2, 3, 4$, was less than 0.5, and there were at least 4 legislators in a pair of Congresses.

[c] A blank entry indicates that there were less than 4 legislators in common for a pair of Congresses.

Subsequent to the Civil War, there are no $t+1$ correlations below 0.8 for the House. In the Senate, there are some low correlations for the 1930s (for Senates 72–74 [1931–37]), during the party realignment in mass voting that was due to the Great Depression. But these are minor effects. The party realignments in mass voting in the 1890s and 1930s were reflected in congressional voting as changes in the center of gravity along an existing dimension and not in any structural change of the voting dimensions. (See chapter 5.) The first dimension is remarkably stable; the stability persists except for two Senates between 1955 and 1962, when a second dimension was also important.

Stability of Individuals

It is possible to obtain high correlations when individuals are moving in the space. If members serving at a particular time, *t,* all had nearly equal trend coefficients, their coordinates would remain highly correlated even if they were moving in relation to members elected later than that time.

To assess the stability of individual positions in the space, we computed for each legislator the annual movement implied by the estimated trend coefficients in our two-dimensional, linear estimation. Given that the space we estimate is identified only up to translations and rotations, one has to interpret the movements in relative terms. The trend coefficient tells us whether a member is moving in relation to legislators whose careers have overlapped this member's.

Average trends for each Congress are shown in figure 4.7. The figure shows only legislators who served in at least 5 Congresses—roughly a decade or more. (Similar curves for legislators with shorter careers would appear systematically above those plotted in the figure.) Movement decreases with the total length of service. Two hypotheses are consistent with this observation. On the one hand, legislators with abbre-

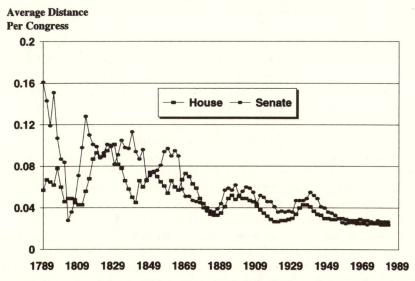

Figure 4.7. Movement of representatives and senators in the space. This figure shows the average distance moved by a member over a two-year period for those members serving at least 5 Congresses. The distance move is computed from the linear trend coefficients for the two dimensions. Although the House and Senate are scaled independently, their patterns of movement have been highly similar since 1880. Movement has declined dramatically in both houses.

viated periods of service tend to be unsuccessful legislators; their movement may reflect their attempts to match up better with the interests of constituents. On the other hand, short-run changes in the central issues before Congress—such as the Vietnam War or free trade—may make the spatial position resemble an autoregressive random walk. In this case, the estimate of the magnitude of the true trend will be biased upward, with greater bias for shorter service periods.

Although legislators with shorter careers tend to have larger time trends, spatial position is not related to length of career. The correlation between length of service and the absolute value of the first-dimension position is only -0.08 in the House and -0.12 in the Senate.[14]

Another result—one we see as more important than the finding that spatial movement is limited for legislators with long careers—is shown in figure 4.7. For the period before the Civil War, there is a choppy pattern in the figure, most likely, in part, a consequence of the smaller number of legislators who served in this period. Not only was Congress smaller, but a smaller proportion of its members served long terms. Our central result is for Congresses after the Civil War. Spatial movement, which was never extensive in relation to the span of the space, has been in secular decline, except for small upturns in the 1890s and the period following the Depression. Since roughly the mid-1950s, biennial movement has amounted to a little over 0.2 units. This represents just 1 percent of the diameter of the space.[15] In addition, the patterns for the House and Senate are very similar over the post-Reconstruction period. The correlation between the House and Senate for Congresses 46 through 99 is 0.85.[16] Whatever forces are working to produce spatial stability have been operating on both chambers with equal intensity. Contemporary members of Congress do not adapt their positions during their careers but simply enter and maintain a fixed position until they die, retire, or are defeated.

Indeed, this stability is so great that, even in their last Congress, members typically do not alter their liberal/conservative positions. Similarly, they generally don't alter their positions if they are redistricted. The major change in behavior is that exiting members vote less often. This is shown in a study by Poole and Romer (1993). They used the absolute value of a representative's change in position from House $t-1$ to House t, in the static single-House scalings, as their dependent variable.[17] Their principal independent variables were those that indicated the types of exit from the House of Representatives from 1947 through 1984.[18] Poole and Romer's regression analysis shows that, controlling for absenteeism, the type of exit—including voluntary retirement—has no effect on a member's position in the member's last Congress. Table 4.3 shows a portion of the Poole and Romer analysis.

None of the exit-indicator variables is statistically significant.[19] (A representative who remained in Congress and was not redistricted has a 0 score on all indicator variables.) Although there may in fact be shirking, it appears to be in the form of not working so hard (not showing up for roll calls) rather than a case of indulging one's personal ideology or preferences at the expense of those of the constituency. Similarly, changing the composition of a representative's district has no significant effect on the representative's liberal/conservative position. The representative does not shirk by indulging a personal ideology only in the last period of service, but, on the contrary, maintains a well-defined ideology—even if his district's boundaries are changed—throughout his career.

Table 4.3 Change in Liberal/Conservative Positions of House Members (1947–1984): Regressions with Absolute Value of the Coordinate Change on the First Dimension, from Congress $t-1$ to Congress t, as Dependent Variable

Variable[a]	Coefficient		Variable Definition
	(1)	(2)	
APPOINT	0.018		Appointed to higher office
	(0.009)[b]		(1= appointed, 0= otherwise)
DIED	0.008		Died in office
	(0.006)		(1= died, 0= otherwise)
HIRUN	0.003		Ran for higher office
	(0.004)		(1= ran, 0= otherwise)
LOST	0.004		Lost primary or general
	(0.003)		election (1 = lost, 0 = otherwise)
RETIRE	0.0009		Voluntary retirement
	(0.003)		(1= retired, 0 = otherwise)
NOTVOTE	0.029*	0.034*	Fraction not voting
	(0.008)	(0.007)	in House t
REDIST	0.0004		Redistricted
	(0.002)		(1= redistricted, 0 = otherwise)
VOTESHR	−5.17E-06		Share of two-party vote in
	(4.31E-05)		previous election

Fixed-effect variables only	(1)	(2)	
0.107	0.110	0.110	Adjusted R^2
0.055	0.055	0.055	Standard error of regression
45.221	31.988	43.999	F-statistic
	0.061		Mean dependent variable
	6,288		Number of observations

[a] Not shown: 18 fixed-effect indicator variables for each pair of Congresses from 80–81 through 97–98 (all statistically significant with two-tail p-values < 0.001 in all equations).

[b] Standard errors are in parentheses.

* Statistically significant with two-tail p value < 0.001

Indeed, further evidence on this score is shown in table 4.4. Using the fraction of roll calls in which the representative did not vote—*NOTVOTE*[20]—as a dependent variable and regressing the other seven variables on it yield very interesting results. All coefficients on the five exit variables are positive and highly significant, with two-tail p values of less than .001. (The largest coefficient is for the indicator variable *DIED*, which makes sense in this context.)[21] When a member knows he is going to exit, he votes less but, as table 4.3 shows, his voting pattern, when he does vote, remains the same. In other words, shirking is not an ideological matter; it is simply voting less.[22] In any event, shirking, interpreted as indulging one's own preferences, rather than representing the district's preferences, is, at best, a second-order phenomenon.

The coefficient for the redistricting variable, *REDIST*, is positive and has a two-tailed p value of 0.058, quite close to the traditional 0.05 level of statistical significance. This means that changing the geographic boundaries of a representative's district produces a slight increase in his abstention record. This increase could be due to

Table 4.4 Abstentions of House Members (1947–1984): Regression with NOTVOTE, the Fraction of Roll Calls in Which the Representative Did Not Vote in House t, as Dependent Variable

Variable	Coefficient	Variable Definition
C	0.056[a] (0.005)[b]	Intercept term
APPOINT	0.080 (0.014)	Appointed to higher office (1 = appointed, 0 = otherwise)
DIED	0.096 (0.009)	Died in office (1 = died, 0 = otherwise)
HIRUN	0.152 (0.006)	Ran for higher office (1 = ran, 0 = otherwise)
LOST	0.054 (0.005)	Lost primary or general election (1 = lost, 0 = otherwise)
RETIRE	0.105 (0.005)	Voluntary retirement (1 = retired, 0 = otherwise)
REDIST	0.004 (0.003)	Redistricted (1 = redistricted, 0 = otherwise)
VOTESHR	0.0006 (0.00007)	Share of two-party vote in previous election
	0.160	Adjusted R^2
	0.089	Standard error of regression
	172.028	F statistic
	0.117	Mean dependent variable
	6,288	Number of observations

[a] All variables except *REDIST* are statistically significant with two-tailed p values < 0.001. Two-tailed p value for *REDIST* is 0.097.

[b] Standard errors are in parentheses.

the representative's spending more time in the new district than he normally would and, therefore, to his voting less often than he normally would.

Finally, the *VOTESHR* coefficient is positive and statistically significant. This finding implies that the higher his previous election margin, the freer the representative feels to vote less. Indeed, electorally safe representatives appear to vote less, but the effect is very small. (We treat not-voting in detail in chapter 10.)

Further evidence of the stability of members' positions comes from examining members who served in both the House and the Senate. In particular, we examined the 134 members who, after the passage of the 17th Amendment (which provided for the popular election of senators), first served in the House and then were elected to the Senate. Given the stability of position that was detailed above, we used the constant (static) coordinates estimated simultaneously for all 99 Congresses (see table 3.1). In this model, each legislator was constrained to a constant spatial position throughout his or her career.

The correlation between a legislator's position in the House and his or her later position in the Senate is 0.90 on the first dimension. This high correlation indicates not only that representatives die in their ideological boots, but that they do not change them when they run for the Senate. In contrast, the correlation for the second dimension is only 0.66. This lower correlation for the second dimension is not surprising, given the structural differences between the two chambers on the second dimension.[23]

Replacement and Stability

A reasonable inference from the discussion above is that replacement and stability might be related. The potential sources of any statistical relationship are both real and artifactual. A true relationship might result because high rates of replacement would

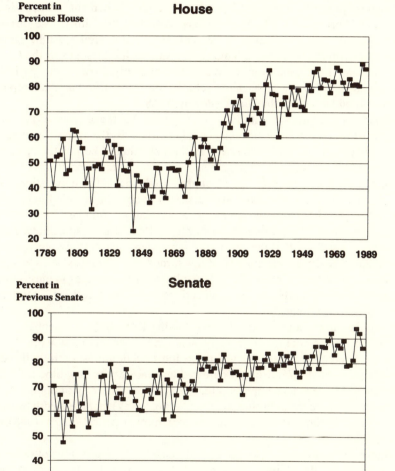

Figure 4.8. Percentage of the current House and Senate members that served in the previous House and Senate. The Senate historically had less turnover than the House as a result of six-year terms; in both houses, turnover began to decrease in the 1870s and 1880s.

indicate periods of political instability, when legislators have strong incentives to adjust their positions in order to win reelection. The potential artifactual relationship comes from the fact that, when turnover is high, there are few legislators with which to tie adjacent Congresses together in the D-NOMINATE estimation. The instability of the legislature might be accompanied by unstable, biased estimates with overlarge time trends.

Figure 4.8 shows the proportion of members of each House and Senate that served in the previous Congress. The proportions for the Senate are higher in the nineteenth century simply because of the six-year term. But a sudden change takes place in the House after the 54th Congress (1895–96). The average proportion that continues to the next House jumps from about 55 percent to around 70 percent in the period from 1897 through World War I. The Republicans controlled the 54th House through the 61st (1895–1910) with 200 seats or more in all but the 56th House. At the same time, the Democrats controlled all but a handful of seats for the 11 states of the Confederacy. Consequently, the conditions were ripe for longevity. Finally, this period is the one immediately following what many scholars have identified as the beginning of the "professionalization" of the House (Polsby, 1968).[24]

A comparison of figure 4.8 with table 4.2 suggests that the absence of turnover and the stability of individual positions may be related. That is, the proportion that continues to serve from a particular Congress to the next should be positively correlated with the correlations (some of which are shown in table 4.2) in positions of members who continue to serve from that same Congress to the next. The correlations of these two series are indeed positive, but only very weakly so—the correlation is only 0.26 for the Senate and 0.29 for the House. The correlations for the twentieth century (which begins with the 57th Congress) are only 0.11 and 0.19, respectively. This finding leads us to conclude that the decline in movement that is shown in figure 4.7 is genuine and not simply a consequence of low turnover in Congress. We speculate that the decline in movement is more likely to result from how changes in mass communications have affected representatives' incentives to establish roll call voting reputations with their constituents.

An immediate implication of this spatial stability from the post-Reconstruction period of the nineteenth century until the present (and especially after World War II) is that changes in congressional voting patterns must occur almost entirely through the process of *replacement* of retiring or defeated legislators with new blood. Politically, selection should be far more important than adaptation. One way of approaching this problem is to compare the coordinates of new (or entering) members with those of exiting members. We do this for the post-Reconstruction period (1879–1988) for the House in figure 4.9.

The figure shows the effects on the first dimension of the positions of entering and exiting members of the House, including northern Democrats, southern Democrats, and Republicans. By *exiting,* we mean those members who were in the previous House but are not in the current House. For the northern Democrats, there is no clearcut pattern until 1897 (after the 1896 elections). Between 1897 and 1909, entering northern Democrats were slightly to the Left of those who had entered from 1879 to 1895. Beginning with the 1908 elections, entering northern Democrats were at least as conservative as exiting northern Democrats for 12 consecutive elections (ending with the 1928 elections). Interestingly, the northern Democrats elected in 1930, 1932, and 1934 were indistinguishable from those elected between 1914 and 1928. Beginning with the 1936 elections, however, entering northern Democrats were to the Left of exiting northern Democrats for 10 of the next 11 elections (ending with the 1956 elections). Members elected in the 1970s tended to be more conservative, whereas those in the 1980s tended to be more liberal.

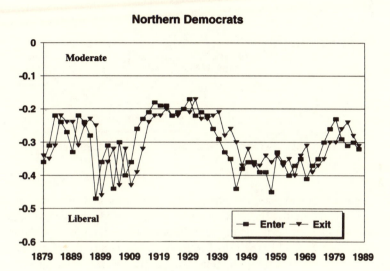

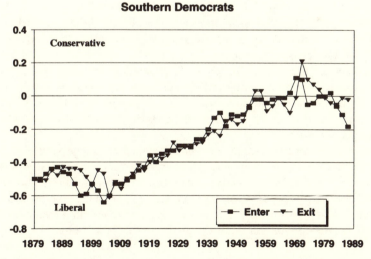

Figure 4.9. Mean first-dimension positions of entering and exiting members, House of Representatives (1879–1988). Entering northern Democrats were consistently more liberal than those leaving Congress during the New Deal era. In recent times, entering Republicans have been more conservative than those leaving, reversing the pattern at the turn of the century and immediately after World War II. Since the civil-rights legislation of the Great Society, new southern Democrats have been relatively liberal.

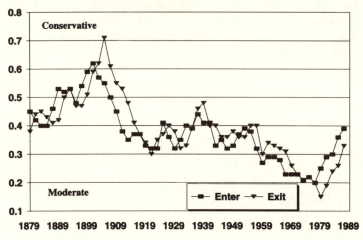

Figure 4.9. (*continued*)

For the southern Democrats, the effects of the positions of entering and exiting members are quite dramatic. In 22 of 33 elections from 1904 through 1968, entering southern Democrats were to the Right of exiting southern Democrats. The effects of the civil-rights laws passed in the mid-1960s can been seen in the last 9 elections in our series—those from 1970 through 1986. In these 9 elections, entering southern Democrats were to the Left of exiting southern Democrats in 7 elections and indistinguishable from them in one other election; the most dramatic leftward movement occurred in the last 3 elections.

The pattern for the Republicans is also very interesting. After the turn of the twentieth century, the Republican entrants were sharply to the Left of their exiting counterparts all the way through the Progressive era (1901–16) and World War I. Entering Republicans tended to be more conservative during the New Deal, but the pattern is not very dramatic. Beginning with the 1954 elections, however, entering Republicans are either to the Left of, or the same as, exiting Republicans all the way through the 1976 elections. In the final five elections in our series, entering Republicans become much more conservative.

The patterns we have described for replacements are largely parallel to those we described earlier for the party means. The party means change mostly because the composition of the party delegation changes, not because individual members change. Of course, given party polarization, far greater changes in positions and in policy occur when constituencies replace a representative with a member of the opposition party. We now take a more detailed look at the evolution of party polarization.

Party Polarization and Dispersion

Figures 4.3–4.6 show that the distances between the mean positions of the two major parties can vary considerably during the three periods of relative stability that we analyzed above. The distance between the major party means is one aspect of party polarization. Polarization is accentuated when party members are concentrated around the party mean.

Polarization thus has two highly related, but quite distinct, aspects. For parties to be polarized, they must be far apart on policy issues, and the party members must be tightly distributed around the party mean. Clearly, if the two parties have a high degree of overlap—with the Left wing of the "conservative" party overlapping the Right wing of the "liberal" party—then they are less polarized than if they have no overlap whatsoever.

Figure 4.10 shows our first measure of party polarization, which is a measure of overlap. This is the proportion of legislators of each major party who are closer to the opposing party's centroid (for example, a Democrat who is closer to the centroid of the Republicans). The periods of high overlap in the 1820s (the Era of Good Feelings) and in the early 1850s correspond exactly to periods we discussed earlier, in which the spatial structure of voting broke down because of the disintegration of one or both of the major political parties (the Federalists and the Jeffersonian Republicans, in the first instance; the Whigs, in the second). We truncate the graph at 0.20 so that the other periods can be seen more clearly.[25]

The period from after the Civil War until about 1920 was one of almost complete polarization of the Democratic and Republican parties—almost no overlap. In the House, where agendas are more controlled and leadership is stronger, polarization was almost perfect until the 1960s. In contrast, overlap began to increase in the Senate

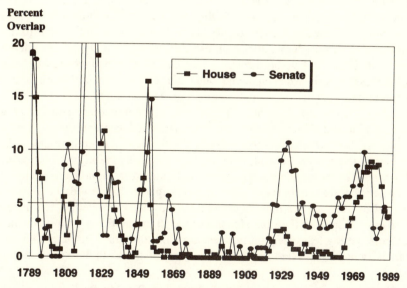

Figure 4.10. Overlap of the two major parties: percentage of a party's members that are closer to the centroid of the opposing party than to the centroid of their own party (1789–1988). Overlap was almost totally absent at the turn of the century. Overlap increased during the Kennedy, Johnson, and Nixon presidencies but has fallen sharply since then. The missing values for the House for 1817–23 are, in order, 0.34, 0.46, 0.45, and 0.36. The missing values for the Senate for 1819–23 are 0.26, 0.22, and 0.24.

in the 1920s because of the small group of midwestern Republicans we discussed earlier. Again, we see that issues related to civil rights for African-Americans affect the increase in overlap in the 1960s: Some moderate Republicans are closer to the Democratic party mean, and some southern Democrats are closer to the Republican party mean. Note that after 1979, overlap again begins to fall as liberal Republicans become rarer and southern Democrats move closer to northern members of the party.[26] The House and Senate patterns are highly similar. The correlation between the two over the 100 Congresses is a substantial 0.77.

For our next two measures of party polarization, we look at how far apart the members of the two major parties are, and how tightly dispersed the members of the two major parties are around their respective party means. To measure how far apart the members of the parties are, we compute the average distance (in two dimensions) between all pairs of members of opposing parties.[27] To measure the dispersion of the parties, we compute the average distance between all pairs of members of the same party.[28] Figure 4.11 shows these measures for the post-Reconstruction Democrat-Republican party system for the House and Senate.

The patterns for the House and Senate are very similar. The period of greatest polarization was that surrounding the presidential election of 1896 and the party realignment of the mass electorate in the 1890s. By World War I, polarization had fallen dramatically, and it was relatively stable until the 1960s, when it began to increase at the end of our series. The correlation between the House and Senate measures of between-party polarization is 0.90, indicating again that the same political-economic macroforces are at work in both chambers.

The two chambers present, nonetheless, two interesting differences. First, the Republican-controlled Senate was very highly polarized throughout the post-Reconstruction period of the nineteenth century. This division was largely due to the fact that the 11 former Confederate states almost always sent two Democrats each to the Senate. In addition, the five border states that had also been slave states (Missouri, Kentucky, West Virginia, Maryland, and Delaware) also sent mostly Democrats to the Senate throughout this period. Consequently, the Democratic party in the Senate was dominated by southerners. In contrast to the Senate, the more balanced, but typically Democratic-controlled House of Representatives reached its highest level of polarization only after its northern seats fell to the Republicans in the realignment at the end of the nineteenth century. Second, even though the series are highly correlated, between-party distances are *always* greater in the Senate than in the House. This is surprising, given that we see, in figure 4.10, that throughout this period, the Senate had a higher level of overlap than the House. The two results, put together, tell us that the Senate is more dispersed than the House. Although the parties are far apart on average, senators, voting less along party lines, are more dispersed. In particular, the Republican party has always had greater within-party distances in the Senate than in the House.

In contrast to the between-party polarization measure, our measure of dispersion shows that the Republican party had not only a higher level of dispersion in the Senate than in the House but a distinctly different pattern. In the House, Republican within-party distances were always quite low, oscillating in the 0.2–0.4 range. In contrast, the dispersion of the Republican party in the Senate increased greatly through the Progressive era, and this dispersion persisted until the late 1930s. This pattern is

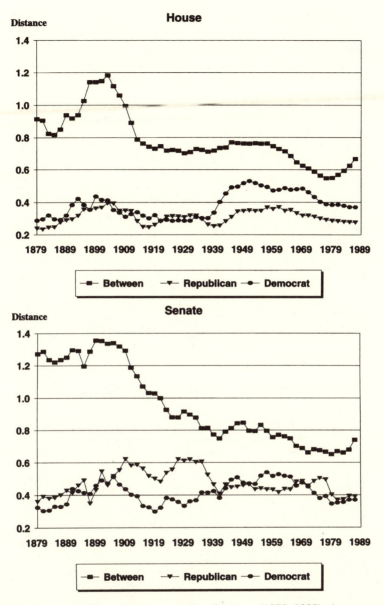

Figure 4.11. Average within- and between-party distances (1879–1988). Averages are computed for all pairs of members from the two-dimensional, linear-trend model. The within-party distances have always been much smaller than the between-party distances. The within-party distances have also been more stable than the between-party distances. Between-party distances declined sharply after 1900, but recently, the parties have shown increased polarization, particularly in the House.

due in part to the group of midwestern Republican senators that we discussed above. No such pattern occurred in the House. Further, the correlation for the Republican-party dispersion measures between the two chambers is only 0.17.

The Democrats are quite a different story. For them, the correlation between the two chambers is 0.79. The increase in their dispersion, due to the split of the party into northern and southern camps in the late 1930s, is clearly evident in both chambers.

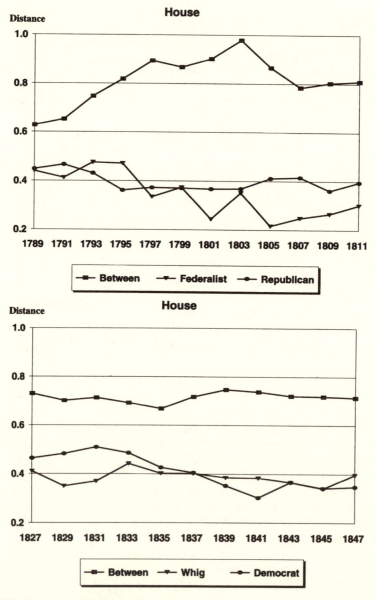

Figure 4.12. Average within- and between-party distances in the first two-party systems, House of Representatives. The results are quite similar to those in the previous figure.

We show in figure 4.12 our polarization measures for the House of Representatives for the Federalist-Jeffersonian Republican period and the Whig/Democratic period we analyzed in figures 4.5 and 4.6. Not surprisingly, as the Federalist and Republican parties coalesced, polarization increased steadily, peaking in Jefferson's first term. In contrast, the Whig/Democratic system was very stable throughout. Polarization in the first two party systems was, measured by within-party distances, much more similar to that in the post-Depression Congresses than to the highly polarized system that followed Reconstruction. The dispersion within parties, from Jefferson's presidency onward, was similar to that within the Democratic party in the House in the post–World War II period, reflecting the important role of the second dimension in separating the northern and southern wings of each party.

Finally, figures 4.10 and 4.11, taken together, indicate that the current Democratic/Republican party system is becoming increasingly polarized. As the southern Democrats are replaced by Republicans, with the remaining southern Democrats representing urban southern areas, the two parties will likely gravitate toward a system more polarized than at any time since the early 1920s.

Summary

The high degree of stability of legislator positions since the end of World War II may be due in part to the role of reputation in American politics.[29] On the one hand, politicians might choose to adapt to changes in issues, demographics, incomes, and other considerations that are relevant to their constituency; on the other hand, the process of adaptation may result in voters believing that the politician is less predictable. In turn, risk-averse voters will value predictability (Bernhardt and Ingberman, 1985). Therefore, a politician faces a trade-off between maintaining an established reputation and taking a position that is closer to the current demands of the constituency. Politicians also may find a reputation useful in cultivating campaign contributors. Some mixture of a reduced change in constituency demands, increased incentives to maintain a reputation, and perhaps other factors is manifest in the stability of legislator positions.

Although legislator positions, particularly in recent times, are stable in the basic space, political change occurs through replacement. Because party positions have been polarized in each of the three major-party systems in American history, very substantial swings in policy—shown by the positions of roll call outcomes—can take place when majority control changes, even though the center of gravity of the space is relatively stable. Replacement, which can result in large differences in spatial positions for successive representatives from the same district (see chapter 6), causes changes in the positions of the parties and in the dispersion of these parties; these changes cause fluctuations in polarization. But the major changes in the space correspond much more to important events in American history, such as the conflicts over slavery and civil rights and the Great Depression.

The greatest changes in the space are represented not by the periods of stability captured in the party systems but by the periods of spatial collapse that separate the party systems. We now turn to an examination of these periods and to a comparison of them with other major events where, even though the mass electorate may have been realigned, the party system and the structure of the basic space were not.

5

Party Realignment in Congress

A realignment represents a fundamental change in the way substantive issues map onto the spatial model we described in chapter 2. Our findings differ from those presented in the realignment literature in political science, which has largely drawn its evidence from the voting behavior of the *mass electorate* rather than from the roll call record of the *congressional elite*. In contrast to the usual finding that three major realignments have occurred since Jackson's presidency, we claim there has been only a single *legislative* realignment. This realignment was produced by the conflict over slavery, and the critical years are 1851–52, well before the Civil War.

There was no major realignment in either the 1890s or the early 1930s. Nevertheless, the Democratic landslides of the 1930s initiated a minirealignment, or perturbation, of the space. Like the conflict over slavery, this minirealignment arose over matters related to the rights of African-Americans. In contrast to these race-related issues, most issues in American politics are simply absorbed into the major dimension of political conflict. Indeed, the politics of race has, for much of American history (including the contemporary period), also been encompassed by the major dimension.

In this chapter, we present a simple model of realignment that is based on the spatial model in chapter 2. We then seek evidence in the roll call voting behavior of realignments in Congress that would be concurrent with changes in the mass electorate that occurred during the 1850s, 1890s, and 1930s. We find that only in the early 1850s does a major change in the structure of congressional voting occur; the realignments of the 1890s and 1930s occurred along the line of cleavage that had solidified after the Civil War. The late 1930s did witness the birth of a second realignment, which focused on the issue of civil rights for African-Americans. But as this second realignment proved to be less intense than the first (and only a temporary one), we describe it, more appropriately, as a perturbation.

We also examine the nature of issue change more generally. We investigate how new issues are accommodated within an existing spatial structure. Most of the galaxy of policy issues that confront Congress are neither as intense nor as enduring as the question of race, which led to the realignment of the 1850s and to the perturbation that occurred from the 1940s to the 1970s. If an issue is to result in sustained public policy, we hypothesize that the policy must eventually be supported by a coalition that can be represented as a split on the first, or major, dimension. Policy developed by coalitions that are nonspatial or built along the second dimension is likely to be transient and unstable. We analyze several issue areas, including abortion and prohibition, and find considerable support for our hypothesis.

The Realignment Literature

E. E. Schattschneider, in his classic *Party Government* (1942, p. 1), wrote that the "political parties created democracy," and that "modern democracy is unthinkable save in terms of the parties." Schattschneider argued that freedom of association and the guarantee of regular elections with plurality winners made the development of two mass-based political parties inevitable. American political history can be written almost entirely around the conflict between and within political parties because the parties have acted as mirrors of the great social and economic conflicts that have divided the country. When the political parties failed to mirror such conflicts, they have been torn apart and replaced by new parties that represent mass opinion.

The realignment literature in political science is concerned with such changes in the mass support for the political parties and with how the leaders of the parties responded to the changes. The prevailing view in this literature is that there have been three major realignments since Jackson assumed the presidency: one in the 1850s over the issue of the extension of slavery to the territories; one in the 1890s over the issue of currency inflation (greenbacks and bimetallism); and one in the 1930s because of the collapse of the economy in the Great Depression.[1]

The most complete statement of this thesis is by Sundquist (1983, p. 4). He argues that a realignment is a durable change in patterns of political behavior. His basic model of realignment emphasizes that a new issue emerges that cuts across the existing cleavage and reorganizes the political parties around it. He notes (1983, p. 37): "The party system has a new rationale, an old conflict has been displaced by a new one for a segment of the electorate, and that segment of the electorate has formed . . . new party attachments on the basis of that rationale. If the segment is large enough, . . . a new party system supplants the old one."

Sundquist marshals an impressive body of evidence for his thesis—including changes in party registration and voting at the county level in various states. There can be little debate about the fact that major changes in the mass electorate occurred during the 1850s, 1890s, and 1930s. The evidence is convincing. Less convincing is Sundquist's argument that these changes in the mass electorate "shifted" the party system on its axis. In Sundquist's model, if a new issue does not seriously divide the political parties *internally,* then "the crisis will be reached and resolved relatively quickly," and the scale of the realignment "will be relatively minor" (1983, pp. 44–45). In other words, the severity of a realignment is a direct function of the internal divisions of the parties.

In Sundquist's work, the mass electorate and the professional politicians are part and parcel of the same process. Sundquist's evidence comes from changes in the mass electorate. We draw our evidence from changes in congressional voting behavior as revealed by our dynamic spatial model.

We set forth here a simple model of realignment based on the spatial model of party competition and offer evidence that the realignments of the 1890s and the 1930s did not change the basic structure of congressional voting that preceded these realignment periods. Indeed, the basic structure set in place during the 1870s was not changed by either realignment. A fundamental change in the structure of congressional voting occurred in only two realignments in American history.[2] The first was the 1850s realignment due to the extension of slavery to the territories. The second began in the *late* 1930s with voting on the minimum wage (see chapter 6) and then intensified with voting during World War II over the voting rights of blacks in uniform. This later realignment was only indirectly the result of the Great Depression. Indeed, the large Democratic majority created by the economic catastrophe split over the race issue. The realignment forced by the North-South conflict was (as we noted earlier) less intense than the 1850s realignment and only a temporary one; so we more appropriately call this realignment a perturbation of the long-run liberal/conservative conflict.

Interpreting Realignment with the Spatial Model of Voting

Realignment, as defined by Sundquist, is easily accommodated by the dynamic spatial model we outlined in chapter 2. For example, before a realignment is initiated, roll call voting should be stable and organized around the cleavage of the last realignment. In terms of spatial theory, this means that the policy space is stable—the same dimensions structure voting over time, and legislators' ideal points should show little change from Congress to Congress. A new issue then emerges, which splits the political parties internally and begins the process of polarization. It can be modeled as a new dimension—orthogonal to the stable structure of legislators in the current voting alignment—across which both political parties become increasingly polarized. The realignment is due partly to the replacement of members—the newly elected members are more attuned to the new issue—and partly to modifications of the spatial positions of continuing members (see figure 4.7). As the process continues, more and more of the voting is concerned with the new issue, so that the old stable set begins to wither away. Finally, the old spatial structure collapses entirely, and a new alignment emerges in which the major dimension is coterminous with the new issue.[3]

Figure 5.1 shows the realignment process at five stages—the early, middle, and late stages of the old alignment; the period of spatial collapse; and the new alignment. Two political parties are shown as contour maps over a space of two dimensions, with most members being located near the center of the contours. One dimension is the original line of cleavage, and the other is the new, realignment issue. Early in the process, as shown by part A of the figure, the parties are relatively homogeneous, with some diversity. The new issue has not yet produced polarized factions within the parties. The legislators, as a whole, are centrally distributed over the original dimension, and because the new issue has only recently emerged, not all members have been forced to take positions on it. Then, as the issue heats up within the electorate and becomes more salient, the legislators begin reacting more forcefully and polarization begins, as shown in part B. Part C of the figure shows the process in its later stage: Both political parties are now polarized. The new dimension is now the primary focus of voting, and the legislators are bimodally distributed across it. The parties are highly divided internally.

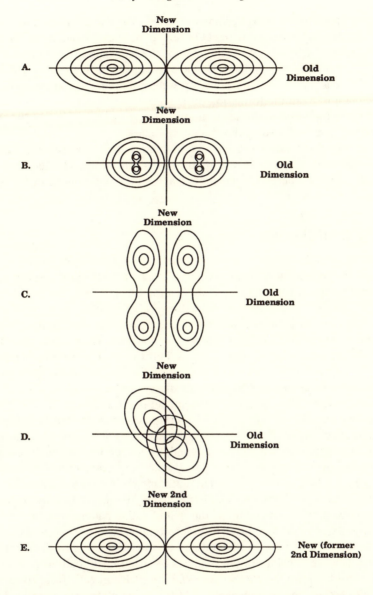

Figure 5.1. Spatial realignment. The contours in the figures show the distribution of legislators' ideal points, with legislators concentrating near the more central concentric contours. Before a realignment (part A), legislators have a largely unidimensional distribution. The major parties are clusters on the dimension. As a new issue arises, it polarizes the parties on the second dimension (parts B and C). When the new issue becomes too intense for the old alignment to survive, the party system collapses (part D). A new system forms, with the new dimension as the first dimension (part E).

When internal party divisions become too strong, the space can collapse, as shown in part D—parties are no longer distinct clusters in the space. In addition, the fit of the model (which cannot be seen from the map of the legislators' ideal points), will be poor. (See, for example, the evidence on the 31st House, in figure 3.6.) Voting alignments within the legislature are unstable. After the collapse, the political system is reorganized, possibly with the formation of new parties. The contours in the new system, part E, are the same as those in the old system (part A), except that the first dimension is now represented by the realigning issue.

Below, we test this model with our two-dimensional D-NOMINATE scaling. We first discuss our scaling results for the 1850s, 1890s, and 1930s. We then cover the period from the 1940s to the 1970s and show that a minor realignment, or perturbation, occurred after World War II.

Evidence of Realignments?

Our realignment model has three potential implications: continuing members should be more volatile in the space, making more changes in their positions; replacements should position themselves distinctly from continuing members; and the realignment issue should change its orientation in the space.

The evidence on continuing members was already presented in figure 4.7. The situation for the 1890s and the 1930s is clearest. In the figure, there is an uptick for both houses of Congress for both of these periods, but it is small. Position changes never reach the levels observed from the initiation of the Era of Good Feelings (1815) through the emergence of the Whig/Democratic system in the elections of 1836, or, particularly for the Senate, during the realignment in the 1850s and 1860s. Nevertheless, two caveats are in order. First, it is difficult to compare the upticks of the 1890s and 1930s to the antebellum realignments, because there has been a secular increase in the stability of legislators' positions. Second, the antebellum picture is less systematic than the postbellum one—in large part because replacement, rather than adjustment, is the major vehicle for realignment in the antebellum period (see figure 4.8).

In order to analyze realignments and issue change in more detail, we select all roll calls on the relevant issue and examine the spatial voting patterns for the issue across time. In particular, we focus on how well the voting on each roll call is accounted for by the first dimension of our estimation and on the increase in fit that results from adding the second dimension. In our analysis of specific roll call votes later in this chapter, we will focus on the *PRE1* and *PRE2* for each roll call. To analyze an issue area, we will compute the aggregate *PRE* (*APRE*) using all the scaled roll calls in the area.

Comparing the *APRE* for one dimension (*APRE1*) with the *APRE* for two dimensions (*APRE2*) gives a good indication of the spatial character of the roll calls. If *APRE1* is high and *APRE2* − *APRE1* is small, then the votes are concerned primarily with the first dimension. If *APRE1* is low and *APRE2* − *APRE1* is large, then the votes are along the second dimension. If both *APRE1* and *APRE2* are low, the votes are poorly fit by the model (or very lopsided). In our figures below, we focus on these sorts of differences by issue areas.

Note that, for a specific roll call, it is possible for *PRE2* − *PRE1* to be negative, for two reasons. First, our scaling maximizes a likelihood function, not classification.[4]

Second, the legislator coordinates are chosen as a function of all the votes, and not just the vote on one roll call; therefore, two-dimensional coordinates can improve the fit of the model overall, while decreasing the fit on some individual roll calls.

Slavery and the Realignment of the 1850s

Slavery, of course, was the issue that produced the realignment of the 1850s. By the 1850s, slavery was not a new issue but a very old one that had become more intense in both the North and the South. Indeed, slavery was already an issue in the writing of the Constitution, which reflects a compromise: the counting of each slave as three-fifths of a person, for purposes of congressional apportionment, and the ending of importation of slaves in 1808. Slavery fits nicely into our model of realignment, but not exactly, as many other issues surfaced between 1789 and the 1850s. Indeed, before the spatial collapse of the 1850s, the space also collapsed in the Era of Good Feelings. As we look at slavery, therefore, we will have to keep in mind other "shocks" to the political system.

A total of 891 roll calls concerning slavery were included in our scaling of the House and 386 for the Senate.[5] For every Congress in which there were at least 5 scaled roll call votes concerning slavery, we computed *APRE1* and *APRE2*.

In the first 14 Congresses, the slavery compromise embodied in the Constitution held. During this period, we coded only 27 slavery roll calls for the House. Although some of these concerned two issues—fugitive slaves and slavery in the District of Columbia, which would remain active issues until the eve of the Civil War—the bulk of the roll calls concerned the taxation of slaves and, in particular, slave imports. In fact, 13 of the 27 roll calls were held on slave imports in 1806 and 1807. But this issue vanished when the constitutional ban on slave imports became effective in 1808. Subsequent to the end of the 9th Congress in March 1807, no slavery roll calls occurred for a decade.

Slavery roll calls were slightly more frequent in the Senate, where 34 roll calls were coded. A very large part of these were represented by 11 roll calls early in 1804, when the Senate was drafting legislation to organize the land acquired in the Louisiana Purchase. These roll calls can be used to illustrate part A of figure 5.1. The closest roll calls were two 16–12 decisions on a provision to bar the bringing of slaves into the territory, except by settlers who were slaveholders. Consistent with slavery not being a salient issue in the old alignment, the *PRE2* is low for these roll calls. The higher *PRE2* occurs on a January 31, 1804, vote (VOTEVIEW number 49) and is only 0.25.

This vote is illustrated in figure 5.2. Throughout our discussion of slavery, in the figures, lowercase letters represent antislavery positions; and uppercase letters, proslavery. Parallel to part A of figure 5.1, the parties are distinctly separated on the first dimension; the second dimension shows little overall dispersion; and the parties are smoothly clustered around a central point. Although the cutting line on the roll call passes through the heart of the Jeffersonian Republicans, there is also a proslavery vote among the Federalists. Moreover, as the United States map panel in the figure shows, except for New England, Tennessee, and Georgia, proslavery and antislavery voters could be found on both sides of the Mason-Dixon line. (South Carolina's two senators did not vote.) Southern legislators, particularly those from the middle

Senate: Louisiana Slavery

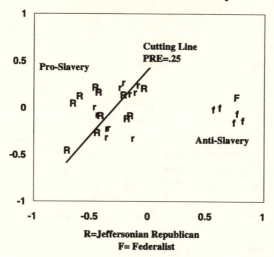

R=Jeffersonian Republican
F= Federalist

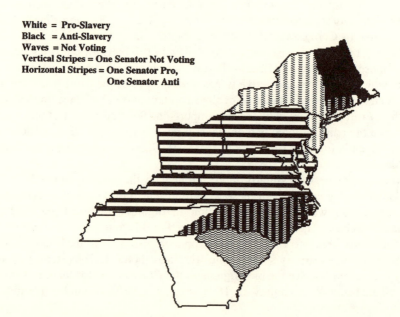

Figure 5.2. Vote on the prohibition of slavery in Louisiana Purchase lands, January 31, 1804 (VOTEVIEW number 49). Proslavery legislators' ideal points are shown in uppercase; anti-slavery, in lowercase.

and border states of the South, were not yet prevented from expressing mild antislavery positions, as they would be later (Freehling, 1990).

The relative peace that preceded the 15th Congress was not to continue. Figure 5.3 displays *APRE1* and *APRE2 − APRE1* for the House from the 15th Congress to the 38th (1815–65). The corresponding graph for the Senate is similar but less smooth. We begin with a discussion of the period before 1831—there were only 39 additional

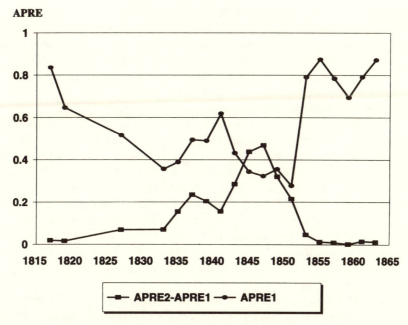

Figure 5.3. Slavery votes in the House of Representatives (1815–65). The first dimension becomes weaker (*APRE1*) and the second becomes stronger (*APRE2 − APRE1*), in accounting for slavery votes, until the old alignment collapses. In the 32nd House (1851–52), the two dimensions together fail to account for the votes. By the 33rd House (1853–55), the new alignment is largely in place and slavery has become the major dimension.

roll calls in the House and 20 in the Senate between 1817 and 1831. The remaining 823 House roll calls and 332 of the 386 Senate roll calls came after 1832.

Nearly three fourths of the roll calls, in both the House and the Senate, in the 1817–31 period came in the 15th and 16th Congresses. The central issue at the time was slavery in Missouri. This proved far more explosive than any previous slave issue because each new state influenced the balance of power in Congress and in the Electoral College (Weingast, 1991). Figure 3.1 shows that the 15th and 16th Congresses (elections of 1816 and 1818) occurred in the period of spatial collapse constituted by the Era of Good Feelings, with the 17th Congress—in both houses—being the worst-fitting Congress in American history. Yet, as illustrated by figure 5.4, slavery votes in the 15th and 16th Houses fit very well in one dimension. Even in the Senate, where the fits are poorer, the 16th House has the best slavery fits in one dimension before the 33rd Congress. Indeed, the level of House fits in the 16th House would have been even higher were it not for several lopsided procedural votes or votes unrelated to Missouri with very low and even negative *PRE*s. The critical votes all exhibited a high degree of spatial structure.[6]

What explains these results is that the spatial collapse of the Federalist/Republican system was unrelated to slavery but arose when the end of the Napoleonic Wars eliminated the foreign-policy issue dividing the parties and when the economic issue was eliminated by a partial Republican embrace of Alexander Hamilton's economic viewpoint. But slavery remained active as a divisive issue. Indeed, an examination of all roll calls for the 16th House revealed that slavery was the only issue with a high degree of fit. Without the slavery votes, the classifications in figure 3.1 would have been even worse. Because slavery was the only strongly spatial issue at the time, it defines the first dimension when there is a spatial collapse on most issues.

To illustrate this period, we use the critical vote on the Missouri Compromise in the House, which took place on March 1, 1820. The compromise admitted Missouri as a slave state for the South and admitted Maine as a free state and banned slavery north of 36°30′latitude in the Louisiana Purchase lands for the North. The compromise was actually passed as two votes—one admitting Missouri and Maine, which allowed the North to take antislavery positions by voting against, and the other, on the 36°30′line, which allowed the South to take proslavery positions by voting against. The first vote was close, 90–87, and fit the model well, with only 10 classification errors; it is illustrated in figure 5.4. The ideal point distribution resembles the spatial-collapse panel, part D, of figure 5.1. The parties, in contrast to figure 5.2's picture for 1804, are no longer well differentiated. The vote indeed splits both parties (the Federalists: 12 Yeas and 14 Nays; the Republicans: 78 Yeas and 73 Nays). Yet there was a solid southern vote in favor, and there were only a few northern defections (but strategically sufficient to guarantee passage).

The Missouri Compromise did not give the South a long-run commitment to maintain a free state/slave state balance in the Senate. (Our view here contrasts with that of Weingast [1991], who argues that such a commitment existed until 1850, when California entered as a free state and no slave state was admitted.) On the contrary, be-

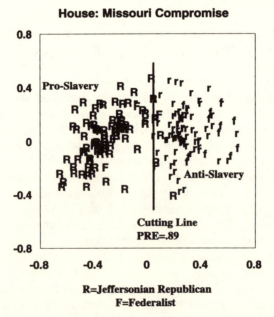

Figure 5.4. Critical vote on the Missouri Compromise in the 16th House, March 1, 1820 (VOTEVIEW number 18). Proslavery legislators' ideal points are shown in uppercase; antislavery, in lowercase.

cause slavery was banned in most of the territories, the compromise placed the South at a long-run disadvantage that it sought to undo. The compromise succeeded, in the short run, in our view, largely because the pace of settlement slowed down. The next states admitted, Arkansas and Michigan, entered only in 1836 and 1837. There were no sufficiently populated areas outside the existing states to make slavery an intense issue for many years after the Missouri Compromise. There were fewer than five slavery roll calls in the 17th, 18th, 21st, and 22nd Houses, and none at all in the 19th.

Consequently, the collapse of a well-organized party system in the Era of Good Feelings (evident in figure 5.4) did not occur because slavery was the new, destabilizing dimension. The Federalist/Republican system collapsed largely because the previously salient foreign-policy and economic issues had waned. The movement of settlers into Missouri made slavery, for a brief period, a salient issue with strong regional divisions. Both the success of the compromise and the absence of new settlements in the 1820s and 1830s implied that the Whig/Democratic system was able to arise along an economic dimension. However, slavery never completely vanished as an issue. Voting on slavery intensified just as the Whig/Democratic system emerged.

Indeed, the great bulk of all slavery roll calls were cast after 1835, during the period of the Whig/Democratic political-party system. Voting on slavery fell increasingly along the second dimension. In line with the scenario outlined in figure 5.1, the gap between *APRE2* and *APRE1* trends upward from 1835 until the late 1840s (during Congresses 24–30) and then drops to nearly zero after the 33rd Congress (1851–52). In addition, *APRE1* climbs dramatically after 1852, and the gap between *APRE2* and *APRE1* disappears, indicating that the first dimension is now the slavery dimension. The picture is clear: As the conflict within the country grew, the Whig and Democratic parties split along North-South lines *along the second dimension,* and the first dimension continued to divide the Whigs from the Democrats on traditional economic issues (for example, tariffs, internal improvements, the national bank, and public lands). By 1853, this economic dimension collapsed and was replaced by the slavery dimension.

The 32nd Congress (1851–52) was pivotal. By then the conflict had become so intense that it destroyed the spatial structure of congressional voting—the spatial model simply does not fit, or fits very poorly, voting in the 32nd Congress.[7] Outside Congress, the Compromise of 1850 was unraveling. Northern resistance to the Fugitive Slave Law was at first scattered, but with the publication of Harriet Beecher Stowe's *Uncle Tom's Cabin* in 1852, northern disregard for the law increased. The number of fugitive slaves was never very large (only about 1,000 out of a population of 3,000,000 in 1850 [Hofstadter et al., 1959]), but the law had great symbolic importance for southerners. Northern aid to the fugitives was seen as evidence of hostility toward the South and only deepened suspicions between the regions.

The realignment was sealed by the passage of the Kansas-Nebraska Act in May 1854 by the 33rd Congress. Both parties were badly split. The Whigs were primarily against the bill, and the Democrats mostly for it. Senator Stephen A. Douglas, an Illinois Democrat, tried to buy southern votes for a northern (as against a southern) route for the transcontinental railway. He introduced a measure that would have allowed the Nebraska territory, which was north of the Missouri Compromise line, to enter as two states. One, Kansas, would be a slave state, and the other, Nebraska, would be free, even though slavery was almost certainly economically unworkable in Kansas. The bill passed, after being pushed by the longstanding Democratic party alliance in which the current Middle West traded votes on slavery for votes on economic matters (Weingast, 1991).

Douglas thought that the act would settle the territorial question once and for all by repealing the Missouri Compromise of 1820 and by allowing the new states that were to be formed in the territories to decide the issue for themselves (popular sovereignty). Douglas evidently thought that by repealing the Missouri Compromise and thereby removing the federal government from deciding the slavery issue, the act would mollify southerners. Since most of the territories would undoubtedly be settled by migrants from the more populous northern states, popular sovereignty would ensure free-soil victories in the new states, thereby pleasing the northerners. Unfortunately for Douglas, however, regional divisions were much more powerful than he thought.[8]

Voting on the act was along regional lines; and the spatial structure of the voting is very coherent (see figure 5.8). Slavery became the primary dimension of voting. Northern politicians unwilling to trade away the slavery issue, displaced the old political class of the Whig/Democratic party system. The Republican party, and its 1860 presidential candidate, Abraham Lincoln, came to power, sealing the spatial realignment.

The realignment is illustrated by figures 5.5 to 5.9. Because slavery was already present as a salient issue when the Whig/Democratic system arose, there is no equivalent, in these figures, to part A of figure 5.1 or to figure 5.2. The phases of the realignment corresponding to parts B and C (of figure 5.1) are shown by figures 5.5 and 5.6.

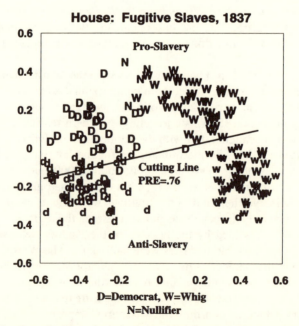

Figure 5.5. Motion for a fugitive-slave resolution, December 13, 1836 (VOTEVIEW number 357). Proslavery legislators' ideal points are shown in uppercase; antislavery, in lowercase.

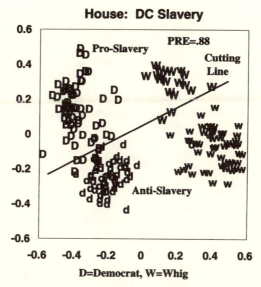

Figure 5.6. Vote on a petition about slavery in the District of Columbia, December 10, 1844 (VOTEVIEW number 433). Proslavery legislators' ideal points are shown in uppercase; antislavery, in lowercase.

Part B is illustrated by figure 5.5, which shows the vote on a fugitive-slave resolution on December 13, 1837 (VOTEVIEW number 357); part C, by figure 5.6, which shows a vote on whether to accept a petition concerning slavery in the District of Columbia, on December 10, 1844 (VOTEVIEW number 433).

The cutting lines are quite similar in the two figures, with both showing the influence of the second dimension on slavery votes. Both fit the model well—the *PRE2* is 0.76 for 1837 and 0.89 for 1844. In both figures, the first dimension separates the Whig and Democratic parties, and the second dimension separates the representatives into southerners (on the top) and northerners (on the bottom). The spatial structure shown in the figures held from approximately 1832 to 1849. The main difference in the figures—parallel to the differences between parts B and C of figure 5.1—is that the parties are more strongly separated into regional blocs by 1844.

After the passage of the Compromise of 1850, however, a spatial collapse transpired quickly, as illustrated by a vote on March 1, 1852, calling for support of the fugitive-slave provisions of the compromise.[9] Although this vote had the highest turnout of any slavery roll call in the 32nd Congress, the *PRE2* was a relatively meager 0.53. Figure 5.7 shows, consonant with part D of figure 5.1, the overlap in party positions.[10] Minor parties are prolific in figure 5.7. The cutting line has rotated considerably from its location in the two previous figures. Strategic voting has much to do with the poor fit. Many northern Democrats, seeking to maintain their party's dominance of national politics, voted Yea. On the other hand, although only 7 southerners voted Nay, 5 of these (and 2 abstainers as well) came from the most strongly proslavery delegation, that of South Carolina. Note further that, consistent with an earlier discussion of figure 5.1, the South Carolina delegation moved from the top of the plot in figure 5.6 to the left-most positions in figure 5.7.

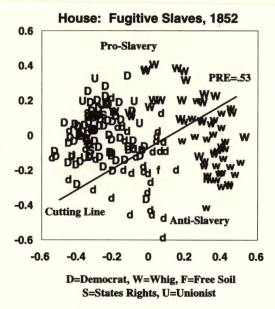

Figure 5.7. Vote to support fugitive-slave provisions of the Compromise of 1850, March 1, 1852 (VOTEVIEW number 71). Proslavery legislators' ideal points are shown in uppercase; antislavery, in lowercase.

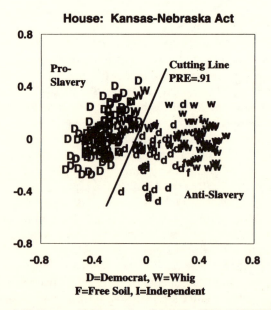

Figure 5.8. Passage of the Kansas-Nebraska Act, May 22, 1854 (VOTEVIEW number 309). Proslavery legislators' ideal points are shown in uppercase; antislavery, in lowercase.

The collapse of the party system is illustrated again in figure 5.8, which shows the vote that passed the Kansas-Nebraska Act on May 22, 1854.[11] Although most minor parties have vanished in figure 5.8, the Democratic and Whig parties are mixed together in the center of the space, which is similar to part D of figure 5.1. The cutting line has, compared to figures 5.5 and 5.6, become more vertical, foreshadowing slavery's emergence as the main dimension of the realigned space. Indeed, unlike the fugitive-slave vote and other votes in the preceding Congress, the Kansas-Nebraska Act votes have high degrees of fit—the *PRE* for the illustrated vote is 0.91.

Finally, figure 5.9 shows the first slavery roll call in the 35th House, which took place on February 2, 1858. The vote was on a proposal by the Democratic majority to postpone consideration of the president's message on Kansas. The vote has a *PRE2* of 0.81 and is now fully on the first dimension. The move to postpone failed (105–109) because of defections of moderate Democrats, as the figure shows; these were all northerners. (The only slave-state representative to vote against the motion was an American-party member from Baltimore.) The realignment was complete by this time, and the new party—the Republicans—was tightly clustered, in line with part E of figure 5.1. Southern representatives for the next 80 years remained on the Left on the major dimension, with views on the treatment of African-Americans being highly correlated with views on economic regulation, the tariff, and monetary policy (as seen later in this chapter and in chapter 6).

Figure 5.3 and figures 5.5 through 5.9 show that the 1850s realignment within Congress was sudden and was initiated *before* the Republican party became a real force in American politics. This result questions some recent work by political economists and historians.

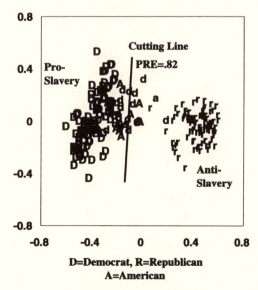

House: President's Kansas Message

Figure 5.9. Vote to postpone consideration of the president's message on Kansas, February 2, 1858. Proslavery legislators' ideal points are shown in uppercase; antislavery, in lowercase.

Fogel (1990) studies the realignment that produced Lincoln's electoral victory by comparing the elections of 1852 and 1860. But, at least in Congress, we see that the old Whig system had largely disintegrated by the time of the elections of 1852. To compare the old system to the new, 1848 would appear to be a better benchmark.

Weingast (1991) correctly identifies 1850 as a crucial date in the slavery conflict. The old spatial alignment collapsed in the 1851–52 House and Senate. But Weingast attributes the sudden change to a single event—the destruction of a credible commitment to slavery in the South by the breaking of the North-South balance in the Senate after the admission of California in 1850. We show that the tension over slavery had built gradually over time, as shown by the steadily rising importance of the second dimension in the 1840s. The realignment of the 1850s was more a matter of a process that gradually increases stress until a breaking point is reached than one of a single overwhelming event.

This pattern does fit Sundquist's (1983) model rather nicely. A new issue (actually a version of a very old issue)—the extension of slavery into the territories—emerges, cutting across the existing line of cleavage (conflicts over economic policy) and causing the two political parties to polarize. One party is destroyed in the process, and a new party system is formed around the new issue. In spatial terms, a stable two-dimensional, two-party system becomes unstable. The first dimension disappears, and its place is taken by the old second dimension.[12]

Gold and Silver and the "Realignment" of the 1890s

Sundquist (1983) notes that in the aftermath of the Civil War, the new dimension of conflict was concerned with Reconstruction, secession, black rights, and related issues. The groups shut out of the system were the farmers and the emerging labor movement. The 1866–97 period saw a persistent, long-run deflation accompanied by falling commodity prices (Friedman and Schwartz, 1971). This was the driving force behind the inflation issue; and according to Sundquist (1983), this issue represented the new line of cleavage that culminated in the realigning election of 1896, in which the Gold Democrats deserted the Democratic party for the Republican party. The Silver Republicans were not able to overcome their aversion to the Democrats because of the Civil War and remained in the Republican party. This shift made the Republican party the majority party until the 1930s.

The inflation issue had its roots in the tremendous expansion of the money supply during the Civil War. The cost of the Civil War forced the Union government to borrow heavily and print "greenbacks." Although some of the colonies had experimented with fiat money (paper money with no specie backing [Weiss, 1970]), the issuance of greenbacks in 1862 marked the first time that the United States had resorted to paper money not backed by specie. The expansion of the money supply during the war caused inflation and the abandonment of the gold standard. By the war's end, inflation had approximately doubled the overall price level.

The efforts of the government to deal with the inflation problem immediately after the war became an issue in the 1868 presidential election, prefiguring the splits within and between the two major parties that were to recur for the next 25 years. The effort by Secretary of the Treasury Hugh McCulloch to contract the money supply by withdrawing greenbacks from circulation contributed to postwar deflation. Heeding the protests of midwestern farmers, the Democrats proposed in their 1868 party platform that the greenbacks be reissued to redeem war bonds that did not specifically require redemption in gold. This was the first of many inflationary, or "soft money," proposals, and it became known at the time as the "Ohio Idea."[13]

A total of 481 roll calls in the House and 523 roll calls in the Senate were cast on banking and currency during the 1865–1908 period (39th to 60th Congresses). For every House in which there were at least 5 roll calls on banking and currency, we computed *APRE1* and *APRE2*. The results are shown in figure 5.10, which is done in the same format as figure 5.3.

The pattern for the currency issue is quite different from the one for slavery in that there is no *sustained* gap, for the former, between *APRE1* and *APRE2*. Rather, the gap peaks in the 43rd to 45th Congresses and in the 52nd to 53rd Congresses. These two peaks coincide with the financial panics of 1873 and 1893. (Once again, the pattern for the Senate is similar to that for the House.)

The financial panic of September 1873 produced a contraction in the money supply and generated demands for inflation. Before the panic, farmers were, in general, suspicious of paper money. After 1873, however, farmer support for greenbackism increased (Unger, 1964, pp. 228–33). The result was the Inflation Bill of 1874, which

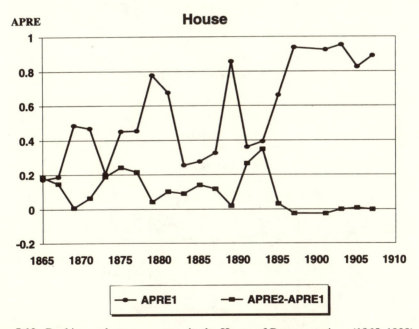

Figure 5.10. Banking and currency votes in the House of Representatives (1865–1908). The first dimension gradually becomes stronger over time. The second dimension never clearly becomes the more important dimension. A realignment does not occur. (*APRE2* − *APRE1* is sometimes slightly negative because the two-dimensional model actually resulted in a lower correct-classification rate than the one-dimensional model. For all roll calls in a Congress, however, the two-dimensional model always improves classification.)

was passed by the 43rd Congress and vetoed by President Grant. Figure 5.11 shows the final passage votes in the House and the Senate in April 1874 on the Inflation Bill.[14]

Voting on the bill split both political parties along the second dimension. Prefiguring the splits that were later to occur on the silver question, the opposition to the inflation bill was concentrated in the New England states and New York; the proponents came primarily from the South and the Midwest. During this period, however, the regional coalitions were not yet completely solid. All the representatives and senators

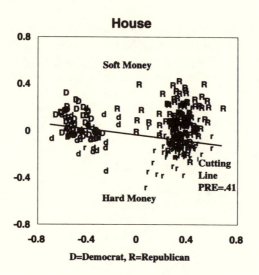

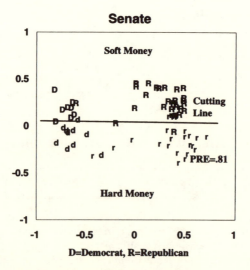

Figure 5.11. Final passage of the Inflation Bill of 1874. The House vote (VOTEVIEW number 126) was on April 14; the Senate vote (VOTEVIEW number 119) was on April 6. A soft-money vote is shown in uppercase; a hard-money vote is in lowercase.

from Nevada and Texas and all the representatives from California (the senators from California did not vote) opposed the inflation bill.

After the 1876 elections, the focus of the inflationists shifted from greenbacks to remonetizing silver. The tremendous increase in silver production in the western states that occurred after the Civil War produced a decline in the price of silver in the 1870s. This drop produced a coalition of convenience among the Western mining interests, farmers, and greenbackers. The result was the Bland-Allison Act of 1878, which was passed in the 45th Congress. It required the Treasury to purchase between 2 million and 4 million ounces of silver per month and to coin it into silver legal-tender dollars. Figure 5.12 shows the votes of February 28, 1878 in the House and the Senate that overrode the veto of President Hayes.[15]

Voting on the act was primarily along the second dimension, which was now clearly a regional dimension. Only 7 representatives and 4 senators from the western and southern states voted to sustain Hayes's veto, whereas only 10 representatives and no senators from New York and New England voted to override.

With the triumph of the "soft money" forces, voting on banking and currency issues from 46th Congress through the 51st (1879–90) reverted to a more normal pattern—that is, voting was more along party lines, and therefore the gap between *APRE1* and *APRE2* is small.

In the 1888 elections the Republicans gained control of both the Congress and the presidency. The blessings of a unified government allowed them to admit to the Union only those parts of the frontier that would be firmly in the Republican camp. Although relatively heavily populated Arizona and New Mexico were denied statehood, Washington, Idaho, Montana, Wyoming, North Dakota, and South Dakota were admitted in 1889 and 1890. They promptly sent an additional 12 Republican senators to Washington.[16] The entry of the western states created great pressure within the Republican party for further action to increase inflation. The Republicans responded by pushing through a logroll which included the McKinley Tariff, the Sherman Anti-Trust Act, and the Sherman Silver Purchase Act, all in 1890.

In return for western votes in the Senate and the House in favor of the McKinley Tariff, the eastern Republicans supported the Sherman Silver Purchase Act, which was passed in both houses in July by straight party-line votes. In effect, the Sherman Silver Purchase Act obligated the government to buy nearly the entire output of the western silver mines. But even this measure did not brake the decline of the price of silver. The falling price of silver only further encouraged people to exchange silver and paper money for gold. The result was a steady drain of the Treasury's gold reserves.

The financial panic that began in May 1893 was touched off, in part, by the drop in the nation's gold reserves. The resulting crisis led to the repeal of the Sherman Silver Purchase Act in October 1893. Figure 5.13 shows that voting on the repeal served to again split the two political parties along regional lines.[17]

In the Senate, 6 southern Democrats and 4 western Republicans along with all the senators from New England, New York, and New Jersey, voted to repeal. In the House, 11 of the 18 Republicans who voted against repeal were from the western states, whereas 31 southern Democrats—mostly from Kentucky, Virginia, North Carolina, and Texas—voted for repeal. New England, New York, New Jersey, and all the representatives from the major eastern cities—New York, Boston, Philadelphia, and Baltimore—voted for repeal.

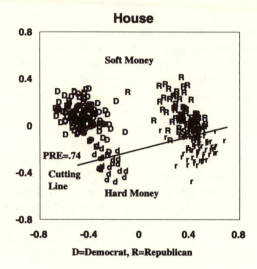

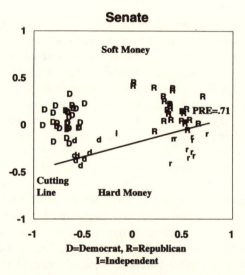

Figure 5.12. Votes to override President Hayes's veto of the Bland-Allison Act. The House (VOTEVIEW number 93) and Senate (VOTEVIEW number 153) both voted on February 28, 1878. A soft-money vote is shown in uppercase; a hard-money vote is in lowercase.

With the repeal of the Sherman Silver Purchase Act by the 53rd Congress, the banking and currency issue again reverted to a more normal pattern of voting along the first dimension. Indeed, after the 53rd Congress, the gap between *APRE2* and *APRE1* disappears, and *APRE1* climbs above 0.8 in both chambers, indicating that the banking and currency issue is absorbed into the first dimension after the 53rd Congress. (See figure 5.10 for the House results.)

What killed the inflation issue was not the "realignment" of the 1890s, but inflation itself. Farm prices started to go back up in 1896, and the general price level began to

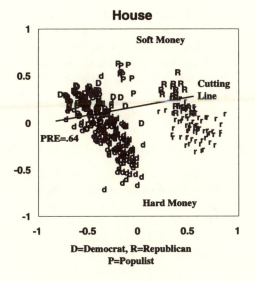

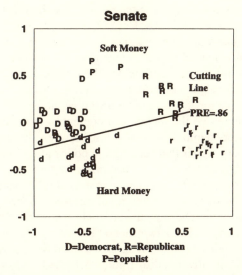

Figure 5.13. Votes to repeal the Sherman Silver Purchase Act. The House vote (VOTEVIEW number 60) was on November 1, 1893; the Senate vote (VOTEVIEW number 80) was on October 30. A soft-money vote is shown in uppercase; a hard-money vote is in lowercase.

increase shortly thereafter. Several major gold discoveries and the introduction of a cheap cyanide process for extracting gold from tailings dramatically increased the money supply after 1896 (Hofstadter et al., 1959; Friedman and Schwartz, 1971).

That the issue was finally drawn into the first dimension does not mean that the regional differences disappeared. Indeed, an examination of the spatial maps for Congresses throughout the post-Civil War period shows that the second dimension tended to separate westerners from easterners—and the effect was greater within the Republican party. In addition, this separation was maintained after the 1896 elections.

In sum, the evidence indicates that the status of inflation as an issue changed. That is, the basic configuration of the House and Senate was fairly stable throughout this period, but the *mapping* of inflation changed—inflation slowly changed from a two-dimensional issue to a strongly one-dimensional issue over the period. Unlike the 1850s, though, the first dimension was never replaced. The realignment at the level of congressional voting did not change the basic structure of voting; rather, as an issue, inflation evolved until voting on it lined up along the first dimension.

The Great Depression and the "Realignment" of the 1930s

The collapse of the stock market in October 1929 was followed by an economic slide that turned into the Great Depression of the 1930s. By the summer of 1932, industrial production was down 50 percent, commodity prices were down 50 percent, and unemployment was around 24 percent. The consequences for the Republican party were equally severe: The four congressional elections between 1930 and 1936 resulted in a massive replacement of Republicans by Democrats in Congress. By 1937 the Democratic party held a 334-to-88 margin over the Republicans in the House (13 congressmen belonged to minor parties), and a 76-to-16 lead in the Senate (4 came from minor parties). This wholesale replacement is the result of realignment in the voting behavior of the mass electorate in the 1930s. Never before or after this period were the Democratic and Republican parties so imbalanced in Congress during peacetime.[18]

The economic catastrophe changed the agenda of Congress. Before the Great Depression, providing relief for the destitute was the function of private and religious organizations, not the federal government. Moreover, the New Deal altered for good the role of the federal government in regulating the economy. Sinclair argues that the New Deal agenda "increased the ideological content of American politics" and produced "a much clearer ideological distinction between the congressional parties" (1977, p. 952). Ginsberg argues that "changes in policy after 1933 are in keeping with voter choices favoring alterations in the economic system and redistributions of opportunities in favor of urban working class elements" (1976, p. 49).

There is no question that the congressional agenda changed radically during the 1930s. The real question is: Did the change in content bring with it a change in the spatial structure of voting? The answer is no. The change in agenda was accommodated within the existing framework. What *did* change was the ratio of Democrats to Republicans. This fact is illustrated in figures 5.14 and 5.15, which show the estimated positions of representatives in the 71st House (1929–30) and the 74th House (1935–36), respectively. In both figures, southern Democrats (denoted by a capital S) represent the left wing of the Democratic party. The shape of the Republican cluster changes but largely as a result of the elimination of a part of the cluster.

The spatial structure of figure 5.14 is essentially repeated in figure 5.15, indicating that the Depression did not result in an immediate realignment of congressional voting patterns. In addition, through this period, the fit of the two-dimensional dynamic model to the roll call data is quite good. That is, the results in figure 3.1, for this period, do not show a dramatic drop in PRE, like the ones in the 16th and 31st Congresses. The second dimension through this period picked up a weak Western-versus-Eastern-states effect, along with the voting on the social issues of the day—prohibition and immigration.

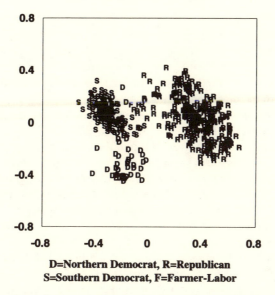

D=Northern Democrat, R=Republican
S=Southern Democrat, F=Farmer-Labor

Figure 5.14. Ideal points of representatives in the 71st House (1929–30). On the first dimension, the southern Democrats are slightly to the left of the northern Democrats.

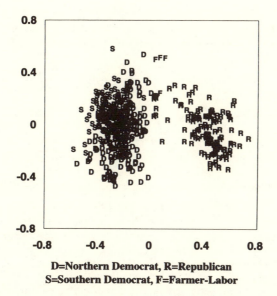

D=Northern Democrat, R=Republican
S=Southern Democrat, F=Farmer-Labor

Figure 5.15. Ideal points of representatives in the 73rd House (1933–34). Although there are many more northern Democrats here than in the previous figure, the relative positions of southern Democrats and northern Democrats have shown no substantial change. Indeed, the Great Depression did not produce an immediate realignment in Congress.

The stable spatial structure shows that the legislation of the *first* New Deal was indeed largely accommodated within the spatial structure that had prevailed since the end of Reconstruction. The legislation reflected either new issues that mapped readily onto the old lines of conflict or old issues, latent during the period of the Democrats' prolonged minority status, that could be brought to the table as new measures and passed into law with the new Democratic majorities.

A good illustration of the absence of realignment in the Depression is provided by roll call voting in the labor area, shown in figure 5.16. In the House, 276 such roll calls were cast from the 59th Congress through the 100th. For every House for which there were at least 3 roll calls on labor regulation, we computed *APRE1* and *APRE2*. Not until the battle over the Fair Labor Standards Act—the original minimum-wage bill—in 1937–38 (75th Congress) did the second dimension influence legislation in the labor area. When the second dimension did come into play, it closely tracked the North-South division within the Democratic party over the race issue. Similar results are found for the Senate.

Another illustration of the absence of realignment in the Depression is roll call voting within Clausen's social-welfare category, shown in figure 5.17 for the House (results for the Senate are similar to those for the House). We removed voting on liquor regulation and immigration from this category because they were strongly two-dimensional issues *before* the Depression. (See figures 5.20 and 5.21; these issues will be discussed further below.) In the House, 1,775 roll calls were cast on social welfare

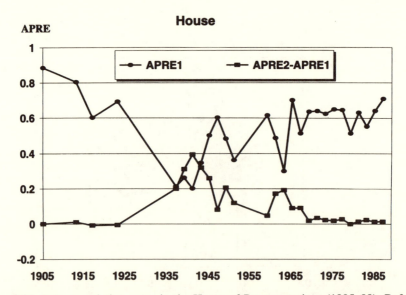

Figure 5.16. Labor-regulation votes in the House of Representatives (1905–88). Before the second New Deal, votes on labor were rare but were fit by the first dimension when they did occur. After the second New Deal perturbed the position of southern Democrats in the space, labor votes became almost entirely first-dimension votes. (*APRE2* − *APRE1* is sometimes slightly negative because the two-dimensional model actually resulted in a lower correct-classification rate than the one-dimensional model. For all roll calls in a Congress, however, the two-dimensional model always improves classification.)

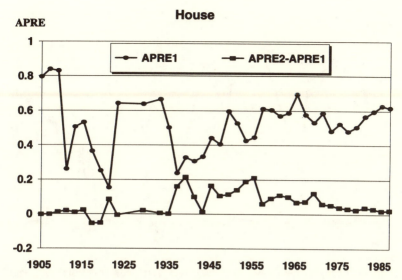

Figure 5.17. Votes coded in Clausen's social-welfare category, House of Representatives (1905–88). These votes have always been predominantly first-dimension votes. They have been, since the second New Deal, an increasingly good fit for the dimension.

during the 1905–89 period (the 59th Congress through the 100th). For every House for which there were at least 3 roll calls on social welfare, we computed *APRE1* and *APRE2*. Social welfare has been largely a first-dimensional issue throughout the century, with occasional minor increments arising from the second dimension. These increments occurred in the late 1930s, the 1950s, and the 1960s. There is no evidence of a realignment brought about by the Depression.

Civil Rights and the Perturbation of the Space, circa 1940–1970

In perhaps a classic illustration of Riker's (1962) size principle, the extraordinarily large Democratic majority of 1937 was too big to last. Northern Democrats, who outnumbered southern Democrats 219 to 115, embarked on the second New Deal. Many of the new programs were not to the liking of the South. The conflict is most evident in the area of civil rights for blacks.

Roll calls on civil rights are shown in figure 5.18. Totals of 486 roll calls in the House and 742 in the Senate were taken on civil rights from the 37th Congress through the 100th (1861–1989). In the Senate, very few votes were taken on civil rights from the 46th Senate through the 75th. Consequently, we focus on the House, for which we computed the *APRE1* and *APRE2* for every Congress in which there were at least 3 roll calls on civil rights.

During the Civil War and Reconstruction (the 37th House through the 44th), civil-rights votes were highly structured on the first dimension. During the Civil War, there were many votes on the role of African-Americans in the military. The Reconstruction period saw votes on the Bureau of Freedmen and civil-rights bills. Between Reconstruction and the New Deal, votes on civil rights had somewhat lower PREs, but the voting was picked up on the first dimension. This is largely because being left on eco-

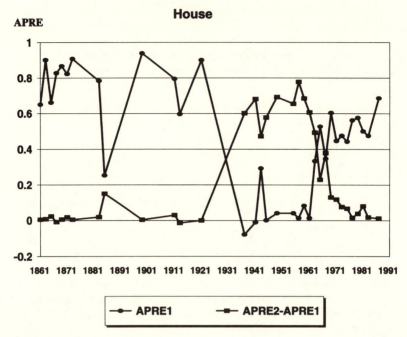

Figure 5.18. Votes on civil rights for blacks, House of Representatives (1861–1988). Having traditionally been first-dimension votes in postbellum America, civil-rights votes became entirely second-dimension votes (with the *APRE1* near zero) during the era of the three-party system. After the passage of the Civil Rights Act and the Voting Rights in the 1960s, this issue area returned to the first dimension as the civil-rights agenda shifted toward issues of economic redistribution.

nomic issues meant favoring redistribution from richer whites in the Northeast to poorer whites in the South.[19] The split on economic issues happened to match, with reverse logic, the split on a host of antilynching roll calls in 1921 and 1922 (the 67th House).

Between 1922 and 1937 (the 68th Congress through the 74th), there were only two civil-rights roll calls in the House. Only one fell in the first Roosevelt administration. By the time votes on lynch laws recurred, in 1937 and 1940, and were joined, during World War II, by roll calls on the poll tax and voting rights in the armed forces,[20] there was a horde of northern Democrats who voted left on economic issues. A second dimension became necessary to differentiate northerners and southerners on civil-rights votes.

The economic agenda itself became infused with the conflict over race. Although the South's opposition to the minimum-wage legislation introduced in 1937 and passed in 1938 might have been motivated by the economic interest of a low-wage area,[21] southern white congressmen also explicitly opposed minimum wages as favoring southern blacks (see chapter 6). To accommodate the South, the tobacco industry and other sectors of the economy concentrated in the South (and in areas where competition with the North was not an issue) were kept out of the initial minimum-wage coverage. Even so, southerners largely opposed the labor legislation of the second

New Deal. Consequently, labor also had an important second-dimension component from the late 1930s onward. (See figure 5.16, and the discussion of minimum-wage legislation in chapter 6.)

As economic issues also turned from redistribution among whites to redistribution from whites to blacks, particularly in the South, the southern Democratic delegation in Congress gradually became more conservative on the first dimension as it began to define a pole on the second dimension. By the late 1950s, this realignment of southern Democrats meant that the first dimension alone was largely sufficient to classify roll call votes, greatly reducing *PRE2 − PRE1* on most labor issues. By 1970, first-dimension *PRE* levels returned to those found in the twenties and thirties (see figure 5.13).

Civil rights remained a second-dimension issue longer than labor did. Economic conservatives in the Republican party joined northern Democrats to pass the Civil Rights Act of 1964 and the Voting Rights Act of 1965. After these two events, civil rights could increasingly be accounted for by the first dimension. In signing the legislation and "delivering the South to the Republicans for 50 years," Lyndon Johnson signaled a realignment in mass voting behavior. But this did not lead to a spatial realignment in Congress. Rather, it ended the perturbation of the space by the civil-rights issue. As southern Democrats took on a black clientele, they became increasingly like northern Democrats. Unlike the 1920s, there is now a consistent right-wing position, personified by Jesse Helms, on economics and race. Not a single southern Democratic senator failed to vote to override President Bush's veto of the Civil Rights Bill of 1990. The veto was sustained by conservative Republicans, from the North and the South. Indeed, the bill involved substantial economic redistribution, and its impact would have been nationwide.

Figure 5.19 shows the override vote in the 101st Senate. The configuration of senators was produced by running W-NOMINATE on the 101st Senate. What is striking about the configuration is the fact that the southern and northern Democrats are no longer clearly separated on the second dimension. The most extreme southern Democrats are now indistinguishable, along the main dimension, from liberal Republican senators such as Bob Packwood of Oregon. Indeed, the second dimension adds only 2 percent to the 83 percent of the total choices classified by the first dimension. The second dimension has been gradually disappearing since the middle of the 1970s, and the trend has continued into the 1990s (see chapter 11).

The civil-rights episode, lasting roughly from 1940 to 1966, is instructive in regard to spatial realignment. Although substantively race and economics are quite distinct, only one dimension was needed before 1940. This was just fortuitous, as conservative positions on race and economics just happened to be strongly, albeit negatively, correlated. The breakup of the overlarge Roosevelt coalition and the subsequent enfranchisement of Southern blacks took place in a framework of spatial perturbation. A second dimension was needed to capture the resolution of this conflict, but the conflict never managed to dominate the basic economic conflict inherent in democracy. Voting never became chaotic, as in 1851–52. The perturbation ended with legislation that induced a strong positive correlation of conservative positions on race and economic policy. Converse's (1964) view of constraint in ideology is now reflected in a basically one-dimensional political space in Congress.

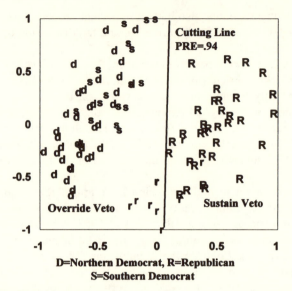

Figure 5.19. Senate vote to override President Bush's veto of the 1990 Civil Rights Bill. Lowercase letters denote votes to override; uppercase, votes to sustain. Southern Democrats are no longer distinctly separated from northern Democrats, as all southern Democrats voted to override. There are only three classification errors.

Incorporation of Substantive Issues into the Basic Space

As we noted earlier, most of the galaxy of policy issues that confront Congress are neither as intense nor as enduring as the race question that led to the realignment of the 1850s and to the perturbation of the 1950s. How are these issues accommodated in the basic space?

We indicated earlier that if an issue is to result in sustained public policies, we hypothesize that the policies must eventually be supported by a coalition that can be represented as a split on the first, or major, dimension. Policy developed by coalitions that are nonspatial or built along the second dimension is likely to be transient and unstable.

To investigate this hypothesis requires us to sharpen our focus and look at issue areas that are relatively narrowly defined, permitting us to keep substance relatively constant. Our first effort of this type was a detailed study of the history of minimum-wage legislation (Poole and Rosenthal, 1991b; see also chapter 6 of this book). Before World War II, the minimum-wage issue was relatively poorly mapped onto the space. Even using two dimensions, the classifications were much worse than they were after the war. Indeed, after the war, the minimum wage became a first-dimensional issue with a high degree of classification accuracy.

An example of an issue in the initial, ripening phase is the abortion issue. Between 1973 and 1989 (the 93rd Congress through the 100th), a total of 61 roll calls in the House and 67 in the Senate were cast on abortion. Figure 5.20 shows the *APRE* values for each House and Senate for which there were at least 3 roll calls on abortion. As

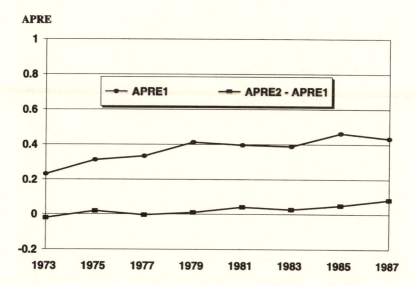

Figure 5.20. Abortion roll calls, House of Representatives (1973–88). Abortion is slowly becoming a liberal/conservative, first-dimension issue, with a better fit for the spatial model.

shown in figure 5.20, when abortion was first put on the agenda, shortly after the Supreme Court's *Roe* v. *Wade* ruling in 1973 (the 93rd Congress), the issue did not fit the existing spatial dimensions very well—it falls along the first dimension but with a low level of *APRE*. However, the *APRE* has gradually increased. Part of this increase has resulted from well-known flip-flops, such as the conversion by Richard Gephardt (D-MO) to a pro-choice position. It no longer seems possible that abortion policy can be decided by single-issue politics because it is slowly being drawn into the first dimension.

The prohibition issue is a nice counterpoint to the abortion issue. The temperance movement was a classical example of single-issue politics. Seventy-three roll calls in the House were taken on liquor regulation from the 59th Congress through the 74th (1905–36). For every House for which there were at least 3 roll calls on liquor regulation, we computed the *APREs*. Unfortunately, there were not enough Senates with 3 or more liquor regulation roll calls to make a comparison between the House and Senate.

Figure 5.21 shows that voting on the passage of prohibition (unlike repeal) did not map at all onto the first dimension and had only a moderately high level of *APRE* on the second dimension. Although the special-interest coalition in this case was strong enough to amend the Constitution, it did not produce a lasting element of public policy.

Although much more work is required to determine how specific issues map onto the basic unidimensional structure of congressional voting, the results from the minimum-wage, abortion, and prohibition issues (and, in an earlier period, from that of monetary policy) support our hypothesis that stable policy coalitions are built on the first dimension.

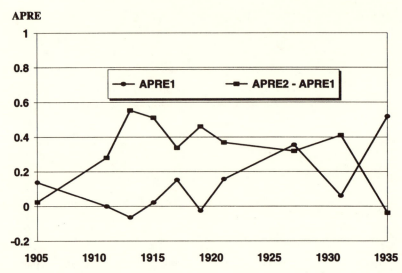

Figure 5.21. Alcoholic-beverage roll calls, House of Representatives (1905–36). Single-issue politics prevail, with *APRE1* actually negative at times, until Prohibition is enacted. Voting is largely on the second dimension, until repeal.

Summary

Major changes in the voting behavior of the mass electorate occurred during the 1850s, 1890s, and 1930s. Only in the 1850s, however, is there evidence that these changes produced a corresponding shift in the structure of congressional roll call voting. The congressional changes of the 1890s and 1930s were mainly the massive replacements of legislators of one party by new legislators from the opposing party. These replacements did not change the basic structure of congressional voting in the late 1890s and early 1930s. The great changes in the voting behavior of the mass public at these times produced new majorities but not a fundamental alteration of how issues mapped onto the space.

Beginning in the late 1930s, however, a perturbation of the space did change the structure of congressional voting. The overlarge Roosevelt coalition gradually fell apart over the old issue of race. It gave rise to the three-party system with distinct clusters for northern Democrats, southern Democrats, and Republicans (see figure 3.3). This division peaked in the 1960s and then slowly faded away. Southern Democrats are now to the Left of most of the moderate Republicans.

Our results suggest a general model for issue change. We have found that the first dimension, throughout most of American history, has captured the main economic conflicts between the two major political parties. During normal periods, a weak second dimension is usually present, capturing the social, or regional, issues of the day. New issues that have staying power will eventually be drawn into the existing one- or two-dimensional alignment because it is easier to build stable coalitions within the existing stable structure of voting.

6
Issues, Constituency Interests, and the Basic Space

We have demonstrated that the great bulk of congressional roll call voting can be accounted for by the simple one- or two-dimensional spatial model. How is this so, given the complex and diverse interests that must be addressed by every session of Congress?

In this chapter, we suggest some answers to this problem and illustrate our answers with five important substantive examples: (1) House voting that initiated the food-stamp program in 1964 and renewed it in 1967; (2) the development of railroad regulation from 1874 to 1887, culminating in the passage of the Interstate Commerce Act; (3) minimum-wage legislation from the initial passage of the Fair Labor Standards Act in 1937 through the 1990 increase in the minimum wage; (4) strip mine legislation in 1974; and (5) Senate votes on the Occupational Safety and Health Administration in 1975.

These topics have been intensively studied by other researchers. Ferejohn (1986), in his case study of food stamps, stresses the importance of logrolling, which, we believe, is critical to the process that projects specific economic issues onto the abstract, low-dimensional space. In contrast, Gilligan et al. (1989) analyzed railroad regulation in relation to economic interests specific to the railroad issue; a similar approach was taken by several researchers who studied the minimum wage.[1] With respect to strip mining, Kalt and Zupan (1984) made the seminal attempt at comparing a detailed model of economic interests with an ideological explanation of roll call voting.[2] As a measure of ideology, they constructed a pro-environment index from votes supported by the League of Conservation Voters (LCV), a single-issue environmental group. Kalt and Zupan, controlling for ideology, find that most other variables are of minor importance. We go one step further and find that the general D-NOMINATE measure of ideology does just as well as the LCV measure that is related to the topical issue. We also find that ideology dominates economic-interest measures for railroads, minimum wages, and food stamps. A similar result is obtained in comparing ideology to a set of economic and demographic variables used in analyzing a large set of roll calls in the manner of Peltzman (1984). In all the analyses presented in this chapter, D-NOMINATE (or W-NOMINATE) scores are the variables that have the most influence on individual roll call votes.

One important reason that our scores are such powerful variables is their ability to incorporate party-line voting. As previously seen in figures 3.3, 3.4, and 5.2 to 5.15, throughout nearly all of congressional history, the parties are represented as two distinct clusters of legislators in the space. Cutting lines that separate the clusters represent party-line votes. When the party whip enforces the long-term logroll that is represented by party affiliation, members vote in a manner that is consistent with spatial voting even if they appear to be voting against their constituency's issue-specific economic interests.

Moreover, parties do not just impose discipline but also package logrolls. Although votes on particular roll calls may appear contrary to the constituency's economic interests, the package, as a whole, may be beneficial. For example, Ferejohn (1986) points out that on food stamps, southern Democrats were bought off by northern Democrats' support for agricultural subsidies. When we attempt, below, to explain voting on food stamps solely in terms of a constituency's economic interests on food stamps alone, à la Gilligan et al. (1989), or Kalt and Zupan (1984), we find, at best, weak support for the proposition that members vote purely on the basis of constituency interests. But, in a larger context, members used a logroll to further constituency interests. If the constituency orientation is captured in a logroll that is spatially clustered, D-NOMINATE will capture the logroll.

Indeed, the spatial logrolls need not be constructed wholly on party lines. Because the Democrats had a healthy majority in the House in 1964, they did not require unanimous support from their southern wing to pass food-stamp legislation. The most conservative Democrats, nicely demarcated by D-NOMINATE, defected. Similarly, the House coalition for railroad regulation in the 1880s was built through the Democratic party but included some agrarian Republicans from the Middle West and did not include many northeastern Democrats. The Democratic majority, in any case, was large enough to pass a regulation bill. Members of both parties were allowed to vote on the basis of sectional economic interests. In chapter 1, we quoted Representative Hewitt to illustrate that sectional economic interests on the railroad issue were correlated with interests on many other economic issues, such as free silver and antitrust legislation. Although such broad sets of economic interests may be difficult to measure directly,[3] they are captured in the D-NOMINATE scores.

Our analysis of House voting on railroads will illustrate that major bills are very complicated packages with a slew of provisions. This complexity is characteristic of legislation, even on bills that, unlike the food-stamp measure in 1964, are not packaged as part of a larger deal. On any major piece of legislation, therefore, the bill manager's role is to keep a bill coalition together and not allow it to break apart on amendments which appeal to specific economic interests. In the case of the interstate commerce bill, there were articles with respect to pooling (sharing of revenues), rebates (discounts or "kickbacks" typically given to large shippers), short-haul versus long-haul pricing (not charging a price on a short route that is higher than the price on a longer route which includes the short route), and enforcement (in courts rather than in a regulatory commission). Each of these articles had provisions with different impacts for different constituencies. For example, wheat farmers west of Chicago might have supported the pooling clause, which prevented price-fixing, but not the short-haul-pricing clause, which disadvantaged long-haul shippers. Farming interests east of Chicago might have acted more favorably toward short-haul pricing constraints. But the cutting lines on amendments to all the economic provisions of the bill were very similar, attesting to the manager's ability to maintain a logroll of interests on the bill.

Logrolls, of course, are not invulnerable, and attempts are made to destabilize a logroll using killer amendments that introduce another salient issue.[4] In chapter 7, we show how the Republicans nearly killed railroad regulation in the House by introducing an amendment to end racial discrimination in passenger service. To avoid destabilization of the railroad bill, the bill manager, after forcing a party-line vote that led to an adjournment at a critical juncture, regrouped and engaged in strategic behavior that allowed the South to accept a regulatory bill that contained a separate-but-equal clause on racial discrimination. (On this issue, see also chapter 7 and, especially, Poole and Rosenthal, 1994a.)

Although the Interstate Commerce Act roll calls thus involved a substantial degree of strategic behavior, this behavior still resulted in votes that are captured by the spatial model. In particular, the antidiscrimination votes are accounted for by D-NOMINATE because positions on the race issue in the 1880s are nicely picked up by the first dimension. The South, the economic Left at the time, also acted favorably toward Jim Crow policies. Much of the strategic behavior simply involved moving the cutting line by getting first-dimension moderates to vote for the separate-but-equal provision but against fully eliminating discrimination.

The House votes on railroads in the 1880s and on food stamps in the 1960s demonstrate that roll call voting behavior typically incorporates party pressures and issue-specific economic interests, both of which are correlated with the more general interests and personal ideology captured by D-NOMINATE.[5] The importance of party depends, to some extent, on the closeness of the partisan division in a chamber. When the division is close, the majority party has more of a need to use the whip. Consequently, a substantive issue can have cutting lines with different angles in the two chambers. For example, in contrast to the House, where the Democrats had a substantial majority in the late 1880s, the Republicans controlled the Senate, but by a slimmer margin. The large Democratic majority in the House permitted substantial position-taking based on economic interests, with the result that the roll calls on railroad regulation divided both parties internally. In contrast, the regulatory votes in the Senate were strictly party-line votes, with the cutting line separating the parties.

The blending of interests into a bill, either along party lines or via an interparty logroll, need not occur as soon as the issue appears on the national agenda. Indeed, the history of the minimum wage and railroads will illustrate the point that new issues typically fit the spatial model less successfully than mature ones—ones in which enduring logrolls have been constructed.

Moreover, economic interests can change the nature of the coalition behind a bill, even though the roll call votes continue to be captured by D-NOMINATE. We illustrate this point with the food-stamp program. As constituents in moderate Republican congressional districts began to receive food stamps, their representatives became "hooked" on the program. In contrast to 1964, when food stamps were opposed by nearly all Republicans, increased Republican support by 1967 removed the need for southern Democratic support. Although voting on food stamps continued to fit the D-NOMINATE model, *economic interests had shifted the cutting line*. In addition, even when the cutting-line angle does not change, a change in the perception of economic interests can affect the mapping of an issue onto the D-NOMINATE space. Thus, although liberals have always been the core of support for the minimum wage, a diminished general level of support has led to a lowering of the real value of the minimum wage. To show this, we will examine voting on the minimum wage by pivotal members over a period of several years. We will argue that their ideal points for the real value of the minimum wage have shifted downward over time. This drop in support was culminated by the Clinton administration's failure to raise the minimum wage even in the two years of unified Democratic government. (The modest increase proposed in 1996 would still leave the real wage at a low level.) Sometimes, as we will show for legislation on inspection levels for the Occupational Safety and Health Administration, the mapping can change in a few months.

In this chapter, then, we will argue that the presence of spatial voting is not inconsistent with voting on the basis of economic interests. Economic interests, though difficult to measure, can influence how issues are mapped onto the space captured by D-NOMINATE. Moreover, members of Congress will express these interests strategically, voting by the use of logrolls, implicit or explicit, in which various interests are packaged. We thus find only a few dimensions of voting, not because legislators are simple-minded with respect to the multitude of issues that arise, but because they are strategic actors, seeking to enter into coalitions that further their own, or their supporters', interests on the issues.

Although we recognize the role of economic interests, we also argue that these interests are neither the same as the interests of a median or pivotal voter in each constituency nor the same as the interests of pivotal voters for each of the major parties in each constituency. A very simple analysis demonstrates that, even were economic interests perfectly measured, pivotal-voter models would fail, dramatically, as models of congressional voting. Below, we show, using comparisons of the two senators from each state, that purely economic models based on pivotal or representative voters can be discarded. On the other hand, once the legislator's ideology in the basic space has been taken into account, there is evidence that points to a modest degree of representative-voter influence on roll call voting behavior. We show the limits of this auxiliary role by comparing the success of economic models and D-NOMINATE. We then show the short-term stability of coalitions by indicating that cutting lines on diverse economic provisions of a bill maintain the same angle across a sequence of votes. In contrast, the projection of economic issues onto the space can vary as underlying preferences on economic policy change. This is shown by changes in the projection for regulation by OSHA, for the minimum-wage level, and for food stamps. The projection, as we show with regard to railroads, is also affected by the trade-off between maintaining party discipline and allowing legislators to engage in position-taking that appeals to constituents.

Purely Economic Theories of Voting: A Failed Idea

In economic approaches to roll call voting (for example, Peltzman, 1984, 1985), the legislator is considered the agent of a constituency. In the simplest version, the agent would look at the constituents' interests on each roll call and vote those interests. The decision on each roll call would be uninfluenced by (that is, independent of) decisions on other roll call votes. Basically, in this standard, simple economic model of roll call voting, each issue is its own dimension and there is no linkage across votes.

This very simple model leads to a straightforward test for the Senate. Each state's two senators should vote the same way on all roll calls because they have the same constituency. The test is as follows: On every roll call on which both senators from the state "vote" in the form of an actual vote, pair, or announced vote intention, if both vote Yea or both vote Nay, count two successes.[6] If they vote differently, count one success and one error. If one were able to perfectly measure economic interests on an issue, this error rate would amount to the minimum a purely economic model could possibly hope to achieve. The test guarantees a success rate of at least 50 percent. It does not count as errors some votes that are against constituency interests, such as two Nays in a case where the senators should have both voted Yea.

The results of this test are shown in figure 6.1, for the first 100 Congresses, and in figure 6.2, for Congresses 80 to 100, as the constituency model. The success rate since the 80th Congress is above 75 percent only once. For our method of counting errors, a success rate of 75 percent results when the two senators from a state agree on half the roll call votes and disagree on the others. Thus, the two senators disagree on half of all roll call votes!

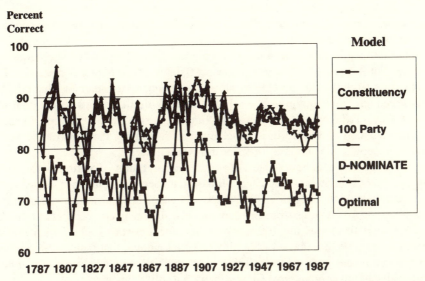

Figure 6.1. Classification success for Senate roll calls (1789–1988). The optimal model is a one-dimensional, ordinal-classification model for each Congress, analyzed separately. D-NOMINATE refers to the two-dimensional, linear-trend-in-position model. We refer to the 100-party model as predicting that two senators from the same party and the same state will vote the same way. When a state's delegation is split, the votes of the two senators are always counted as successes. The constituency model is referred to as predicting that two senators from the same state will vote the same way. It is clearly bettered by the other three models throughout the history of Congress. The 100-party model does not better the other two models, despite being less parsimonious and less precise.

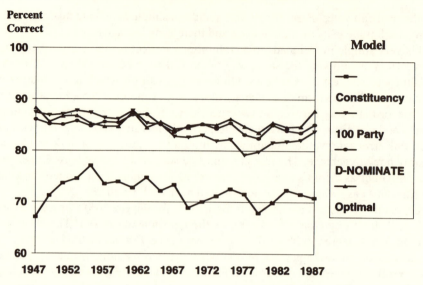

Figure 6.2. Classification success for Senate roll calls (1947–88). The models are the same as in figure 6.1. This figure shows that the optimal model betters all the other models after 1973.

The pure constituency model cannot be saved by claiming that senators could disagree because one senator sold his vote or logrolled in the state's interest. The two senators should still operate as a team and bundle the pricing of their two votes. The buyers of votes should seek out the cheapest states from among the sellers. Thus, pairs of votes from the cheapest states should be bought up to the point where the buyers have enough votes to win on the roll call vote. With the possible exception of the last vote that is to be bought, one senator from a state should be involved in a trade if the other senator is involved in a trade. Even with trading, the constituency model would be expected to be correct for 99 of the 100 senators.

A way out for proponents of an economic interpretation of voting is to hold, as Peltzman (1984) suggests, that each senator represents a state-party constituency rather than the constituency of all the voters in a state. Therefore, we would count as errors only discordant votes from two senators in a state who are members of the same party. We refer to this as the 100-party model (for 2 parties times 50 states), as it claims, for example, not that all Republicans vote together, just that two Republicans from the same state vote together. This model must do better than the constituency model, as it can never be in error for a state with a split delegation.

The 100-party model does not better the classifications of either the two-dimensional D-NOMINATE model with a linear trend or the optimal-classification model in one dimension. (The latter technique is described in chapter 2.) In particular, its classification percentage is worse than that for the optimal model in Congresses 93 to 100. It is also a very unparsimonious model since it requires 50 "parameters" (one per state) per roll call, or, for q roll calls, $50q$. In contrast, optimal classification requires one location for each of 100 senators and q midpoints. Since $q + 100$ is much less than $50q$, the 100-party model is clearly a bad starting point for the analysis of roll call voting.

If economic models must be, on their own, utter failures, they may play an auxiliary role once ideology is taken into account. The marginal relevance of economic factors is nicely shown by Loomis (1995). Loomis modified W-NOMINATE to make it a probit model rather than a logit model (see chapter 2 and appendix A). This modification permitted him to view the errors in voting as being correlated across senators from the same state and to estimate the degree of correlation.[7] He estimated one correlation, ρ_S, which applied to all pairs of senators who belonged to the same political party, and another correlation, ρ_D, which applied to all senators who belonged to different parties. If the senators are agents of "median voters," $\rho_S = \rho_D > 0$; if senators are agents of the "100 parties," $\rho_S > \rho_D = 0$; and if elements of both median and party representation are active, then $\rho_S > \rho_D > 0$. The results of the estimation are shown in figure 6.3.

The "median" model receives only weak support. The correlation of the errors in cases where the senators are from the same state but different parties averages only around 0.2. The 100-party model fares better, as the same party correlation, ρ_S, averages around 0.5. Monte Carlo work by Loomis (1995) shows that the ρ_D's, though small in magnitude, still are at least three times the level of their standard errors. Consequently, it is clear that, if one controls for ideology, the two senators from the same state do not vote independently. Still, most of what W-NOMINATE does not explain cannot be explained by the common interests of the two senators from the same state, even when they are from the same party. A clear indication of the weakness of the economic approach can be obtained by looking directly at the influence of economic factors. This is the focus of the next section.

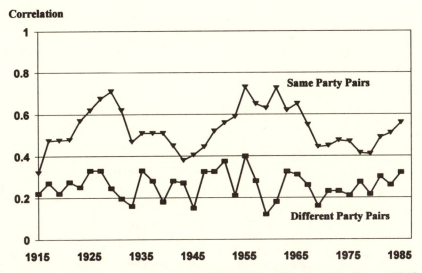

Figure 6.3. Correlations of errors in the W-NOMINATE utility function, Senate (1915–86). The estimates of the correlations come from a probit version of W-NOMINATE. "Same Party Pairs" refers to two senators from the same party in the same state. The moderately high correlations suggest that their votes reflect common interests that are independent of ideology. These common interests are much weaker for different-party pairs, when the two senators belong to different parties. Source: Loomis (1995).

The Horse Race: Economic versus Ideological Models

To compare how D-NOMINATE fares against standard models of constituency interests, we use a standard methodological technique. We evaluate the fit of each model
separately and then test a combined model, within which both the economic models
and D-NOMINATE are "nested." If D-NOMINATE, as a stand-alone model, outperforms the economic-variables model, and if the impact of the economic variables is
greatly diminished in the combined model, we can safely say that the D-NOMINATE
model better accounts for the data than do the economic variables.

The Interstate Commerce Act

We start with the critical vote (see Gilligan et al., 1989) in the House that preceded the
passage of the Interstate Commerce Act (ICA). On July 30, 1886, the Reagan (D-TX)
bill was paired against a bill that had recently passed in the Senate, the Cullom (R-IL)
bill. The Reagan bill, which was a stronger, more antirailroad regulatory measure than
the Cullom bill, passed by a 134-to-104 margin.[8]

To simplify the discussion, in table 6.1, we present linear regressions, where the dependent variable is the vote, with 1 being the value corresponding to a vote for the
Reagan bill and 0 being the value corresponding to a vote for the Cullom bill. The coefficients show the effect of each independent variable on the vote. For example, in

Table 6.1 The House Vote on the Reagan Bill versus the Cullom Bill (1887)

Variable[a]	D-NOMINATE Model	Economic Model	Combined Model
Constant	0.502**	1.182**	0.700**
	(0.012)	(0.063)	(0.057)
1st dimension	−0.917**	—	−0.831**
	(0.035)		(0.052)
2nd dimension	0.980**	—	0.661**
	(0.141)		(0.175)
CENTER	—	−0.066	−0.124
		(0.077)	(0.053)
WEST	—	−0.696**	−0.122
		(0.122)	(0.107)
CAP	—	−1.223**	−0.384**
		(0.131)	(0.127)
ROI	—	−0.043**	−0.012**
		(0.005)	(0.004)
LAND	—	0.996**	0.316*
		(0.163)	(0.152)
R^2	0.702	0.375	0.737

Note: Estimates are from linear-probability model. White (1980) asymptotic standard errors are in parentheses. N = 238.

[a] Economic-variable definitions (see Gilligan et al. [1989] for greater detail): *CENTER:* 1 for district with a major rail center, 0 otherwise; *WEST:* 1 for district north and west of Chicago, 0 otherwise; *CAP* is a measure of railroad capitalization;
ROI is a measure of railroad return on investment; *LAND* is a measure of the value of farmland.

* One-tail significant at the 0.05 level.

** One-tail significant at the 0.01 level.

the D-NOMINATE-model column, the constant of 0.502 shows that a representative with a zero score on both the first dimension and the second would have voted for Reagan with a probability of 0.502. In the economic-model column, a representative from a major rail center would have 0.066 less of a chance of voting for the Reagan bill than a representative whose district did not contain a rail center.[9]

Among the independent variables, we include the D-NOMINATE scores on the first and second dimensions.[10] The constituency-interest variables are the five variables used by Gilligan et al. (1989) in their study of the Interstate Commerce Act. These include *CENTER* (which equals 1 for districts with a major rail center, and 0 otherwise); *WEST* (which equals 1 for states north and west of Chicago, and 0 otherwise); *CAP*, a measure of railroad capitalization; *ROI*, a measure of railroad return on investment; and *LAND*, a measure of the value of farmland.[11]

On the railroad vote, the results of the horse race between the constituency-interest model and D-NOMINATE are apparent from the table. By itself, D-NOMINATE does quite well. The R^2 value of 0.70 indicates that D-NOMINATE scores explain 70 percent of the variation in the vote. The two coefficients are very precisely estimated; both are over 8 times their estimated standard errors.[12] The set of five economic variables has far more limited success, with an R^2 of only 0.38. The *CENTER* variable is not statistically significant. Moreover, the combined model shows that the constituency-interest model adds little to D-NOMINATE, increasing R^2 only from 0.70 to 0.74; and the *WEST* and *CENTER* variables are not statistically significant at conventional levels. The effect of the economic variables is also noticeably less. The magnitudes of the economic variables in the combined model drop considerably. They are only about one-third of their values when the D-NOMINATE scores are not included. In contrast, the magnitudes of the D-NOMINATE-score variables drop much less. Clearly, as measured, constituency interests are less important than ideology on railroad voting.

There are several reasons to view these initial results with skepticism.

- Have we chosen a vote particularly favorable to D-NOMINATE?
- Is a bias introduced by the use of the Reagan-versus-Cullom vote and later votes in the estimation of the D-NOMINATE scores?
- Is R^2 misleading as a measure of evaluation?
- Does the use of linear regression distort the comparison?

The answer to all these questions is no. Table 6.2 captures the essence of the answer. It shows the results for all votes on the Cullom bill, the Reagan bill, and the final passage of the Interstate Commerce Act in the 49th House. Restricting the ideological model to just the first-dimension score, it compares the results from using the D-NOMINATE score to those from using a score produced by applying the W-NOMINATE algorithm to just the first 161 roll calls in the 49th Congress that preceded the first ICA vote.[13] In model evaluation, it uses the percentage of votes correctly classified rather than R^2. Finally, table 6.2 is based on logit estimates rather than linear probability.

The results in the table are not sensitive to our earlier choice of the Reagan-versus-Cullom vote. The improvement in classification that is brought about by adding the economic variables is typically no better for the other 6 votes in table 6.2 than

Table 6.2 Classification on the 49th House's ICA Roll Calls, by Model

Model[a]	Percentage Correctly Classified by Logit Estimation						
	VOTEVIEW Number for Roll Call[b]						
	177	190	191	192	193	231	239
One-dimension D-NOMINATE	93	83	87	86	84	90	83
One-dimension NOMINATE 161	93	82	87	84	83	90	83
Combined (D-NOMINATE)	93	88	93	92	89	91	84
Combined (NOMINATE 161)	92	87	92	90	90	91	85

[a] D-NOMINATE is the first-dimension score from the full D-NOMINATE estimation. NOMINATE 161 is the first-dimension score from 161 roll calls preceding the ICA votes (see note 11 in this chapter, for further details).

[b] Description of roll calls (VOTEVIEW number is sequential for each House):

    177—Hiscock motion, Reagan bill versus Cullom (Senate) bill, July 27, 1886.

    190—Reagan: ordering of the previous question, July 30, 1886.

    191—Reagan bill versus Cullom bill, July 30, 1886.

    192—Recommittal of Reagan bill, July 30, 1886.

    193—Passage of Reagan bill, July 30, 1886.

    231—Crisp motion to consider conference-committee report, January 17, 1887.

    239—Final passage: acceptance of conference-committee report, January 21, 1887.

it was for Reagan versus Cullom. Classifications are also only slightly affected by the sample used to estimate the ideological scores. Correct classifications average under 1 percent less when we use the sample of 161 votes than when we use the D-NOMINATE scores. Using classifications as the measure of success in the logit estimates echoes the results based on R^2. Several votes, even when the D-NOMINATE model is based on just one dimension, show almost no improvement in classification in the combined model.

The comparison between D-NOMINATE and the economic variables in Gilligan et al. (1989) indicates a preference for the spatial model rather than a model based on aggregate economic indicators. One could argue that better economic horses, in the form of better measures of constituencies' economic interests, might run a better race. But we have already shown that bettors would want very good odds to back even the best possible measures of such interests.

Food Stamps

The much higher explanatory power found for D-NOMINATE variables in comparison to standard economic variables on railroad roll calls in the nineteenth century is replicated in the analysis of three 1960s and 1970s issues: food stamps, the minimum wage, and strip mining.

Our food-stamp analysis focuses on two key House votes (Ferejohn, 1986) on the food-stamp program. The first was the April 8, 1964, vote on passage of the Food Stamp Act in 1964; the second, the September 19, 1967, vote on the conference-committee report extending the program. In both cases, voting Yea represented the pro-food-stamp position. The dependent variable is coded as 1 for Yea, 0 for Nay. The logit model is used for estimation.

As we did for railroads, we use the two D-NOMINATE coordinates in the set of independent variables. The independent variables also include—as is typical for constituency-interest studies—all variables that we could tap that were potentially relevant to the pursuit of economic interests. These included:

- Food-stamp payments per capita: Higher levels of food-stamp payments should make a representative more likely to support food stamps. Recipients of food stamps clearly represent a constituency that supports the program.
- Federal farm subsidies per capita: The presence of the farm bill in the initial logroll; the administration of the program by the Department of Agriculture; and the subsidy that food stamps represent to agricultural producers—these factors suggest that agricultural interests would support the program.
- Farm income per capita: Like the previous variable, this is a measure of agricultural interests.
- AFDC (Aid to Families with Dependent Children) payments per capita: The poor, even if a food-stamp program were not present in a district, would represent a constituency for the program.
- Personal income per capita: Wealthier states could be less inclined to support a redistribution program.
- Wheat-cotton states: Because the logroll was used with a farm bill in which wheat and cotton supports figured prominently, representatives from major wheat- and cotton-growing areas should be more inclined to vote for food stamps. The value of this variable equals 1 if a district is in a wheat-cotton state; 0, if not.

Note that the economic variables are all measured at the state level, a problem we address below.

In addition to economic variables, political-party affiliation is often included as an independent variable in research papers that adopt a constituency-interest perspective. We not only follow the literature in this respect but also break down the Democrats into northern and southern contingents. Because food stamps represented an intraparty logroll in 1964, it is important to see whether party affiliation identifies a propensity to support food stamps that is not contained in the D-NOMINATE scores. Party affiliation is measured as follows:

- Southern Democrat: The value of the variable equals 1 if the representative is a Democrat from a southern state; 0, otherwise.
- Northern Democrat: The value equals 1 if the representative is a northern Democrat; 0, otherwise.

The data analysis based on these variables is shown in table 6.3. The "Separate" column for each year shows the results of two logit estimations—the D-NOMINATE coordinates in roman type; and the other variables, run separately as a set, in italics. Clearly, D-NOMINATE fits the data much better than do the economic/party variables.

The results of the logit estimation for the full set of variables are shown in the "Full" columns of table 6.3. None of the economic variables is significant for 1964, and just two, food-stamp payments and farm income, are significant for 1967. One of

Table 6.3 Food Stamps in 1964 and 1967—Logit Estimates

Variable	1964			1967		
	Separate[a]	Full	Final	Separate	Full	Final
Constant	0.590*	3.440	1.364*	1.466**	4.776	3.029**
	(0.228)[b]	(2.996)	(0.669)	(0.291)	(3.143)	(0.865)
1st Dimension	−12.043**	−15.533**	−13.269**	−14.372**	−26.178**	−24.953**
	(1.270)	(2.412)	(1.587)	(1.691)	(3.983)	(3.534)
2nd Dimension	4.592**	10.026**	7.989**	−0.415	6.070*	6.498**
	(0.646)	(2.517)	(1.627)	(0.688)	(3.056)	(2.150)
Southern Democrats	*3.474** *	−3.455*	−2.260*	*1.127** *	−5.872**	−5.050**
	(0.677)	(1.41)	(0.991)	*(0.432)*	(1.798)	(1.389)
Food-stamp	*1.057*	1.301	1.959*	*0.562* *	1.553*	1.660**
payments	*(1.080)*	(1.291)	(0.998)	*(0.261)*	(0.551)	(0.473)
Farm income	*0.064*	0.402	−0.041	*−0.045*	0.398*	0.304**
	(0.319)	(0.429)	(0.156)	*(0.104)*	(0.106)	(0.093)
Farm subsidies	*−0.022*	−0.051		*0.013*	−0.017	
	(0.028)	(0.041)		*(0.011)*	(0.016)	
AFDC payments	*0.132* *	0.113		*0.017*	−0.077	
	(0.063)	(0.082)		*(0.026)*	(0.054)	
Income	*−0.001*	−0.0008		*0.001*	−0.0003	
	(0.001)	(0.001)		*(0.001)*	(0.001)	
Wheat-cotton state	*0.022*	−0.760		*0.038*	0.944	
	(0.409)	(0.549)		*(0.359)*	(0.604)	
Northern Democrats	*6.963** *	−1.488		*5.601** *	−0.489	
	(0.787)	(1.430)		*(1.021)*	(2.099)	
Log likelihood	−84.021	−72.509	−77.763	−89.889	−63.211	−65.792
	−107.991			*−155.453*		
Pseudo R²	0.712	0.751	0.733	0.633	0.742	0.732
	0.629			*0.366*		
Number of observations	423	423	423	357	357	357

Note: For data sources, see note to table 6.5.

[a] Italicized figures refer to economic-variables model; roman figures, to D-NOMINATE model. Constant is reported for D-NOMINATE model only.

[b] Asymptotic standard errors are given in parentheses.

* Significant at the 0.05 level.

** Significant at the 0.01 level

the party variables—southern Democrat—is significant. Southern Democrats, even in the presence of the 1964 logroll, were more opposed to food stamps than was expected from the D-NOMINATE coordinates. In contrast, there is no distinction between northern Democrats and the residual group of Republicans, once spatial position has been taken into account.

This is a common finding. For example, party affiliation is insignificant if added in the railroad example discussed earlier. *The effects of party are typically contained in the D-NOMINATE measures.*[14] Party is largely just a very coarse encoding of spatial position, except for some special circumstances, such as southern Democrats' votes on food stamps.

The economic variables may have been individually insignificant in 1964 simply because we used a large set of highly intercorrelated variables. In the "Final" column of table 6.3, we show the estimates obtained when we drop all variables not statistically significant in either year. The dropped variables, judged by a standard likelihood-ratio test, are also not significant as a set. In the "Final" regressions, food-stamp payments are significant in 1964 and 1967; farm income, in 1967. The standard pseudo-R^2 measure discloses that the logit regressions explain about 73 percent of the voting on food stamps.

Of all the variables, the D-NOMINATE coordinates, particularly the first dimension, have the greatest effect on voting behavior. This is disclosed by table 6.4, where we show how the estimated probability of a pro-food-stamp vote is influenced by a one-standard-deviation change in the independent variable, holding all other variables at their sample means. Clearly, ideology predominates. A change in the first dimension affects probabilities at least five times more than a similar change in either food-stamp payments or farm income.

A caveat is in order: The fact that the other variables are less important than D-NOMINATE variables does not mean that they are unimportant. For example, instead of looking at the southern-Democrat variable, through its standard deviation—which is only 0.43 in 1964 and 0.41 in 1967—one can simply compare the probability of a pro–food-stamp vote for southern Democrats to that for other representatives, holding all other variables at their means. In 1964, this probability was 0.36 for southern Democrats but 0.89 for others. In 1967, reflecting the breakup of the logroll and the increased attractiveness of food stamps in the North, the disparity was greater; the probability dropped to 0.05 for Southern Democrats and increased to 0.96 for others. The high level for others reflects the increased mean level of food-stamp payments, which rose from 15 cents per capita in 1964 to 51 cents per capita in 1967. Even though the coefficient of food stamps declined slightly from the estimates for 1964 to those for 1967, the total impact of food stamps increased, as representatives became "hooked" through the higher mean levels. The sample standard deviation of payments also increased, from 24 cents in 1964 to 66 cents in 1967, resulting in the change in probability shown in table 6.4—a doubling, from 0.09 in 1964 to 0.18 in 1967. Thus, although overall ideology is the major influence on a legislator's voting behavior on food stamps, ideology is deflected to some extent by factors captured in regional-economic measures.

Table 6.4 Change in the Probability of a Pro–Food-Stamp Vote

Variable	Change in Probability[a]	
	1964	1967
First dimension	−0.69	−0.94
Second dimension	0.36	0.24
Southern Democrat	−0.18	−0.41
Food-stamp payments	0.09	0.18
Farm income	−0.01	0.10

[a] Changes are for a one-standard-deviation change in the variable, centered on the mean of the variable, with the other variables being held at their mean values.

We now discuss the methodological problem raised by our use of state-level variables to measure the economic variables. Because the level of income in a congressional district will, for example, differ from that in the state, we have a classic error-in-the-variables problem that will downwardly bias our estimate of the economic effects. To put the D-NOMINATE measures and the economic variables on an equal footing, we reran the "Final" analysis for a state's delegation voting for food stamps. That is, the dependent variable is *ln(PRO/CON)*, where *PRO* is the number of pro-food-stamp voters in the state and *CON* is the number against.[15]

This aggregated analysis basically confirms the previous results, as we see in table 6.5. Again, the first D-NOMINATE dimension is the most important variable. As the "Economic" column of the table indicates, there is very little stand-alone explanatory power in the three economic variables (one of which is just southern Democrat) retained in the final model of the disaggregated analysis. In the "Combined" columns, food-stamp spending is again significant, with similar magnitudes in both years, and farm income is significant in 1967, but the southern Democratic variable no longer has much punch. In contrast to the disaggregated analysis, the behavior of southern Democrats, who were part of a logroll in 1964 but not in 1967, is captured by the second dimension, which is highly significant in 1964 but not in 1967. Thus, the analysis

Table 6.5 Log of the Odds Ratio of a State Delegation Voting in Support of Food Stamps

	1964			1967		
Variable	D-NOMINATE Model	Economic Model	Combined Model	D-NOMINATE Model	Economic Model	Combined Model
Constant	0.141*	0.286	−0.003	0.315***	0.363	−0.258
	(0.075)[a]	(0.204)	(0.060)	(0.112)	(0.264)	(0.067)
First dimension	−4.345***		−4.349***	−4.917***		−5.825***
	(0.555)		(0.579)	(0.737)		(0.758)
Second dimension	2.349***		2.216**	0.431		0.145
	(0.360)		(0.925)	(0.689)		(1.159)
Southern Democrats		0.682**	0.143		−1.121**	0.134
		(0.266)	(0.507)		(0.437)	(0.596)
Food-stamp		−0.010**	0.607*		0.401*	0.428***
payments		(0.528)	(0.377)		(0.218)	(0.149)
Farm income		−0.132**	−0.003		−0.053	0.118***
		(0.065)	(0.052)		(0.053)	(0.042)
Adjusted R^2	0.62	0.14	0.66	0.51	0.11	0.61
Number of states	50	50	50	50	50	50

Sources: Food-stamp-payment data were obtained from USDA, Food and Nutritional Service, in a report of bonus coupons issued for the 1960s by participating counties and cities. Government farm subsidies and farm income for each state came from USDA, Agricultural Marketing Service, Farm Income Statistics, found in the *American Statistical Index (ASI)*. AFDC payments came from the "Public Assistance" table in the *ASI,* supplied by the Department of Health, Education and Welfare. Personal income per capita came from *ASI,* using information from the U.S. Bureau of the Census, *U.S. Census of Population 1970,* vol. 1. The variable Southern Democrats was created by multiplying a dummy variable for southern states (1 if South, 0 otherwise) times the proportion of state congressional delegation which is Democratic. Thus a value of 1 means a southern state with all Democratic representatives. The proportion of a state delegation that favored food stamps is calculated on the basis of delegation members who voted or were paired or announced.

[a] Asymptotic standard errors are given in parentheses.

* Significant at the 0.10 level, two-tail.

** Significant at the 0.05 level, two-tail.

*** Significant at the 0.01 level, two-tail.

of the state averages further supports the claim that roll call voting is largely accounted for by the spatial model.

The Minimum Wage

The story for the minimum wage parallels that for railroads and food stamps. We are able to compare our results to those of three other studies: Bloch (1980); Silberman and Durden (1976); and Krehbiel and Rivers (1988). The work of these authors has shown that measures of constituency interests, represented by wage levels, unemployment levels, and union membership, are far less important to voting decisions than is party membership. For example, Krehbiel and Rivers, in their analysis of 1977 Senate votes on minimum wage amendments, found that Democrats, ceteris paribus, would prefer a minimum-wage increase of 17 cents to 22 cents higher than Republicans would, whereas a 10 percent increase in the percentage of the labor force belonging to unions in the state would induce a preferred increase in the minimum wage of only 4 cents to 8 cents. Similar conclusions can be drawn from Bloch's work on 1966 and 1974 Senate voting. In probits run separately for each party, Bloch found that neither the wage variable nor the union variable was significant at the conventional 0.05 level in 1966. To put matters simply, two senators from the same state will tend to oppose each other on the minimum wage if they are from different parties. The partisan effect overwhelms aggregate measures of constituency interests.

The importance of ideology, as against simple party-line voting, is apparent when we consider the D-NOMINATE analysis. In our detailed study of the minimum wage (Poole and Rosenthal, 1991b), we showed that D-NOMINATE correctly classified 85 to 90 percent of all individual voting decisions made on the minimum wage since the first bill was passed in 1938.

More important, minimum-wage votes tend to split both parties. Some liberal Republicans join northern Democrats, but southern Democrats historically vote with the Republicans. In the political-science literature on Congress, the alliance of the southern Democrats and the Republicans is known as the "conservative coalition." The minimum wage was, until recently, a conservative-coalition issue. Although a three-party model (northern Democrats, southern Democrats, and Republicans) will classify much better than a two-party model, figure 6.4 shows that a three-party model is still inferior to a spatial model. The figure shows the two votes used in the Silberman and Durden (1976) study. The votes divide both southern Democrats and Republicans. The three-party model fails to tell us which southern Democrats are likely to oppose the minimum-wage bill and which Republicans are likely to break party ranks and support the bill. In contrast, the spatial model can capture the diversity within party and regional blocs.

Models that use economic variables are far less successful than D-NOMINATE in accounting for roll call voting on minimum wages, as illustrated by the Krehbiel and Rivers (1988) essay.[16] These authors studied Senate votes on the Bartlett and Tower amendments to the minimum-wage bill in 1977.

The Bartlett amendment was for a sharp reduction in the increase in the minimum wage that was contained in the bill proposed by the Democrats. The Tower amendment was for a more moderate reduction. Staunch conservatives could be expected to vote Yea on both amendments; moderates, Yea on Tower, but Nay on Bartlett; and liberals, Nay on both. No one, as was in fact, the case, should vote Nay on Tower but Yea

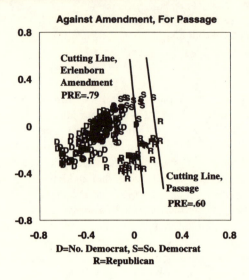

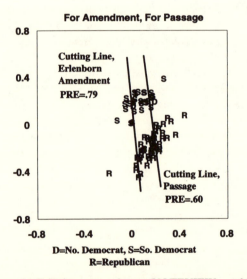

Figure 6.4. The votes on the Erlenborn amendment (VOTEVIEW number 119) and on passage of the minimum-wage bill (VOTEVIEW number 129) in the House of Representatives on June 6, 1973. Members against the amendment and for passage are overwhelmingly to the left of the amendment cutting line. Members for the amendment and against passage are preponderantly to the right of the passage cutting line. Members in favor of both the amendment and passage are concentrated between the two cutting lines, which are close to parallel. (The figure excludes Nay–Nay votes and members who voted on only one of the two roll calls.)

on Bartlett. Thus, the three categories of voting patterns could be ordered by the degree to which they favored high minimum wages.

   Krehbiel and Rivers (1988) estimated an ordered probit model of the probability a senator would fall into the three categories. They used the following independent variables: party, union membership, wages, unemployment, the South, and the per-

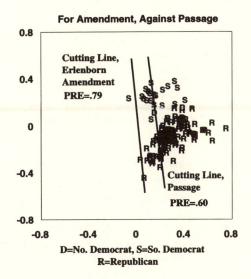

For Amendment, Against Passage

Figure 6.4. (*continued*)

centage of population that is black. These variables include two, party and the South, that are arguably more ideological than economic, particularly when union membership, wages, and percentage black are also present in the equation. Even so, Krehbiel and Rivers succeed in classifying only 74 percent to 76 percent of the observations, depending upon the specification chosen. The relevant benchmark prediction for their study is the modal category, Nay on both amendments, which included 68 percent of the 91 senators voting or announced on both roll calls. The improvement afforded by use of economic variables is slight. In contrast, the D-NOMINATE two-dimensional predictions (no senator is predicted as Nay–Yea) for these three categories results in an 86 percent classification rate. Only 13 of the 91 senators are misclassified. The results are summarized in table 6.6.[17]

Although we did not conduct the complete horse race that we carried out for railroads and food stamps, our 13 classification errors seem unlikely to be residuals that can be reconciled by appealing to standard economic-interest considerations. To illustrate this point, we ask whether union membership—an independent variable used by Krehbiel and Rivers—or the presence of a right-to-work law might account for the 13 errors.[18] Our two most serious errors were those for Danforth (R-MO), who voted Yea–Yea when he was predicted to vote Nay–Nay, and for Garn (R-Utah), who voted Nay–Nay when predicted Yea–Yea. Neither deviation would seem consistent with an economic interpretation. Missouri in 1977 was above the national average in union membership and did not have a right-to-work law, while Utah had a low degree of unionization and a right-to-work law.[19] The other Republican senator from Utah, Hatch, voted Yea–Yea, as predicted. Any economic considerations that would explain Garn's vote would not explain Hatch's. A similar inspection of the 11 less serious errors (Nay–Yea predictions that fell into the other two categories or vice versa) also failed to disclose any consistent pattern in either unionization or right-to-work laws. The errors of the spatial model are likely to be linked as much to internal logrolling within Congress as they are to constituencies' economic interests that are specific to minimum wages.

Table 6.6 Classification Accuracy on the Bartlett and Tower Amendments in 1977

Model	Percent Correctly Classified
D-NOMINATE, two-dimensional	85.7
Krehbiel-Rivers (1988), various specifications	73.9–76.1
Marginals (percent that voted no on both amendments)	68.1

Note: N = 91, the number of senators voting or announced on both the Bartlett and Tower roll calls.

We also looked at the two Senate roll calls, one from 1966 and the other from 1974, studied by Bloch (1978). We achieved classification success of 90 percent and 86 percent, respectively, for these two roll calls. Bloch does not report classification success, but it is unlikely his models would better D-NOMINATE, as his independent variables are a subset of those used by Krehbiel and Rivers.

The final previous study we compared to the ideological model represented by D-NOMINATE is Silberman and Durden (1976). Like Krehbiel and Rivers, these authors used an ordered probit approach. They studied two 1973 roll calls: on the Erlenborn amendment and final passage by the House.[20]

Silberman and Durden used five independent variables: South; labor's campaign contributions to 1972 congressional winners; contributions by small business organizations; and measures of low-wage workers and of teenage workers. It is difficult to compare this study to the spatial model, as the authors report only the estimated coefficients. Two points can be made. First, the most statistically significant coefficients are South and the two campaign-contribution coefficients. In this respect, we note that campaign contributions and region cannot be specifically linked to minimum wages but are relevant to a whole set of interests that are captured by our spatial coordinates. Indeed, campaign contributions, particularly by labor, are highly related to spatial position, as shown by Poole and Romer (1985); by Poole, Romer, and Rosenthal (1987); and by McCarty and Poole (1995). In other words, there is an identification problem. Region and campaign contributions have a logical relationship to minimum-wage interests. On the other hand, they relate to a whole set of other interests as well. Since southerners, for example, tend to vote as a bloc on a whole set of issues, it is difficult to distinguish the economic impact specific to the minimum wage from general regional interests.

Second, campaign contributions do not measure within-constituency interests. Because the contribution variables are contributions to a winning candidate, variable values for individual districts will be highly sensitive to the outcomes of House races. For example, labor contributions are likely to be far higher if the winner is a Democrat rather than a Republican. In a swing district, a small shift in district preferences, expressed, in turn, in a small shift in the congressional vote, can make a large difference to the labor-contribution variable. Moreover, many contributors, such as the United Auto Workers or the National Association of Manufacturers, are not local groups.[21] So if the Silberman-Durden probit equation is to be believed (instead of a Bloch equation or a Krehbiel-Rivers equation), we will have to believe that although economic interests may matter, they are not median voter interests.

In figure 6.4, we have plotted the cutting lines and shown the cross-tabulation of the two roll calls. Table 6.7 contains our classification analysis. Excluding (therefore

Table 6.7 Comparison of D-NOMINATE–Predicted and Actual Votes for the 1973 House Minimum-Wage Roll Calls

Vote Predicted by D-NOMINATE	Actual Vote		
	Against Erlenborn, for Passage	For Erlenborn, for Passage	For Erlenborn, against Passage
Against Erlenborn, for passage	188	16	3
For Erlenborn, for passage	11	35	27
For Erlenborn, against passage	2	17	102

mimicking Silberman and Durden) legislators voting against the amendment and against passage, and legislators voting on only one of the roll calls, we correctly classify 81 percent of the joint decisions. The most serious errors occur in the upper-right and lower-left corners of the table—these represent only 1 percent of the representatives. (Classification of the two roll calls separately shows 89 percent for Erlenborn and 87 percent for passage.)

More research would need to be done to see if the Silberman-Durden variables would account for the errors of the spatial model. One of them clearly will not, at least on its own. An inspection of figure 6.4 shows that southern Democrats are spread out over the three vote categories. There is not a strong pattern to the classification errors for southern Democrats.

In the studies considered here, there appears to be little interest in using economic models once the spatial nature of voting has been recognized. Perhaps the failure of economic models of roll call voting on minimum wages lies with the problem of measuring economic interests. Ideally, one would like to calculate the general equilibrium implications of a change in the law. The change would leave some people better off— for example, those working at the old minimum who saw their real wage increased and maintained the same number of hours of employment—and others worse off, such as workers who became unemployed as a result of the change, or certain holders of capital. Thus, in any constituency, there is likely to be a mixture of winners and losers. After one had calculated the winners and losers, one would have to determine whose preferences were decisive for a particular member of Congress. Given the complexity involved in constructing a realistic *economic and political* model of minimum-wage voting, it is not surprising that naive attempts are inferior to the spatial model based on persistent patterns of voting.

Strip Mining

Even the most careful attempts at measurement are, however, unlikely to meet with success. We will illustrate this point with another example—Kalt and Zupan's (1984) study of the Surface Mining Control and Reclamation Act.[22] This act both regulated strip mining and clarified property rights in strip-mining areas. Votes on the act would appear to be strong candidates for finding evidence of economic influences. At the same time, more broad, ideological views about the role of government in economic and environmental regulation might also be important.

Kalt and Zupan's dependent variable was an index of opposition to strip mining, "*ANTISTRIP,*" which they constructed from 21 Senate roll call votes in 1977.[23] The formula for the index for each senator *i* was:

$$ANTISTRIP_i = ln \left[\frac{U_i + 0.5}{F_i + 0.5} \right],$$

where U_i is the number of votes cast by the senator that were unfavorable to strip mining, and F_i is the number favorable to strip mining. Only recorded Yea and Nay votes were used to construct this index.

Kalt and Zupan also carefully constructed six economic variables to measure the direct economic costs and benefits that would relate to the interests of both underground and surface coal producers; electric utilities and other coal consumers; noncoal land users; and environmentalists. These variables and their variants are:[24]

MC	The regulation-induced increase in the long-run average cost of surface mining in each coal-producing state
SURFRES	The state's surface reserves of coal
UNDERRES	The state's underground reserves of coal
SPLITR	The agricultural- and timber-revenue yield of surface acreage underlain by potentially strippable coal
ENVIROS	Fraction of voters who are active environmentalists
UNREC	Prospective value to noncoal interests of strip-mined unrestored acreage
CONSUME	Fraction of state's electricity generated from coal
HSURF	The Herfindahl index for surface coal producers in each state
HUNDER	The Herfindahl index for underground coal producers in each state
HENVIROS	The Herfindahl index for active environmentalists in each state
HCONSUME	The Herfindahl index for coal consumers in each state

The measure of ideological positions was a *PROLCV* (for pro-League of Conservation Voters) index based on 27 votes selected by the League of Conservation Voters.[25] These votes all dealt with environmental issues *other than* strip mining. The index used a formula similar to that for *ANTISTRIP.*

The horse-race results for the *ANTISTRIP* regressions are quite similar to those for railroads and food stamps. The level of fit of the economic variables is relatively low, but most of the estimated coefficients have the anticipated signs, as shown in the first data column of table 6.8.

When *PROLCV* is included, as seen in column 2 of table 6.8, explanatory power increases dramatically. (R^2, adjusted for degrees of freedom, rises from 0.21 to 0.53.) The estimated coefficient of *PROLCV* is of the correct sign and is more than 10 times its standard error. Even a specification that includes only *PROLCV* and a constant (see column 3 of table 6.8) outperforms the model of column 1.

When we compare the results in the first three columns with those in the last two, where the D-NOMINATE first dimension is substituted for *PROLCV* as a measure of ideology, we obtain a striking result. As a single independent variable, our dimension outperforms *PROLCV* (compare columns 3 and 5) and does as well when ideology

Table 6.8 Regression Estimates for Kalt and Zupan's Anti-Strip Index (N = 100)

Variable[a]	Economic	Economic and *PROLCV*	*PROLCV*	Economic and D-NOMINATE	D-NOMINATE
			Model		
Constant	−0.154	1.414*	0.712*	0.704	0.659*
	(0.468)[a]	(0.494)	(0.058)	(0.476)	(0.058)
MC	−0.513*	−0.375*		−0.350*	
	(0.107)	(0.108)		(0.108)	
SURFRES	−16.765	−17.196		−14.865	
	(10.073)	(10.073)		(10.075)	
UNDERRES	12.512*	14.132*		11.330	
	(5.972)	(5.974)		(5.973)	
SPLITR	−26.548	68.478		29.323	
	(48.083)	(49.004)		(48.385)	
ENVIROS	83.373*	0.497		31.115	
	(18.602)	(20.349)		(19.275)	
UNREC	0.019*	0.015*		0.011*	
	(0.005)	(0.005)		(0.005)	
CONSUME	−0.0035	−0.0044		−0.0023	
	(0.0024)	(0.0024)		(0.0024)	
HSURF	−0.294	0.018		−0.297	
	(0.237)	(0.239)		(0.237)	
HUNDER	0.305	0.150		0.417	
	(0.277)	(0.277)		(0.277)	
HENVIROS	1.935	−1.287		−0.119	
	(1.085)	(1.132)		(1.103)	
HCONSUME	−0.486*	−0.261		−0.203	
	(0.201)	(0.202)		(0.203)	
PROLCV		0.466*	0.471*		
		(0.046)	(0.040)		
D-NOMINATE				−1.211*	−1.334*
(1st Dimension)				(0.117)	(0.106)
Adjusted R²	0.210	0.531	0.451	0.553	0.490

Source: Poole and Romer (1993). All regressions are weighted.

[a] See text for variable definitions.

[b] Estimated standard errors are in parentheses.

* Denotes coefficient > 2 standard errors.

and economics are combined (compare columns 2 and 4). The reason for this result is disclosed in chapter 8, where we examine the ideological stance of the LCV and other interest groups. There, we find that, in the main, the only distinction between interest groups is where they stand on a single liberal-conservative axis. Nothing specific distinguishes the evaluations of environmental groups from those of labor groups, business groups, civil-liberties groups, and so on. What counts is where the group stands in the basic space discussed in chapter 2.

Our discussion of strip-mining votes reinforces, in an important way, our previous analyses of railroads, food stamps, and minimum wages. Even the most serious attempts to find economic influences on roll call voting will tend to find that the representative's general liberal/conservative orientation is the primary influence on roll call voting behavior.

A "Fishing Expedition"

Partly to check whether strip-mining roll calls were just an odd set of roll calls fit badly by constituency models, we conducted a Peltzman (1984) "fishing expedition" (his apt term) using broad economic and demographic variables for 568 Senate roll calls in 1977.[26] Eight of these were made available to us by Kalt and Zupan from their study. These were party, income, growth, education, urbanization, union membership, age, and manufacturing. To these we added percentage of nonwhites. Party, is of course, a dubious choice as an "economic" variable, but we deliberately included it to load the dice in favor of the constituency-interests hypothesis. This set of variables closely follows that used by Peltzman (1984).

Peltzman estimated a logit equation for each roll call. Such a procedure can be interpreted as stating that individuals' ideal points vary across roll calls, so an individual senator i has an ideal point x_{ij} on roll call j, $j = 1, \ldots, 568$. The ideal point takes the form:

$$x_{ij} = \gamma_{0j} + \gamma_{1j}v_{i1} + \gamma_{2j}v_{i2} + \ldots + \gamma_{9j}v_{i9}$$

where the v_i's are the 9 constituency-interest variables for the senator's state and the γ's are coefficients estimated. Such a fishing expedition lacks parsimony, as it estimates $10 \times 568 = 5{,}680$ parameters. We refer to the fishing expedition as the LINEAR model.

A more parsimonious constituency-interest model would hold that voting is one-dimensional, and that the ideal point is the same linear function for all roll calls:

$$x_i = \gamma_0 + \gamma_1 v_{i1} + \gamma_2 v_{i2} + \ldots + \gamma_9 v_{i9}$$

This model is equivalent to W-NOMINATE, except that the ideal point is constrained to be a linear function of the constituency variables. When it is estimated, one estimates a signal-to-noise ratio and the two outcome coordinates for each roll call (see chapter 2), in addition to the 10γ coefficients. Therefore, there are $1 + 2 \times 568 + 10 = 1{,}147$ parameters for this CONSTITUENCY model. The basic W-NOMINATE model has only slightly more parameters. Since there are 100 senators in the estimation, one estimates the 100 ideal points directly rather than the 10γ coefficients. This leads to a total of 1,237 parameters.

Although one can compare the fit of the W-NOMINATE model to that of the two constituency-interest models, there is no direct way to combine the models. To evaluate what ideological models add to constituency-interest models, we use a measure of ideology that is independent of the 1977 roll call data: the 1976 Poole and Daniels (1985) coordinates for senators who served in 1976 and the 1978 coordinates for senators who entered in 1977. The Poole-Daniels coordinates have a very high degree of correlation with those from W-NOMINATE, as we explain in chapter 8. We define a new independent variable as the residual from the regression of the Poole-Daniels coordinates on the constituency variables. That is, the residual is only that part of ideology that is not picked up by constituency factors. In the estimations, the constituency effect will be exaggerated, because some purely ideological effects will be counted as constituency effects. The LINEAR model, with the residual added as an independent variable, is termed LINRES; the CONSTITUENCY model, CONRES.

The performance of the various models is compared in table 6.9. The constrained CONSTITUENCY model performs very poorly without party. Even with party

Table 6.9 Logit Estimation for All Senate Roll Calls (1977)

Model[a]	Number of Estimated Parameters	Percentage Correctly Classified	Geometric Mean Probability
CONSTITUENCY, without party	1,146	73.2	0.585
CONSTITUENCY, with party	1,147	78.2	0.633
CONRES	1,148	81.0	0.668
NOMINATE	1,237	82.3	0.680
LINEAR	5,680	82.8	0.690
LINRES	6,248	86.2	0.740

Note: 568 roll calls, with more than 2.5 percent of votes on the minority side.

[a] *CONSTITUENCY* and *LINEAR* independent variables were income, growth, education, union membership, age, manufacturing, nonwhite population, and party. *CONSTITUENCY* constrains coefficients on independent variables to be identical across roll calls. In *LINEAR*, coefficients are unconstrained. *LINRES* and *CONRES* add an ideological residual as an independent variable to *LINEAR* and *CONSTITUENCY*. *NOMINATE* constrains ideal points to be identical across roll calls and estimates ideal points and roll call outcome locations

included, it is inferior to W-NOMINATE, providing further evidence that the W-NOMINATE coordinates contain far more information than political-party and constituency characteristics.[27] Moreover, the very unparsimonious LINEAR model betters W-NOMINATE by only one-half of 1 percent in classification and by 0.01 in geometric mean probability. Clearly, a parameter-expensive fishing expedition is not more productive than a simple spatial model of voting. Finally, the ideological residual substantially increases the performance of both the CONSTITUENCY and LINEAR models. Indeed, the residual is statistically significant at the 0.001 level, or better, in 239 of the 568 roll calls for the CONSTITUENCY model, and 286 for the LINEAR model, whereas it would, under the standard null hypothesis, be expected to be significant in less than one roll call.[28]

These findings suggest that Peltzman (1984) overinterpreted his results in support of the constituency story. Clearly, ideology plays an important independent role even when the constituency variables are allowed to do as much work as possible. Moreover, the simple spatial model, by itself, does very nearly as well as the atheoretical fishing expedition represented by the LINEAR model. One would expect even stronger results in favor of ideological voting in periods of history that did not include the 1960s and 1970s "textbook" Congresses, where local interests have been said to predominate.

The Projection of Economic Issues into the Basic Space

Projection and Parallel Cutting Lines

The results discussed above, supporting ideological models over constituency models, are consistent with the primary argument of this book: Complicated issues, including those involving economic conflict, can be represented as simple projections into a one- or two-dimensional space. If a quantitative variable, such as the minimum-wage level, is a projected issue, the cutting lines for votes between alternative values of the variable should be parallel. In figure 6.4, we provided a graphical illustration of parallel cutting lines for the Erlenborn-amendment vote and the bill-passage vote in the House in 1973. Cutting lines are also roughly parallel for the Bartlett- and Tower-amendment votes in 1977 that were analyzed by Krehbiel and Rivers. Another example, used in the theoretical discussion in chapter 2, was provided by votes on the minimum number of employees that subject a firm to inspection by the Occupational Safety and Health Administration. The OSHA votes are discussed in greater detail later in this section.[29]

Parallel cutting lines can also occur on amendment voting on a bill when several different economic dimensions are active. For example, in regard to railroads, in the 48th Congress, the Reagan version of the Interstate Commerce Act was debated, section by section, under a relatively open rule that allowed minority amendments. (The bill was passed in the House but not acted on by the Senate.) Five votes were taken on rebates, on the short-haul-pricing constraint, and on whether the regulations should be enforced by the courts or an independent commission. These issues, although distinct, were anticipated, and the cutting lines on all these votes, and on two economic votes in the 49th House, had angles that fell within the narrow range of 34°to 58°(see Poole and Rosenthal, 1994a, for further details). In contrast, the amendments dealing with racial discrimination, which were not anticipated when the logroll was constructed, had sharply different angles, being vertical cutting lines (see chapter 7 for a further discussion). Railroad regulation, OSHA, and the minimum wage illustrate the point that economic issues, even if complex packages, appear, in the short run, as projections into our basic space.

But our spatial model is not a model of how these projections occur. A dramatic example is the contentious rejection of Robert Bork as a nominee for the Supreme Court, which was preceded by the confirmation, with only one dissenting vote, of the arguably equally conservative Antonin Scalia. But Scalia is only arguably as conservative as Bork. An even more compelling example is the bill on OSHA firm-inspection levels, which the Senate voted on twice within a five-month period in 1972.

The OSHA bill considered by the Senate had no provision concerning the size of firms that could be inspected; therefore, if one presumed some bill would pass, the status quo was that all firms with employees were subject to inspection. The 1972 votes on inspection levels are summarized in table 6.10. Senator Carl Curtis (R-NE) attempted to exempt smaller firms by attaching an amendment that would bar expenditures on inspection of any firm with 25 or fewer employees. Like all voting on the firm-size issue, this vote was a conservative-coalition vote, with a cutting line of approximately −45°. The amendment failed, with 44 votes being cast against the amendment to 41 in favor of it, on June 27, 1972. On the very next roll call, Curtis obtained a vote for barring inspection of firms with 15 or fewer employees, again against the status quo of all firms being subject to inspection. This time, Curtis received more votes, in line with our discussion in chapter 2. Lowering the minimum level from 25 to 15 should have produced, and did produce, more votes against the status quo. The level of 15 employees passed, by a vote of 46 to 43.

The bill came up again in October. Senator Clifford Case (R-NJ), a liberal Republican, proposed to strike the Curtis amendment. That is, the status quo was now 15, and Case got a revote on 15 against the old status quo of "all firms." Case's motion passed, by a vote of 47 to 33. Curtis then proposed a still lower limit of 7 employees. This failed by a 38-to-43 vote, as did an attempt at a limit of 4 employees, which lost on a tied 39-to-39 vote. Finally, Curtis succeeded with a 3-employee limit by a 50-to-28 margin.

Table 6.10 Minimum Number of Employees That Allow OSHA to Inspect a Firm (1972 Votes)

VOTEVIEW Number	Date	Senator Making Motion	Number of Employees	For/Against Inspection		Errors	PRE2[a]
				Actual Vote	With Pairs and Announced		
653	June 27	Curtis	25	44–41	46–42	10	0.76
654	June 27	Curtis	15	41–45	43–46	7	0.84
895	Oct. 13	Case	15	47–33	51–38	9	0.76
896	Oct. 13	Curtis	7	45–41	43–38	13	0.68
898	Oct. 13	Curtis	4	39–39	42–42	13	0.81
900	Oct. 13	Curtis	3	28–50	31–53	13	0.58

[a] *PRE2* is the proportionate reduction in error for the two-dimensional, linear-trend D-NOMINATE model (see chapter 3).

In June, Curtis had been able to get a 15-employee limit passed; in October, he had to settle for a limit of 3. The angles of the cutting line were quite stable. Nonetheless, the projection of the issue into the basic space had changed. Senators' ideal points in the projection had shifted in a liberal direction. Undoubtedly, senators were responding to lobbying efforts by labor unions. Even though the votes can be accounted for by the basic space, economic interests helped to define the projection of the issue.

A change in projection can also reflect longer-run forces. For example, in the 1970s and the 1980s, persistent discussion of the negative employment effects of the minimum wage, coupled with declining union membership, may have reduced congressional preference for a higher minimum wage. Making such an inference is difficult because each minimum-wage bill is in fact a multiattribute item. As a result, we do only some rough, back-of-the-envelope calculations.

We find that the cutting lines of the Tower-amendment vote in 1977 and of the GOP substitute-bill vote in 1989 both separated Senator Lugar, who took the conservative position, from Senators Hatfield, Packwood, and Heinz, who voted with the liberals. The four senators were reasonably close to both cutting lines. Therefore, if we can map a wage onto a cutting line in both cases, we can get a rough estimate of how the preferences of moderate Republicans have changed over time.

As Krehbiel and Rivers (1988) point out, the 1977 vote on the amendment of John Tower (R-TX) was in fact a vote between the proposals of Tower and Harrison Williams (D-NJ). These differed most sharply in their proposed wages for 1980, $3.05 in Tower and $3.15 in Williams. Using these two alternative 1980 wages, we impute a value of $3.10 to the cutting line. In 1967 dollars, this amounts to a value of $1.25 for the cutting line.

The corresponding comparison for 1989 is between the 1991 wage of $4.55 in the Democratic bill and the wage of $4.25 in the GOP substitute. The imputed cutting-line value is $4.40 or $1.07 in 1967 dollars. Comparing the $1.25 figure from 1977 to $1.07 for 1989 suggests an ebbing support for the minimum wage. On the other hand, the differential would be less important if one argued that senators were conditioning their votes with a view toward adopting a bill that would win presidential approval. Carter's acquiescence to labor demands and Bush's firmness may have influenced the spatial mapping in the legislative branch. Nonetheless, it is quite possible that the minimum-wage ideal points of senators shifted downward.

In a nutshell, economic interests are important because they affect projections as well as logrolls. Even when there is a stable projection, economic interests can change the mapping of quantitative alternatives onto the projection.

Evolution of the Angle of Projection

The angle of the projection into the basic space can evolve over time. In some cases, this evolution will simply reflect changes induced by the overall evolution of the political system. This type of change in the cutting-line angle is well illustrated by minimum-wage legislation, where the angle of minimum-wage-bill votes was influenced by the changing ideological positions of southern Democrats. Another type of change is endogenous change, where prior legislation creates an economic constituency that influences the later voting behavior of the legislator. We illustrate this "hooking" effect with food stamps.

To begin our discussion of a change in the cutting-line angle, we consider the entire set of minimum-wage roll calls that occurred in the House of Representatives during the period spanned by our dynamic estimation. The first roll call occurred in the 75th House in 1937; the last, in the 98th House in 1983.

The spatial model provides a better accounting of minimum-wage voting after World War II than of votes before it. Voting on the minimum wage occurred before the war in the 75th Congress, when the initial legislation was passed, and in the 76th, when revisions were considered. Subsequently, new legislation was made moot by the command economy of the war. Divided government occurred in 1947–48, with a Republican Congress and a Democratic president. In the labor area, the Republicans devoted their energies to overriding Truman's veto of the Taft-Hartley Act. Minimum wages did not get considered until the 81st Congress.

Consequently, we can divide the roll calls neatly into pre–World War II and post–World War II samples. Correct classification of minimum-wage roll calls, using only the one-dimensional dynamic model, is at a very high level after World War II, averaging 88.2 percent, but is much lower, at 71.2 percent, before World War II.[30] Moving to a two-dimensional model improves matters considerably before World War II. Correct classifications jump to 82.0 percent, but are still below the 88.6 percent obtained for the postwar period.[31]

The finding that the second dimension is the key to the classification of minimum-wage voting before World War II shows that, initially, the minimum wage was an unusual, nonstandard issue that was not part of the main line of liberal-conservative conflict. The finding that, even in two dimensions, minimum-wage voting does not fit the spatial model particularly well before World War II is indicative of the potential multidimensionality of most economic legislation. Because, for example, the level of the wage can be traded off against what type of employment will be covered, a vote between two alternative bills may not fit readily into the preexisting spatial pattern of voting. The complex nature of such trade-offs should, we suggest, be most apparent in the initial legislative handling of an issue. Eventually, however, the multidimensionality is put into a package and shoehorned into the spatial structure.

The packaging indeed results, at any one point in time, in minimum-wage voting being nearly unidimensional. In figure 6.5, we plot the cutting-line angles in chronological order. If the votes were unidimensional at a point in time, all the angles for a

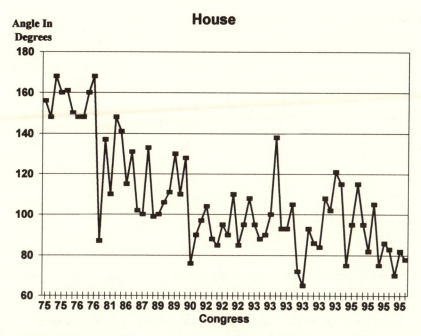

House

Figure 6.5. Cutting-line angles on minimum-wage roll calls in the House of Representatives. Angles are for all vote margins closer than 65 to 35. The minimum wage shifts from a second-dimension issue before World War II (angles are just under 180°) to a first-dimension issue (angles are near 90° as southern Democrats adopt conservative positions).

year would be identical. There is some variation within years, but it is quite small, particularly for roll calls with close (less than 65-to-35) margins.

In contrast, the angles vary strongly and linearly over time. In table 6.11, we present the results of a regression of the angle against a constant, calendar year and roll call margin. The angle declines sharply over time, especially for close roll calls.[32] The standard error of the estimate of 14.5° indicates the small variability in the angle within a given year.

The results presented in chapter 4 help us understand why the angle has gradually shifted. At the beginning of the New Deal, positions of northern and southern Democrats did not show significant differences. The Roosevelt coalition represented a reasonably coherent voting bloc. The civil-rights issues introduced significant and increasing polarization within the party. The passage of the Voting Rights Act in 1965, however, marked the beginning of a period in which southern Democrats drifted back toward the party mainstream.

The changing position of southern Democrats is evidenced in figures 3.4 and 5.15. By 1940, some of the separation of the southern delegation had occurred. They had moved above the northern Democrats on the vertical dimension but had not moved to the right on the horizontal dimension. By 1960, a time when civil rights began to dominate American domestic politics, southern Democrats had made the full transition. By 1977, there was less separation.

The spatial movement of southern Democrats is tracked by the minimum-wage cutting lines. The opposition of southern Democrats, and of Republicans, to the initial

Table 6.11 Minimum-Wage Votes: Cutting-Line Angles, Time, and Vote Margin

	Model	
Variable	(1)	(2)
Constant	3385.37	3291.22
	(268.11)[a]	(260.56)
Calendar year	−1.667	−1.622
	(0.136)	(0.132)
(Year × margin)/100[b]		0.8059
		(0.336)
Adjusted R²	0.679	0.703
Standard error of estimate	15.037	14.467

Note: Dependent variable is the cutting-line angle in degrees.

[a] Standard errors are in parentheses.

[b] Margin = percent Yea − percent Nay.

minimum-wage legislation led to a nearly horizontal cutting line before the war. As southern Democrats, flush with the manna of public works and military bases provided by the New Deal, switched from seeking to alleviate their economic situation vis-à-vis the North to seeking to protect the internal status quo vis-à-vis blacks, they became more conservative on the economic dimension. The cutting-line angle echoed this movement. The votes in the immediate postwar period, as was typical of conservative-coalition votes, gave more emphasis to the first dimension. With more liberal southern Democrats, the cutting line became nearly vertical in the 1970s, as illustrated by figure 6.4. In the 1980s, the cutting line had an angle smaller than 90°, showing that party-line voting was occurring on minimum wages, with the South's historical opposition to minimum wages now being expressed by an increasing number of southern Republicans.

Although a standard economic explanation for the opposition of the South is that minimum wages cause low-wage regions to lose their comparative advantage in attracting investment, an alternative view is that enfranchised whites in the South sought to maintain disenfranchised blacks in a low-wage situation. When the first minimum-wage roll calls took place in 1937, Congressman Martin Dies (D-TX) was unambiguous on this point: "There is a racial question involved here. Under this measure whatever is prescribed for one race must be prescribed for the others, and you cannot prescribe the same wages for the white man as the black man."[33]

Later developments support the view that the race issue was a central one. As southern Democrats acquired a black constituency, in the 1970s, more of them began to favor increased minimum wages, even though southern states had low levels of unionization and nearly all had right-to-work laws. Only one southern Democrat voted against passage of the 1989 bill in the House, and only three supported the GOP substitute in the Senate.

The change in the angle for minimum-wage votes is thus largely one of the projection adjusting to the perturbation of the space (see chapter 4) that is induced by the reappearance of race as a salient issue in American politics. The story is quite different for food stamps.

The change in the angle for food-stamp votes is shown in the comparison of the top panel of figure 6.6, which shows the 1964 vote, and the bottom panel, which shows

1964 Vote

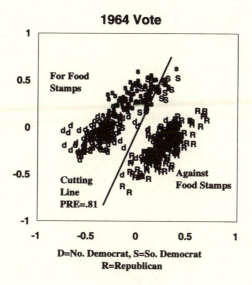

D=No. Democrat, S=So. Democrat
R=Republican

1967 Vote

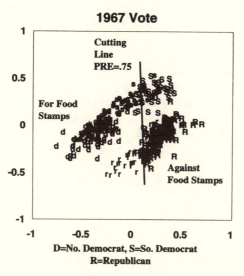

D=No. Democrat, S=So. Democrat
R=Republican

Figure 6.6. Votes on passage of the 1964 Food Stamp Act (VOTEVIEW number 149) and on the 1967 conference report extending the food-stamp program (VOTEVIEW number 134). The 1964 vote is nearly a party-line vote, while the 1967 vote is a conservative-coalition vote.

the 1967 vote. The 1964 vote is nearly a party-line vote; this makes the cutting line nearly perpendicular to the conservative-coalition votes that occurred on the minimum wage at this time. Northern Democrats supported food stamps nearly unanimously (141 to 2); more than three-fourths of southern Democrats also voted for passage (75 to 24); but the Republicans were nearly united (13 to 163) in opposition. By 1967, the food-stamp program could be renewed because the northern Democrats (113 to 1) had enough Republican support (45 to 113), even though a majority of southern Democrats (38 to 41) were now against food stamps. The internal party logroll was no longer necessary, perhaps because of the "hooking" discussed previously. In 1967, food-stamp programs were far more widespread in the North than in the South. State and local southern politicians, who were aware that blacks would be beneficiaries of food stamps, had frequently failed to implement a food-stamp program. As a consequence, the effect of food-stamp payments was smaller in the South than in the North, and southern Democrats and northern Republicans shifted votes in opposite directions on food stamps. The cutting-line angle changed to reflect the new coalition supporting the program.

Coalition Politics and the Angle

The need to build majority coalitions means not only that the projection of an issue can change in time but also that it can be different, at the same time, in the two houses of Congress. The Interstate Commerce Act votes illustrate this possibility.

We have previously noted that all economic-issue votes on railroad regulation in the 48th and 49th Houses had similar angles. The votes resembled the splits on bimetallism studied in chapter 5. Some Republicans from the current Middle West joined a core group of Democrats in supporting the various provisions of the Reagan bill, and some northeastern Democrats joined Republican opponents of the bill. The Democratic majority in the House was large enough so that Reagan's bill would pass; both parties could afford position-taking votes where regional economic interests went against the party line.

In contrast, in the Senate, especially when absences were taken into account, Cullom could count on only small Republican margins, particularly on critical votes concerning a strong-versus-weak short-haul pricing constraint. These votes, all in 1886, can be seen in table 6.12. The first four votes were won by the Democrats. On the first vote, the Democrats benefited from Republican defections. Subsequently, on the next four votes—critical ones—party ranks closed and there were never more than four defections from the two parties. The first five votes turned around the question of whether short hauls should receive the relatively strict regulation proposed by Johnson Camden

Table 6.12 Senate Votes on Short-Haul Pricing (1886)

Roll Call	Date	Yea–Nay Vote						PRE1	PRE2[a]	Topic
		All		Democrats		Republicans				
		Y	N	Y	N	Y	N			
155	May 5	29	24	24	2	5	22	0.75	0.75	Camden (D-WV) amendment (committee of whole)
156	May 5	32	27	30	0	2	27	0.89	0.89	Cameron (R-PA) motion (committee of whole)
163	May 12	23	24	1	23	22	1	0.89	0.89	Edmunds (R-VT) amendment
164	May 12	26	24	23	1	3	23	0.75	0.82	Camden (D-WV) amendment
165	May 12	27	24	2	23	25	1	0.85	0.85	Edmunds (R-VT) amendment
166	May 12	20	29	2	21	18	8	0.55	0.50	Deletion of short-haul-pricing section

[a] *PRE1* (*PRE2*) is the proportionate reduction in error for the one-dimensional (and two-dimensional) linear-trend D-NOMINATE model.

(D-WV) or the laxer regulation proposed by George Edmunds (R-VT). The Democrats were able to win votes 156, 163, and 164—in large part because they had more actual voters than Republicans even though the Republicans had a majority in the Senate. The Edmunds amendment finally passed when the Republicans produced a majority on the floor. Following passage, Republican stalwarts who were opposed to any form of short-haul-pricing regulation were allowed a position-taking vote (vote 166).

In contrast to the short-haul votes in the House, which had angles of approximately 45°, all the short-haul votes in the Senate had angles in excess of 90°. But, because of the strong spatial separation between the legislators of the two parties at this time in the Senate, the votes would have been classified just as well by a vertical cutting line. Indeed, table 6.12 shows that adding a second dimension provides no improvement in the classification of the Senate votes, consistent with figure 3.1 which shows that a second dimension does not improve the fit of party-line votes during this period. Thus, the cutting-line angles differ between the House and Senate, not because of differences of constituency interests on railroads but because of the differential exercise of party discipline in the two chambers.

Summary

The analysis in this chapter began by demonstrating that at no point in American history could a model of appropriately measured constituency interests outperform a simple spatial model of voting. This striking result holds even if the two major parties are viewed as representing distinct constituencies in each state. True, the work of Loomis (1995) disclosed that the constituency-interest model might explain a part of what the spatial model does not explain. But the correlations between two senators from the same state and party were sufficiently modest that most of what is unexplained by ideology remains unexplained by the constituency-interest model. The results were confirmed by a direct confrontation of economic and ideological models in a variety of domestic-policy areas.

On the other hand, the chapter provides some evidence that economic interests are important in the framing of the projection of issues into the space. Even when the angle of the mapping is relatively stable, as has been true for the minimum wage in the past two decades, the mapping may change as all legislators tend to shift their ideal points in a common direction. The angle itself may change as different coalitions are built, either around a major issue, such as civil rights, that influences voting on a wide variety of economic issues, or as a result of endogenous changes brought about by the effects of government spending, as seems to have been the case for food stamps. The angle is, however, influenced not only by economic interests but by the imposition of party discipline.

The finding that the spatial model, rather than constituency models, describes the data is an important regularity. Although this and previous chapters have documented the regularity, it is important to understand how projection of issues occurs. Of the next three chapters, two rule out some potential possibilities. Chapter 7 shows that strategic behavior other than party discipline is not a major influence on issue projection. Chapter 9 shows that committees are unlikely to introduce major distortions in legislation. Chapter 8, in contrast, shows that interest groups have extreme preferences. These extreme preferences may be reflected in the extremity of winning outcome projections analyzed in chapter 4.

7

Sophisticated Voting and Agenda Manipulation

In this chapter, we examine the evidence that indicates whether there is strategic or sophisticated voting in Congress. A basic premise of this book is that on each roll call, legislators vote as if they were choosing sincerely between a Yea outcome and a Nay outcome. That is, those who prefer the policies associated with the Yea outcome actually vote Yea, while those who prefer the policies associated with the Nay outcome vote Nay. Preference is determined by the legislator's Euclidean distance to the alternatives and by random disturbances (see chapter 2).

The alternative to sincere voting is strategic or sophisticated voting. We need to consider two types of strategic behavior: vote trades and sophisticated voting on agendas. Vote trades occur when one actor says to another, "Let's make a deal." The deal might be a logroll, of the type explored in chapter 6, where votes on one issue (such as agricultural price supports) are traded for votes on another (food stamps). Another possible deal is represented by a White House phone call with an implicit promise that the legislator will acquire chips that can be cashed in in the future. Still another would be the trading of a vote in response to campaign contributions, endorsements, or threats. A wide range of interest groups, from the National Rifle Association (NRA) to the America-Israel Political Action Committee, are alleged to be particularly successful in manufacturing trades. Nevertheless, the traders are likely to be legislators close to the "sincere" cutting line on an issue because the votes of these people, who are nearly indifferent on the issue, represent the cheapest votes. The most liberal members of Congress are unlikely to succumb to NRA threats to work against their reelection; the most conservative don't need to be pushed. Similarly, as we argued in chapter 2, logrolls are likely to take place between spatially adjacent actors. Vote trades involving actors close to sincere cutting lines largely preserve spatial voting. Such trades will not significantly influence the estimation of legislators' ideal points. Of course, the estimated cutting-line and outcome locations can, depending on the extent of trading, differ substantially from those produced by sincere behavior.

Strategic behavior also arises when there is a series of votes on the agenda for a specific bill. Strategic voters look ahead to future votes. When future votes are considered, a self-interested voter may vote against his or her immediate preferences. The calculation is basically that a vote for one's first choice today may be wasted if it means an empty cupboard tomorrow. Instead, one votes for one's second choice, recognizing that half a loaf is better than no loaf. Sophisticated behavior with respect to agendas, unlike logrolls, does not require implicit or explicit trades among legislators.

Strategic calculations make sense only if one anticipates a sequence of votes. In chapter 2, we indicated that the spatial model would still apply if there was a finite, binary agenda and both the agenda and voter preferences were known in advance. Voters would simply replace the ostensible alternatives with sophisticated equivalents and continue to vote along spatial lines. Such sophisticated voting would not bias our estimation of the legislator coordinates. The outcome coordinates estimated would be those of the sophisticated equivalents rather than the true mappings of the alternatives.

In this chapter, we first look for sophisticated voting using a one-dimensional model. We argue that truly sincere voting should almost always be observed, largely because the framers of bills should be able to anticipate how to draft their legislation to command a majority. Consistent with this hypothesis, our search of the literature on strategic voting found very few bothersome needles in our haystack of the 37,000 roll calls in the first 100 Congresses. In the few instances where the literature points to sophisticated voting, we find that the predictions of the complete-information model—with preferences and agenda known in advance—are disconfirmed, indicating that some voters vote in a sophisticated fashion while others continue to vote sincerely.

The presence of a mixture of voting types suggests that the basic one-dimensional voting model with a single midpoint might be improved on by a two-point model in which extremists on both ends vote one way and moderates vote the other. This so-called both-ends-against-the-middle voting might also arise because extremists are position-taking or expressing alienation. For example, Jesse Helms voted against a moderating Republican amendment to the minimum-wage bill in 1990, thereby expressing his opposition to a minimum wage of any form. In this chapter we show, however, that a two-point model cannot improve vote classifications beyond the amount expected from the random-error process assumed by D-NOMINATE.

When there is a mixture of sincere and sophisticated types, agenda manipulation is possible. There are in fact a few dramatic examples of successful killer amendments. These all involve race and are the final topic of this chapter.

Saving Amendments, Killer Amendments, and One-Dimensional Voting

The basic framework for the analysis of strategic voting can be developed by the simple voting tree shown in figure 7.1. In this tree, B stands for a bill, A stands for an amendment, and Q stands for the status quo. The first vote involves the amendment and the bill, with the winner being put against the status quo. Suppose that the unamended bill, B, would lose to the status quo, whereas the amended bill, A, would defeat it. That is, A **>** Q and Q **>** B, where the use of the bold face **>** in A **>** Q means A is preferred to Q by a majority. If A, B, and Q are one-dimensional—that is, they lie on a line through the basic space—A **>** Q and Q **>** B implies that A **>** B. Therefore, if everyone voted sincerely, the amendment would pass and then defeat the status quo—the amended bill would indeed be the winner.

To fix matters, let Q be a minimum wage of $3.35, let B be a minimum wage of $4.75, and let A be a minimum wage of $4.25. Sincere voting would have only liberals who preferred $4.75 to $4.25 voting against the amendment and only conservatives who preferred $3.35 to $4.25 voting against the amended bill. (To denote the

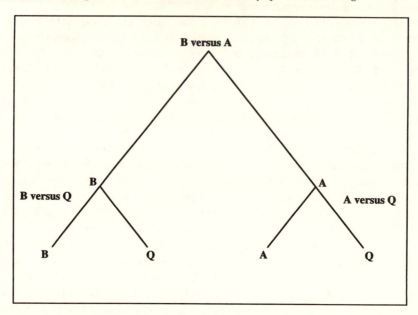

Figure 7.1. A simple agenda tree. An amendment (A) is voted on against the bill (B). The winner of this vote is then voted on against the status quo (Q).

preference of an individual, we use the nonbold face >.) As figure 7.2 illustrates, we can have only four voter types with one dimension. Assume there were 20 voters with preferences of B > A > Q (that is, B was preferred to A and A preferred to Q); 20 with A > B > Q; 20 with A > Q > B; and 40 with Q > A > B. These are consistent with A > Q (by a vote of 60 to 40) and Q > B (by a vote of 60 to 40). If the Q > A > B types, the most conservative members, saw all other types voting sincerely, they could vote for the $4.75 wage on the initial vote. This would win, combining 20 B > A > Q votes and 40 Q > A > B votes. Then, on the final vote, Q would defeat B. Clearly, sophisticated behavior would pay for the conservatives.

Sophisticated behavior by conservatives poses a dilemma for legislators with a preference ordering of B > A > Q. If they vote for the bill on the first vote and they win, then they lose to the status quo. They are faced with a choice of either compromising their principles or "going down in flames." If they do choose to compromise and look ahead, they will realize, as explained in chapter 2, that the initial vote is really a vote between A and Q, the sophisticated equivalent of B. When all voters vote on the basis of the sophisticated equivalents, A wins the initial vote 60 to 40 and the final vote 60 to 40.

Three related observations are pertinent to this situation. First, A plays the role of a saving amendment, introduced when it is clear that the original bill will be defeated. Second, on the initial vote, liberals and conservatives flip-flop when they vote in a sophisticated fashion. Liberals vote for the lower wage, $4.25; conservatives vote for the higher wage, $4.75. Third, on a saving-amendment agenda, the initial vote and the final vote should be identical. In our example, there should be two 60-to-40 votes, with Q > A > B types forming the minority in both cases.

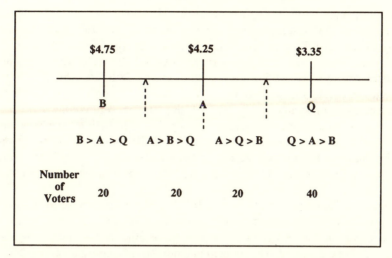

Figure 7.2. The minimum-wage example. The bill (B) with a high wage of $4.75 is at the liberal end of the continuum. The amendment (A) has a more moderate proposal of $4.25. The status quo (Q) is $3.35. In one dimension, there are only four types of strict preferences. The number of voters of each type is shown under the type.

We argue that one should only rarely observe saving amendments, the reason being that the managers of bills should draft a bill that can win. One would expect few proposals with the property Q > B. Much more often, one should see agendas where B > Q.

If B > Q, there might be amendments where A > B. Hence, in one dimension, A > Q. Such amendments would occur in cases where the bill managers report a bill that can defeat the status quo but where opponents can come up with a measure that is more appealing to the median voter in the chamber. In this case, the sophisticated equivalents on the initial vote are simply the ostensible alternatives, A and B. The initial vote will be a sincere vote between A and B; and the second vote, a sincere vote between A and Q. Or, alternatively, one could see proposals where B > A > Q. In this case, the opposition is proposing amendments as a matter of position-taking. But again, the initial choice will be a sincere vote between A and B. A good illustration of this situation is provided by the Erlenborn amendment on the minimum wage, shown in figure 6.4.

An even more hopeless position-taking amendment would have the characteristic B > Q > A. In this case, the initial vote will be a sophisticated vote between B and Q, and the second vote will be a sincere vote between B and Q. Consequently, if voters are sophisticated, the initial and final vote should have identical cutting lines. So if bill managers exercise care in making proposals, one should find only sincere voting, unless some legislators prefer to engage in position-taking and to "go down in flames."

Empirical tests do not reject the proposition that most voting is sincere. In chapter 6, we summarized the Romer and Rosenthal (1985) study of Senate voting on amendments to the bill concerning the minimum size that opened a firm to inspection by the Occupational Safety and Health Administration and the Poole and Rosenthal (1991b) study of amendment voting on minimum wages. Such amendments provide a direct test of sincere voting because the amendments are altering a quantitative parameter of a bill. With sincere voting, as the firm size is made smaller, the pro-OSHA vote should decrease, and as the minimum-wage level is made higher, the pro-minimum-wage vote should decrease. In both cases, the evidence was consistent with sincere voting. Ladha (1991, 1994), using a model derived from NOMINATE, carefully studied all amendment voting in the 95th Congress through the 98th, for which, as with minimum wages or OSHA inspections, an a priori quantitative ordering could be given to the alternatives. Almost all cases he studied supported sincere voting.

Three important exceptions that illustrate sophisticated voting have been identified by Enelow and Koehler (1980) and Enelow (1981). How do these well-known examples—the Common Situs Picketing Bill in 1974, the Panama Canal Treaty ratification in 1978, and Title IV of the 1966 Civil Rights Act—appear in the D-NOMINATE estimation?

Consider the Common Situs Picketing Bill, which was discussed in chapter 2. The situation was exactly as diagrammed in figure 7.1. The key vote was on the Sarasin amendment, which was designed to weaken the original bill—which most members believed would be defeated. The Sarasin amendment passed by a vote of 246 to 177, but then the amended bill lost 205 to 217.[1] Figure 7.3 shows the two votes.

The spatial model accounts very well for the two votes. The *PRE* for the Sarasin amendment was 0.74, and for the final-passage vote, the *PRE* was 0.75. Note that the two cutting lines are almost parallel, and that the representatives that represent voting errors tend to be clustered near the cutting lines. The Sarasin amendment was drafted to gain support among southern Democrats and Republicans. This objective was achieved—the cutting line passed through the southern Democrats and liberal Republicans. The party splits on the amendment vote were northern Democrats, 184 to 10; southern Democrats, 33 to 52; and Republicans, 29 to 115. In contrast, the splits on the final-passage vote were northern Democrats, 171 to 23; southern Democrats, 20 to 65; and Republicans, 14 to 129.

The voting patterns shown in figure 7.3 are consistent with sophisticated voting (on each vote) by both the extremes—the liberals and conservatives; and with sincere voting by the moderates—the group between the two cutting lines. For the moderates to be voting sincerely, their preferences would have to be the same as those of their more conservative brethren to the right of the Sarasin cutting line—namely, a preference ordering of Q > A > B. On the Sarasin amendment vote, the liberals and conservatives vote for the sophisticated equivalents (A versus Q), whereas the moderates vote sincerely on A versus B. On the final passage, the moderates now vote for Q. This behavior is consistent with the fact that the cutting lines are not identical. Indeed, since the status quo won the final vote, the Sarasin amendment was not a saving amendment, with A > Q.

Enelow and Koehler (1980, p. 406) note that the defeat of the amended bill "surprised both supporters and opponents of the bill alike." Suppose, however, as Enelow and Koehler claim (p. 407), that the amendment did not seriously weaken the bill—that is, A was almost as liberal as B. It is then possible that voters recognized that Q > A. In this case, because Q always wins in the final vote regardless of whether it faces A or B, voters can vote either way on the initial vote. Note, however, regardless of whether Q > A or A > Q, if all parties are certain that Q > B, liberals cannot be worse off by voting for A on the initial vote, and conservatives cannot be worse off by voting for B. Therefore, they can be expected to be sophisticated voters.

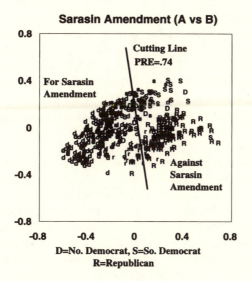

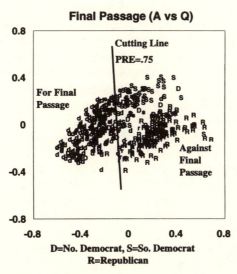

Figure 7.3. House voting on the Sarasin amendment and on passage of the Common Situs Picketing Bill. Those voting with a majority of the Democrats are shown in lowercase letters. (VOTEVIEW numbers 82 and 83; March 23, 1977.)

Among those representatives with preferences Q > A > B, those with relatively moderate D-NOMINATE scores appear, as we argued earlier, not to have followed their more conservative brethren and instead to have voted sincerely. The end result is nonetheless a vote along spatial lines, although the cutting line on the initial vote has neither the interpretation of being generated by sincere voting nor the interpretation of being generated by sophisticated equivalents. Instead, the cutting line reflects both types of behavior. Ironically, the final outcome would have been exactly the same if all voters had voted sincerely.

An amendment whose purpose is exactly opposite to that of a saving amendment is known as a killer amendment. A killer amendment is designed to sink a bill (so that $Q > A$) that would defeat the status quo were it not amended (so that $B > Q$). Since $B > Q$ and $Q > A$, in one dimension, $B > A$. Even with sincere voting, the killer amendment would fail. Sophisticated voters will treat the initial A-versus-B vote as a Q-versus-B vote, implying that B would defeat A on the first vote. Hence, in one-dimensional voting killer amendments must always fail!

Enelow and Koehler (1980) discuss several amendments offered by conservatives as killer amendments to the Panama Canal Treaties of 1978.[2] Although the intent of the conservatives was directly opposite to that of the saving Sarasin amendment favored by liberals, the voting patterns were similar. The amendments were of the "motherhood and apple pie" variety. For example, one concerned a cemetery in the Canal Zone where U.S. citizens were buried. The strategy of the conservatives was very simple: propose something that it is embarrassing to vote against; then the amended bill also passes. But if any of the "motherhood and apple pie" amendments passed, the amended treaty would require a renegotiation with Panama. A renegotiation would be preferred by the conservatives because, at a minimum, it would force a delay in the implementation of the main treaty provisions.

Placing "motherhood and apple pie" in our basic ideological space is somewhat problematical because, when voted on sincerely, such proposals might attract unanimous support. Because voters voted strategically, however, the actual voting behavior on the Panama Canal Treaty amendments fits into a one-dimensional framework.

Figure 7.4 shows one of these amendments along with the final-passage vote on the Panama Canal Neutrality Treaty. The amendment concerned the right of the United States to maintain military bases in the Canal Zone if the United States were at war. It was offered by Senator James Allen (D-AL), and then Senator Frank Church (D-ID) made a motion to table it. The motion to table passed by a vote of 57 to 38 on March 1, 1978, and the neutrality treaty was later passed by a vote of 68 to 32 on March 16, 1978.[3]

Both votes fit the spatial model well. The *PRE* for the Church motion was 0.68, and the *PRE* on the final passage was 0.59. The two cutting lines are close to being parallel, indicating unidimensional voting on the issue; and the overall pattern is very similar to that shown in figure 7.3 for the Common Situs Picketing Bill, but the interpretation of it is quite different.

Any vote for the Allen killer amendment can be interpreted as a sincere vote, since the amendment was of the "motherhood and apple pie" variety. But such a vote was also in accord with the strategic interests of conservatives who voted for the amendment (that is, against the Church motion to table) but against the treaty. Liberals who voted against the amendment but for the treaty were, in voting against "motherhood and apple pie," acting strategically, accepting an embarrassing vote in return for preserving the treaty.

The interesting case concerns the moderates in between the two cutting lines who voted both for the amendment and for the treaty. Although one could see them as being sincere voters, they may well also have been strategic ones. They wanted the treaty and may have been willing if necessary, "to take the fall" on the amendment, but they could presume that liberals wanted the treaty even more than they did. Moreover, there were enough liberals to defeat the amendment, leaving the moderates free to take the patriotic position on the amendment.

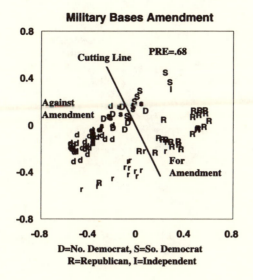

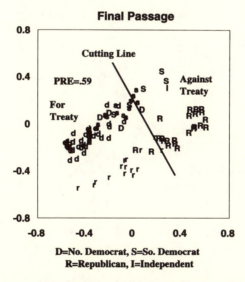

Figure 7.4. Senate voting on the Church motion to table military-bases amendment and on passage of the Panama Canal Neutrality Treaty. Those voting with a majority of the Democrats are shown in lowercase letters. (VOTEVIEW numbers 673 and 702; March 1 and March 16, 1978.)

Enelow (1981) shows another interesting case where, unlike the Common Situs Picketing Bill, there was a successful saving amendment. The case is Title IV, the open-housing provision of the 1966 Civil Rights Bill. Title IV was aimed at prohibiting discrimination in the sale, rental, or financing of housing. Representative Charles Mathias (R-MD)[4]—who supported Title IV—offered a saving amendment to weaken Title IV enough for it to survive an attempt to delete it from the bill. Figure 7.5 shows

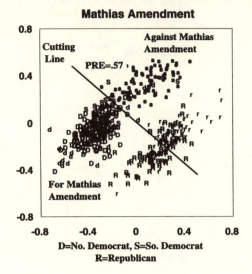

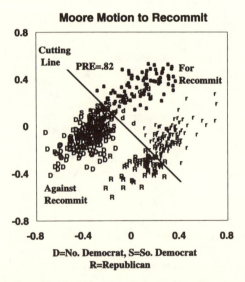

Figure 7.5. House voting on the Mathias amendment to Title IV, the open-housing provision of 1966 Civil Rights Bill, the Moore motion to recommit, and passage. (VOTEVIEW numbers 289, 292, and 293, respectively; August 9, 1966.) Those voting with a majority of the Democrats are shown in uppercase letters.

the three critical votes in the sequence: the Mathias amendment, which passed by a vote of 237 to 176; the motion by Representative Arch Moore (R-WV) to recommit the bill with instructions to delete Title IV, which failed on a vote of 190 to 222; and the final-passage vote of 259 to 157.[5] The expectation of Mathias was that the original bill, B, would lose to the motion to recommit, R, but that the amended bill, A, would defeat both R and the status quo, Q.

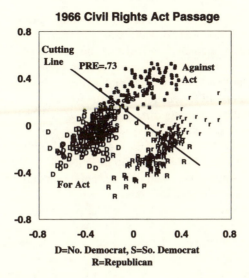

1966 Civil Rights Act Passage

D=No. Democrat, S=So. Democrat
R=Republican

Figure 7.5. (*continued*)

Two things stand out in figure 7.5. The three cutting lines are roughly parallel, again suggesting a single active dimension, but the fit of the spatial model is poor for the Mathias amendment. On the Moore motion and on the final-passage vote, the spatial model performs very well in that the errors are quite close to the cutting line. Not so for the Mathias amendment—the *PRE*s were 0.57, 0.82, and 0.73, respectively.[6]

The expected-utility theory of sophisticated voting developed by Enelow (1981) predicts that the only groups that may split their votes on a saving amendment are the extreme liberals and/or conservatives. Even if it means an eventual defeat for the bill, some of the extremist legislators may not be able to bring themselves to compromise their principles. In short, the two-outcome spatial model we fit to the roll calls may not work well for this type of roll call.

The Mathias amendment is an example. Note that a number of liberal Democrats quite distant from the cutting line voted against the amendment (the lowercase "d"s in the lower left quadrant). In contrast to the Sarasin and Allen amendments, where strategic voting led to a spatial, cutting-line pattern of voting, voting of the Mathias-amendment-vote type would, if pervasive, run counter to the basic premise of this book. Consequently, it is important to check whether "both ends against the middle" voting is prevalent.

Both-Ends-against-the-Middle Voting

The both-ends-against-the-middle type of voting on the Mathias amendment does not appear to occur very often. Among the examples of sophisticated voting that we found in the literature—more of which we discuss below—it is in fact the only one that shows this pattern. In addition, in chapter 3, we showed that the voting error from D-NOMINATE closely matches the theoretical-error distribution—especially on roll calls with at least 20 percent on the minority side.

To get a better measure of how frequently two-ends-against-the-middle voting oc-curs, we performed a simple experiment using a version of the optimal-classification method we described in chapter 2. Recall that the first step is to begin with an arbi-trary ordering of the legislators. The optimal cutting point is found by making a sim-ple search of the midpoints between adjacent legislators. These roll call midpoints are then fixed, the optimal point for each legislator is found, and so on.

Here, we perform the same experiment, only now each roll call is represented by *two* cutting points. We now search *all pairs* of cutting points to find the optimal clas-sifying pair. This allows for the two-ends-against-the-middle Y-N-Y (Yea-Nay-Yea) and N-Y-N patterns. It also allows for the simple Y-N and N-Y patterns, where the two cutting points are the same. These roll call midpoint pairs are then fixed, the optimal point for each legislator is found, and so on.

Because the one-point model is a subset of the two-point model, the latter is guar-anteed to do better. Accordingly, we show the classification gain provided by the so-phisticated two-point model over the one-point model for the House of Representa-tives in figure 7.6. Given our results in chapter 3, it is not surprising that the two-point model does not have much punch—for 65 Houses, it added 1 percent or less to the classifications; and for 86 Houses, it added 1.5 percent or less.

To see whether an increase of 1 percent is a meaningful result, we performed a Monte Carlo analysis by applying the two-point classification procedure to artificial data created from legislator and roll call coordinates from D-NOMINATE. We intro-duced errors into the individual utility functions at roughly the level encountered in the actual roll call data. The two-point model always showed an increase of about 1

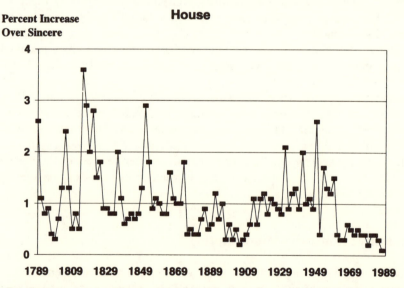

Figure 7.6. Increase in classification when both-ends-against-the-middle voting is allowed (1789–1988). Optimal classifications with two cutting points on each roll call are compared to standard optimal classification with one cutting point. Allowing for both-ends-against-the-mid-dle voting does very little to improve classification, particularly after the late 1950s.

percent over the one-point model. In short, two-ends-against-the-middle voting is undeniably occurring, but it clearly has a low-level effect.

Killer Amendments in Two Dimensions

Until this point, we have considered strategic voting in the context of unidimensional issues. In the unidimensional case, the distinction between sincere and sophisticated voting has limited policy relevance. With a truly saving amendment, a majority should prefer the amendment to the bill, and a majority should prefer the amended bill to the status quo; so the amended bill should win even with sincere voting. If there were a truly unidimensional killer amendment (in contrast to the "motherhood and apple pie" amendment), the amendment should never pass in one dimension. If the original bill is liberal in relation to the status quo, for example, the killer amendment needs to be even more liberal. In this case, a sincere majority would prefer the original bill.

Possibilities are quite different in two dimensions. Reconsider figure 2.6. There are now, in contrast to the four voting types in one dimension, six possible types of strict preferences. If there were 32 A > B > Q types, 2 A > Q > B types, 2 B > A > Q, 31 B > Q > A, 31 Q > A > B, and 2 Q > B > A, we would have Q > A by a 64-to-36 vote; B > Q by 65 to 35; and A > B by 65 to 35. That is, we would have a voting cycle in which there would be no one alternative that defeated all others under majority voting. In particular, it is possible to have B > Q and A > B but Q > A. Sincere voting would lead to the amendment's killing the bill.

In contrast, voting on sophisticated equivalents would lead to the recognition that the initial vote is truly one between B and Q; so B would win. Therefore, if voters vote strategically, killer amendments won't work in either one or two dimensions. If voters are sincere, the amendments might well succeed, but only in two or more dimensions. Not surprisingly, therefore, the interesting cases of killer amendments in the literature all involve two dimensions. Given that (in chapter 3) we identified race as the second dimension in those periods of American history where a second dimension was most important, it is also not surprising that the examples all involve race.

A killer amendment discussed by both Enelow (1981) and Riker (1982) was the Powell amendment. The amendment was offered by Adam Clayton Powell, Jr. (D-NY) to the 1956 School Aid Bill. The amendment "barred federal funds from going to states that had failed to comply with the decisions of the Supreme Court" (Enelow, 1981, p. 1080) and therefore would have denied aid to segregated schools. The amendment passed by a vote of 225 to 192 (northern Democrats voted 77 to 42; southern Democrats, 0 to 104; and Republicans, 148 to 46) on July 5, 1956, and the amended bill then failed by a vote of 194 to 224 (ND 116-3; SD 3-102; R 75-119) on that same day.[7] Note that, as an African-American, Powell himself may have been more interested in position-taking than in strategic legislative activity. Presumably, Powell wanted both school aid and desegregation. His actions suggest that he preferred position-taking on desegregation to a half-loaf consisting of school aid.

The Powell amendment transformed the debate from one over the level of school aid to one over both school aid and school desegregation. The status quo, Q—no school aid and segregated schools in the South (in spite of the 1954 *Brown* v. *Board of*

Education ruling)—would appear to be near the conservative pole on both dimensions. The unamended bill, B, had a combination of school aid and (implicitly) the status quo, segregation. That is, the bill was relatively liberal on one dimension and conservative on the other. The amended bill, A, was liberal on both dimensions. So if the Powell amendment were attached to the School Aid Bill, then southern Democrats would clearly vote for segregation, the status quo, while many Republicans would vote for the status quo of no school aid. According to our issue analyses in chapters 4 and 5, segregation, the status quo, would be near the top of the second dimension with the southern Democrats, and the status quo of no school aid would be on the right side of the first dimension with the conservative Republicans. The status quo was thus a conservative position on both dimensions.

Figure 7.7 shows the two votes. The *PRE*s were 0.60 and 0.71, respectively. The southern Democrats voted almost unanimously against both motions and were clearly sincere voters on both. The southern Democrats were probably a mix of the orderings of B > Q > A and Q > B > A because, no doubt, some southern representatives would have liked the school aid if there were no strings attached (Riker, 1982, p. 154). The Powell amendment split the northern Democrats, with the liberals voting for the amendment and the moderates voting, along with the southern Democrats, against the amendment. The ordering of northern Democratic liberals was clearly A > B > Q, and that of the northern Democratic moderates was probably B > A > Q, so both groups were voting sincerely on both motions. In addition, the Democratic party fits the spatial model very well.

Not so for the Republicans—the cutting line for the Powell amendment produces the prediction that almost all the Republicans will vote for the amendment. This occurs because 96 Republicans voted for the Powell amendment but against final passage—indeed, they were Y-N voters. These Y-N voters were clearly voting in a sophisticated fashion if their preference ordering was Q > B > A, and sincerely if their ordering was Q > A > B (Riker, 1982, p. 155). Most of these Y-N voters were moderates and conservatives. Of the 96 Y-N voters, 79 were above the cutting line on the final-passage vote and 17 were below the cutting line. These 17 below the cutting line represent errors, according to the spatial model, but they are quite close to the cutting line, and they are adjacent to the Y-Y voters, all of whom were liberals. These 17 Y-N voters could have had the ordering Q > A > B because the liberal Republican Y-Y voters they were next to were undoubtedly sincere voters with the ordering A > B > Q or A > Q > B. This would be consistent with the liberal Republicans, continuing in the nineteenth-century civil-rights tradition of their party. If some were more fiscally conservative than the others, then it is plausible that they would have had the ordering A > Q > B. Nevertheless, the bulk of the 79 Y-N Republicans above the cutting line were clearly sophisticated voters.

In sum, the preference orderings, from top to bottom, for the Republicans were in all likelihood Q > B > A, Q > A > B, A > Q > B, and A > B > Q; and for the Democrats, Q > B > A, B > Q > A, B > A > Q, and A > B > Q. Overall, everyone voted sincerely except the conservative Republicans, who were split—most voted sophisticatedly, while a minority voted sincerely. Note that these preference orderings *require* the presence of two dimensions; no one-dimensional ordering can produce them.

Riker (1982) cites the Powell amendment as an example of a voting cycle produced by sophisticated voting. The bill was killed because northern Democrats voted sin-

Powell Amendment

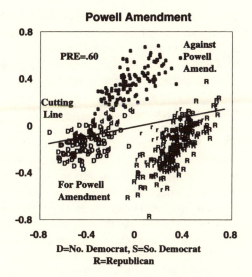

D=No. Democrat, S=So. Democrat
R=Republican

1956 School Aid Passage

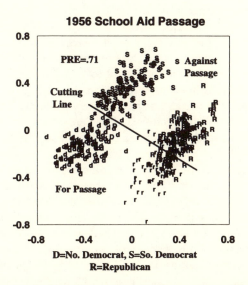

D=No. Democrat, S=So. Democrat
R=Republican

Figure 7.7. House votes on the Powell amendment and on passage of the 1956 school aid bill. (VOTEVIEW numbers 122 and 124; July 5, 1956.) Those voting with a majority of the Republicans are shown in uppercase letters. The Powell amendment operated as a killer amendment since 96 Republicans voted for the desegregation provisions of the amendment but voted against passage.

cerely and Republicans voted sophisticatedly. Even though the status quo, Q, prevailed, as Riker shows, it was probably the case that B > Q. For figure 7.7, without the Powell amendment, the cutting line on passage probably would have been higher on the second dimension. Only 15 of the more moderate southern Democrats near the cutting line would have been needed to pass the School Aid Bill.

Riker (1982) cites two other examples of cycles—the Wilmot Proviso, and the DePew amendment to the constitutional amendment for the popular election of senators. In 1846, President Polk, a Democrat, wanted a quick victory in the war with Mexico. Intending to bribe the Mexican military commanders, he asked Congress to appropriate $2 million for that purpose. Polk should have gotten the $2 million without much difficulty, because the Democrats had firm control of the 29th Congress. In the House, the division was 142 Democrats, 79 Whigs, 6 American party members, and 1 vacancy. In the Senate, the division was 34 Democrats, 22 Whigs, and 2 vacancies. Unfortunately for Polk, Representative David Wilmot (D-PA) offered an amendment—which became known as the Wilmot Proviso—that prohibited slavery in any territories taken from Mexico. This amendment was passed by the House on a series of votes on August 8, 1846. The amended bill later died in the Senate.

As we discussed in detail in chapter 5, slavery, by this time, had emerged as a second dimension that divided both the Whigs and the Democrats. Consequently, just as was the case for the Powell amendment 110 years later, the status quo had two aspects. One involved providing no appropriation for the bribe; and the other meant, at a minimum, leaving the slavery question in the territories taken from Mexico as an open issue to be decided at a later date. Given the unified control of the government by the Democrats, the bill to provide funds for bribery would undoubtedly have passed in the absence of the Wilmot Proviso (Riker, 1982, p. 225).

The critical vote analyzed by Riker was on a procedural motion that would have killed the Proviso, so a Nay vote is for the Proviso. In the vote, shown in figure 7.8, the procedural motion failed by a vote of 79 to 93 (northern Democrats, 13 to 51; southern Democrats, 47 to 0; northern Whigs, 5 to 35; southern Whigs, 14 to 2; American party 0 to 5).[8] The vote was almost purely a sectional one. It was very representative of literally hundreds of other roll calls that were taken, through this period, on a variety of slavery-related issues. (Compare figures 7.8 and 5.6.) The *PRE* on this roll call was 0.85.

Because the House was rushing toward an adjournment, and a filibuster in the Senate prevented a final vote, the only pairing observed was A versus B and A > B by 93 to 79. As we noted above, clearly B > Q because of unified control by the Democrats. Riker (1982, p. 227) argues that the southern Democrats and the southern Whigs would certainly have voted for Q over A, and because most of the northern Whigs opposed the war, they would also have probably voted for Q. Hence, Q probably would have gotten the 47 southern Democrats and 14 southern Whigs who voted against the Wilmot Proviso, along with the 35 northern Whigs who voted for the Proviso. This yields a total of 96 votes, so that Q > A.

In effect, a unified Whig party, plus the southern Democrats, would have defeated the bill as amended by the Wilmot Proviso. This would be consistent with a cutting line in figure 7.8 that passed through the Democrats, as it does for the Wilmot Proviso vote, but at a sharper downward angle so as to include all or most of the northern Whigs. Sincere position-taking on slavery by northern Democrats would have led to the defeat of Polk's proposal.

The other example of a voting cycle discussed by Riker involves the DePew amendment to the constitutional amendment to permit the direct election of senators (which became the 17th Amendment). The DePew amendment is yet another example of the power of race in American politics—once again, the introduction of race, via an

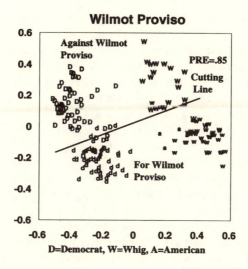

Wilmot Proviso

D=Democrat, W=Whig, A=American

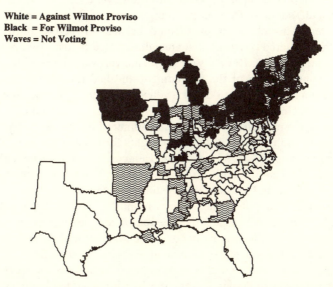

White = Against Wilmot Proviso
Black = For Wilmot Proviso
Waves = Not Voting

Figure 7.8. House voting on the Wilmot Proviso. (VOTEVIEW number 456; August 8, 1846.) Those voting with a majority of northerners are shown in lowercase letters. The sectional nature of the vote is shown on the map. Only two slave-state representatives from the border state of Kentucky supported the proviso.

amendment to a bill, created a voting situation with a two-dimensional status quo. In this situation, it had the interesting effect of derailing a bill that, unamended, had more than a two-thirds backing in the Senate. DePew's clever maneuver had the effect of creating a voting cycle.

Riker (1982, p. 195) estimates that at least 64 of 86 senators (or 88, after Oklahoma was admitted to the Union in November 1907) supported the constitutional amendment. Even with the two-thirds requirement for constitutional amendments, clearly

B > Q. The DePew amendment was offered by Senator Chauncey DePew (R-NY) as a device to derail the amendment. The southerners interpreted the DePew amendment as giving the federal government the authority "to send the army into the South to register blacks and enforce their voting rights" (Riker, 1982, p. 194). During the lame-duck session of the 61st Congress in early 1911, the constitutional amendment reached the floor of the Senate. Opponents offered the Sutherland amendment, the negative equivalent of the DePew amendment, to strike language from the constitutional amendment that guaranteed white supremacy in the South.[9] Hence, a vote for the Sutherland amendment was equivalent to voting for the DePew amendment. The Sutherland amendment passed by a vote of 50 to 37 on February 24, 1911 (NDs, 0 to 7; SDs, 1 to 22; Rs, 49 to 8), and the constitutional amendment, as changed by the Sutherland amendment, failed by a vote of 54 to 33 on February 28, 1911, because a two-thirds vote was required (NDs, 7 to 0; SDs, 14 to 9; Rs, 33 to 24).[10]

Figure 7.9 shows the DePew-Sutherland amendment, along with the final-passage vote. The *PRE*s were 0.92 and 0.41, respectively. The DePew-Sutherland amendment was opposed by all the Democrats and a few progressive Republicans and supported by most of the Republican party. The constitutional amendment was then opposed by many (but not all) southern Democrats and northeastern Republicans.

The recorded votes tell us that A > B and, because of the two-thirds requirement, Q > A. But the unaltered constitutional amendment clearly had a two-thirds support in the Senate, so that B > Q. DePew's clever maneuver was first used in 1902 during a committee's consideration of the amendment and had the effect of preventing the amendment from reaching the floor for a vote (Riker, 1982, p. 193). Since it was clear that from then on DePew (or someone else) would offer his amendment, it had the effect of delaying the passage of the 17th Amendment for nine years because Republicans were united in their support of voting rights for blacks. It was finally passed by the 62nd Senate on June 12, 1911, after the Democrats had made enough gains in the 1910 elections to defeat the Sutherland amendment. The amendment was sent to the states in 1912 and ratified by 36 of the 48 states on May 31, 1913.

The three successful killer amendments found by Riker are the only ones mentioned in the literature. We suspect that the reason they are not more common is that potentially successful killer amendments are derailed either by strategic voting or by the introduction of subsequent saving amendments by bill managers.

An example of a saving amendment introduced by a bill manager occurred in the voting on the Reagan Interstate Commerce Bill in the 48th Congress. The Reagan bill eventually passed in the House but the Senate did not act.[11] During the House debate on interstate commerce, James O'Hara, an African-American Republican member from North Carolina, moved to eliminate racial segregation in passenger rail service. As with the Powell amendment in the twentieth century (discussed earlier), the O'Hara amendment passed with the support of northern Democrats and Republicans. The O'Hara amendment was modified, however, by a saving amendment that banned discrimination but held that "separate but equal" seating was nondiscriminatory. The language allowed just enough northern Democrats to switch from position-taking to strategic voting, so that the amendment to the amendment passed by a bare 8-vote majority. As a consequence, the Interstate Commerce Bill was not killed, as it would have been if it had been turned into a race issue for southern representatives.

Depew-Sutherland Amendment

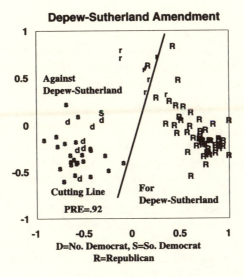

Constitutional Amendment

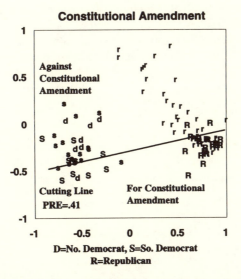

Figure 7.9. Senate voting on the Depew-Sutherland amendment and on passage of the constitutional amendment for popular election of senators. (VOTEVIEW numbers 244 and 248, respectively; February 24 and February 28, 1911.) Those voting with a majority of the Republicans are shown in uppercase letters. Republicans voted for the amendment, which concerned blacks' voting rights in the South, and against passage. Southern Democrats voted overwhelmingly against passage.

This example shows that the supporters of killer amendments try to take advantage of the unwillingness of some of a bill's supporters to compromise their principles and vote strategically. At the same time, supporters can be clever in finding alternative language that circumvents the strategy of their opponents. In any event, there are relatively few observations of voting cycles in Congress.

Summary

Our analysis suggests that sophisticated voting is not pervasive in Congress. We found some saving and killer amendments that could be analyzed as essentially one-dimensional. Our examination of these amendments disclosed only one example, the Mathias amendment, where voting strayed from a one-dimensional spatial pattern and became a case of both ends against the middle. Such voting is rare, however, as disclosed by our analysis of the two-point model.

Voting is sophisticated in another fashion, as illustrated by William Riker's examples: the Wilmot Proviso, the DePew amendment, and the Powell amendment. The examples are separated by approximately 60 years, but each involves the same maneuver: the introduction of an amendment that taps into the second great organizing dimension of American politics—race; and the destabilization of the winning coalition along the primary dimension of voting. The Wilmot Proviso split the Democratic party, which was a winning coalition that controlled the entire government in 1846. The DePew amendment caused a split between the Democratic party and progressive Republicans, thereby reducing the winning coalition to below a two-thirds size. Finally, the Powell amendment split the Democratic party internally in a rerun of 1846 and defeated the School Aid Bill, which had majority support. These three examples suggest that strategic manipulation of the agenda can have important effects when some legislators feel bound to engage in position-taking, sincere voting. But, as the interstate commerce example showed, additional manipulation can short-circuit manipulative strategies. On balance, strategic behavior appears to be a destabilizing force only very rarely. We thus continue to find that the spatial model is a reasonable summary of roll call voting behavior.

8
Roll Call Voting and Interest-Group Ratings

We will now extend our analysis of legislative behavior to incorporate the role of interest groups. We have previously established that there is a polarized distribution of legislator preferences. This polarization has been increasing since the 1960s. Polarization, when coupled with party discipline and majority rule, results in relatively extreme swings in policy outcomes. Policy outcomes are rarely close to the ideal point of the median legislator in one dimension or close to the center of the space in two dimensions. And in chapter 6, we presented very strong evidence indicating that legislators could not be viewed as representing middle-of-the-road interests in their constituencies. It is interest groups that may well direct the polarization process.

The potentially polarizing role of interest groups is evident in the research of Kirkpatrick (1976) and of McCloskey et al. (1960). They found that convention delegates and political activists had extreme opinions relative to those of the mass public. This finding is quite consistent with the theory of rational abstention. According to this theory, active political participation, in the form of time and money spent in promoting group causes, is far more costly than simply voting. Theoretically, of course, moderates should be the ones who do not participate, since they have less to lose from a disliked extreme outcome than do extremists.[1] If activism, of which interest groups are one form, implies extremism, and if politicians are responsive to activists, polarization will result. Since the beginning of the Clinton administration, there has been substantial anecdotal evidence to support this view. The president, by responding to elements of his support coalition, drew substantial flak over his policies concerning gays in the military, health care, and Haiti. Senator Bob Dole, in his quest for the Republican nomination in 1996, initially ran toward the Right, not the center. The new Republican majorities in Congress have kowtowed to the National Rifle Association.

Attempts by politicians to take a moderate position often come under attack from interest groups at both ends of the spectrum on an issue. Consider the problems of California governor Pete Wilson, a former senator, in dealing with the abortion issue:

> Press aide Dan Schnur said . . . Wilson had long opposed federal funding for abortion, . . . [but]Wilson does support state tax spending on abortion because a 1981 California Supreme Court ruling guaranteed poor women access to abortion through Medi-Cal. . . . Wilson's comments sparked a negative reaction from both sides of the abortion debate. Proponents of abortion rights and their foes characterized the governor's remarks as waffling. . . . Susan Culman, national chairwoman of the Republican Coalition for Choice,

said she was surprised to learn that "the only reason [Wilson] has supported state funding was because it's the law." . . . But the most vociferous criticisms came from anti-abortion advocates. . . . "Our concern would be that he's posturing himself for the presidential race," said Kenda Bartlett of Concerned Women for America. If those are truly his deeply felt feelings, . . . he would be actively pursuing some way to change [state law].[2]

A politician who, like Wilson, is blasted by both of the extreme sides on an issue, may choose to take a polarized position, thus avoiding one source of criticism.

In this chapter, we present systematic evidence indicating that a large set of visible interest groups have extreme policy positions. We accomplish this by integrating their ratings with the roll call data.

Many interest groups rate members of Congress on a 0-to-100 scale. The raters include groups with a broad ideological orientation, such as the Americans for Democratic Action (ADA), groups with a special public-interest mission, such as the League of Conservation Voters; labor unions, such as the United Auto Workers; business and industry associations, such as the Chamber of Commerce of the United States; and farm organizations, such as the National Farmers Union. In this chapter, we integrate the evaluations of the interest groups into the spatial model of legislative choice that underlies this book. In a nutshell, interest groups are treated as roll call voters. The combined analysis of the "votes" of interest groups, and of the choices of representatives and senators, leads to an important substantive conclusion: Interest groups, particularly labor unions and ideological groups of the Left and Right, are more extreme than members of Congress. If interest groups succeed in pulling legislators away from middle-of-the-road or moderate positions, they may be an important factor in the increasing polarization of American politics that we cited in chapter 4.

This chapter also provides three important methodological results. First, we validate the earlier D-NOMINATE estimates of spatial positions. Second, we are able to make direct comparisons of the House and Senate results because the interest groups effectively "vote" in both houses. In contrast, if just roll call voting data are employed, one must perform separate scalings of the House and Senate, with the consequence that the estimated locations of representatives and senators are not comparable. With the interest-group data, we obtain a common scaling of the House and Senate. Third, we use the results to discuss whether interest-group ratings, which are widely used in professional journals in economics and political science, fulfill their intended purpose as reasonable measures of liberalism/conservatism or ideology.

Interest-Group Ratings

Interest groups, as part of their efforts to influence the political process, regularly publish ratings of members of Congress.[3] To construct its ratings, an interest group selects a set of roll calls. These typically number between 10 to 40 roll calls in each House. If a member of Congress supports the interest group's position on all the selected roll calls, the member receives a score of 100. Members who always oppose receive a score of 0. More generally, a legislator's rating equals the percentage of the selected roll calls in which the legislator took the interest group's position.[4]

In this chapter, we study the 96th Congress (1979–80).[5] In table 8.1, we list 28 interest groups that issued ratings during the 96th Congress, along with the number of roll calls each group used in its ratings. (Also included in the table is CARTER, which refers to the *Congressional Quarterly* rating of support for President Carter's legislative program.)

Does the information provided by the interest groups accord with the story laid out in the previous chapters? The answer is a quite positive one; in particular, the main liberal/conservative dimension found by D-NOMINATE is closely matched by the interest-group ratings. The ratings correlate very highly with our first dimension.

Table 8.2 shows the Pearson correlations between the ratings of the groups and both dimensions of D-NOMINATE.[6] Correlations are provided for all members, for Democrats only, and for Republicans only. The correlations for all members between the first dimension and the ratings most commonly used by researchers—such as the ADA, COPE, the ACA, and the ACU—are all above 0.9. No first-dimension correla-

Table 8.1 Interest Groups That Evaluated Congressional Votes in 1979–1980

Group	Abbreviation	Number of Votes Selected[a] Senate	House
American Civil Liberties Union	ACLU	15	15
American Conservative Union	ACU	44	47
Americans for Constitutional Action	ACA	53	50
Americans for Democratic Action	ADA	38	38
American Farm Bureau Federation	AFBF	—[b]	9
American Federation of State, County and Municipal Employees	AFSCME	13	14
American Federation of Teachers	AFT	11	15
American Security Council	ASC	10	10
Bread for the World	BFW	10	10
Building and Construction Trades Department (AFL-CIO)	BCTD	12	13
Congressional Quarterly presidential support votes	CARTER	276	235
Chamber of Commerce of the United States	CCUS	58	52
Child Welfare League of America	CWLA	16	16
Christian Voice	CV	14	14
Coalition for a New Foreign and Military Policy	CFNFMP	14	17
Committee on Political Education (AFL-CIO)	COPE	38	39
Congress Watch	CW	65	70
Consumer Federation of America	CFA	21	24
Friends' Committee on National Legislation	FCNL	21	28
League of Conservation Voters	LCV	30	50
League of Women Voters	LWV	20	20
National Alliance of Senior Citizens	NASC	20	20
National Council of Senior Citizens	NCSC	20	20
National Farmers Organization	NFO	16	19
National Farmers Union	NFU	23	18
National Federation of Independent Business	NFIB	18	15
National Women's Political Caucus	NWPC	—[b]	13
United Auto Workers	UAW	35	31
United Mine Workers	UMW	11	10

[a] All votes used by the interest group in either 1979 or 1980.

[b] This group did not evaluate the 96th Senate.

Table 8.2 Correlations of Interest-Group Ratings with D-NOMINATE Dimensions

	Senate						House					
	All		Democrats		Republicans		All		Democrats		Republicans	
Group	1[a]	2[b]	1	2	1	2	1	2	1	2	1	2
ACLU	−.74	−.58	−.88	−.84	−.81	−.82	−.80	−.49	−.83	−.74	−.68	−.68
ACU	.95	.22	.88	.79	.94	.87	.96	.17	.91	.63	.87	.58
ACA	.96	.14	.84	.76	.95	.82	.96	.09	.91	.56	.87	.53
ADA	−.93	−.30	−.91	−.84	−.90	−.87	−.93	−.39	−.93	−.81	−.76	−.65
AFBF[c]							.77	.24	.64	.56	.60	.43
AFSCME	−.70	−.33	−.59	−.55	−.70	−.73	−.81	−.32	−.79	−.62	−.70	−.32
AFT	−.75	−.26	−.63	−.56	−.74	−.69	−.87	−.35	−.85	−.71	−.64	−.56
ASC	.89	.21	.84	.83	.77	.76	.88	.35	.88	.76	.60	.57
BFW	−.85	−.45	−.83	−.82	−.87	−.91	−.91	−.22	−.86	−.61	−.75	−.60
BCTD	−.74	.19	−.14	−.01	−.65	−.43	−.75	−.02	−.56	−.33	−.51	−.14
CCUS	.94	.08	.84	.73	.88	.76	.84	.33	.82	.74	.40	.44
CWLA	−.85	−.42	−.81	−.80	−.89	−.84	−.94	−.19	−.90	−.62	−.78	−.49
CV	.91	.30	.84	.78	.92	.85	.89	.23	.83	.60	.73	.60
CFNFMP	−.79	−.45	−.84	−.82	−.78	−.77	−.84	−.50	−.87	−.83	−.62	−.71
COPE	−.94	−.22	−.86	−.83	−.92	−.82	−.92	−.18	−.87	−.66	−.74	−.41
CW	−.82	−.41	−.81	−.81	−.80	−.80	−.88	−.43	−.87	−.87	−.62	−.65
CFA	−.88	−.37	−.91	−.86	−.83	−.81	−.89	−.39	−.87	−.83	−.63	−.56
FCNL	−.88	−.45	−.88	−.88	−.90	−.90	−.91	−.43	−.92	−.83	−.75	−.70
LCV	−.65	−.63	−.84	−.84	−.72	−.81	−.85	−.55	−.86	−.89	−.74	−.70
LWV	−.78	−.58	−.88	−.88	−.81	−.92	−.87	−.45	−.89	−.79	−.72	−.62
NASC	.94	.16	.85	.79	.90	.80	.94	.21	.92	.70	.72	.51
NCSC	−.88	−.33	−.81	−.74	−.88	−.84	−.93	−.22	−.90	−.69	−.75	−.48
NFO	−.78	−.08	−.30	−.38	−.80	−.65	−.59	.06	−.33	−.11	−.61	−.06
NFU	−.89	−.11	−.69	−.53	−.86	−.71	−.68	.17	−.32	−.01	−.62	.00
NFIB	.88	.13	.71	.60	.86	.76	.87	.18	.84	.63	.43	.11
NWPC[c]							−.89	−.20	−.82	−.59	−.71	−.54
UAW	−.95	−.24	−.88	−.83	−.92	−.88	−.94	−.27	−.92	−.72	−.79	−.54
UMW	−.77	−.19	−.56	−.49	−.79	−.68	−.88	−.35	−.85	−.80	−.68	−.43

Note: Our data are for 101 individual senators, including 59 Democrats, 41 Republicans, and 1 Independent. The corresponding figures for the House are 438 Representatives—278 Democrats and 160 Republicans. Senators total more than 100 and representatives total more than 435 because of within-Congress replacements.

[a] Correlations are with the first-dimension D-NOMINATE coordinates.

[b] Correlations are with the second dimension.

[c] This group did not publish ratings for the 96th Senate.

tion is below 0.59 in magnitude. Liberal groups have a negative correlation; conservative groups, a positive one. Note further that, on the first dimension, the House correlation is positive if and only if the Senate correlation is also positive. This finding demonstrates that the interest groups are consistent in evaluating the two houses.

The correlations with the second dimension for all members are much smaller; none exceeds 0.65 in magnitude. For all interest groups and for both houses, the magnitude of the first-dimension correlation always exceeds the magnitude of the second-dimension correlation. No group issues ratings that primarily tap the second dimension. This result supports our view (expressed in chapter 3) that American politics, particularly in the contemporary period, is largely unidimensional. We explore this finding in more detail later in this chapter.

When separate correlations are computed for each party, the first-dimension correlations remain high, but the second-dimension results change dramatically. This is no surprise. As first discussed in chapter 3, in the modern period, liberal Democrats lie at one end of the first dimension, and conservative Republicans, at the opposite end (see also figures 8.5 and 8.6). Moderates from both parties are in the middle. Thus, the first dimension and the liberal/moderate/conservative positioning of the ratings correlate highly, overall. In contrast, moderate Democrats tend to be at one end of the second dimension; moderate Republicans, at the other; and extremists from either party tend toward the middle. This alignment produces a low *overall* correlation between the D-NOMINATE second dimension and the interest-group ratings. In contrast to the overall pattern, *within* each party, the second dimension—as well as the first—discriminates along liberal/conservative lines, distinguishing liberal from moderate Democrats, and moderate from conservative Republicans. Within each party, there are relatively high correlations on both dimensions.

The pattern of the correlations is reflected directly in the D-NOMINATE scores. Even though the overall correlations between the first and second dimensions were virtually zero, the correlations between the D-NOMINATE first and second dimensions for 1979–80 were 0.90 for the Senate Democrats, 0.88 for the Senate Republicans, and 0.71 and 0.43 for the respective party contingents in the House of Representatives.

As noted above, ratings of individual interest groups appear frequently in professional journals in economics and political science as measures of the liberalism/conservatism or the ideology of legislators.[7] Whether these ratings are being used as measures of preferences in a particular policy area or as general measures of ideology, the implicit assumption being made is that the group that issues the ratings *is at the periphery of the space spanned by the legislators.* That is, if the ADA rating measures liberalism with a score of 100 indicating the most liberal legislator and a score of 0 indicating the least liberal, all members with less than perfect scores must be more conservative than the ADA. In short, the ADA has to anchor one end of the scale.

To see the effect of this assumption, suppose that some interest group is truly a centrist group—for example, its ideal legislator is someone like Senator David Boren of Oklahoma. What would the ratings of such a group look like? Clearly, centrist legislators like Boren would receive scores near 100. If the centrist interest group were to evenly balance its ratings by including a number of roll calls with midpoints to its left and an equal number with midpoints to its right, both the very liberal Ted Kennedy types and the very conservative Jesse Helms types would receive scores near 50. This interest group's ratings would cover a range from moderates to extremists. (Recall that, in one dimension, the roll call midpoint is the point equidistant between the Yea and Nay outcomes.)

If an interest group is instead exterior to the legislators, its ratings act much like a thermometer: Just as a thermometer tells us that 60° is hotter than 50° but cooler than 70°, an ADA rating of 60 is a less liberal one than an ADA rating of 70, but a more liberal one than an ADA rating of 50. Hence the legislators can be ordered by their "thermometer reading."

The upshot of the statements above is that the way researchers have used interest-group ratings implies a simple one-dimensional spatial model in which the interest group and the legislators can be represented as points on a line, where the point representing the interest group is the farthest left or right point. Figure 8.1 shows a hypothetical situation in which the ADA is to the left of six legislators—A, B, C, D, E, and F. In this situation, legislator A would receive the highest score and F would receive the lowest score. Now, suppose our hypothetical centrist interest group were positioned between legislators C and D, as shown in figure 8.1. Then C would get the highest rating, followed by D, with F getting the lowest rating. As the figure shows, this is akin to defining a new dimension by *folding* the original dimension back onto itself at the location of the centrist interest group. Notice that if the centrist group's ratings could be *unfolded,* then they would be equivalent to the ADA ratings.

The folding problem is one reason that, even if the interest-group ratings were based solely on votes that have cutting lines perpendicular to the first dimension, the correlations in table 8.2 would not be 1.0. (Recall that the cutting line is the two-dimensional analog of the midpoint; it is the locus of points equidistant from the Yea and Nay outcomes.) A folded group in the center of the space would have a correlation near 0. Conservative groups that were near the end of the space would have a correlation that was positive but less than one. Another reason that the ratings would not produce perfect correlations is that, because they are based on a fairly small number of roll calls, the ratings are not very fine-grained (Kiewiet and McCubbins, 1991).

Looking at figure 8.1, if legislator A receives a 100 rating based on 10 roll call votes, then A votes with the ADA position 10 out of 10 times. By assumption, the ADA is to the left of A. Hence, if there is perfect spatial voting (no errors), legislator A must be to the left of the midpoint of all 10 roll calls. Suppose that not only A but also B were rated 100 and that legislators E and F were both rated 0. These ratings imply that, among the roll calls selected by the ADA, the farthest left midpoint is to the right of B, and the farthest right midpoint is to the left of E. This situation is shown in figure 8.2.

Figure 8.2 demonstrates that the implicit assumption that the interest group is exterior to the legislators can be more accurately phrased: In a perfect voting world, if an interest group is exterior to the midpoints of its chosen roll calls, then the ordering of the legislators is weakly monotone with the true ordering. Stated simply, the orderings are identical, except that the coarseness of the ratings leads to ties. And the presence of ties will reduce correlations. More generally, the ratings are influenced by the distribution of the roll calls selected (Snyder, 1992a). For example, as in figure 8.2, if the midpoints are concentrated in the center of the distribution of legislators, then the ratings will be bimodally distributed even if the legislator distribution is unimodal. Even if the interest group uses many roll calls, if the midpoints of the selected roll calls are all close to one point in the space, there will be a relatively low correlation between the ratings and the true legislator positions.

To illustrate the effect of an interest group's selection of a relatively small number of roll calls, with cutting lines that are heavily clustered in the space, we examine the ratings of the highly liberal ADA and the highly conservative ACA, two interest groups unlikely to be affected by the folding problem. The top portions of figure 8.3 shows the distribution of their ratings for the 96th House against the first dimension of D-NOMINATE. In both cases, a large number of ratings at or close to 0 and 100

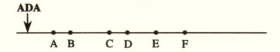

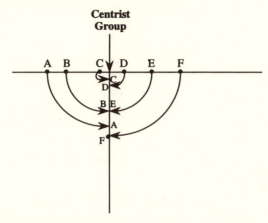

Figure 8.1. The folding of legislators' ideal points in interest-group ratings. A, B, C, D, E, and F denote the ideal points of legislators. An extremely liberal interest group like ADA (in the top part) rates legislators in a way that preserves the liberal/conservative order of the legislators. In contrast, the centrist interest group (in the bottom part) is about equally distant from the extreme liberal A and the extreme conservative F. The centrist group gives A and F similar ratings. These ratings "fold" the ideal points.

lead to S-shaped curves. Distinctions that D-NOMINATE makes among both the most liberal representatives and the most conservative are lost in the ratings, leading to the flat portions of the S shapes. The bottom portion of the figure shows the distribution of the midpoints for the roll calls selected by the two groups, vis-à-vis the distribution of the representatives. In both instances, the midpoints are disproportionately drawn from the center of the legislator distribution. Concerns about bias in interest-group ratings (Snyder, 1992a) are well founded.

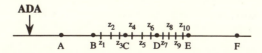

Figure 8.2. Ratings are biased by the roll calls selected by the interest group. If the ADA uses only the 10 roll calls with midpoints $z_1, z_2, \ldots, z_{10}$, legislators A and B and legislators E and F will vote (errors aside) identically on all 10 roll calls. The ratings for A and B and for E and F will then be identical, even though A is more liberal than B and F is more conservative than E.

HOUSE

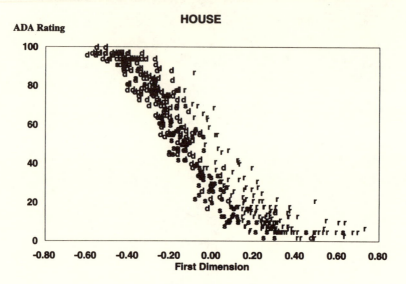

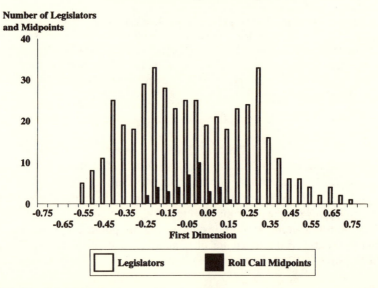

Figure 8.3. The D-NOMINATE scores for the 96th House of Representatives (1979–80) and the ratings of the Americans for Democratic Action (ADA) and the Americans for Constitutional Action (ACA). The top portions plot the ratings against the scores, with the letter *d* indicating northern Democrats; *s*, southern Democrats; and *r*, Republicans. The S shape of both

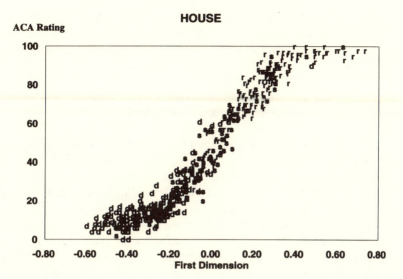

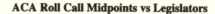

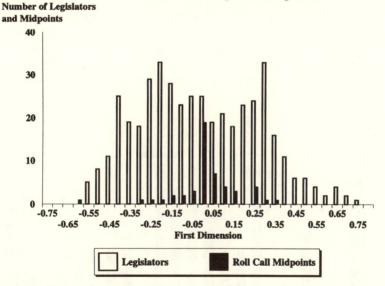

curves shows how the ratings fail to differentiate among extreme liberals and among extreme conservatives. This failure results, as the bottom portions show, from the interest groups' construction of their ratings from roll calls with midpoints near the center of the space.

Figures 8.1, 8.2, and 8.3 raise two related issues. First, can we test the assumption that the interest group is to the exterior of the legislators; and second, can ratings be unfolded to recover a common ordering of interest groups? We deal with these issues in the next two sections.

Are Interest Groups Exterior to the Legislators?

Using W-NOMINATE, we can test whether the interest groups are exterior to the legislators by treating the interest groups as legislators. For the 96th Congress, we identified every roll call vote used to compute the ratings of the 28 interest groups shown in table 8.1.[8] If an interest group uses a roll call in its rating, it has stated its position and has thus "voted." These "votes" allow us to treat the interest groups as legislators and include them in a W-NOMINATE scaling of the 96th Congress that combines the actual votes of the members of Congress and the "votes" of interest groups. (Given that the maximum number of roll calls selected by an interest group was 70 [see table 8.1], most of the "votes" by the interest groups are abstentions.) In the first scaling we present, we used the 8 interest groups that selected at least 25 votes during the 96th Senate. Figure 8.4 presents the results in one dimension.[9]

As figure 8.4 shows, 7 of the 8 groups are estimated to be at or near the ends of the dimension (-1 and $+1$, respectively). The CCUS is the interesting exception. Its estimated first-dimension position of .86 is the most interior position among the 8 interest groups. It appears to be a genuine case of folding of the sort shown in figure 8.1. Of the 58 roll calls the CCUS used in its Senate ratings, 3 had less than 2.5 percent in the minority and were unscalable.[10] For the remaining 55 roll calls, 8 had midpoints to the

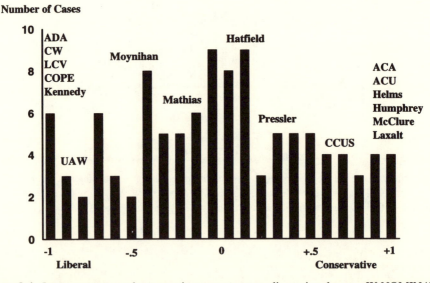

Figure 8.4. Interest groups and senators in a common one-dimensional space: W-NOMINATE scaling for 1979–80. The histogram shows the distribution of both senators and interest groups. All interest groups used in the scaling are named on the plot. Some senators are also named.

right and 47 had midpoints to the left of the CCUS's position. On 54 of the 55 roll calls, the CCUS "voted correctly"—that is, its actual position corresponded with the prediction of the spatial model on 54 of 55 occasions. The selection of roll calls by CCUS fits the spatial model quite well. Because the CCUS has an interior position, however, its ratings are folded. In fact, the 7 senators to the right of the CCUS received an average rating of 87, whereas the 5 senators equidistant to the left of the CCUS (between 0.72 and 0.86) received an average rating of 88.

As to the 7 interest groups at the periphery of the space, the ACA and the ACU, the two groups at the right end, are *perfect*—that is, they are exterior to the midpoints of all their chosen roll calls. At the left end, COPE, the ADA, and the UAW fit the dimension very well. They are not perfect, but they have no more than two voting "errors." There are poorer fits for the LCV and for Ralph Nader's Congress Watch (CW). As we now demonstrate, a second dimension is required to account for their voting patterns.

We noted above that a one-dimensional spatial model with the interest group at the end of the dimension is the implicit model behind the use of interest-group ratings as measures of ideology. If the voting space of the legislators is in fact two-dimensional, and if all the interest groups are using the same dimension through the space to construct their ratings, then the interest groups should lie on a line that runs through the two-dimensional space.

Figure 8.5 shows the W-NOMINATE results for the 96th Senate, in two dimensions.[11] (As explained in appendix A, the space is constrained to be the unit circle.) Once again, 7 out of the 8 groups are on the rim of the unit circle, exterior to the posi-

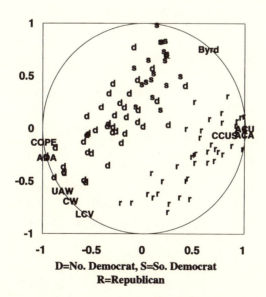

D=No. Democrat, S=So. Democrat
R=Republican

Figure 8.5. Interest groups and senators in a common two-dimensional space: W-NOMINATE scaling for 1979–80. The interest groups and the independent Harry F. Byrd, Jr., are named on the plot. See table 8.1 for identification of the interest groups. The circle shows that W-NOMINATE constrains the estimation to a circle of unit radius. All interest groups are at or near the periphery of the space. They are concentrated along an axis that runs roughly from the UAW to the ACU.

tions of the senators, with the CCUS being in an interior position among the Republican senators. The second dimension dramatically improves the fit of the LCV—it now votes "correctly" on all roll calls, and its geometric mean probability rises from 0.70 to 0.95. Ralph Nader's CW also fits better in two dimensions—its geometric mean probability rises from 0.59 to 0.67, and the number of voting errors drops from 14 to 10.

Note that a line running at a slight angle through the two-space—from the location of the UAW to the location of the ACU in figure 8.5—provides an axis that comes close to capturing the positions of the 8 interest groups. This finding lends rough support to the implicit one-dimensional spatial model that underlies the use of interest-group ratings as measures of liberalism/conservatism. Projection onto the axis would give results very close to those shown in figure 8.4, including the folded position of the CCUS. The locations of the interest groups are also consistent with the correlations reported in table 8.2.

We also need to make two methodological observations about figure 8.5. First, compared to the senators, the interest groups are imprecisely estimated because the number of votes they cast is so small. The estimated number of standard errors for the interest-group locations are, on average, more than 10 times larger than those for the senators.[12] Nevertheless, the extreme positions of the interest groups are not a consequence of the imprecise estimates.[13] Second, adding the interest groups to the roll call data does not affect the recovery of the legislators. The R^2 (squared Pearson correlation) between the estimated first dimensions with and without the interest groups was 0.99 for the Senate and 0.96 for the House. For the estimated second dimensions with and without the interest groups, the R^2s were 0.99 and 0.98, respectively.

Unfolding the Interest-Group Ratings

In our analysis in the previous section, the only information about the interest groups that we used was those roll calls for which they had announced their positions. This is not identical to the information contained in the ratings. Some groups weight some roll calls when they calculate their ratings (for example, the ACU); other groups count absences as Nay votes (for example, the ADA); and still others do not take pairs into account (for example, the LCV). Consequently, in this section we analyze the ratings directly as a check on our results.

Figure 8.1 was deliberately designed to be identical to figure 5.1 in Clyde Coombs's classic book *A Theory of Data* (1964). Coombs labeled the common dimension of legislators and midpoints (individuals and stimuli, in his discussion) a "J scale" and the interest-group ratings (the observed individual preference orderings) an "I scale." Coombs stated the problem: "The data consist of a set of I scales from a number of individuals, and the analytical problem is how to unfold these I scales to recover the J scale."

In our earlier work (Poole, 1981, 1984, 1990; Poole and Daniels, 1985; Poole and Rosenthal, 1986), we developed a method of unfolding and applied it to a large collection of interest-group ratings issued from 1959 through 1981. In this model, the ratings are treated as inverse distances—the higher the rating, the closer the legislator is to the interest group. The aim of the analysis is to estimate points representing the legislators and points representing the interest groups in such a way that the Euclidean distances between the two sets of points reproduce the ratings as closely as possible.[14]

Table 8.3 shows the R^2 between the corresponding legislator coordinates from D-NOMINATE and the interest-group unfolding. Two sets of estimations were analyzed: dynamic estimations for the 1959–81 period and estimations for the 96th Congress only.[15] Like D-NOMINATE, the dynamic unfolding model of the ratings treats the spatial positions of legislators as linear functions of time. The procedure is detailed by Poole and Rosenthal (1986) and Poole (1990).

The unfolding procedure recovers the same first dimension from the interest-group ratings that D-NOMINATE recovers from the whole set of roll calls. The second dimension recovered from the interest-group ratings appears to differ somewhat from that estimated by D-NOMINATE, although the dynamic interest-group analysis for the House—which is based on the largest number of ratings—is closer to the corresponding D-NOMINATE second dimension than are the other estimations.

Why do the D-NOMINATE results and the interest-group-unfolding results from the second dimension differ? The pattern of correlations between individual interest-group ratings and the D-NOMINATE dimensions (presented in the previous section) suggests an explanation: The interest groups are picking roll calls primarily from the first dimension, so that the ratings contain very little information about the second dimension. To test this hypothesis, we separated the roll calls into two subsets—those chosen by the interest groups and those not chosen—and applied W-NOMINATE to both subsets of roll calls and to all the roll calls. Table 8.4 shows the distribution of the percentage of votes, on the majority side, for all the roll calls, for the chosen subset, and for the nonchosen subset. It also shows the R^2s between the estimated legislator coordinates from the three applications of W-NOMINATE.

The distribution of the roll calls chosen by the interest groups is not representative of the overall distribution—it is skewed toward the closer roll calls. Indeed, more than 70 percent of the roll calls selected by the interest groups have winning margins

Table 8.3 R Squares between D-NOMINATE Dimensions and Interest-Group Unfoldings

		Senate			House	
		Dimension			Dimension	
Legislators	n	1	2	n	1	2
Dynamic Coordinates: 1959–81						
All	331	.82	.35	1,352	.90	.61
Democrats	167	.78	.39	772	.82	.61
Republicans	142	.58	.21	580	.74	.42
Static Coordinates: 96th Congress						
All	101	.94	.38	438	.91	.37
Democrats	59	.90	.35	278	.86	.30
Republicans	41	.92	.13	160	.70	.17

Note: The dynamic coordinates are from an analysis of all interest-group ratings issued from 1959 through 1981, reported in Poole and Rosenthal (1986). The static coordinates are from a separate scaling of the 96th Congress.

Table 8.4 Differences between Roll Calls Chosen and Those Not Chosen, by Interest Groups in 1979–1980

| | Distribution of Roll Calls (Percent) | | | | | |
| | Senate | | | House | | |
Majority Percentage	All	Chosen	Not Chosen	All	Chosen	Not Chosen
50–60	32	43	27	27	45	22
61–70	22	30	18	19	26	16
71–80	15	15	14	12	13	12
81–90	11	7	13	11	9	12
91–97.5	9	4	11	14	6	17
97.6–100	12	1	17	16	2	21
All	101[a]	100	100	99	101	100
n (roll calls)	1,054	334	720	1,276	312	964
n (scalable)	928	331	597	1,067	306	761

R-Squares of W-NOMINATE Scalings

| | Senate | | | House | | |
| | All | Chosen | Not Chosen | All | Chosen | Not Chosen |
Legislators						
All	—	—	—	—	—	—
Chosen	.99/.92[b]	—	—	.98/.92	—	—
Not chosen	1.00/.95	.98/.79	—	.99/.96	.94/.82	—
n (legislators)	101			438		

[a]Columns do not total 100 due to rounding.

[b]The first number is the R^2 between the estimated first dimensions; the second number is for the corresponding second dimensions.

of 70 to 30 or less, with over 40 percent at 60 to 40 or less. Even though the sample of interest-group roll calls is skewed, W-NOMINATE recovers essentially the same legislator configuration from both samples. The correspondences of the estimated second dimensions for the two samples are weaker than those for the first, but the R^2 is still quite high (0.79 for the Senate and 0.82 for the House), and the correspondences of the estimated second dimensions with those estimated from the total set are all above 0.92. In addition, the increase in geometric mean probability and the increase in correct classification gained from adding the second dimension are about the same in both sets of roll calls.

In sum, the roll calls chosen by the interest groups contain essentially the same amount of information about the second dimension that is contained in the roll calls they do not select. Given this fact, why isn't the second dimension accurately estimated by the group-unfolding analysis?

For one thing, the second dimension is not very important in relation to the first dimension. During this time period, the first dimension typically classifies about 80–82 percent of the roll call votes correctly. The second dimension typically adds about 2–3 percent to the correct classifications, and the geometric mean probability climbs about 0.02–0.04. All in all, the second dimension, although important, is minor as compared to the first dimension. Consequently, the variation across legislators of the ratings—which are based on relatively small samples of roll calls—due to the addition of the second dimension will be quite small and will be sensitive to voting errors by legislators. The NOMINATE method is less sensitive to errors, even when applied only to the roll calls chosen by the interest groups, because it pools *all* the roll calls chosen by *all* the interest groups in estimating the positions of legislators.

To demonstrate the sensitivity of ratings to the errors of legislators, we performed an experiment in which we constructed ratings based on perfect voting by senators and interest groups on the roll calls the groups chose for the 96th Senate. We used both the roll call coordinates and the legislator coordinates (shown in figure 8.5) estimated by W-NOMINATE. But rather than using the actual votes on each roll call, we used the votes predicted by W-NOMINATE. This procedure generated perfect spatial voting. When the ratings are constructed—using the roll calls actually selected by the interest groups—from perfect voting, the second dimension is recovered almost as accurately as the first (R^2s of 0.88 and 0.85, respectively).

Thus, an unfolding analysis of the ratings in one dimension produces essentially the same results as W-NOMINATE. Beyond the first dimension, the ratings contain very little information because the ratings are noisy evaluations of legislator locations on a second (or higher) dimension. Better results can be obtained by pooling all the information about the voting records of the legislators and the interest groups. This pooling occurs when one treats the interest groups as legislators and analyzes the augmented roll call data with NOMINATE.

Using the Interest Groups to Estimate a Joint House-Senate Scaling

The fact that the interest groups are regarded here as "legislators" who are, so to speak, members of both chambers makes it possible to apply NOMINATE to the House and Senate simultaneously by assuming that the interest groups occupy the same spatial position within both chambers. Ideally, those roll calls for which the substance was identical in both the House and Senate should be treated as a single roll call with 535 voters. Examples include veto-override and conference-report votes.

In the 96th Congress, there were only two veto-override votes—one overrode President Carter's attempt to impose an oil-import fee; and the other was on special pay bonuses for Veterans Administration doctors. The VA-doctor-pay veto was overridden unanimously in the Senate and by a 401 to 5 vote in the House. These margins were too lopsided for the vote to be scaled by W-NOMINATE for either chamber. However, the oil-import vote was scaleable, and we treated it as a single roll call in both chambers.

With respect to conference-report votes, we found only seven roll calls for which it was clear that identical bills were being voted on. Most conference report votes were very lopsided, and many were passed by a voice vote in the Senate, leaving very few votes for analysis.

Even when the *text* of the bill is identical in both houses, however, the political interpretation of the vote within the two chambers may differ. For example, the Panama Canal Treaty was ratified in 1978 by the Senate, but the House felt its prerogatives were being trampled on because the treaty disposed of government property. The 1979 vote on the conference report on implementation of the treaty failed by a close margin of 192 to 203 in the House on September 20. This first vote on the report appeared to exhibit a great deal of position-taking in the "turf war" between the two houses. A vote more directed at the substance of the treaty occurred five days later, and the report was approved by a vote of 232 to 188. On the same day, the twenty-fifth, the Senate, too, passed the report by a vote of 59 to 29; we combined the House and Senate votes on the twenty-fifth into one roll call.

Table 8.5 shows the eight roll calls (one veto override and seven conference reports) that were combined. In the estimation, we used all the groups shown in table 8.1.[16] The two-dimensional results are displayed in figure 8.6. Not surprisingly, the estimated legislator coordinates from the combined scaling are virtually identical to those coordinates estimated in the separate scalings done without the interest groups. The R^2 between the two sets of coordinates for the first dimension for the House of Representatives was 0.99, and for the second dimension, 0.98. The R^2s for the Senate were both 0.99. The distribution of the senators and representatives over both dimensions is approximately the same.[17]

In the combined one-dimensional scaling, 12 of the 28 interest groups are exterior to the members of Congress, and another 6 groups are near the ends. The CCUS is again in the interior, and it is joined by several other labor, business, and farmers' interest groups. Adding the second dimension dramatically increases the number of groups exterior to the legislators—20 of 28 are now indeed on the rim of the space, and the UMW, though not on the rim, is also clearly toward the exterior.

The recovery of the interest groups in the combined scaling is almost the same as that from separate scalings of the House and Senate. A comparison of figure 8.5 with figure 8.6 shows that the interest groups common to the two scalings are recovered in nearly the same positions.

With respect to the eight identical votes, the fit was quite good. Table 8.5 shows the classification results for two dimensions. As expected, constraining the cutting lines to be the same increases the classification errors vis-à-vis the separate scalings. But the respective *PRE*s (recall that the *PRE* controls for the margin of the roll call) are fairly close in magnitude.[18]

Figure 8.6 shows the estimated cutting line for the veto-override vote and for the conference-report vote on the bill to implement the Panama Canal Treaty. The cutting line for the veto override forecasts a nearly unanimous vote because President Carter's veto was overridden by a margin of 335 to 34 in the House and 68 to 10 in the Senate. Of more interest is the Panama Canal Treaty implementation vote. As we noted above, the vote was 232 to 188 in the House and 59 to 29 in the Senate. In the separate scalings, counting pairs and those announced as voting, 362 of 428 representatives were correctly classified, as were 80 of 97 senators, for a total of 83 errors. In the combined scaling, the total number of errors is 91—or an 82.7 percent correct-classification rate.

We estimated President Carter's position by assuming he "voted" on the roll calls chosen by *Congressional Quarterly* to construct its presidential-support score. President Carter's "votes" were a good fit to the spatial model. In one dimension, the geometric mean was 0.71, with 83.4 percent of 463 roll calls being correctly classified. In two dimensions, the geometric mean was 0.72, with 85.1 percent being correctly classified.

In two dimensions, President Carter is positioned almost exactly midway between the northern and southern wings of his party. On the first dimension, Carter is considerably to the left of his party median—18 Democratic senators are to his left and 41 are to his right. The numbers for the House are 52 and 226, respectively. In fact, only

Table 8.5 Identical Roll Calls in the 96th Congress

Roll Call Number and House of Congress	Yeas	Nays	Errors NOMINATE	Errors Combined	PRE[a] NOMINATE	PRE[a] Combined	Subject Matter
House	463[b]	236[c]	192	66[d]	72[e]			Panama Canal implementation
Senate	310	64	33	17	20			
Total		300	225	83	92	0.63	0.59	
House	468	219	205	109	99			Establishment of Department of Education
Senate	309	71	23	16	18			
Total		290	228	125	117	0.45	0.49	
House	527	301	112	78	78			Emergency program of energy conservation
Senate	363	79	18	15	23			
Total		380	130	93	101	0.28	0.22	
House	672	254	138	87	85			Chrysler loan guarantees
Senate	506	43	37	21	24			
Total		297	175	108	109	0.38	0.38	
House	800	305	109	79	77			Windfall-profits tax on crude oil
Senate	575	66	34	12	15			
Total		371	143	91	92	0.36	0.36	
House	885	326	82	31	29			Food-stamp authorization
Senate	644	65	25	14	13			
Total		391	107	45	42	0.58	0.61	
House	945	340	37	37	38			Veto override on oil-import fee
Senate	683	68	12	9	10			
Total		408	49	46	48	0.06	0.02	
House	1,237	213	201	48	65			Budget resolution
Senate	986	50	38	32	34			
Total		263	239	80	99	0.67	0.59	

[a]Proportionate reduction in errors (see chapter 3 for definition).
[b]VOTEVIEW number of roll call.
[c]Includes pairs and announced.
[d]Total number of classification errors from separate NOMINATE two-dimensional scalings.
[e]Total number of classification errors from combined scaling, with roll calls in this table being constrained to a common cutting line in both houses.

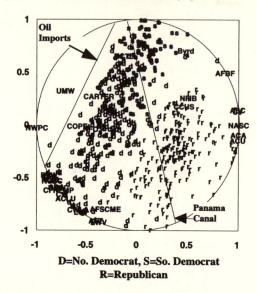

Figure 8.6. Representatives, senators, and 28 interest groups in a common two-dimensional space: W-NOMINATE scaling for 1979–80. The interest groups and Harry F. Byrd, Jr., are named on the plot. The circle shows that W-NOMINATE constrains the estimation to a circle of unit radius. Results are very similar to those in figure 8.5, although a few interest groups have interior positions. The figure also shows the cutting line for roll call votes on oil imports and the Panama Canal.

two southern Democrats, Mickey Leland and Bob Eckhardt, both representatives from Texas, were to Carter's left. On the second dimension, Carter is much closer to his party median—24 senators and 125 representatives are above him, and 35 senators and 153 representatives are below. Of the 105 southern Democrats in both Houses, 86 were higher than Carter on the second dimension. Although one might expect a president with a legislative agenda to adopt, for strategic reasons, positions of moderation, Carter's positions appeared to be more those of a representative agent of his party and certainly not those of a typical southern Democrat.

Summary

We have shown that interest-group ratings confirm this book's basic message that roll call voting is largely accounted for by a low-dimensional spatial model. A major new finding is that most interest groups issuing ratings are to the exterior of the legislators. This is good news for previous studies of Congress that have used ratings as measures of ideology. Although these measures are coarse, they show a high degree of correlation with the W-NOMINATE estimates.

The exterior nature of interest groups is important because, to the extent the interest groups influence legislators, they will be polarizing, moving the legislators away from middle-of-the-road positions. On the other hand, the interest groups that issue ratings are a select group among all interest groups. They are overwhelmingly either labor unions, public-interest organizations, or ideological groups like Americans for Constitutional Action.

Our methods could be applied, however, to a wider array of evaluating groups, because the key to using the methodology is not having quantitative ratings from a group but having positions on a reasonable number of roll calls. For example, newspapers frequently take positions on legislation before Congress. They, too, are effectively voting on roll calls. Consequently, newspapers could be integrated with the roll call voting base just as we have integrated interest groups. This approach would be particularly attractive in dealing with American history before World War II when interest-group ratings are hard to come by but when American cities had several newspapers.

A variant of the NOMINATE methodology, called PAC-NOMINATE, provides information about interest groups—including those that do not issue ratings—from the contributions of their political action committees (PACs). In PAC-NOMINATE, the interest groups are treated as legislators who vote on incumbents and challengers, both playing the role of roll calls. (For a detailed discussion, see McCarty and Poole, 1995.) Labor PACs, consistent with their ratings, are concentrating their money overwhelmingly on liberal Democrats. But the bulk of PAC money comes from corporations and trade and industry associations. With the exception of oil firms, which are ideologically focused, business PACs seem as concerned with buying access as with policy. (Or, to put it differently, they are more concerned with policies that affect their immediate interests than with national policy.) Since their contributions tended to exclude only the most liberal Democrats, business PACs were estimated to have moderate conservative positions. But it is an open question whether the business PACs were truly centrist, or—since in the 1970s and 1980s, the Democrats were presumed likely to control the House indefinitely—are merely acting strategically. In any event, the ideologically oriented interest groups, as this chapter demonstrates, are forces of extremism.

9
Committees and Roll Calls

Congressional committees are critical in the framing of the roll call vote choices that we analyzed in previous chapters. A committee system by its very nature carves up the policy universe into jurisdictions. Members should gravitate toward the committees with jurisdictions closest to their interests. These interests are predominantly ones that further the members' chances of reelection (Fenno, 1973, 1978; Mayhew, 1974; Fiorina, 1989).

Shepsle (1978), in his study of the committee-assignment process in the House, found that members do self-select. The assignment process generally respects seniority, somewhat overrepresents the majority party, and is constrained by the limited size of the most desirable committees; but the preferences of individual members are important. If, indeed, members do self-select, then the committee system should produce systematically biased policy. That is, in comparison to the House as a whole, the Agriculture Committee will be more proagriculture; the Veterans' Affairs Committee, more proveteran; the Armed Services Committee, more pro-defense contractor or promilitary; and so on. Thus, the committees will tend to be "preference outliers" with respect to the chamber as a whole.

The basic logic of Shepsle's approach is that committees are opportunities to reward special interests that are highly important to certain members. As a result, policy is distorted from that which would be produced by a majority-rule legislature without a committee system (Niskanen, 1971). A quite opposite view of the committee system is found in the work of Gilligan and Krehbiel (1990).[1] These authors recognize that the chamber is sovereign. A chamber would not delegate policy formation to a committee that systematically distorted policy from the chamber's wishes, unless such distortions were in the chamber's interests. Indeed, their view of the raison d'être of committees is not that committees arise for the selective allocation of benefits but that committees arise as a result of a classical division of labor. Policy formation requires information; committees are specialized information-gathering bodies. Because committees composed of preference outliers with private information have an incentive to distort their reports to the full chamber, the chamber prefers committees that are *not* composed of outliers. Committee preferences should closely mirror chamber preferences. As noted by Gilligan and Krehbiel (1990, p. 558): "Organization of informative committees by a rational legislature is *not* a process culminating in committees that are composed of preference outliers."

Cox and McCubbins (1993) take a position somewhat similar to that of Gilligan and Krehbiel, except that they argue that the focus should be on the match between party contingents on the committees and the party as a whole. In particular, they argue that parties will allow self-selection but will also pay very close attention to committees whose jurisdictions affect large numbers of voters and, hence, bear heavily on the electoral prospects of all party members, not just those on these important committees. For example, decisions of the Appropriations Committee affect everyone. This committee, and others like it,[2] should have party contingents reflective of the whole party.

These diverse theoretical views have sparked a series of empirical studies of whether committees are preference outliers (Krehbiel, 1990, 1992; Hall and Grofman, 1990; Londregan and Snyder, 1994; Groseclose, 1994b; Maltzman, 1994; Maltzman and Smith, 1994). And the empirical literature has given rise to a lively debate.

The outlier debate has usually been conducted on the assumption—either explicit or implicit—of a one-dimensional model of policy preferences. The outlier question is then decided by evaluating whether there is a significant difference between the committee medians and the chamber median on the dimension.[3] To measure positions on the dimension, Krehbiel (1990) and Groseclose (1994b) use jurisdiction-specific interest-group ratings; Hall and Grofman (1990) use "corrected" interest-group ratings; Cox and McCubbins (1993) use D-NOMINATE scores; and Londregan and Snyder (1994) use a variety of interest-group ratings and W-NOMINATE scores.[4]

The results of these efforts are mixed. Londregan and Snyder (1994) claim that about one-third of committees in the 82nd House through the 98th are preference outliers. Cox and McCubbins (1993) find strong support for their party-support model, with only the Veterans' Affairs Committee as an outlier. Krehbiel (1990) and Groseclose (1994) find few committee outliers; Hall and Grofman (1990, p. 1154) argue that "roll call data will understate committee-chamber differences" and that the diversity of most committee jurisdictions raises formidable measurement problems; and Maltzman (1994) finds that "party committee contingents are frequently more extreme and rarely more moderate than their caucus."

We join this debate with the D-NOMINATE scores for the first 100 Congresses—our methodology is presented below. Readers interested only in the substantive punch line may choose to skip to the subhead "Are Committees Preference Outliers?"

All the literature cited above is concerned only with the period since the Legislative Reform Act of 1946, which greatly reduced the number of committees in both chambers. With respect to the debate over this period, we find that there are a moderate number of committees that are outliers, largely because the Democratic contingents on four committees (Agriculture; Armed Services; Education and Labor; and Veterans' Affairs) are outliers with respect to the median member of their party.

Our major finding, however, arises from extending the period of analysis to include all of the first 100 Congresses. Before the 80th Congress, outlier committees are rare. There are even fewer outliers prior to the 80th Congress, under a more stringent and substantively relevant test. This test looks at party contingents on a committee. If a party-contingent median had a significantly extreme position in one Congress, we required that it have a significantly extreme position in the same direction, in the preceding Congress, to be counted as an outlier. This is because the self-selection hypothesis on committee formation predicts a persistence in the types of legislators who join committees. This persistence would be absent, for example, if the Republican contingent on the Armed Services Committee went from being unusually conservative in one Congress to being unusually liberal in the next. Under our measure of consistent outliers, only once in each chamber (the 71st House and the 74th Senate) does the proportion of outliers exceed 5 percent before the 80th Congress.

In contrast, after 1946, we find that a small but important minority of House committees are either exceptionally liberal or exceptionally conservative. Because a handful of committees is not representative of the full House, for most Houses after the 80th, we overwhelmingly reject the null hypothesis that the entire committee structure is representative. The pattern for the postwar Houses is *not* echoed in the Senate. Most important, when we look for consistent outliers, we find no evidence, with the exception of the 98th Senate, supporting the self-selection hypothesis.

The whole debate, however, might be framed differently. Legislators who especially value military bases in their constituency might, quite aside from their general liberal/conservative preferences, be prone to join the Armed Services Committee, in the hope of influencing the geographic allocation of defense spending and the global level of spending. We agree with Krehbiel (1990), Hall and Grofman (1990), and Shepsle and Weingast (1994), who find that such interests are difficult to discern in overall voting patterns. Consequently, we analyze whether committee members vote differently on bills within their committee's jurisdiction than on other legislation. We find that common interests are evident in the fact that committee members are, ceteris paribus, more likely to support committee bills than are noncommittee members. However, the comparison of the roll call voting of committee members and noncommittee members also supports the informational theory of committees. We thus suggest that committees advance self-selected interests of members with specialized information.

Measuring the Representativeness of Committees

To perform a statistical test of whether congressional committees are representative of the chamber from which they are chosen, the measure that is used as a basis of evaluation, the evaluation statistic, and the sample space must all be specified.

Measuring Preference

A member's one-dimensional D-NOMINATE score is the measure of preference we use to assess whether committees consist of preference outliers.[5] Although using a one-dimensional measure has limitations that we address below, it is, as indicated earlier, standard in the literature. Moreover, even a one-dimensional measure has the potential for disclosing important differences across committees. For example, conservative guns seekers could choose to join the Armed Services Committee, while liberal butter seekers could choose the Public Works and Transportation Committee.

Any measure of preference will contain some error. The real question is how serious a problem the measurement error is. Kiewiet and McCubbins (1991) and Londregan and Snyder (1994) point out that most of the measures used in the literature, such as ADA ratings, are inappropriate because they contain a significant degree of selection bias and measurement error. (See chapter 8.) Londregan and Snyder (1994, p. 235) assess the measurement error by averaging the Congress-by-Congress W-NOMINATE scores across a large number of Congresses and by then treating the year-to-year variation in the scores as the measurement error. They find that the measurement error is very small in relation to the span of the space. Their technique overestimates the measurement error because some of the intertemporal variation in scores is the result of a genuine change in liberal/conservative preferences. To allow for some intertemporal change while retaining the benefits of averaging, we use the D-NOMINATE scores from the estimation in which legislator positions change linearly over a career (see chapter 2 and appendix A). We can safely treat these scores as having no measurement error, given not only the results of the study by Londregan and Snyder (1994) but also our own bootstrap estimates of the standard errors of the estimated scores (see table A.1). Since the D-NOMINATE scores are, unlike the ratings, based on the entire set of roll calls,[6] the selection-bias problem also disappears.

The Statistic of Evaluation

In assessing whether a specific committee is a preference outlier, we compute the magnitude of the difference between the committee median and the median of the whole chamber.[7] We also assess whether major party contingents are outliers. Here, we compute the magnitude of the difference between the median of the party contingent on the committee and the party median in the whole chamber. This comparison of medians is standard. An outlier committee, or an outlier party contingent on a committee, is one for which the discrepancy between the committee and the chamber is so large as to be statistically significant. When we examine whether the *entire committee structure* of a chamber reflects preference outliers, we use the sum of squared differences between the committee medians and the chamber median

The Sample Space

The critical issue in assessing outliers is the specificiation of the sample space. The concept of statistical significance presupposes a sample space from which a random sample is drawn. Londregan and Snyder (1994) do not deal with this problem. If there is *no measurement error,* they treat any difference between the committee median and the chamber median as significant. Such an approach is clearly inappropriate and is guaranteed to find that most committees are outliers. To see why, consider the 100th House. It had 22 standing committees, but no member had more than 4 committee assignments. Since a member of, at most, 4 of the 22 committees could thus represent the chamber median, at least 18 must, in the Londregan-Snyder approach, be outliers. Such a conclusion is, to say the least, not very helpful.

Congressional scholars know, even without resorting to elaborate methodologies, that individual committee assignments are limited and that committee medians must invariably differ from chamber medians. The relevant question is whether the actual distribution of committee medians—or the median on a given committee—could have arisen simply as the outcome of a purely random assignment process or if, alternatively, the assignment was likely to have arisen only if there was a deliberate tilt toward producing outlier committees. Specification of a random process defines a sample space. In order to test the a priori alternative hypothesis that the median of, for example, the Armed Services Committee was significantly different from the House median, standard two-tailed p values can be used (see the Technical Terms box). The real issue is: What is the appropriate random-assignment process?

Defining the sample space is somewhat tricky. As indicated above, the random-assignment process must reflect the fact that a given legislator receives very few committee assignments. Consequently, there is an interdependence in committee assignments—for example, once a member is assigned to the Armed Services Committee, the chances of this member's being assigned to any other committee are reduced. In addition, party imbalances on committees must also be accounted for. The majority party is typically somewhat overrepresented on a committee. Finding that committee medians differ from chamber medians because of this overrepresentation would not be very interesting. Therefore, letting the random assignment process reflect overrepresentation is appropriate.

There are two related aspects of committee formation that we do not deal with directly. The first is that assignments to some committees, such as the Appropriations Committee, are almost universally more valued than assignments others, such as the Post Office Committee. Obtaining one plum, such as Appropriations, may affect the likelihood that a second or third assignment is another plum, such as Rules. Since our interest pertains to the *effects* of committee formation on the preference makeup of committees, we eschew any attempt to model the details of committee formation.[8] But because the *FULL* model below reproduces the actual distribution of legislators across committees, trade-offs between plums and lemons are captured indirectly. The second aspect is seniority. Because seniority is only weakly related to D-NOMINATE scores (see chapter 4), not stratifying on the basis of seniority is not of major consequence to the analysis. Therefore, we have restricted our sampling methods to controlling for party overrepresentation and for a limited number of committee assignments per individual member.

The relevance of these controls is nicely illustrated by considering the simpler question of whether committee *chairs* are representative. Because chairs must be from the majority party, even if chairs were randomly chosen from the majority, they would obviously not be representative of the floor. Chairs would be distributed around the party median, not the floor median. For this reason, we would want to define the sample space with respect to the majority party, not the whole chamber.

How should we sample the majority party? Suppose the majority party has *D* members and there are, as in the 100th House, 22 committees. We could draw the 22 committee chairs from an urn filled with *D* balls—each ball being labeled with a D-NOMINATE score—*with replacement*. If we did this thousands of times, we would obtain, for each committee, a distribution of chair D-NOMINATE scores that could be used to test whether the position of an actual committee chair was significantly distinct from the party median.[9] But sampling with replacement ignores the constraint that no person can head more than one committee. This constraint has an effect on any test of

---

Technical Terms

p value: When committee medians are compared to chamber medians, the *p* value measures the probability that a random assignment of legislators to committees would produce a difference between the committee median and the floor median that is greater than, or equal to, the observed difference. The magnitude of the difference is used in calculating the *p* value because the randomly assigned committee could be either a liberal outlier or a conservative outlier. That is, in the jargon of statistics, the *p* values are "two-tailed." Similar *p* values are calculated for the differences between the median of a party's committee contingent and the party's floor median.

Standard Error: The standard error is a measure of the precision of the estimate of a parameter (for example, the D-NOMINATE estimate of a legislator's ideal point); the larger the standard error, the less precise the estimate.

Combinations $\binom{D}{d}$: This notation denotes the number of distinct ways of forming a group of d individuals from a larger group of D individuals. It is well known that $\binom{D}{d} = \dfrac{D!}{d!\,(D-d)!}$ where $D! = D(D-1)(D-2)\ldots(2)(1)$.

Multiplication with an Index: $\prod_{j=1}^{n} x_j = x_1 x_2 x_3 \ldots x_n$

Summation with an Index: $\sum_{j=1}^{n} x_j = x_1 + x_2 + x_3 + \ldots + x_n$

---

whether the set of 22 committee chairs constitutes a set of preference outliers. Consequently, we must sample *without replacement*.

To illustrate the difference, assume we have a very, very small legislature, with $D = 3$ and 2 committees. Suppose the three legislators had D-NOMINATE scores of -0.5, 0, and $+0.5$. Our null hypothesis is random assignment; the alternative hypothesis is that the extremists get the chairs. We then observe that the two extremists are the committee chairs. If we sampled with replacement, there would be $3 \times 3 = 9$ possible ways of assigning the chairs, 4 of which have two extremists heading the committees. So the *p* value would be 4/9. If we sampled without replacement, there would only be $3 \times 2 = 6$ ways of assigning the chairs, with 2 ways having extremists heading both committees. In this case, the *p* value would be 2/6 or 3/9, which is less than the sample with-replacement value of 4/9.

We now extend these ideas, developed for the simple case of chairs, to the analysis of committee medians. After we define the appropriate sample spaces, we report the results of Monte Carlo experiments designed to test the representativeness of committees. As with chairs, we need to incorporate real-world structure into the experiment. Because we focus not on an individual characteristic (chairing), but on a distributional characteristic (the committee median), our sampling scheme must reflect the actual number of representatives on each committee. Moreover, we must use the actual number of Republicans and Democrats on the committee. The reason for this is directly analogous to our sampling only from among the majority party when we consider chairs. The party percentages on committees are skewed from those in the full House. For example, in the 100th Congress, the Rules Committee was 69 percent (9 of 13) Democratic, whereas Democrats had only 59 percent (258 of 435) of the seats in the House.

To define the sample space in a way that incorporates the party allocations to committees, let j be an index for committees, let D be the total number of Democrats; let D_j be the number of Democrats on the jth committee; R_j be the number of Republicans on the jth committee; and R be the total number of Republicans. Therefore, the number of ways to form the jth committee, with D_j and R_j unique members, is:

$$\binom{D}{D_j}\binom{R}{R_j}$$

Now, if each committee is formed the same way, then the number of ways to construct n committees—that is, the number of elements in the sample space—is:

$$\prod_{j=1}^{n}\binom{D}{D_j}\binom{R}{R_j} \tag{1}$$

The sample space implied by equation (1) would be appropriate for tests of whether *individual* committees are made up of preference outliers. But it is not a realistic model with which we can test hypotheses about the *overall structure of the committee system*. After one committee is formed, members of the next committee are drawn *with* replacement. Thus, each member has a chance of serving on all the committees. But in practice, all members have a limited number of committee assignments. We therefore introduce constraints that reproduce the observed distribution of committee assignments. For example, across the 22 standing committees in the 100th House, 66 Democrats and 51 Republicans had only one committee assignment; 155 Democrats and 113 Republicans had two committee assignments; and 34 Democrats and 12 Republicans had three committee assignments. One Democrat, Chester Atkins of Massachusetts, had assignments on four committees—Budget, Education and Labor, Foreign Affairs, and Standards of Official Conduct. In addition, the mix of the assignment types varies across the committees. For example, there were 26 Democrats and 17 Republicans on the Agriculture Committee. Of the 26 Democrats, 1 had only one assignment, 19 had two assignments, and 6 had three assignments; of the 17 Republicans, 3 had one assignment, 13 had two assignments, and 1 had three.

Let $D^{(T)}$ be the total number of Democratic seats on all committees; let $D^{(1)}$ be the number of Democratic-party members with one assignment; let $D^{(2)}$ be the number of members with two assignments; and so on. Now, to choose a committee contingent randomly, we increase the number of Democrats from D to $D^{(T)}$ by cloning those members with multiple committee assignments. That is,

$$D^{(T)} = \sum_{t=1}^{T} tD^{(t)} = \sum_{j=1}^{n} D_j > D = \sum_{t=1}^{T} D^{(t)}$$

In the 100th House, for example, $D^{(T)} = 66 + 2 \times 155 + 3 \times 34 + 4 \times 1 = 482$ and $R^{(T)} = 313$.

Because the number of Democratic committee seats and the number of Democratic "members" are now the same, the committee contingents can be drawn without replacement. The first step is to randomly assign the D and R D-NOMINATE scores to the types corresponding to $D^{(1)}$, $D^{(2)}$, $R^{(1)}$, $R^{(2)}$, and so on. That is, an actual D-NOMINATE score is drawn at random from the scores for Democrats and assigned as a one-committee-assignment type. Then, without replacement, another D-NOMINATE score is drawn at random and also assigned as a one-committee-assignment type. The process continues until the number of assigned scores equals $D^{(1)}$. Continuing without replacement, one next allocates the two-committee-assignment types, and so on. A similar process takes place with Republican scores. The number of ways of assigning all the scores can be written as the product of two multinomial coefficients:

$$\frac{D!}{\prod\limits_{t=1}^{T} D^{(t)}!} \frac{R!}{\prod\limits_{t=1}^{T} R^{(t)}!} \tag{2}$$

The next step is to allocate the randomly assigned members to seats that correspond to their types. That is, a randomly selected person with one committee assignment is assigned to one of the committee seats actually held by a real member with only one committee assignment. Assignments continue, *without* replacement, until all the seats for one-assignment types are filled. Next, a randomly selected member with two assignments is allocated to one of the committee seats actually held by real members with two committee assignments and is also randomly assigned to a similar seat on another committee. The process continues until all committee seats are filled.

The possible committee assignments for the randomly drawn one-assignment members are easy to calculate. There are $D^{(1)}!$ and $R^{(1)}!$ ways that they can be assigned to the $D^{(1)}$ and $R^{(1)}$ committee seats held by one-assignment types. Note that this cancels a term in the denominator of equation (2). Hence, the number of possible assignments that satisfies the constraint of assigning a member with t committee memberships to seats held by actual members with t committee memberships is given by:

$$\frac{D!}{\prod\limits_{t=2}^{T} D^{(t)}!} \frac{R!}{\prod\limits_{t=2}^{T} R^{(t)}!} N_{d2} N_{d3} \ldots N_{dT} N_{r2} N_{r3} \ldots N_{rT} \tag{3}$$

where N_{d2} is the number of ways the $D^{(2)}$ Democrats can be assigned to $2D^{(2)}$ seats; N_{d3} is the number of ways the $D^{(3)}$ Democrats can be assigned to $3D^{(3)}$ seats; and so on.

To illustrate how the assignments are made, consider the case of Democrats with 3 assignments in the 93rd House. In the actual House, 8 Democrats, whom we label a, b, ... , f, each had 3 assignments. These assignments were spread over 16 committees, which we label A, B, ... , P. The assignment problem can be specified as one of constructing an 8-by-16 matrix of zeros and ones where the rows sum to 3 and each column sums to the number of three-assignment members on the committee. One solution for this assignment problem is shown on the next page:

	Total Number of Assignments ↓	A	B	C	D	E	F	G	H	I	J	K	L	M	N	O	P
	a 3	0	0	0	0	0	0	1	1	0	0	0	0	0	1	0	0
	b 3	0	0	0	0	0	0	0	0	1	0	0	0	0	0	1	1
	c 3	1	0	1	1	1	0	0	0	0	0	0	0	0	0	0	0
	d 3	0	0	0	0	0	0	0	0	0	1	0	1	1	0	0	0
Representative	*e* 3	0	0	0	1	0	0	0	0	0	0	1	1	0	0	0	0
	f 3	0	0	0	1	0	0	0	0	0	1	0	0	0	0	1	0
	g 3	0	1	0	1	0	1	0	0	0	0	0	0	0	0	0	0
	h 3	0	0	0	1	1	0	0	0	0	0	1	0	0	0	0	0
	24	1	1	1	5	1	1	1	1	1	3	1	2	1	1	2	1

Committee ← Total Number of Committee Members with 3 Assignments

Given a solution, clearly any permutation of the $D^{(3)}$ rows is also a solution. Hence $D^{(3)}!$ is one of the terms in N_{d3}. This reasoning holds for any assignment type with two assignments or more. Note that this will cancel the denominator factorials in equation (3), which allows us to write equation (3) in a simpler form:

$$D!R!\, M_{d2} M_{d3} \ldots M_{dT} M_{r2} M_{r3} \ldots M_{rT} \tag{4}$$

where, with reference to the example above, M_{d3} is the number of ways of filling the matrix with 0's and 1's such that the row and column marginals are satisfied. Although the complexity of the assignment process prevents us from giving formulas for the M's, it is straightforward enough to generate elements of the sample space by a random-assignment process.[10] We refer to this process, which preserves the *structure* of committee assignments, as the *STRU* model.

As an alternative to equation (4), we impose some additional structure by fully replicating the observed pattern of committee assignments—simply replacing each member's actual D-NOMINATE score with a randomly assigned one. This *FULL* model is just a simple people-and-chairs permutation. For example, some Democrat may be assigned to both the Agriculture and the Armed Services committees. We replace the member's true score with a randomly drawn one (from the set of Democrat D-NOMINATE scores for that House). We do this, without replacement, for each member, and the total number of combinations is simply:

$$D!R! \tag{5}$$

Before we turn to a historical summary of our results, we will illustrate the tests we have conducted with a discussion of the 100th House. Results for both the *STRU* and *FULL* models are shown in table 9.1. The table was generated, for each sample space, by 1,000 Monte Carlo random assignments of committees.

At the top of the table, we present overall results of the test of the joint null hypothesis that the observed committee medians are produced randomly. The entries are *p* values. The first entry is for the full committees, the second is for the Democratic contingents, and the third is for the Republican contingents. Because this is a test of whether the committee structure, as a whole, is nonrepresentative, the test statistic does not use the magnitude of the difference between a single committee median and a floor median. Instead, for each experiment, we calculated the sum of squares of the artificial committee medians around the House median and compared it with the actual sum of squares. The *p* value is the proportion of the 1,000 experiments for which the artificial sum of squares exceeded the actual sum of squares. For example, 155 of the 1,000 experiments using the *STRU* model each produced a sum of squares of artificial Republican committee contingents around the House Republican median larger than the actual sum of squares; therefore, we would not reject the null hypothesis that Republican assignments are representative of the entire Republican party at the traditional 5 percent level. In contrast, the House members as a whole and the Democratic contingent appear to have been assigned in a nonrepresentative fashion.

Even if committee medians are significantly different from the true median in a statistical sense, the difference may not have important policy consequences if the difference is small in relation to the dispersion of legislators' ideal points. Consequently, we report "Dispersion" in the final column of table 9.1. "Dispersion" is a statistic that normalizes the dispersion of committee medians around the true median by the dispersion of all legislators around the true median. More precisely, "Dispersion" is the ratio of the average absolute difference between the overall House median and the true medians of the 22 committees to the average absolute difference between the overall median and the legislators. For example, for the Democrats, this is the ratio of the average absolute difference between the 22 Democratic-party-contingent medians and the Democratic-party median to the average absolute difference between the score for each Democrat and the Democratic-party median. The closer this number is to zero, the more representative the 22 committee medians are of the chamber/party contingent.

Individual committee results also appear in the table. Each committee entry shows the proportion of the 1,000 experiments that produced a median that was farther from the House median than the true committee median was. Each committee for each House also has three entries—one for the entire committee, one for the Democrats, and one for the Republicans. For example, for the Agriculture Committee in the 100th House in table 9.1, 484 of the 1,000 experiments using the *FULL* model produced committee medians farther from the House median than the actual median of the committee was. For the Democrats, only 15 random-contingent medians were farther from the overall party median than the actual contingent median was, and for the Republicans, the corresponding number was 500.

The numbers for the committees in the table are quite literally two-tailed *p* values for the null hypothesis that the corresponding committee is *not* an outlier. Values that are at or below 0.055 are signed according to whether the actual median is above or below the House median. If the sign is negative, this means that the committee is significantly (at the traditional 5 percent level) to the left of the House median; vice versa, if the sign is positive.

Under the "Dispersion" column for individual committees, we report the ratio of the difference between the committee median and the floor median to the average absolute difference between the legislators and the overall median. For example, for the Agriculture Committee Democrats, this is $(-0.154 - -0.257)/0.147 = 0.701$; where -0.154 is the median of the 26 committee Democrats; -0.257 is the overall Democratic-party median; and 0.147 is the average of the absolute differences between all Democrats and -0.257.

The results for the *STRU* and *FULL* models in table 9.1 are different for two reasons. First, the Monte Carlo draws are different; second, with reference to "All Committees," the different sample spaces affect the results. With reference to individual committees, results should be identical except for the variation introduced by the

Table 9.1 100th House: Committee-Outlier Two-Tailed *p* Values

Committee	Sample Space		*p* Value Is for:	Dispersion
	STRU Model	*FULL* Model		
All	.004	.004	All	.257
	.007	.009	Dem.	.436
	.155	.137	Rep.	.400
Agriculture	.511	.484	All	.110
	+.021	+.015	Dem.	.701
	.513	.500	Rep.	−.215
Appropriations	−.020	−.028	All	−.382
	.940	.951	Dem.	−.017
	.167	.197	Rep.	−.403
Armed Services	+.008	+.010	All	.437
	+.000	+.000	Dem.	1.284
	.674	.696	Rep.	−.118
Banking, Finance, and Urban Affairs	.991	.985	All	−.002
	.718	.750	Dem.	.085
	.361	.366	Rep.	−.270
Budget	.629	.622	All	.028
	.286	.286	Dem.	−.403
	.713	.700	Rep.	.126
District of Columbia	−.004	−.007	All	−1.001
	.186	.180	Dem.	−.810
	.655	.683	Rep.	−.270
Education and Labor	.062	.086	All	−.366
	−.023	−.019	Dem.	−.816
	−.038	−.040	Rep.	−.821
Energy and Commerce	.532	.546	All	−.091
	.972	.966	Dem.	−.010
	.380	.380	Rep.	.318
Foreign Affairs	−.051	−.047	All	−.354
	.059	.056	Dem.	−.556
	.420	.413	Rep.	−.252
Government Operations (Expenditures in the Executive Branch)	.337	.339	All	−.165
	.526	.522	Dem.	−.193
	+.001	+.001	Rep.	1.162
House Administration	.181	.193	All	−.375
	.657	.649	Dem.	−.200
	.267	.253	Rep.	.570
Interior and Insular Affairs (public lands)	.248	.248	All	−.210
	.177	.162	Dem.	−.471
	.073	.058	Rep.	.662

Table 9.1 *(continued)*

Committee	Sample Space		P Value Is for:	Dispersion
	STRU Model	*FULL* Model		
Judiciary	.265	.282	All	−.203
	.525	.507	Dem.	−.220
	.186	.174	Rep.	.511
Merchant Marine and Fisheries	.256	.264	All	.182
	.061	.062	Dem.	.566
	.404	.427	Rep.	−.289
Post Office	−.040	−.041	All	−.506
	.341	.384	Dem.	−.417
	.088	.069	Rep.	−.858
Public Works and Transportation	.828	.806	All	.034
	.392	.356	Dem.	−.257
	.306	.314	Rep.	.318
Rules	.144	.155	All	−.535
	.811	.809	Dem.	−.136
	.803	.788	Rep.	.170
Science, Space, and Technology	.815	.795	All	.033
	.605	.629	Dem.	.125
	.242	.252	Rep.	.348
Small Business	.608	.596	All	−.079
	.071	.082	Dem.	.532
	.206	.202	Rep.	.466
Standards of Official Conduct	.471	.509	All	.392
	.212	.207	Dem.	−.745
	.923	.910	Rep.	−.052
Veterans' Affairs	.378	.391	All	.160
	.061	+.043	Dem.	.654
	.181	.210	Rep.	.533
Ways and Means	.912	.937	All	−.019
	.267	.252	Dem.	−.403
	.855	.830	Rep.	.067

Number of Committees That Are Preference Outliers

Significance Level	*STRU* Model	*FULL* Model	Results Are for:
5%	4	4	All
	3	5	Dem.
	2	1	Rep.
10%	6	7	All
	7	8	Dem.
	4	2	Rep.

Note: The p values at or below 0.055 receive a + sign if the committee is a conservative outlier; a − sign if the committee is a liberal outlier. See the text for an explanation of the computation of p values and the dispersion measures.

Monte Carlo draws.[11] Thus, the comparison of the *STRU* and *FULL* results for individual committees indicates how much sampling variability remains after 1,000 experiments.

Because the results for the *STRU* and *FULL* models are very similar, we present results for Houses 80 to 100 only for the *FULL* model in table 9.2. As we will see in the next section, these Houses contain most of the outliers in American history. Note that it is possible that a full committee can appear as an outlier even when both party con-

Table 9.2 Committee Outliers, Using Medians: Sample Space Defined by Full Model

Committee	House										
	100	99	98	97	96	95	94	93	92	91	90
All	.004	.000	.000	.000	.049	.002	.004	.000	.005	.007	.000
	.009	.001	.000	.000	.000	.000	.001	.005	.040	.009	.001
	.137	.350	.650	.377	.038	.009	.002	.046	.003	.036	.104
Agriculture	.484	.955	.809	.761	.364	.310	.584	.267	.099	+.041	.061
	+.015	+.010	+.028	+.055	+.030	+.014	+.042	+.010	+.003	+.002	+.000
	.500	.398	.930	.802	.762	.671	.455	.743	.067	.279	.218
Appropriations	−.028	−.046	.123	.109	.353	.736	.623	.842	.582	.927	.967
	.951	.492	.324	.916	.803	.245	+.035	.070	.211	+.032	+.038
	.197	−.043	.271	.967	.308	.832	.864	.770	.558	.578	.229
Armed Services	+.010	+.002	+.015	+.031	+.002	+.001	+.000	+.018	.107	.222	.844
	+.000	+.000	+.000	+.000	+.000	+.003	+.001	+.000	+.003	+.003	+.053
	.696	.629	.405	.960	.911	+.054	.308	+.016	.158	.487	.754
Banking, Finance,	.985	.534	.486	.356	.136	−.054	.198	−.001	.194	.637	.345
and Urban Affairs	.750	.877	.892	.351	.638	.622	.445	.372	.318	.565	.352
	.366	.392	.803	.223	.740	−.043	.789	.120	.260	.484	.911
Budget[a]	.622	.473	−.007	.549	.113	.115	.971	−.028			
	.286	.100	.306	.749	.237	.226	.622	.387			
	.700	.156	.787	.519	.577	.338	.623	.384			
District of	−.007	−.000	−.001	−.000	.460	.531	.157	.065	.483	.566	.691
Columbia	.180	−.054	−.022	−.007	−.017	.264	.545	−.048	.076	.060	.119
	.683	.747	.906	.643	−.011	−.000	−.001	.802	.468	.672	.391
Education	.086	−.053	−.005	−.039	−.047	.069	.080	−.004	−.002	−.001	−.000
and Labor	−.019	−.022	−.022	−.045	.069	.174	.056	−.054	−.037	−.025	−.054
	−.040	−.011	.085	.191	.514	.058	−.030	−.037	−.052	.139	.193
Energy and	.546	.913	.256	.084	.278	.213	.777	.467	.607	.710	.677
Commerce	.966	.861	.565	.360	.298	.374	.671	.507	.304	.486	.649
	.380	.505	.402	.968	.631	.563	.794	.623	.681	.996	.986
Foreign Affairs	−.047	−.009	−.039	.321	.381	−.002	−.052	−.003	−.025	−.003	−.014
	−.056	−.011	−.046	.339	.200	−.052	.173	.638	.646	.227	.162
	.413	.394	.411	−.002	.159	.431	.157	−.035	.168	.967	.938
Government	.339	.771	.647	.703	.734	.587	.139	.079	−.014	−.017	−.023
Operations	.522	.199	.655	.433	.099	−.026	.096	.331	.306	.371	.812
	+.001	.186	.901	.601	.692	.738	.176	.076	.122	−.030	.416
House	.193	.108	.092	.112	.286	.422	.570	.914	.857	.844	.302
Administration	.649	.765	.750	.869	.398	.647	.225	.675	.971	.776	.228
	.253	.439	.832	.632	.510	.561	.189	.777	.295	.909	.389

Table 9.2 *(continued)*

Committee	House										
	100	99	98	97	96	95	94	93	92	91	90
Interior	.248	.516	.164	.695	.867	.181	.130	.421	.822	.975	.180
	.162	.149	.159	.332	.211	.397	.815	.572	.951	.768	.659
	.058	.160	.118	.271	.820	.359	.521	.788	.802	.586	.533
Internal Security								.423	.057	.682	+.035
								.298	.821	.181	.063
								.398	+.012	+.030	+.033
Judiciary	.282	.285	.301	.571	.501	.395	.375	.316	.172	.267	.358
	.507	.278	−.021	.464	−.012	.136	−.033	−.004	−.019	.106	.593
	.174	.134	.120	.312	.371	.665	.753	.333	.158	−.025	.138
MerchantMarine	.264	.199	.797	.859	.744	.947	.757	.479	.889	.699	.777
and Fisheries	.062	.122	.127	.078	.861	.947	.665	.935	.539	.664	.369
	.427	.227	−.015	−.016	.097	−.055	−.007	−.001	−.001	−.010	.123
Post Office	−.041	−.052	−.042	−.024	.371	−.025	.164	.810	.476	.121	.075
	.384	.115	.169	−.050	.463	.193	.143	.217	.973	.411	.282
	.069	.504	.268	.535	.828	.249	+.027	.356	.123	.819	.717
Public Works and	.806	.925	.745	.445	.076	.080	.101	.584	.160	.451	.802
and Transportation	.356	.615	.899	.477	+.020	.072	.739	.904	.972	.566	.533
	.314	.480	.608	.435	.371	.280	.343	.200	.493	.519	.480
Rules	.155	.066	.120	.101	.170	.319	.532	.135	.123	.154	.129
	.809	.380	.410	.354	.296	.306	.394	.561	.684	.705	.499
	.788	.553	.288	.160	.142	.072	.108	.099	.121	.146	.114
Science, Space,	.795	.979	.794	.389	.941	.269	.671	.956	.943	.777	.833
and Technology	.629	.241	.350	.524	.179	.094	.806	+.012	.727	.626	.725
	.252	.749	.907	.704	.950	.617	.161	.656	.115	.169	.404
Small Business	.596	.859	.536	.996	.730	.572	.603				
	.082	.147	.088	.891	.536	.357	.995				
	.202	.338	.496	.153	−.009	−.015	−.022				
Standards of	.509	.448	.304	.712	.775	.351	+.017	+.029	.181	.176	.290
Official Conduct	.207	.211	.101	.734	.354	+.013	+.001	.082	+.053	.072	.318
	.910	.349	.969	.697	.193	.476	.383	.168	.197	.235	.418
Veterans Affairs	.391	.331	.433	+.020	+.000	+.007	.243	.320	.278	.252	.760
	+.043	+.047	.131	+.000	+.003	+.002	.829	.095	.442	+.032	+.008
	.210	.182	.340	.924	.784	.900	.562	.175	.755	.648	.135
Ways and Means	.937	.806	.804	.554	.458	.862	.838	.587	.780	.495	.282
	.252	.486	.200	.394	.679	.568	.785	.703	.966	.969	.695
	.830	.732	.951	.972	.646	.468	.137	.490	.618	.513	.326
Number of Committees That Are Preference Outliers											
5% All	5	6	6	5	3	5	3	6	3	4	4
5% Dem.	4	6	6	6	6	6	5	6	5	6	5
5% Rep.	2	2	1	2	2	5	5	4	3	4	1
10% All	6	7	7	7	4	7	5	8	5	4	6
10% Dem.	7	7	8	7	8	8	7	9	6	7	6
10% Rep.	4	2	2	2	3	7	5	6	4	4	1

[a]Blank entries occur when a committee did not exist.

Table 9.2   *(continued)*

	House									
	89	88	87	86	85	84	83	82	81	80
All	.000	.000	.000	.001	.098	.164	.089	.378	.079	.026
	.015	.000	.018	.044	.031	.009	.009	.154	.249	.004
	.073	.001	.001	.006	.400	.536	.032	.168	.487	.159
Agriculture	+006	.090	.087	.065	.232	.492	+.013	.870	.718	+.008
	.117	.074	+.036	+.019	.075	.135	+.038	+.031	+.022	.333
	.233	.222	.286	.973	.194	.283	.329	.669	.922	.710
Appropriations	.838	.717	.813	.117	.725	.366	.062	.181	.962	.154
	+.052	.332	.151	+.050	.145	.849	.176	.714	.412	.899
	+.027	+.055	+.031	+.026	.284	.912	+.010	.276	.775	.548
Armed Services	.133	.602	.561	.292	.690	.424	.777	.680	.663	.851
	+.030	+.041	.094	.169	.182	.303	.128	.327	.117	.174
	.729	.549	.266	.421	.348	.182	.739	.950	.911	.981
Banking, Finance,	.169	−.004	−.001	−.009	−.002	−.049	.108	−.009	−.006	.073
and Urban Affairs	.172	.182	−.032	.059	.058	−.014	−.016	.289	.264	.305
	.301	.633	.862	.237	.534	.461	.564	.580	.734	.683
Budget										
District of Columbia	+.032	.221	.270	+.045	.205	.173	.785	.645	.112	.210
	.905	+.000	−.001	+.048	+.006	+.001	.260	.138	.124	.074
	.564	.187	.251	.274	.169	.117	.124	.141	.767	.836
Education and Labor	−.029	−.000	−.001	−.001	−.017	−.001	.535	.634	.287	.260
	−.020	−.019	−.036	−.017	.088	.058	.146	.787	.161	−.019
	.533	.729	.492	.952	.673	.365	.699	.057	.520	.259
Energy and Commerce	+.039	.636	.553	.168	.893	.652	.548	.902	.626	.278
	.950	.195	.178	.084	.623	.861	.792	.919	.231	.964
	.774	.206	.239	.837	.856	.355	.573	.421	−.025	.225
Foreign Affairs	.204	.546	.076	.062	.085	.338	.357	−.041	.495	−.009
	.134	.279	.196	.056	.707	.757	.372	.113	.272	−.006
	.561	.516	−.026	.440	.882	.621	.275	.074	.087	.203
Government	.383	−.040	.134	.407	.677	.190	.515	.121	−.035	.394
Operations	.944	.862	.625	.599	.187	−.027	−.001	.108	.072	.306
	.539	−.040	.514	.622	.086	.317	.955	.687	.638	.715
House	.237	.422	.761	.227	.963	.899	.571	.840	.357	+.030
Administration	.607	.392	.638	.399	.643	.971	.515	.535	.983	+.010
	.941	.655	.270	.915	.972	.527	.988	.936	.831	.598
Interior	.893	.133	.226	.766	.918	.834	.136	.517	.793	.913
	.369	.589	.983	.785	.476	.244	.405	.901	.288	.644
	.758	.351	.950	.765	.313	.551	.564	+.036	.578	.845
Internal Security	+.005	+.000	+.028	+.007	.253	.240	.158	.156	.134	.740
	+.044	+.007	.359	.392	.621	.640	.980	.841	.590	.168
	.060	+.001	+.002	+.010	.435	.161	.107	.569	.791	.488
Judiciary	.296	.638	.973	.696	.666	.870	.159	.637	.969	.798
	.987	.994	.703	.540	.813	.858	.743	.699	.313	.388
	.412	.909	.773	.922	.547	.193	.320	.404	.191	.300

Table 9.2   *(continued)*

	House									
	89	88	87	86	85	84	83	82	81	80
Merchant Marine	.933	.829	.944	.506	.518	.146	.306	.343	.801	.449
and Fisheries	.818	.923	.705	.938	.453	.071	.207	.057	.367	.076
	.093	−.020	−.055	−.024	−.023	.625	.076	.748	.235	.224
Post Office	.296	.464	.435	.987	.677	.295	.706	.638	.198	.539
	.313	.746	.214	.918	.994	.776	.538	.445	.609	.995
	.969	.944	.758	.722	.476	.282	.209	.418	.087	.216
Public Works and	.703	.139	.059	.276	.318	.095	.126	.293	.560	.538
Transportation	.459	.707	.882	.686	.208	.180	.639	.767	.977	.341
	.964	.302	.653	.430	.762	.512	.535	.601	.323	.403
Rules	.736	.096	.082	.788	.354	.621	.221	.999	.319	.136
	.527	.699	.644	.819	.644	.552	+.047	.818	.495	.270
	.100	.096	+.039	.102	.297	.432	.794	.457	.444	+.032
Science, Space,	.331	.755	.551	.962						
and Technology	.790	.368	.424	.406						
	−.045	−.029	.097	.107						
Small Business										
Standards of										
Official Conduct										
Veterans Affairs	.082	.676	.923	.971	.692	.582	.982	.625	.743	.263
	+.004	+.004	+.045	.347	.212	.984	.176	+.006	.629	.903
	.082	.068	−.044	−.033	.248	.697	−.000	.090	.411	.111
Ways and Means	.761	.226	.165	.540	.107	.236	.656	.077	.252	+.054
	.923	.334	.672	−.019	−.014	−.007	.258	.209	.507	.721
	.161	.122	.092	.048	.260	.430	.155	+.032	+.023	+.020
Number of Committees That Are Preference Outliers										
5% All	5	4	3	4	2	2	1	2	2	4
5% Dem.	5	5	5	4	2	4	4	2	1	3
5% Rep.	2	5	6	5	1	0	2	2	2	2
10% All	6	6	7	6	3	3	2	3	2	5
10% Dem.	5	6	6	8	5	6	4	3	2	5
10% Rep.	5	7	8	6	2	0	3	5	4	2

tingents on the committee have medians very close to the overall medians of their parties—the reason is that the committee median is typically determined by the moderate tail of the distribution of the majority party in the committee. Even if the median Democrat on the committee is close to the party median, a conservative Democrat could represent the committee median. Consequently, the committee as a whole could be an outlier, but the two party committee medians could be representative of the respective parties. An example of this is the Agriculture Committee in the 80th and 89th Houses.

Similarly, a party contingent can be an outlier in relation to the overall party median, and the overall committee median can still be quite close to the chamber median. Again, the Agriculture Committee provides the example—in 14 of the 21 Congresses shown in table 9.2, the Democratic contingent on the committee was a conservative outlier, but the overall committee was not.

Are Committees Preference Outliers?

Having set forth our methodology, we now focus on the central question of this chapter: Are committees preference outliers? We define an outlier committee as one where the median member's position is sufficiently far to the left or the right that it would have been produced by a random-assignment process less than 1 time in 20. In other words, the committee median has a p value of less than 0.05.

Figure 9.1 shows the proportion of outlier *committees* for the House and the Senate, for Congresses 1 to 100.[12] In the House, there is a clear change in the proportion of outlier committees after the passage of the Legislative Reform Act in 1946. Before the 80th House (1947–48), the proportion of outliers oscillates around 5 percent, rarely exceeds 10 percent of the committees, and never goes over 15 percent. In 35 of the first 79 Houses and in 22 of the first 79 Senates, fewer than one-twentieth of the committees—the fraction expected from pure chance—are significant outliers.

After the reforms of 1946, which cut the number of committees from 47 to 19 in the House, the proportion of outliers begins to rise to around 20 percent. In the Senate, the proportion of outlier committees appears to increase after the passage of the 17th Amendment, in 1913, which mandated the popular election of senators (the 64th Senate was the first to be affected by the amendment); nevertheless, the increase is not very large, and there is no coherent pattern after the 80th Congress, which there is in the House. (The reforms of 1946 cut the number of Senate committees from 33 to 15.)

Figure 9.2 shows the proportion of outlier *party contingents* for the twentieth-century Houses. The change (after 1946) in the proportion of outlier committees that is shown in figure 9.1 appears to be a result of a dramatic shift toward less representative committee contingents among the Democrats after the 83rd House. Table 9.2 shows the Democratic outliers to be concentrated primarily in four committees: Agriculture, Armed Services, and Veterans' Affairs are conservative outliers, whereas Education and Labor is a liberal outlier. In addition, the District of Columbia contingent tends to be a liberal outlier after the 93rd House.

If self-selection along the lines suggested by Shepsle (1978) is taking place, then this implies that the party contingents should be biased in the same direction over time. Table 9.2 suggests this is the case. Note, for example, that the Agriculture Committee's Democratic contingent has a significant conservative bias in 16 of the 21 Congresses and never has a significant liberal bias. To better measure this form of bias, we count the number of committee party contingents that are same-direction outliers in the current and previous Houses and Senates.[13] Figure 9.3 shows the proportion of these consistent-bias committees over time. The difference between the House and Senate is striking. The Senate shows no pattern, but the House clearly changed in the 1950s. What is interesting about these results for the House is that they run counter to the expected consequence of a reduction in the number of committees after 1946. The larger the number of committees, the greater the opportunity for self-selection; with fewer committees, the committees must be larger and more representative of the chamber. Therefore, the proportion of consistently biased committees

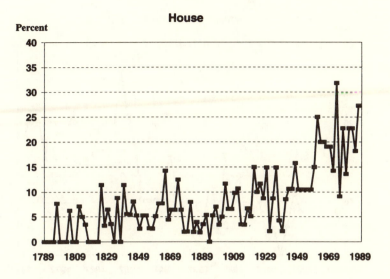

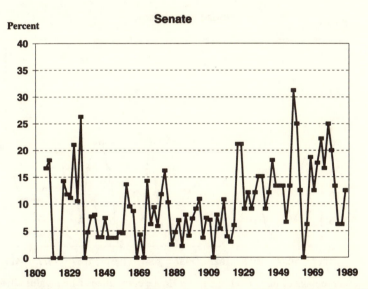

Figure 9.1. Percentage of committees with *p* values less than 0.05 for testing the null hypothesis that the committee members are randomly assigned from the floor membership (1789–1988). By chance, 5 percent of the committees should have *p* values less than 0.05. The Senate has never witnessed a prolonged period where committees are systematically not representative of the floor. About 20 percent of the committees in the House were not representative in the period beginning with the 85th House (1957–58).

should be higher before the 80th House than after it if self-selection were taking place in both periods. It is not higher.

As a check on these results, we compared *p* values, controlling for committee size over time by performing simple linear regressions of committee size on the corresponding *p* value. We tried a variety of specifications using committee size, the

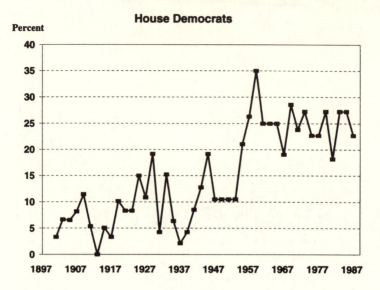

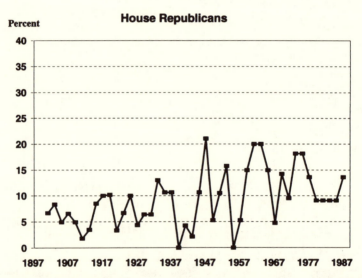

Figure 9.2. Percentage of party contingents on House committees with p values below 0.05 for testing the null hypothesis that the delegation is randomly assigned from party members on the floor (1901–1988). By chance, 5 percent of the delegations should have p values below 0.05. The figure shows that the outlier committees in the House, after 1956, resulted from the Democrats' delegations being nonrepresentative. Republican delegations were always largely representative of the party.

square of committee size, and time as independent variables and found nothing of consequence. Separate regressions for the first 79 Houses, Houses 80 to 100, and all Houses were performed for the entire committee and for majority- and minority-party contingents. In no specification were the coefficients on committee size statistically significant.

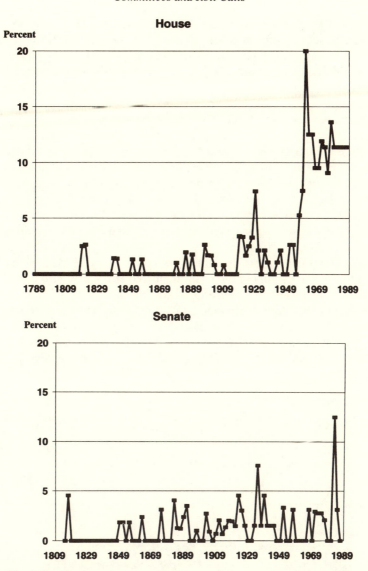

Figure 9.3. Consistent bias in committees. This shows the percentage of committees that had *p* values less than 0.05 in a particular Congress and in the preceding Congress, and that were biased in the same direction in both Congresses (conservative in both or liberal in both). The Senate shows no periods where bias persists. About 12 percent of House committees are consistently biased, but again, only starting in 1957–58.

To check whether or not the dramatic change in our *overall p* values for the entire committee system that occurred after the 80th Congress was affected by the majority- and minority-party ratios, we formed random committees in the same way that we did for the *FULL* model, except that we first randomized the D-NOMINATE coordinates across all members. In effect, we used $(D + R)!$ as a sample space. This experiment produced results very similar to those produced by the *FULL* model for the overall committee medians. The reason is that the average majority- and minority-party ratios on committees have tracked the actual party ratios fairly closely throughout the twentieth century.

In sum, the changes shown in figures 9.1, 9.2, and 9.3 are not due to changes in the size of committees or party ratios. Other explanations have to be found.

Do Committee Members Have Common Interests?

Self-selection implies that committee members have a greater stake in their committee's success on the floor than do legislators who are not on the committee. Presumably, if self-selection is at work, then the members of a committee have a set of common interests that, at times, may overpower their party affiliation. When a committee bill is on the floor, these common interests suggest that the minority-party contingent will vote with the majority-party contingent more often than they would if they were not members of the committee.

We tested this proposition with data collected by Cox and McCubbins (1993) on the committee origin of bills in the even-numbered Houses 82 through 98. For each committee, we computed an agreement score—much like the *Congressional Quarterly* party-support or conservative-coalition-support scores—to determine whether members voted with the committee majority, using all committee-related roll calls. We then aggregated the scores across committees for committee members and nonmembers. Figure 9.4 shows the difference between these aggregated agreement

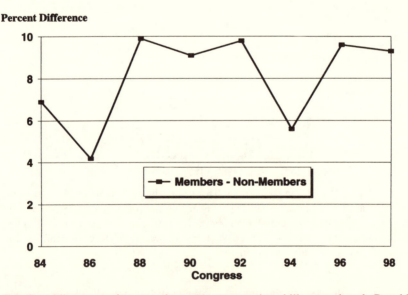

Figure 9.4. Republican committee members support committee bills more than do Republican nonmembers. This figure shows the difference between the percentage of committee members who support committee bills and the percentage of nonmembers who support. The data are aggregated across all committees and bills coded by Cox and McCubbins (1993). They coded roll calls, by committee origin, only for even-numbered Congresses from the 84th through the 98th.

scores for the Republicans (always the minority party in the House) over the course of the eight even-numbered Congresses.

The agreement-score results provide striking evidence supporting the hypothesis that legislators with common interests choose committee assignments that reflect these interests. Republicans on a committee vote with a majority of committee Democrats on 8 percent more of the roll calls than do Republicans who are not committee members. As a benchmark, this 8 percent figure can be compared to the fact that Democratic committee members vote with a majority of committee Democrats on 10 percent more of the roll calls than do Democrats who are not committee members. This discrepancy is not surprising since the committee majority shapes bills within the committee's jurisdiction. What is surprising is that the pull on minority members, relative to other members of their party, is nearly as great.

An alternative test of committee behavior comes from looking at the D-NOMINATE classification errors. In the spatial model, if self-selection is at work, then the Republicans should be making more voting "errors" because of their defections—that is, the Republican committee members are occasionally voting contrary to their basic beliefs but in favor of their constituents' interests. Put somewhat differently, the cutting line on roll calls will tend to divide Democrats and Republicans. If Republican committee members support the committee position, they will be making errors with respect to the spatial model. On the other hand, if Democratic committee members support the committee position, they will typically be voting correctly. Figure 9.5 shows the difference between the correct classifications of the committee members and of the noncommittee members, by party, for the committee-related roll calls.[14]

On average, the Republican committee members are making about 2 percent more voting "errors" than the noncommittee Republicans. For the Democrats, the situation is reversed. The committee Democrats make about 1 percent fewer errors than the noncommittee Democrats on committee-related roll calls. This is most likely an information effect. Committee members have more information than noncommittee members and, therefore, can more accurately map the outcome of the committee-related roll call into their basic beliefs. Checking these findings for earlier periods of history, for which we do not have information on the committee origin of bills, can be done indirectly because if there was a change in behavior after the 80th House, then it should be detectable in the classification results for *all* roll calls when we control for the majority-versus-minority-party factor.

The upper panel of figure 9.6 shows the difference between the majority-party and minority-party classification successes for the House for all Congresses. The period after the 80th House stands out clearly. In the constituency-service era (Cain, Ferejohn, and Fiorina, 1987; Fiorina, 1989; Alford and Brady, 1993), all 21 of the Houses from 80 to 100 show a positive difference between the majority- and minority-party classification results. The minority party exhibits more spatial voting errors, arguably because constituency interests force legislator defections to support majority-sponsored bills. Before the 80th, 60 of the 79 Houses showed either no difference or, in most cases, negative differences due to the fact that the minority party members were more cohesive—they voted together more often as a bloc ("we either hang together or hang separately")—than did the majority party. This fact is displayed in the lower panel of figure 9.6, which shows the difference between the majority- and minority-

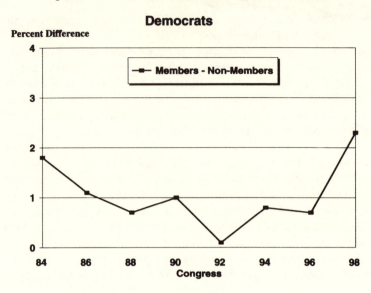

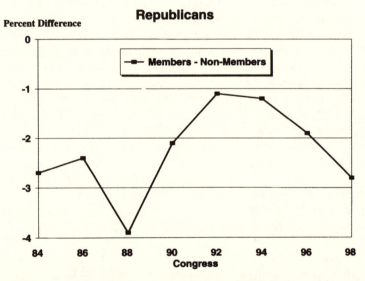

Figure 9.5. Difference in classification success for committee members and nonmembers on committee bills. Classifications are from the D-NOMINATE two-dimensional model with a linear trend. Democrats on committees always vote more in accord with the spatial model on their own bills than do nonmembers. The reverse is true for Republican committee members, who tend to become classification errors by supporting the committee position. The data are aggregated across all committees and bills coded by Cox and McCubbins (1993). They coded roll calls, by committee origin, only for even-numbered Congresses from the 84th through the 98th.

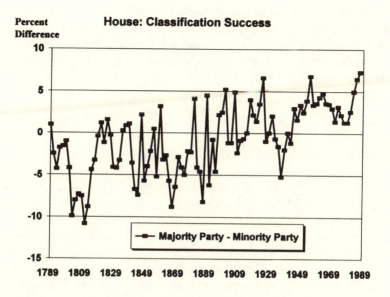

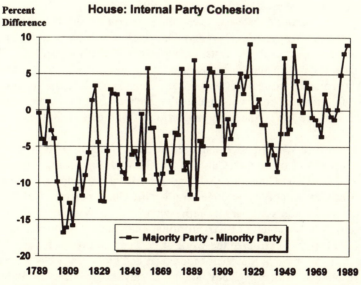

Figure 9.6. Majority and minority parties compared on classification success and cohesion. The top portion shows the difference between the percentage of decisions correctly classified by D-NOMINATE for the majority party and the minority party. The minority party is, typically, better classified before 1946, but subsequently the majority party is better classified. The bottom portion shows differences in cohesion—the percentage of party membership that votes with the party majority on a roll call. In the first 50 Congresses, the minority party was frequently far more cohesive than the majority party. In the next 50 Congresses, the minority was relatively less cohesive, particularly after 1946.

cohesion scores.[15] Until approximately the 80th Congress, the cohesion graph shows that the minority party is typically more cohesive than the majority. In the modern period, this distinction is muted. Correspondingly, the correlation between the classification difference and the cohesion difference for Houses 1 to 79 is 0.89, whereas the correlation for Houses 80 to 100 is only 0.63.

Summary

Something changed fundamnetally in House committees after the Legislative Reform Act of 1946. It is not clear that the change was due to the Reform Act—indeed, as we noted above, if self-selection existed before the reforms, there should have been more outliers as a proportion before the 80th Congress than after it. The Republicans controlled the House in the 80th and 83rd Congresses, and figures 9.1 to 9.3 show that the change occurred approximately between the 85th and 86th Houses (during Eisenhower's second term), very early in the 40-year period of uninterrupted Democratic-party control of the House. The timing of the change closely coincides with the increase in constituency-service representation in the House of Representatives and with the emergence of a seemingly permanently divided government in the United States (Fiorina, 1992; Alesina and Rosenthal, 1995).

The committee-outlier debate has been concerned only with the House committee system during and after the 80th Congress. Our findings for this period generally support the view that the committee system is representative of the chamber. This is certainly the case for the Senate; in the House, the proportion of outlier committees is small. If a reasonably stringent definition of *outlier* is used—namely, looking at the proportion of committee party contingents that are biased in the same direction, from one Congress to the next—then the proportion of outlier committees is further reduced.

In the post–World War II period, our evidence is consistent with the party-support model developed by Cox and McCubbins (1993). With the notable exception of the House Veterans' Affairs Committee's Democrats, all of the committees that they define as "uniform externality committees" reflect the whole party. Since committees as well as party contingents are largely representative, the evidence is also consistent with Gilligan and Krehbiel's (1990) informational theory. However, Shepsle and Weingast (1994, p. 175) criticize the work of Gilligan and Krehbiel and that of Cox and McCubbins by arguing that their theoretical and empirical work rests on the assumption of unidimensionality. They attempt to salvage the Structure Induced Equilibrium view of congressional committees by arguing for the need of "a comprehensive, spatially organized theory in many dimensions."

The many-dimensions view of the world fails, as we have shown earlier, to be at all helpful in understanding roll call voting decisions. If preference outliers are of great importance, they should be present among the dimensions that organize roll call voting. That they are not is bad news for the view that committees exist to solve equilibrium problems with majority voting. The many-dimensions view can, however, lay claim to some role, given our findings that minority-party committee members tend to support the committee's position and to make spatial voting errors in doing so. But since this finding pertains only to the post-1946 period, the findings provide more evidence of strengthened "electoral connections" (Mayhew, 1974) than of the fundamentals of legislative committees. The fundamentals seem to be that committees are tools of the majority party (Cox and McCubbins, 1993) and that the tools are used to develop information (Gilligan and Krehbiel, 1990).

10
Abstention from Roll Call Voting

In previous chapters, we have shown that, throughout nearly all of the history of the United States, the bulk of individual congressional roll call voting decisions can be accounted for by a low-dimensional spatial model. In this chapter, we analyze the decision to *abstain* rather than choosing between Yea and Nay—that is, equivalently, we study turnout in congressional roll call voting.

A framework for our analysis is provided by the theory of rational abstention. The theory suggests several hypotheses:

- Turnout should be inversely related to the degree of indifference, as measured by spatial utilities (see chapter 2 and appendix A) computed from D-NOMINATE coordinates.
- Turnout should be higher when preferences on a roll call are evenly divided rather than being lopsided.
- Turnout should decrease as the cost of voting increases.
- Turnout should be higher on the minority side of an issue than on the "silent" majority side.
- Turnout should decrease as the number of members of the legislative body increases.[1]

Even though we were aware that the abstention data had the potential to substantially enrich our analysis, we ignored information on abstentions in the development of D-NOMINATE. We did this, in part, as a way of simplifying the construction of the scaling algorithm and, in part, because, particularly in the modern period, when abstention is quite low (see figure 10.1), considering abstention would have little effect on our estimates of the ideal points of the legislators or of the locations of the roll call alternatives.[2] If we have, with D-NOMINATE, indeed succeeded in capturing the *preferences* of the legislators on each roll call vote, we can use the D-NOMINATE results to test the hypotheses mentioned above.

In this chapter, we summarize the predictions of the abstention theory we seek to test and discuss the variables we use to measure indifference, cost, and closeness. We then specify a logit model that is used for hypothesis testing; and, finally, we present the empirical results.

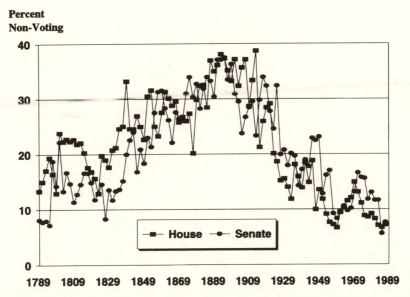

Figure 10.1. Nonvoting in Congress (1789–1988). The percentage abstaining is the percentage of members absent or present but not voting, and announced, on all roll calls with over 2.5 percent in the minority.

Tests of the Theory of Abstention

Congressional roll calls are similar to two-candidate elections in that they are choices between two alternatives. For this case, the decision-theoretic model is expressed in the following well-known equation (Downs, 1957; Riker and Ordeshook, 1968):

$$R = PB - C + D$$

In this equation, R is the net reward from voting. It equals the *instrumental* benefit of voting, PB, minus the fixed costs, C (such as the opportunity cost of the time spent in voting), plus the fixed benefits, D (such as a sense of a citizen's duty). The instrumental benefit is simply the voter's utility gain if the side he or she favors wins, B, multiplied by the subjective probability, P, that the voter assigns to his or her chances of casting the decisive vote.

If, without loss of generality, the utility of abstention is set at zero, then voting takes place if and only if the reward is positive or $R > 0$. It is common to focus only on the net fixed cost, $c = C - D$. We thus obtain:

Vote if and only if $R = PB - c > 0$

Testing the decision-theoretic model requires measuring P, B, and c. The easiest part is the B term, because the maintained hypothesis of the D-NOMINATE model is that $E(B)$, the expected value of B, is the absolute value of the difference in the utility of the Yea and Nay outcomes:

$$E(B) = |\Delta U|$$

where $\Delta U = U(\text{Yea}) - U(\text{Nay})$

We will, therefore, estimate B by using the spatial utilities calculated from the D-NOMINATE model.[3] The term P is difficult to measure, especially because subjective probabilities may depart sharply from objective probabilities (Tversky and Khaneman, 1974). There are at least three ways to compute P empirically. First, we could view P as a decreasing function of the actual margin on the roll call.[4] Second, we could view P as a decreasing function of the margin if everyone had voted as predicted by the D-NOMINATE estimates. Third, we could view P as a decreasing function of the expected margin implied by the probability of a Yea vote the model assigns to each legislator. In the second and third approaches, one could or could not include abstainers in the computation. We have chosen the first method for simplicity. We suspect that all alternative measures would be strongly correlated with the actual margin.

The cost variable, c, is also difficult to measure. Maintaining a good overall turnout record on roll calls may benefit one's reputation among constituents, but the value of the benefit may vary across individual legislators and over time. Similarly, the cost of being present in Washington may vary over time and cross-sectionally, particularly because different members have different travel times from Washington to their constituencies.

The direct cost of travel should be closely approximated by using the distance to the constituency. As an independent variable in our analysis of the House, we used *LNDIS,* the natural logarithm for the distance from the congressional district to Washington.[5] The relationship of *LNDIS* to both turnout and travel time is an ambiguous one. If each member were to spend the same number of days in the district, more distant members would miss more votes since they, particularly in the era prior to air travel, would spend more time in transit. However, for the more distant districts, the travel times might be prohibitive, in which case the more distant members would miss fewer votes. Consequently, we use *LNDIS* only to explore whether *LNDIS* influences the level of turnout.

The theoretical ambiguity of a distance measure illustrates how difficult it is to measure cost. Nonetheless, it is important to control for variations in cost in order to assess the effect of the P and B terms in the voting calculus. A good indicator of the value of c is provided by a legislator's prior turnout record. We use two indicators: The variable *ABSPREV* equals 1 if the legislator abstained on the previous roll call and equals 0 if the legislator voted; and the variable *ABSAVG* is the fraction of times the legislator abstained on the 2nd through 26th preceding roll calls.[6] (When these variables are used, our analysis will be confined to the 27th roll call, and later ones, of each Congress.)

These two *ABS* variables will pick up costs induced by illness or trips to the constituency. They are also a potential way of proxying for the effects of other roll calls. As we do throughout most of this book, we make the simplifying assumption that decisions on successive roll calls are independent ones.[7] If, in contrast, a legislator decided to be present for a critical vote on a trade treaty, the legislator would find it cheaper to be present for other roll calls on the same day. This type of interdependence would be picked up by our two *ABS* variables. But in a detailed examination of the context surrounding each roll call vote on railroad regulation in the 49th Congress (Poole and Rosenthal, 1994a), we did not find any evidence of important effects on turnout and choice that could be traced to the types and the substance of preceding roll calls. This result leads us to conjecture that *ABSAVG* and *ABSPREV* are mainly picking up long-term costs that are not strongly related to the roll call agenda. Nonetheless, the impact of the agenda merits further investigation because railroad-regulation bills in the 49th Congress are but a small slice of the historical record.

In addition to the costs that are captured by the legislator's prior record of absenteeism, other costs may arise for legislators who know they will not be present in the next Congress. Some of those who will not return for the next Congress may be abstaining because they have decided to retire or to pursue another career or higher office. These legislators, particularly those leaving politics, find voting relatively costly, as they no longer have an incentive to present their electorate with a good attendance record. They can thus shirk their duty by not voting.[8] Of course, causality may run the other way. A poor voting record may result in an involuntary exit through an electoral defeat. We can control for the direction of causality by considering only roll calls that occurred after elections for the next Congress. Postelection roll calls always took place in Congresses before the 74th. The traditional lame-duck sessions generally ran in the first three months of the years following elections. With the passage of the 20th Amendment—beginning in the 74th Congress—lame-duck sessions have been rare, occurring in only 8 special sessions in Congresses 74 to 100. In all postelection sessions, costs should be similar for those who had been defeated and those who had retired.

From the basic decision-theoretic equation for the reward for voting, we can make the following four predictions, other things being equal:

1. As net fixed costs decrease, turnout should increase. Abstentions should be positively related to both *ABSAVG* and *ABSPREV.*
2. As the perceived probability of casting a decisive vote increases, turnout should increase. Abstentions should be negatively related to the variables measuring *P.*
3. As the fixed benefits increase, turnout should increase. Abstentions should be negatively related to *B.*
4. As the expected instrumental benefit from voting increases, turnout should increase. Abstentions should be negatively related to *PB.*

Additional predictions result from considering the game-theoretic approach to abstention. In this approach, the decision-theoretic model is embedded in a voting game where the legislators interact strategically. The level of turnout in an equilibrium of the game reflects two forces. One force arises because legislators with Yea preferences compete for a victory with those with Nay preferences. This competitive force, which is increasing in *B* but decreasing in *c,* results in positive turnout. The second force is free riding. Legislators with, say, a Yea preference have an incentive to abstain, as they can free ride on the votes of others with a Yea preference. The interplay between the forces of competition and free riding leads to the endogenous determination of *P.* That is, in the game-theoretic approach, actual probabilities and subjective probabilities of casting the decisive vote must be equal.

The actual probability that a given voter will cast a decisive vote depends on the distribution of benefits, *B,* and of costs, *c,* across the set of legislators. If a substantial number of legislators with negative net costs prefer one roll call outcome and a smaller number prefer the other, the outcome will be lopsided if only members with negative net costs vote. Thus, there can be an equilibrium where no one with positive costs votes, with $P = 0$.

There can also be equilibria where those with positive and negative net fixed costs vote. But in this case, the expected outcome must be close to a tie. If it were not, one of the positive-cost voters would want to abstain. For the outcome to be close to a tie, the expected turnout among those who represent the majority preference must be lower than the expected turnout among those who represent the minority. That is, there must be a relatively silent majority (Palfrey and Rosenthal, 1983). This leads to a fifth prediction:

5. Turnout among those representing the majority's preferred position on a roll call should be lower than among those representing the minority's preferred position.[9]

This prediction needs to be modified because of the constitutional quorum requirement that legislation can be passed only if a majority of the membership is present.[10] The strategic aspects of the quorum requirement have been largely ignored in formal models of rational abstention. If the minority side expects that less than 50 percent of the membership will be present to vote for the majority position, the minority has an incentive to be absent if the minority supports the status quo.[11] That is, when turnout is very low, abstentions may be disproportionately drawn from those on the minority side. This quorum effect is likely to have been most pronounced in the late nineteenth century, when overall turnout levels were low. For example, in the 52nd House, no quorum was present for 34 of the 304 recorded roll calls. Most of these had lopsided majorities, suggesting strategic abstention by the minority. (We take this strategic element into account in our empirical work below.)

The game-theoretic model also predicts (Palfrey and Rosenthal, 1985) that, other things being equal, turnout (as a percentage of the membership) will decline as the size of the legislature increases. This is because P tends toward zero as size increases. Thus, we make two further predictions:

6. At any given point in time, abstention will be greater in the House than in the Senate.
7. As the size of either the House or Senate increases, other things being equal, abstention increases.

Strictly speaking, the game-theoretic model does not account for the data. Because the average majority throughout American history has been around 63 percent of the vote cast, it is hard to believe that a tie is expected on all votes. On most roll calls, only those with negative net costs should be voting. Nonetheless, the game-theory prediction that majorities will be silent is worth investigating.

An alternative theory of abstention has been developed by Cohen and Noll (1991). They observe that "on virtually all roll call votes, the outcome is virtually certain and winning margins are very large. . . . High rates of voting combined with virtually certain outcomes are at odds with a naive instrumental theory of voting."[12] In their model, the behavior of legislators is driven by the reelection motive rather than by a consideration of playing a pivotal role on any one roll call. Legislators view voting as costly because the time spent voting could be used in providing constituency services, raising campaign money, and so on.

The predictions of the Cohen and Noll model differ from those of the rational-turnout model for several important reasons: (1) roll calls vary in salience to constituents; (2) some constituencies have conflicts, in that some constituents are pro, while others are anti, on an issue; and (3) constituents weigh *legislative* losses more heavily than legislative victories. This last feature of their model demands voter behavior that is not always consistent with findings of other studies (such as Wilson, 1980), which argue that constituents have a different concern—specifically, they care more about utility *losses* than utility gains. If the loss/gain view were true, we might find constituents weighing a victory on a motion that protected them from losses (for example, on a motion blocking the closing of a military base) more heavily than a defeat on a motion that promised gains (a new military base). In any event, as we are unable to measure constituency conflict and salience for all issues in American history, we will confine our analysis to predictions from the rational-abstention model.

In the next section, we test the seven predictions stated above. In doing so, we must exercise great caution because a number of institutional factors are at odds with the underlying assumption that each roll call outcome depends on simple majority rule. First, supermajorities are important on some roll calls, including those that involve veto overrides, constitutional amendments, discharge petitions in the House, and filibuster clotures in the Senate. Because votes of this type are a relatively small proportion of the total, we chose, in view of the effort required to screen such votes, to ignore the problem of supermajorities.[13] Second, on occasion, abstention was used strategically—for example, to block the quorum needed for the majority vote to be valid. (We address this problem later.) Third, ICPSR data records announced votes for recent Congresses but not for earlier ones. The issue of announced votes poses a comparability problem in defining the dependent variable, abstention. Although we used announced votes in the scaling, including them as votes in this chapter would distort intertemporal comparisons. Consequently, we define votes as actual individual votes and pairs. Those absent, those present but not voting, and announced voters are treated as abstainers.

A Framework for Empirical Tests

Our first and third predictions (stated earlier) are that turnout should increase as net fixed costs, represented by *ABSAVG* and *ABSPREV,* decrease; and that turnout should increase as the estimated utility difference $E(B) = |\Delta U|$ increases. To test these two predictions in a single framework, for each roll call, we estimated vote probabilities with a trichotomous logit model—the three probabilities were Yea (a Yea vote or a paired Yea); Nay (a Nay vote or a paired Nay); or an abstention (absent, present but not voting, or announced).[14] These probabilities can be viewed as reflecting the comparison of three utilities. Without loss of generality, one can express the utility of abstention simply as zero plus an error term:

$$UA = \text{utility of abstaining} = 0 + \text{error}_{\text{ABSTAIN}}$$

For Yea votes to become more likely as the utility difference increases, and less likely when the cost variables increase, we specify the Yea *differential* utility (relative to abstentions and Nays) as:

$$UY = \beta_{0y} + \beta_{1y}\Delta U + \beta_{2y}ABSPREV + \beta_{3y}ABSAVG + \text{error}_{YEA}$$

Our predictions tell us that we expect $\beta_{1y} > 0$; $\beta_{2y} < 0$; $\beta_{3y} < 0$. The expression for the Nay choice is directly parallel to that for the Yea choice:

$$UN = \beta_{0n} + \beta_{1n}\Delta U + \beta_{2n}ABSPREV + \beta_{3n}ABSAVG + \text{error}_{NAY}.$$

Here, our predictions tell us that we expect $\beta_{1n} < 0$; $\beta_{2n} < 0$; $\beta_{3n} < 0$. Moreover, ignoring, for the time being, the strategic aspects of silent majorities, the symmetry of the spatial model implies that $\beta_{1y} = -\beta_{1n}$; $\beta_{2y} = \beta_{2n}$; $\beta_{3y} = \beta_{3n}$.

Under the standard assumptions about the errors in a logit model, it is well known that the probabilities are given by:

$$\Pr(\text{Yea}) = \frac{\exp(UY)}{1 + \exp(UY) + \exp(UN)}, \Pr(\text{Nay}) = \frac{\exp(UN)}{1 + \exp(UY) + \exp(UN)},$$

$$\Pr(\text{Abstain}) = \frac{1}{1 + \exp(UY) + \exp(UN)} = 1 - \Pr(\text{Yea}) - \Pr(\text{Nay})$$

The bottom line is that once we have estimated the β coefficients, we can calculate the (estimated) probabilities. To illustrate, table 10.1 shows the estimates for one of the thousands of roll calls in our analysis. This is the vote (which we discussed in chapter 6) on the Reagan bill (a House version of the interstate-commerce bill) versus the Cullom bill (a Senate version) that preceded the passage of the Interstate

Table 10.1 Trinomial Logit Estimates for the Reagan-versus-Cullom Vote

	Coefficient	Estimate
β_{0y}	Constant	3.268*
	Yea/abstain	(0.545)[a]
β_{0n}	Constant	3.068*
	Nay/abstain	(0.531)
β_{1y}	D-NOMINATE	9.672*
	Yea/abstain	(2.116)
β_{1n}	D-NOMINATE	−9.845*
	Nay/abstain	(2.107)
β_{2y}	ABSPREV	−3.430*
	Yea/abstain	(0.550)
β_{2n}	ABSPREV	−3.174*
	Nay/abstain	(0.530)
β_{3y}	ABSAVG	−5.289*
	Yea/abstain	(1.058)
β_{3n}	ABSAVG	−4.465*
	Nay/abstain	(0.937)
	Log-likelihood	−134.917

Note: VOTEVIEW number 191, 49th House; n = 322.
[a] Significant at the 0.01 level.

Commerce Act of 1887. For a legislator who had always voted on the past 26 roll calls and who was completely indifferent about the issue ($ABSAVG = ABSPREV = \Delta U = 0$), the estimated probability of abstention was $1/(1 + \exp(3.286) + \exp(3.080)) = 0.02$. Voters with $\Delta U > 0$ were even less likely to abstain, whereas those who had failed to turn out on previous roll calls were more likely to abstain. We developed estimates, like those shown in table 10.1, for every roll call included in the D-NOMINATE scaling.[15]

Empirical Analysis of Abstention in Congress

The overall abstention rates for the first 100 Congresses are plotted in figure 10.1. The patterns for the House and Senate are quite similar and belie any simple predictions about size and turnout. Although initially abstentions increase over time, as the memberships of the House and Senate are also increasing, abstention in the Senate begins to fall after, roughly, the 50th Senate, even though the Senate grew in spurts until the 63rd Senate (when Arizona and New Mexico were admitted) and grew slightly in the 88th Senate (with the addition of Alaska and Hawaii). Similarly, abstention in the House falls, dramatically, after roughly the 60th House, even though membership in the House plateaued at 435 (in the 63rd House).

Further, these data suggest that the trends are mainly reflections of the interaction of improvements in passenger-transportation technology and the representative's need to maintain contact with the constituency. Note that in the first 20 Congresses, the rate of abstentions is relatively low, around 15 percent in the Senate and 20 percent in the House. In this prerailroad period, a journey to Washington was so arduous that once a member arrived for a session, a brief trip back home was out of the question. In 1800, a trip from Washington to New York took three days; to Boston, six days; and to Savannah, nearly two weeks. By 1830, travel times in the East had improved but the nation had expanded. Although New York could be reached from Washington in a little more than one day, it was still nearly a week to Savannah and to Cincinnati. As the rail network developed, a trip back home was feasible but would lead to an absence of several days, particularly for representatives of the newer, more distant states. By 1857, one could reach either Savannah, St. Louis, or Des Moines in under three days. Perhaps as a result, abstentions rose. Further developments in transportation made it possible for representatives to both visit the constituency and get back to Washington for votes.[16]

That technological change, rather than institutions, is the primary force driving intertemporal variation in turnout is confirmed by the strong correlation ($R^2 = 0.71$) between the Senate and House series shown in figure 10.1. (See the first column of table 10.2.)

A further indication of the role of better technology and of better health is provided by figure 10.2. The figure is based on the computation of the longest nonvoting string—that is, the maximum number of consecutive abstentions—for each legislator in a Congress. Votes with an under-55-percent turnout were excluded from the computation in order to eliminate strategic abstentions with respect to the quorum. The strings were computed as a proportion of the total roll calls in a Congress—the figure shows the mean string for each house in each Congress. To eliminate those with very

Table 10.2   Descriptive Regression for Senate Abstention

	Model	
Variable	(1)	(2)
Constant	3.300	−0.782
House abstention	0.805	0.932
	(0.052)	(0.052)
Senate directly elected		3.440
		(1.245)
R²	0.71	0.73

Note: The dependent variable is Senate abstention; n = 100.

prolonged illnesses, legislators voting on less than 50 percent of all roll calls were eliminated from the computation of the mean.

In the first 15 Congresses, legislators were typically absent for large chunks, about 10 percent, of the roll calls in a Congress. As turnout averaged about 85 percent in this period, almost all abstention was indeed the result of prolonged absence. From the 15th to the 45th Congress, there were fewer prolonged absences; typically, legislators missed only about 5 percent of the roll calls. Nonetheless, nonvoting began a steady increase, exacerbated by the increase in prolonged absences from the 45th Congress to the 60th. By the 60th Congress, representatives were missing chunks of votes as

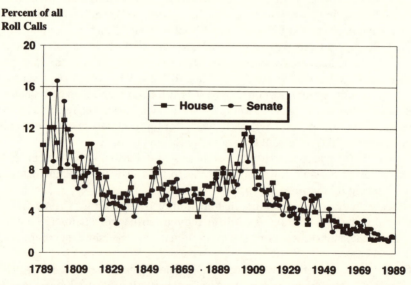

Figure 10.2. Average of the maximum percentage of consecutive abstentions, as a percentage of all roll calls in the Congress (1789–1988). For each member, the percentage is 100 × (the maximum number of consecutive roll calls missed in the Congress) divided by (the total number of roll calls in the Congress). The plot shows the average of these percentages. Large blocks of votes were missed in the early Congresses and at the turn of the century. (Members must have had an overall turnout rate of 50 percent to be included in the computation.)

large as those missed a century earlier. But as modern transportation improved, legislators rarely had prolonged absences. Today, the average longest string of consecutive roll calls missed is just over 1 percent of the total.

How Turnout Responds to Costs

Our first test of how turnout responds to costs is to look at the signs of the abstention coefficients in the trichotomous logit model developed in the previous section. All four of these coefficients should be negative. Indeed, this is overwhelmingly the case—the evidence is summarized in figure 10.3. The figure plots the percentage of roll calls in each Congress for which all four coefficients were negative. The same percentage is plotted for votes that were close—that is, votes having less than a 60-to-40 split. All four signs are correct on over 75 percent of the close votes in the 85 Houses since the 15th and on over 90 percent of the close votes in 59 of the 85 Houses. Missing a recent vote systematically increases the chances of not casting a vote or of being paired. The curve for all votes is not very different from that for close votes. In fact, the average proportion of four correct signs for close votes is only 0.004 greater than for all votes. This similarity suggests that the *ABSPREV* and *AB-SAVG* variables are picking up absences that are largely the result of "prohibitive"

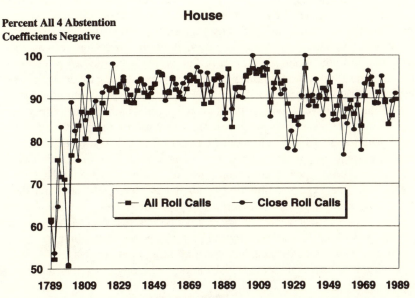

Figure 10.3. Percentage of roll calls for which all four coefficients on the ABSAVG and AB-SPREV variables are negative. By chance, only 25 percent of all roll calls should have all coefficients negative, but, with the exception of the eighteenth century, about 90 percent are as theoretically predicted. Because the pattern for close roll calls is the same as for all roll calls, the ABSAVG and ABSPREV variables should be accounting for illnesses, trips home, and other nonstrategic, non-issue-specific sources of abstention.

costs—those of illness and trips home—that prevent attendance regardless of the legislator's chance of playing a pivotal role.

To ascertain if we could discern any systematic relationship in regard to how travel influenced turnout, we added *LNDIS* terms to the trinomial logit model, estimating coefficients β_{4y} and β_{4n}, in addition to the other coefficients. If both β_{4y} and β_{4n} are negative, representatives from more distant districts vote less. As should be expected, adding *LNDIS* terms introduces substantial correlations among independent variables, which clearly renders our estimates more variable and less precise. The percentage of roll calls for which the utility terms have the appropriate opposite signs drops slightly. A more substantial drop occurs in the percentage of roll calls for which all four coefficients on the *ABS* variables are negative. The *ABS* coefficients are, however, far more negative than positive, indicating that the hypothesized effect of these variables is found even when one controls for distance.

As for distance itself, the pattern of coefficients is mixed, except for one stretch of American history. For the 26 Houses from the 52nd (1891–94) through the 77th (1941–42), there were always more positive coefficients than negative ones. In other words, representatives from more distant districts voted more than those from closer ones. This period represents one in which passenger transportation was largely by rail, before travel was affected by World War II and before the postwar development of airlines. A stay of a given length of time in the constituency would cause a member from, say, Ohio to miss far fewer votes than one from Minnesota. Members from more distant states, apparently trapped in Washington, D.C., voted more. Prior to this period, trips home may have been difficult for nearly everyone; after it, almost all representatives could make short weekend trips to the constituency.

Our second look at the effects of costs on turnout involves a comparison of the turnout rates of members who continued service into the next Congress with the rates of those who did not. When we look at roll calls that occurred before congressional elections, in the House, we find, in figure 10.4, overwhelming evidence that noncontinuing members vote less. The difference between these and continuing members is relatively small, however—typically, between 5 percent and 10 percent in recent Congresses. Moreover, in six Houses (all before the twentieth century), the relationship is reversed. And the difference may indeed be small if marginal members who seek reelection vote frequently to curry favor with constituents. That this is the case is suggested by the data on postelection roll calls, also shown in figure 10.4. Here, the difference is in the expected direction in all but two early Houses, and the difference is substantial, around 15 percent in the twentieth century. (The absence of a point in the figure indicates the absence of a lame-duck session.) Most of the increase in lame-duck shirking has occurred in the past 100 years. In the first 50 Congresses, the difference between continuing and noncontinuing members was only 1.4 percent, but it averaged 8.9 percent in the 32 of the last 50 Congresses that had lame-duck sessions.

The story for continuing versus noncontinuing members in the Senate is about the same as for the House, except that there is more variability, no doubt a reflection of the smaller size of the Senate (see figure 10.4). Thus, there are, for preelection roll calls, 11 Congresses in which continuing Senate members turned out less than noncontinuing members versus only 6 such Congresses for the House. Similarly, continuing members turn out more for postelection votes than noncontinuing members in 6 of

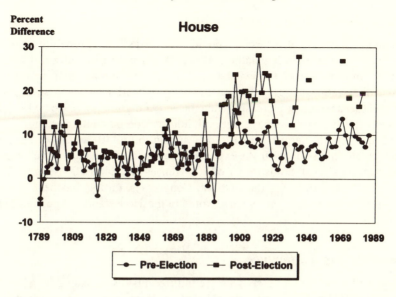

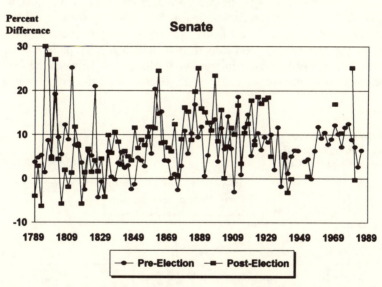

Figure 10.4. Difference in abstention between noncontinuing and continuing members (1789–1988). Noncontinuing members have almost always "shirked" by voting less. The difference is particularly large for roll calls that took place in lame-duck sessions in the twentieth century.

the first 22 Senates. There is also a smaller increase in lame-duck shirking in the last 50 Congresses. Whereas the difference of 1.6 percent in the first 50 Senates is similar to the 1.4 percent for the first 50 Houses, the 3.0 percent in the last 50 Senates is substantially below the 8.9 percent for the last 50 Houses. In both chambers, however, the bulk of the evidence points to considerable shirking of duty by nonreturning members, particularly when their electoral fates are known.

Closeness Counts in Congressional Voting

Our second prediction is that turnout should increase as P, the probability of casting a decisive vote, increases. A legislator's subjective estimate of P for a roll call should be a decreasing function of the legislator's forecast of the margin of the roll call. To the extent that actual margins are, on average, indicative of forecast margins, we should find that abstention increases when the actual margin proves to be lopsided. To show that this is the case, we have, for both houses, computed the abstention rates for close roll calls (with margins equal to or less than 60 to 40) and those for lopsided margins (greater than 60 to 40). As expected, the lopsided roll calls have a higher abstention rate. This result holds for 91 of 100 Houses and 84 of 100 Senates. The data are shown in figure 10.5. For the first 100 Congresses, turnout has been 3.3 percent higher on close votes than on lopsided votes in the House and 2.8 percent higher in the Senate.

Abstention Due to Indifference

Our third prediction is that voters who are indifferent—as measured by a low B term from the D-NOMINATE model—should abstain. If this hypothesis holds, we should obtain a positive coefficient on ΔU in the estimated Yea equation in the logit model and a negative coefficient in the estimated Nay equation. In figure 10.6, we show, for all roll calls, the proportion of roll calls for which the expected pattern of coefficient signs holds. The evidence is most impressive for the period between the 25th and the 60th Congress, when almost always over 95 percent of all the roll calls were as ex-

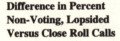

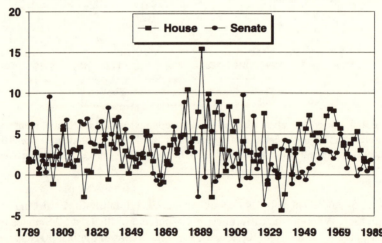

Figure 10.5. Difference between abstentions on lopsided roll calls (majorities greater than 60 percent to 40 percent) and on close roll calls (1789–1988). There are more abstentions on lopsided votes.

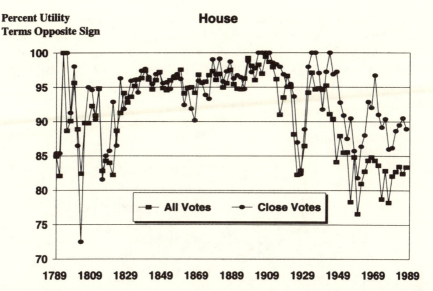

Figure 10.6. Percentage of roll calls where D-NOMINATE utility terms have opposite signs (1789–1988). Most roll calls have the theoretically expected pattern of opposite signs. The pattern is especially true on close roll calls (majorities of no more than 60 percent to 40 percent).

pected. Although always over 80 percent, the percentage of roll calls with the expected pattern was more erratic in the first 25 Congresses, and even more so in modern times, when the percentage of correct coefficient estimates falls as low as 76 percent. Thus, the poorer results occur in periods when the general level of abstention is very high.

With very low abstention levels, the effective sample sizes that distinguish abstainers from voters are small, making coefficient estimates more variable. In addition, the few nonvoters may be "alienated" legislators at the periphery of the space (Hinich and Ordeshook, 1969; Rosenthal and Sen, 1973). The expected pattern of opposite signs on the coefficients arises more frequently on close roll calls, as also shown in the figure. The failure to find the expected pattern on lopsided votes indeed suggests abstention that results from alienation. The fact that, for nearly all Congresses, the expected pattern is more prevalent on close votes supports the fourth prediction: that the *B* term is important only when the perceived value of *P* is high.

Regarding the results on indifference, then, we found that the attractiveness of abstention, relative to voting, is inversely related to the *B* term. And the effect is heightened for close roll calls.

Silent Majorities

To test our fifth prediction—that abstentions are more prevalent on the majority side of an issue—we compared the percentage of legislators, among abstainers, that had been predicted to vote on the winning side (if they had voted) with the percentage that actually voted on the winning side. The difference between these two percentages, plotted in figure 10.7, should be positive. Because the minority is interested in abstaining to block a quorum when turnout is close to 50 percent, we considered only the votes with turnout in excess of 55 percent. Beginning with the 65th House, the difference is always in the expected direction. But results are erratic for the first 64

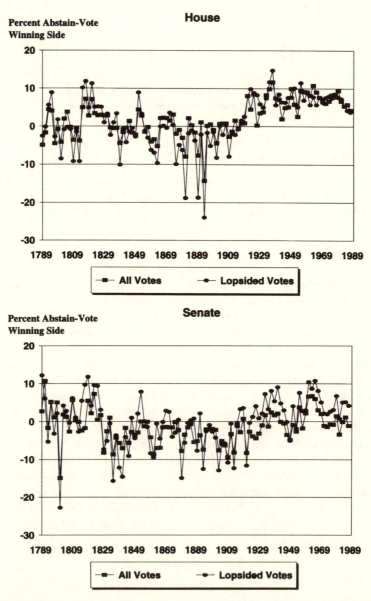

Figure 10.7. Difference between the percentage of legislators, among abstainers, that had been predicted to vote on the winning side and the actual percentage of voters on winning side (1789–1988). The silent-majority hypothesis predicts the difference to be positive. The result is the expected one only for the House since the 65th Congress.

Houses. The general pattern for the Senate is similar to, but weaker than, that for the House. The results are as expected only for lopsided roll calls and, for these, only after the 80th Senate. Thus, the silent-majority hypothesis receives support only in the modern era. Why the hypothesis was not supported in the earlier Congresses is an open question.

Does Size Matter in Turnout?

Our examination of figure 10.1 indicated that it would be difficult, without controls, to find any simple relationship between the size of either legislative body and turnout. Clearly, changes in nonvoting patterns are driven by changes in transportation technology; changes in the relationship between legislators, constituents, partisan support groups, campaign contributors, and party leaders; and, undoubtedly, other factors. Nevertheless, many of the influences on nonvoting patterns can be controlled for by comparing House and Senate turnout within a given Congress. Clearly, transportation technology, communications technology, the size of government, the influence of PACs, and many other factors have similar effects on both chambers at any one time.

Within given Congresses, there are systematic, if relatively small, differences in turnout between the House and Senate that are not apparent in figure 10.1. Over the first 100 Congresses, nonvoting patterns were in line with our sixth prediction, 1.09 percent higher in the House than in the Senate.[17] But this overall difference masks an important variation over time. Before popular election of the Senate, as shown by figure 10.8, the House, indeed, typically had more nonvoting than the Senate—the difference was 2.85 percent over the first 64 Congresses. But after the 65th Congress, the Senate had more nonvoting than the House—the difference was −1.93 percent. Some

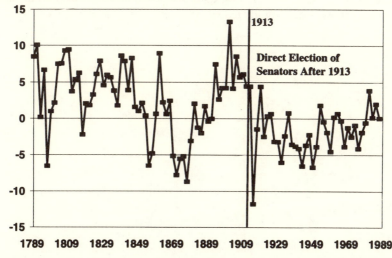

Figure 10.8. Difference in the percentage of legislators abstaining in the House and in the Senate. Since the House is larger than the Senate, this difference is expected to be positive. The actual difference is typically positive until the Senate is directly elected. Subsequently, the difference is typically negative.

of this difference reflects the largest negative difference in the series, -11 percent in the 65th Congress, when many indirectly elected senators were likely to have been shirking. But the difference is still significantly negative, at -1.66 percent, when computed only for Congresses after the 65th.

The same point is made in table 10.2. We regressed Senate abstention on House abstention, a constant, and a dummy variable that equals one for the directly elected Congresses, and zero otherwise. As seen in the table, abstention, after controlling for the level of abstention in the House, is 3.4 percent greater in directly elected Senates than in indirectly elected Senates.

We can only conjecture why direct election of the Senate sharply lowered turnout in the Senate relative to the House. The data suggest that when voters, rather than a state's legislators, are one's constituents, one spends more time at home and less in Washington. How much time one spends at home should be related to the safety of one's seat. If Senate races are generally more competitive than races for the House, senators could well wind up voting less than representatives, even if the Senate is a smaller body than the House. On the other hand, table 4.4 showed that House abstention is very weakly increasing in the safety of the seat. This observation does not provide an explanation for the shift brought about by direct election.

Summary

Our comparison of the House and Senate indicates some difficulties in testing theories of turnout. Although abstentions appear related to cost, closeness to one's constituency, and indifference throughout the history of Congress, the predictions concerning silent majorities and size effects are supported only for some historical periods. Explaining the anomalies is obviously a topic for future research, where more effort can be placed on finding controls—such as electoral margins and campaign contributions—that would create better natural experiments.

11
The Unidimensional Congress

The United States of America, and its Congress, is now entering its third century, with its original institutions modified but largely intact. Such stability, measured against the instability characteristic of most of the world, is truly remarkable.

Stability did not come easily. The Civil War suggests that the Constitution of 1787 was a failure, or at least far from the glorified success story that we ingested in high school. The watershed marked by the Civil War is echoed in our analysis of roll call voting. Prior to the war, as two-party systems arose and then collapsed, there were periods when a spatial model of voting failed to fit the data. In other words, the form of coalition on each roll call varied greatly. Another indication of instability is the fact that far greater changes in the individual positions of legislators occurred prior to the Civil War than in subsequent times.

After the Civil War, the modern party system arose, legislators slowed down in their movement, and the spatial model fit well. Legislators moved a little more than usual during the mass voting realignments of the 1890s and 1930s, but on the whole, the changes in mass voting behavior were reflected in Congress by changes in the location of new members in the space, not by a realignment of the space. A second dimension (as was the case a century earlier) was needed to handle the perturbation introduced by the race issue from the late 1930s to the 1970s, but the basic liberal/conservative configuration was maintained.

Because the low-dimensional spatial model fails to account for roll call voting only in the two periods when the two-party system collapsed, political parties appear to be the critical element in promoting stable voting alignments. Stable patterns of roll call voting are, however, more than just party-related. The many scatter diagrams and histograms of legislators' ideal points that are presented in this book demonstrate that there are very important distinctions within parties. The differences between an Arlen Specter or a Mark Hatfield, on the one hand, and a Phil Gramm or a Jesse Helms on the other, are visibly important to even casual observers of Washington politics. They often, as in the vote to confirm Robert Bork as a Supreme Court justice, or, as in the 1995 vote on a balanced-budget amendment, have a real impact on policy. Our scaling technique makes internal party distinctions in a rigorous manner and does so for all of American history.

Except for two periods of American history, when race was prominent on the agenda, whenever voting can be captured by the spatial model, a one-dimensional model does almost all the work. In large part, this is, as our examination of realignment suggests, because policy objectives must be accomplished largely through the party system. While a balanced-budget amendment may fail when a Mark Hatfield defects, it would never have had a ghost of a chance without solid support from Republican senators. And feminist groups, in moving to align themselves with the Democratic party, have shown their understanding of the game.

After documenting, in chapters 3 to 5, the low-dimensional spatial character of congressional voting and, in particular, the move toward stability of voting patterns after the Civil War, we sought to confront the spatial model with alternative models of roll call voting. Chapter 6 discussed pocketbook voting on constituency interests. We gave constituency-interest models their best possible shot and found them inferior to the spatial model. In addition, we found only a marginal role for economic variables as explanations for voting on minimum wages, strip mining, food stamps, and railroad regulation; the major effects were from the D-NOMINATE spatial utilities. Moreover, as chapter 8 showed, the evaluation of senators and representatives by some major groups with economic interests—namely, labor unions and business and farm organizations—could also be accounted for by our spatial model. We did find a supplementary role for economic interests that was apparent in both the correlations between the voting "errors" of two senators from the same state and, in chapter 9, the tendency of minority members to support the position of the committee majority. We also showed how economic interests, even if they do not distort spatial patterns of voting, influence the mapping of economic issues onto the space.

In chapter 7, we looked at strategic voting as an alternative to the sincere or naïve spatial voting that is assumed in our estimations. One manifestation of strategic behavior, within the context of a one-dimensional model, might be both-ends-against-the-middle voting. We gave the both-ends-against-the-middle concept its best shot, and the spatial model easily withstood the challenge. As illustrated by Jesse Helms' position on minimum wages in 1990, a cantankerous conservative will, on occasion, vote with the liberals, but such out-of-character voting is too rare to be of concern. Moreover, one form of strategic voting—voting on binary-amendment agendas under complete information—is, as argued in chapter 2, fully consistent with spatial voting. The strategic votes will not bias our estimates of legislators' ideal points, but interpretation of roll call outcome coordinates will be affected. We examined the needles of strategic voting the literature has identified in the roll call haystack. Most of these well-known examples produced roll calls which fit the spatial model quite well.

The finding that the spatial model describes the pattern of roll call voting does not pin down the nature of policies produced by Congress. In chapter 4, we found that the average locations of winning outcomes were far more volatile than the average locations of legislators' ideal points. Winning outcomes are consistently pulled away from the congressional center and toward the mean location of the majority party. Party, rather than committees, appears to be the source of this policy distortion. In chapter 9, we found that throughout American history, committees had been representative of the views of the floor of Congress, with the exception of the Democratic contingent on a few committees since the late 1950s. The distinction between the period since the late 1950s and earlier times attests to the value of pursuing a long-term historical study. Much of the current political-economy approach to legislatures has been based on scholars' experience with the textbook Congresses of the 1960s and 1970s. Such a time span is too short for accumulating the stylized facts that need to be explained by a theory of legislatures in general or of Congress in particular. The usefulness of the historical approach was also manifested in our discovery of chaos in a few Congresses, such as the 32nd, where we found convincing examples that there is nothing that guarantees that a one- or two-dimensional model will fit the data. Similarly, while our analysis of abstention in chapter 10 largely verified most predictions developed on the basis of the rational-choice theory of participation, the prediction that the majority side votes less was supported by only the most recent Congresses. Such an anomaly is indicative of the future research agenda that is opened by this book.

There are at least three further directions to follow. First, now that we have the capacity to extract the date of each roll call, we have the opportunity to improve, vastly, the study of dynamics. One important topic in dynamics is learning: Do legislators learn their place in the space, in which case behavior will be more variable on early votes, or do they arrive with prewired ideology? Another is the dynamics of spatial collapse: When and how do stable patterns of voting fall apart? When and how does a new alignment emerge? A second important direction is to incorporate nonvoting into the spatial estimation. A third is to widen the spatial study of Congress to the study of the larger society. This can be done, not only (as we show in our study of interest groups) with newspapers and other sources that take positions but also with mass voting data; citizens have the opportunity to "rate" their representatives every two years.

Epilogue: Congress in Its Third Century

Our study of Congress was restricted to the first 100 Congresses or two centuries of roll call voting. From the turn of the century until the mid-1970s, we have, with some interruptions, seen a decline in party polarization and a shrinking of the space. Toward the end of the period of decline in polarization, a sociologist told us about *The End of Ideology* (Bell, 1961), and political scientists became focused on constituency-service models (Cain, Ferejohn, and Fiorina, 1987).

In contrast, since we started our research collaboration, we have been convinced that contemporary American politics is polarizing around a one-dimensional ideology. Our first published essay related to congressional voting was titled "The Polarization of American Politics" (1984); the work therein was based on a scaling of interest-group ratings (see chapter 8 of this book), rather than on NOMINATE. It was restricted to data that covered only the period from 1958 to 1980. Nonetheless, we were able to discern the increase in polarization in the 1970s and 1980s that we documented in chapter 4—we wrote that "support [coalition] interests . . . are more polarized than ever" (Poole and Rosenthal, 1984, p. 1073). Shortly afterward, we began the work discussed in this book. In an unpublished work (Poole and Rosenthal, 1987b), which was titled "The Unidimensional Congress," our conclusion was based on data that covered the period from 1919 to 1984. Since 1984, the polarized, unidimensional character of Congress has become even more accentuated. The most recent Congresses are highly unidimensional, very polarized, and fit the spatial model extremely well. Figure 11.1 shows the classification percentages in one and two dimensions for the House of Representatives from W-NOMINATE, which was applied separately to each House over the 1887–1995 period (50th to 104th Houses).

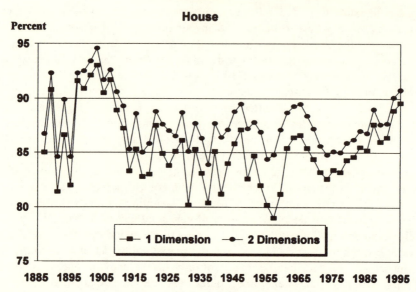

Figure 11.1. Percentage correctly classified by W-NOMINATE in one and two dimensions for the House (1885–1995). The second dimension is increasingly less important after the mid-1970s and only accounts for an additional 1 percent in the 103rd and 104th Houses.

Since the mid-1970s, voting has become increasingly unidimensional, and the percentage of the roll call choices accounted for by the first dimension has climbed steadily. In the 102nd House, the first dimension accounts for about 86 percent of the choices; in the 103rd House, 88 percent of the choices; and for the first session of the 104th House (1995), 90 percent of the choices. In addition, the importance of the second dimension is in a free fall. It peaked during Eisenhower's second term, when it accounted for an additional 6 percent of the choices; it then fell to around 3 percent during the mid-1960s and fell again to around 1.5 percent in the late 1970s and early 1980s. It now accounts for only an additional 1 percent.

In chapter 5 we discussed, at length, the fact that the second dimension, from the late–New Deal period until the early 1970s, was related to voting on race and picked up the division of the Democratic party into northern and southern blocs. What happened to the second dimension? The short answer is that the southern Democratic bloc has splintered into black and white subblocs. The black Democrats, both northern and southern, are at the far Left of the Democratic party, and the white male southern Democrats are at the far Right of the Democratic party. Voting on race-related issues has been absorbed by the first dimension.

Figure 11.2 shows histograms of the W-NOMINATE one-dimensional scaling of the first session of the 104th House in 1995. The figure shows the approximate locations of the means of various groups of the two parties. The polarization of the two political parties is obvious. The bars for Democrats and Republicans, indeed, show a high degree of polarization of the two parties; only three Democrats are to the right of the leftmost Republican, and two of these Democrats have switched to the Republican party. Nonetheless, the parties, particularly the Democrats, have important internal distinctions.

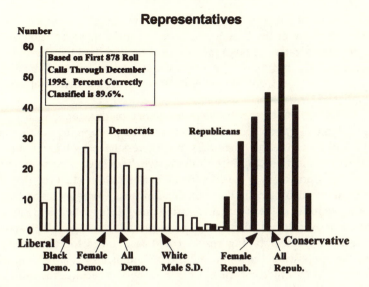

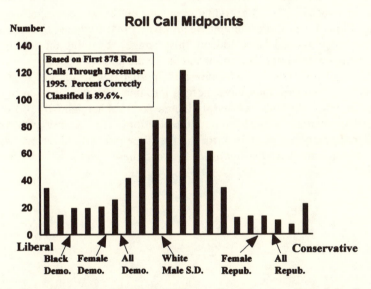

Figure 11.2. Histogram of the W-NOMINATE one-dimensional scaling of the first 878 roll calls in 1995 (the 104th House). The Democrats and Republicans are very polarized; only three Democrats are to the right of the leftmost Republican. The roll call midpoints are concentrated among the conservative Democrats.

The congressional black caucus (there were only 2 black Republicans in the 104th House) anchors the far left, with female Democrats closeby. Reflecting a finding documented in Poole and Zeigler (1985, chap. 5), women in both parties are to the left of their respective party means. The Republicans are far more tightly clustered, reflecting the fact that a large number of conservative freshmen—men and women—were elected in 1994 and the high degree of Republican-party unity during the voting on the Republicans' Contract with America. The distribution of the cutpoints is concentrated in the right wing of the Democratic party, near the mean position of the white male southern Democrats. Although the 1994 elections shifted the House Republican party to the right, the positions of the various subgroups of the Democratic party hardly changed from their locations in the 102nd and 103rd Houses—all that changed was the number of Democrats.

Much has been written since the historic victory of the Republican party in the 1994 congressional elections about the changes taking place in the South. Many local and state politicians and several members of Congress have switched to the Republican party since the elections. Almost all these switchers have been white males. The switching is not surprising in light of figure 11.2, which shows that the Democrats are far more spread out ideologically than the Republicans. Moreover, even though there was a working majority in the House, consisting only of Republicans to the right of all the Democrats, most roll call votes in 1995 were structured to gain the support of the more conservative Democrats. Figures 11.1 and 11.2, taken together, make it more evident that the long-awaited realignment of the South is now finally happening.

Race was drawn into the first dimension in Congress because race-related issues became, increasingly, redistributional ones—welfare, affirmative action, food stamps, and so on. In response, it was only a matter of time before white southerners, who began voting Republican in presidential elections in 1964, switched to the Republican party at the congressional level. Indeed, this change was going on before the 1994 elections, which were simply the straw that broke the donkey's back.

The degree of polarization in Congress is approaching levels not seen since the 1890s. Race and redistribution have merged into one voting dimension in Congress and the polarization on both has sharply increased. This heightened level of conflict will not end, even after the hard-fought 1996 elections. The collapse of the old southern Democratic party has produced, for the first time in nearly 60 years, two sharply distinct political parties. Intense conflict between these two "new" parties will continue.

Appendix A: The NOMINATE Method of Estimating Spatial Models of Voting

In this appendix, we detail the procedures we used to estimate the parameters of the spatial model that is the basis of this book. Our dynamic estimation procedure, D-NOMINATE, was designed specifically for the CYBER 205 supercomputer. The 205's unique architecture was ideally suited to handle the huge combined roll call data sets of the first 99 Congresses. D-NOMINATE was developed from 1986 to 1988, during the early period of the NSF supercomputing initiative, which began in 1985. Later (1991–94), we developed W-NOMINATE, a static (single-Congress) estimation procedure based on our very early (1982-85) presupercomputer work but incorporating many advances we made during our research on the D-NOMINATE algorithm. W-NOMINATE is written in FORTRAN and can be run on a 486 PC or better. It can be obtained from the World Wide Web site discussed in the preface.

Dynamic Nominal Three-Step Estimation (D-NOMINATE)

Our discussion of D-NOMINATE is divided into four sections. In the first, we show the formal development of our spatial model. The second section details the algorithm we developed to estimate the parameters of the model, and the third section deals with statistical issues raised by our estimation procedure. The fourth section discusses various Monte Carlo tests of D-NOMINATE.

Development of the Spatial Model

The spatial model estimated by D-NOMINATE represents, as we indicated in chapter 2, each roll call as two points in a low-dimensional Euclidean space. Each legislator is represented as a point in the same space. A legislator's point is dynamic; it moves as a polynomial function of time. In our model, time is discrete, and is measured by the Congress number. Since our estimation pertains to the first 99 Congresses, time, indexed by t, takes on the integer values of 1 to 99. Thus, a legislator's point is constant over the (typically) hundreds of roll calls in a given Congress but (possibly) "jumps" along a linear or quadratic or cubic or quartic path between Congresses. (Our decision to measure time in integers was in fact a nondecision. When we estimated the model, the ICPSR codebooks were available in a variety of formats that made it impractical to extract the exact date of each roll call. While we have now edited the codebooks in a fashion that would allow one to measure time on a daily basis, we are certain that our major results would be entirely robust to this change. Indeed, it might well be argued that integer measurement is preferable to daily measurement since congressional elections, which induce changes in majorities and committee chairmanships, are discrete events that have a major impact on roll call voting.)

The basic task of the D-NOMINATE estimation algorithm is to produce Euclidean coordinates for the two points of each roll call and a polynomial function for each coordinate of the moving point for each legislator. This task would be much simpler if there were no "missing" data, if every legislator had voted in every roll call in American history. We will often simplify the discussion in this appendix by ignoring the missing-data problem. Similarly, we will often ignore the dynamics and assume the legislators' positions are constant, or static, over time. To be complete in a way that permits replication of our results, we do, where appropriate, provide expressions for the full-blown dynamic model, including missing data.

Our model is a metric one. That is, the coordinates are identified up to a linear transformation. Our algorithm correspondingly constrains coordinates to lie (exactly, in the case of W-NOMINATE; approximately, in that of D-NOMINATE) in a hypersphere of radius one centered at zero.

An alternative to a metric model would be an *ordinal* model. We would only seek to find out if Senator Foghorn is to the left of Senator Bleep who is to the left of Senator Smith, and so on. With more than one dimension, only a metric model is computationally feasible; using a metric model, including a functional specification for probabilistic voting, allows one to apply the powerful "hill climbing" techniques developed for maximum-likelihood estimation. Hundreds of thousands of parameters can be estimated from examining millions of decisions in just a few hours of supercomputer time. On the other hand, for discussion purposes, it is often clearer to pretend that, rather than maximizing likelihood, the algorithm was minimizing classification errors in an ordinal framework. Where necessary, we make the relevant distinctions between ordinal and metric perspectives.

Specification of the Spatial Model

Let s denote the number of policy dimensions, which are indexed by $k = 1, \ldots, s$; let p denote the number of legislators ($i = 1, \ldots, p$); and q denote the number of roll call votes ($j = 1, \ldots, q$). Let legislator i's ideal point be $\mathbf{x}_i$, a vector of length s. Each roll call vote is represented by vectors of length s, $\mathbf{z}_{\mathbf{j}\mathbf{y}}$ and $\mathbf{z}_{\mathbf{j}\mathbf{n}}$, where y and n stand for the policy outcomes associated with Yea and Nay, respectively.

Legislator i's utility for outcome y on roll call j is

$$U_{ijy} = u_{ijy} + \varepsilon_{ijy} = \beta \exp\left[- d_{ijy}^2\right] + \varepsilon_{ijy} \tag{A1}$$

where u_{ijy} is the deterministic portion of the utility function and where ε_{ijy}, the stochastic portion, represents the idiosyncratic component of utility. The utility for outcome n is similarly defined. The d term in the exponent is the Euclidean distance between $\mathbf{x}_i$ and $\mathbf{z}_{jy}$; namely,

$$d_{ijy}^2 = \sum_{k=1}^{s} (x_{ik} - z_{jyk})^2$$

The coefficient, β, is a constant, common to all legislators, and acts as a signal-to-noise ratio. As β increases in value (with d_{ijy} held constant), the deterministic portion of the utility function overwhelms the stochastic portion, and perfect spatial voting is the result. Conversely, as β decreases to zero, voting becomes completely random.

The two roll call policy outcome points can also be written in terms of their midpoint and the distance between them; namely,

$$\mathbf{z}_{jy} = \mathbf{z}_{mj} - \mathbf{d}_j \quad \text{and} \quad \mathbf{z}_{jn} = \mathbf{z}_{mj} + \mathbf{d}_j$$

where $\mathbf{z}_{mj}$ is the midpoint and $\mathbf{d}_j = (\mathbf{z}_{jy} - \mathbf{z}_{jn})/2$.

We found it preferable to estimate the $\mathbf{z}_{mj}$ and $\mathbf{d}_j$ rather than the Yea and Nay outcome points. Why? Consider a vote for which, given the legislators' ideal points, we can obtain perfect classification—that is, we can find, as shown in figure A.1, a hyperplane that perfectly separates the Yea voters from the Nay voters. With a large number of voters, the location of this cutting line is pinned down rather precisely. If the line drawn in the figure is wiggled a little, we can still get perfect classification; but it can't be wiggled very much, or else some legislators will be misclassified. Now the hyperplane we have drawn would result from an infinite number of possible Yea and Nay outcome points. The same separating hyperplane is defined by any pair of points that are equidistant from the hyperplane on a line perpendicular to it. Consequently, while the separating hyperplane is precisely identified with perfect voting, the outcome positions are not identified.

These identification problems persist with noisy voting and maximum-likelihood (as against classification) analysis. The z_{mj}, which are analogous to the hyperplane, are precisely estimated, while the d_j and the outcome points have relatively imprecise estimates. In particular, in one dimension, the midpoint is always (or almost always) precisely estimated,[1] and the convergence of the estimation algorithm is improved by having one of the two roll call parameters precisely estimated. Since our multidimensional estimation procedure is essentially a chaining together of one-dimensional procedures, the z_{mj} and d_j representation also improves the convergence of the multidimensional model.

In our earlier studies (Poole and Rosenthal, 1983; 1985b; 1987a), we used a slightly different deterministic utility function:

$$u_{ijy} = \beta \exp\left[-\frac{w^2 d_{ijy}^2}{2} \right] \tag{A2}$$

where w is a weighting factor common to all individuals. Equation (A2) is simply a normal distribution multiplied by a constant. We found, through extensive experimentation, that it was unnecessary to estimate both w and β because the two parameters are highly—but not perfectly—collinear. For most Congresses, simultaneous estimation of w and β produced values of about 1/2 and 15, respectively. Consequently, we set $w = \frac{1}{2}$ in our later work and just estimated β. This produced a scaling constant of $\frac{1}{2}w^2 = \frac{1}{8}$ in the exponent of the utility function. Because the underlying space can only be identified up to a scaling constant, we could have dropped the 1/8 altogether. However, we retained it so that the β's estimated in our later studies would be com-

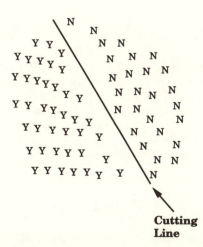

Figure A.1. A perfect roll call in two dimensions. All legislators to the left of the cutting line voted Yea, and all to the right voted Nay.

parable to what we estimated earlier. In equation (A1) above and in our discussion below, we omit the scaling constant in order to simplify the equations.

We assume that the stochastic term, ε, is distributed as the log of the inverse exponential— that is, the "logit" distribution. This allows the probability that legislator i votes for outcome y on roll call j, to be written as:

$$\text{Prob (Yea)} = P_{ijy} = \frac{\exp\left[u_{ijy}\right]}{\exp\left[u_{ijy}\right] + \exp\left[u_{jn}\right]} \tag{A3}$$

To simplify notation, we often replace the mnemonic y with the index 1 and n with 2 and allow the symbol ℓ to be the generic indicator for a roll call outcome. We can thus express the likelihood function as

$$L = \prod_{i=1}^{p} \prod_{j=1}^{q} \prod_{\ell=1}^{2} P_{ij\ell}^{C_{ij\ell}} \tag{A4}$$

where ℓ is the index for y and n, and $C_{ij\ell} = 1$, if choice ℓ is the actual choice of legislator i on roll call j and is zero otherwise.

Equation (A4) is the expression for the static model. To allow for spatial movement, we assume that legislator coordinates are polynomial functions of time. In particular, let $\mathcal{T}$ denote the total number of Congresses in which legislator i served, and let $t = 1, 2 \ldots, \mathcal{T}$ index time for these Congresses.[2] (To be precise, we should use t_i and $\mathcal{T}_i$, but we drop the subscript since the meaning is clear.) Then, the legislator has coordinates:

$$\mathbf{x}_{it} = \mathbf{x}_{i0} + \mathbf{x}_{i1}\psi_{t1} + \mathbf{x}_{i2}\psi_{t2} + \mathbf{x}_{i3}\psi_{t3} + \cdots + \mathbf{x}_{iv}\psi_{tv} \tag{A5}$$

where v is the degree of the polynomial and the time-specific terms—the ψ_t's—are Legendre polynomials. The first three terms of a Legendre polynomial representation of time are:

$$\psi_{t1} = -1 + (t-1)\frac{2}{\mathcal{T}_i - 1}$$

$$\psi_{t2} = \frac{3\psi_{t1}^2 - 1}{2} \qquad \text{for } t = 1, \ldots, \mathcal{T}_i$$

$$\psi_{t3} = \frac{5\psi_{t1}^3 - 3\psi_{t2}}{2}$$

If we estimated a normal polynomial model, the variables t, t^2, t^3, and so on, would all be correlated. Notice that as t goes from 1 to $\mathcal{T}_i$, the linear Legendre variable ψ_{t1} takes on the values -1, $-1 + 2/(\mathcal{T} - 1)$, $\ldots$, $+1$. Thus, this term is proportional to the linear term in a simple powers-of-time framework. The higher-order variables are chosen such that all the ψ's are orthogonal on the interval $[-1, +1]$ (Hinich and Roll, 1981). Since the parameters x_{ik0}, x_{ik1}, $\ldots$, x_{ikv} are estimated simultaneously, orthogonality speeds up convergence.

For the dynamic case, were there no missing data in any Congress, the likelihood function would be:

$$L = \prod_{t=1}^{\mathcal{T}} \prod_{i=1}^{p_t} \prod_{j=1}^{q_t} \prod_{\ell=1}^{2} P_{tij\ell}^{C_{tij\ell}} \tag{A6}$$

where p_t and q_t are the number of legislators and the number of roll calls in Congress t, respectively.

To allow for missing data, let Q_t^i denote the set of roll calls for which legislator i voted at time t. (Votes include pairs and announced votes, as well as actual votes.) Then,

$$L = \prod_{i=1}^{p} \prod_{t=1}^{\mathscr{T}_i} \prod_{j \in Q_t^i} \prod_{\ell=1}^{2} P_{tij\ell}^{C_{tij\ell}} \tag{A6'}$$

The Estimation Algorithm: An Alternating Algorithm for Maximizing the Log-Likelihood

For the dynamic model without missing data and with $\mathscr{T} > v$, the number of parameters to be estimated is:

$$2s \sum_{t=1}^{\mathscr{T}} q_t + sp(v+1) + 1$$

In actual practice, we estimate fewer than $s(v+1)$ parameters for legislators with short periods of service. The number of terms in the polynomial estimated for legislator i is given by $\max\{1, \min\{\mathscr{T}_i - 1, v + 1\}\}$. This allows us to estimate a linear trend for legislators with as few as three Congresses of service, a quadratic for four Congresses of service, and so on.

Following standard practice, we estimate parameters that maximize the log of the likelihood function:

$$\mathscr{L} = \beta \sum_{i=1}^{p_t} \sum_{t=1}^{\mathscr{T}_i} \sum_{j \in Q_t^i} \sum_{\ell=1}^{2} C_{tij\ell} \exp\left[-d_{tij\ell}^2\right] - \sum_{i=1}^{p_t} \sum_{t=1}^{\mathscr{T}_i} \sum_{j \in Q_t^i} \ln\Phi_{tij} \tag{A7}$$

where

$$\Phi_{tij} = \exp\left[\beta\exp\left[-d_{tijn}^2\right]\right] + \exp\left[\beta\exp\left[-d_{tijy}^2\right]\right]$$

If our utility function were linear in the parameters, maximizing equation (A7) would be very easy because the likelihood function would be globally convex. Instead, equation (A1) is nonlinear, and care must be taken to avoid local maxima.

We must depart from conventional methods of maximizing equation (A7) because of the sheer number of parameters. (For example, the two-dimensional linear scaling of the House requires the estimation of 159,523 parameters using 8,110,702 individual voting decisions.) Instead, we use an alternating algorithm in which the set of parameters is divided into three subsets. All the parameters remain fixed except for one subset, which is estimated. Each subset of parameters is estimated in turn while the other parameters remain fixed. This alternating algorithm converges to a solution in which each subset of parameters is at an optimum, given that the other parameters remain fixed.

In our algorithm, we have three subsets of parameters: those for the legislators—the x_i's; those for the roll calls—the z_m's and the d_j's; and the signal-to-noise ratio, β. In outline form, the D-NOMINATE algorithm has three basic steps:

Step 1: Estimate the z_{mj} and the d_j.
Step 2: Estimate the x_i.
Step 3: Estimate β.

Hence the acronym D-NOMINATE—*D*ynamic *N*omi*na*l *T*hree-Step *E*stimation.

Steps 1, 2, and 3 form a global iteration. Global iterations are repeated until the z, x, and d parameters all correlate at 0.99 or better with the set estimated on the previous global iteration. Typically, by this criterion, D-NOMINATE converges within three global iterations.

In step 2, we are able to estimate each $\mathbf{x}_i$ separately. Note that with β and the roll call parameters remaining constant, each $\mathbf{x}_i$ influences the log-likelihood only through the votes of legislator i. The likelihood of a vote by legislator i is thus independent of the parameters for the other legislators. Similarly, in step 1, we can estimate the parameters for each roll call separately. In other words, the second derivatives of the parameters with respect to the other parameters in their subset are all zero.

The BHHH Gradient Method

To estimate the parameters, we utilized a variant of the BHHH algorithm developed by Berndt, Hall, Hall, and Hausman (1974). This gradient method uses only the first derivatives of the parameters in the update formula. Specifically, let Θ be the vector of parameters; let $\mathbf{g}$ be the vector of partial derivatives of $\mathcal{L}$, with respect to Θ; and let ∇ be a matrix which is the sum of the outer products of $\mathbf{g}$—that is,

$$\nabla = \Sigma\, \mathbf{gg}'$$

where the sum is over the number of observations. The update formula is

$$\Theta_{new} = \Theta_{old} + \alpha\nabla^{-1}\mathbf{g} \tag{A8}$$

where α is the step size for the gradient. Note that, because of our use of an alternating algorithm and because of the separability in steps 1 and 2, the vector Θ will always have very few elements. In step 3, there is just a single element, β. In a one-dimensional problem, there are at most $v+1$ elements for each legislator. There are two elements involved when the roll calls are processed.

An iteration is defined as calculating $\mathbf{g}$ and ∇ and finding the optimal step size. We found BHHH to be very efficient and, regardless of what parameters we were estimating, no more than six or seven iterations were required for convergence.

The optimal step size is found with a simple search. On the first three iterations, a step size of one is tried. If the log-likelihood improves, the step size is doubled, and this continues until no further improvement occurs. If the log-likelihood does not improve with a step size of one, the step size is halved, and if the likelihood then improves, the process stops. If halving the step size does not improve the log-likelihood, the step size is halved again, and this process is continued until the log-likelihood improves. After the third iteration, the procedure continues as described above, except that it is much more efficient to use the final step size of the previous iteration as the initial step size.

Estimating One Dimension at a Time

The discussion above did not explicitly address multidimensional estimation. On the surface, it appears to be a simple extension of our framework. For example, suppose we wish to estimate the two dimensional linear model—$s = 2$ and $v = 1$. In step 1, four parameters would be estimated for each roll call—z_{mj1}, z_{mj2}, d_{j1}, and d_{j2}—while all other parameters are held fixed. It is not this simple, however.

For one thing, the likelihood function is so nonlinear that good starting estimates for the parameters are necessary to avoid local maxima. Obtaining good starting estimates for the legislators is easy regardless of the number of dimensions. This is not the case for the roll call parameters.

To see this, consider the simple one-dimensional case and suppose that we have good one-dimensional starting estimates for the legislators. Given a fixed configuration of legislators, it is relatively easy to obtain a reasonable starting value for the roll call midpoint, z_{mj}, by examining the pattern of Yeas and Nays and by placing z_{mj} so as to maximize correct classifications. To illustrate, suppose that the legislators' starts are ordered from left to right, and that a Y is used for each Yea voter and a N for each Nay voter. Suppose the pattern below was observed:

$$YYYYYYYYYYYYYYYYYYYYNY|NNYNNNNNNNNNNNNNNNNNNNNNNNNNNN$$

Placing z_{mj} between the two legislators denoted with the vertical line results in only two classification errors.

In general, a simple method of obtaining a good starting estimate of z_{mj} in one dimension is to iteratively set z_{mj} equal to the midpoint between every adjacent pair of legislators along the dimension and to compute the percentage of correctly classified votes corresponding to that midpoint/cutting point. The starting estimate of z_{mj} is simply the cutting point that best classifies the roll call.[3] Finally, in practice, the starting value for d_j can be a fairly arbitrary one. We found that setting it at a value equal to one fourth of the span of the legislator configuration worked very well (that is, since the span of the space was about two units, we set the d_j's at 1/2).

Unfortunately, in two or more dimensions, starting estimates for $\mathbf{z}_j$ cannot be easily obtained even if the starting estimates of the legislators are very good ones. The simple search procedure we described for one dimension becomes quite cumbersome in two dimensions. In fact, since the search procedure is maximizing classification, the result of the search will not be a cutting *point,* but a cutting *line;* and above two dimensions, it will be a cutting *plane.* Not only is such a search procedure computationally intensive, but it does not yield a point estimate—rather, it produces a line/plane.

We solved these problems by estimating one dimension at a time. Our approach bears a family resemblance to eigenvalue/eigenvector decomposition in that we begin by estimating the one-dimensional configuration that best accounts for the data. Keeping this first dimension fixed, we then estimate a second dimension that best accounts for the remaining "variance," and so on, until the desired number of dimensions is estimated.

We are able to estimate one dimension at a time because the deterministic portion of our utility function can be decomposed into a product of the separate dimensions. (In the remainder of this section, we drop all time subscripts; the extension to dynamic multidimensional models is direct.) That is, $\exp[-d_{ijy}^2]$ from equation (A1) can be written (omitting the i and j subscripts) as

$$e^{-d_{y1}^2}\, e^{-d_{y2}^2}\, e^{-d_{y3}^2} \ldots e^{-d_{ys}^2}$$

where

$$d_{y1}^2 = (x_1 - z_{y1})^2 \cdots d_{ys}^2 = (x_s - z_{ys})^2$$

Now, letting δ be the component of the squared distance on the k-th dimension

$$e^{-d_y^2} = \Psi_y e^{-d_{yk}^2} = \Psi_y e^{-\delta_y^2}$$

where

$$\Psi_y = e^{-d_{y1}^2}\, e^{-d_{y2}^2} \ldots e^{-d_{y,k-1}^2}\, e^{-d_{y,k+1}^2} \ldots e^{-d_{ys}^2}$$

This allows equation (A1) to be rewritten as

$$U_{ijy} = u_{ijy} + \varepsilon_{ijy} = \beta \Psi_{ijy} \exp[-\delta_{ijy}^2] + \varepsilon_{ijy} \tag{A9}$$

The log-likelihood equation is

$$\mathcal{L} = \beta \sum_{i=1}^{p} \sum_{j=1}^{q} \sum_{\ell=1}^{2} C_{ij\ell} \Psi_{ij\ell} \exp[-\delta_{ij\ell}^2] - \sum_{i=1}^{p} \sum_{j=1}^{q} \ln \phi_{ij} \tag{A10}$$

where

$$\phi_{ij} = \exp\left[\beta \Psi_{ijn} \exp[-\delta_{ijn}^2]\right] + \exp\left[\beta \Psi_{ijy} \exp[-\delta_{ijy}^2]\right]$$

Equation (A10) is the same as equation (A7) except for the presence of the Ψ's, which are treated as constants with respect to estimating the parameters for the k-th dimension. When the first dimension is estimated, the Ψ's are all equal to one since all the higher-dimensional coordinates for the legislators and roll calls are initially set at zero. When the second dimension is estimated, the Ψ's are set at

$$\Psi_y = e^{-d^2_{y1}} \qquad \Psi_n = e^{-d^2_{n1}}$$

since the third- and higher-dimensional coordinates for the legislators and roll calls are set at zero. Similarly, when the third dimension is estimated, the Ψ's are

$$\Psi_y = e^{-d^2_{y1}} e^{-d^2_{y2}} \qquad \Psi_n = e^{-d^2_{n1}} e^{-d^2_{n2}}$$

since the fourth- and higher-dimensional coordinates for the legislators and roll calls are set at zero. In general, when the k-th dimension is estimated, the Ψ's are

$$\Psi_y = e^{-d^2_{y1}} \ldots e^{-d^2_{y,k-1}} \qquad \Psi_n = e^{-d^2_{n1}} \ldots e^{-d^2_{n,k-1}}$$

and

$$x_{i,k+1} = x_{i,k+2} = \cdots = x_{is} = 0 \qquad \forall i$$

$$z_{mj,k+1} = \cdots = z_{mjs} = d_{j,k+1} = \cdots = d_{js} = 0 \qquad \forall j$$

The alternating three-step algorithm described above is used to estimate each dimension in turn. The three steps are repeated until all the parameters have converged. If no constraints are placed on the values that the coordinates can take on, the log-likelihood will always improve from one step to the next. However, some constraints are necessary, as we will explain later. The presence of constraints does not seriously affect the total log-likelihood.

Although (without constraints) the log-likelihood always improves within the estimation of a dimension, it does not necessarily improve during the transition from estimating dimension k to estimating dimension $k + 1$. Consider the situation at the end of the estimation of the coordinates for the first dimension. The algorithm has produced legislator points and pairs of points for each roll call along a line. The distances computed between the various points along this line produce the log-likelihood. Now, given these one-dimensional points, consider the problem of estimating a second dimension. Using equation (A10), the log-likelihood, at convergence, can be produced by setting

$$\Psi_{ij\ell} = e^{-d^2_{ij\ell1}} \quad \text{and} \quad \delta^2_{ij\ell} = 0 \quad \text{so that} \quad e^{-\delta^2_{ij\ell}} = 1 \quad \forall\, i,j,\ell$$

On the surface, the transition to the second dimension does not appear to be a serious problem. Simply begin the iterative process with all the δ's set at zero, and by definition, the log-likelihood must improve. However, this is only possible if all the second-dimension parameters are simultaneously estimated. Given the large number of parameters we have to estimate, as before, simultaneous estimation is impractical. We must break the problem into alternating steps. But we cannot carry out the roll call step with all the legislators at zero on the second dimension. The term $\exp[-\delta^2]$ in equation (A10) would be a constant for every legislator, and the likelihood, conditional on the legislators remaining at zero, would be maximized by setting $\delta = 0$ (since $\exp(0) > \exp(-\alpha)$, $\alpha > 0$). Similarly, we could not begin with a legislator step. Therefore, in an alternating algorithm, we must begin the estimation of the second dimension by picking nonzero legislator starts that may lead to a decrease in the likelihood in initial steps.

Our solution to this problem is: First, use starting estimates of the second-dimension coordinates for the legislators, and second, set the roll call coordinates at zero. (We discuss legislator starts later.) Geometrically, the estimation of the second dimension begins with the legislators being dispersed over a plane while the roll call points are on a line through the plane. The starting value for the log-likelihood is produced by substituting

$$\Psi_{ij\ell} = e^{-d^2_{ij\ell1}} \quad \text{and} \quad \delta^2_{ij\ell} = \tilde{x}^2_{i2} \quad \forall\, i,j,\ell$$

in equation (A10), where the $\tilde{x}_{it2}$ are the starting estimates of the legislator coordinates. This starting value for the log-likelihood is not an improvement over the final log-likelihood for the first dimension because $\delta \neq 0$.

Because the first-dimension coordinates remain fixed, the pair of outcome points for a roll call are, in effect, constrained to lie on parallel "tracks" that are $2d_{j1}$ units apart. This fact is illustrated in figure A.2.

As illustrated in parts A and B of the figure, in terms of the cutting line, constraining the outcome points to the parallel tracks does not constrain the location of the cutting line, except at a knife's edge. Any cutting line which is not exactly parallel to the tracks must intersect them. The intersections in the figure represent two outcomes that satisfy the condition of being on the parallel tracks. The knife's edge is that we rule out getting a better cutting line that is parallel to

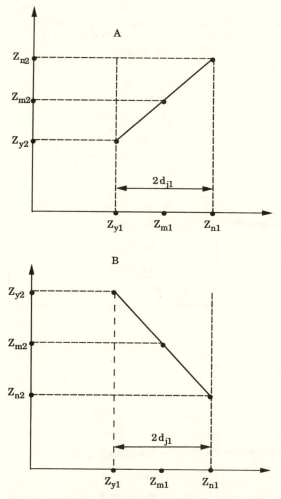

Figure A.2. Dimension-by-dimension estimation of roll call outcome locations. When the second dimension is estimated, the first-dimension outcome coordinates remain fixed at z_{y1}, z_{n1}. This does not constrain the location of the roll call cutting line, as is evident in comparing parts A and B. The outcomes are constrained to lie on the two parallel dashed lines through the points z_{y1}, z_{n1}.

the tracks, and hence the original cutting line in the one-dimensional fit. Were we optimizing classifications rather than a likelihood, this knife's edge would not be a concern. The one-dimensional cutting line would already have been chosen to be an optimum among all cutting lines parallel to it. Consequently, since optimizing classifications and maximizing a likelihood tend to give highly similar results, the knife's edge does not represent an important constraint.

The legislator coordinates on the second dimension are estimated in a similar fashion, with the $\tilde{x}_{i2}$'s being used as the starting estimates. Finally, β is reestimated for the two-dimensional configuration. Note that, except for the transition from the first to the second dimension, the log-likelihood will improve from step to step within each dimension. In practice, even though the log-likelihood worsens during the transition from dimension k to dimension $k + 1$, the log-likelihood is always better after one passage through the three estimation steps on the $k + 1$ dimension.

After estimating s dimensions, one might return to the first dimension, with the Ψ's appropriately defined to now keep all coordinates, except the first dimension, constant. One could then pass through the dimensions again. After some experimentation, we found this unnecessary since it provided extremely small increases in the log-likelihood.

Figure A.3 summarizes the D-NOMINATE algorithm.

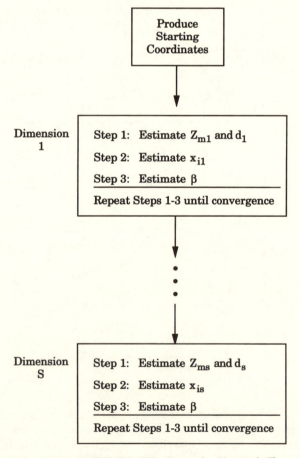

Figure A.3. Summary of the D-NOMINATE (*D*ynamic *Nomina*l *T*hree-step *E*stimation) algorithm.

Obtaining Starting Values for the Parameters

Legislators' Starts. Good starting values for the legislators are crucial to the success of our dimension-by-dimension scaling algorithm. To obtain starting values for the legislators, we use a metric-similarities scaling (Torgerson, 1958; Poole, 1990) of the legislator-by-legislator agreement scores computed from the roll call votes. Specifically, the agreement score for legislators *i* and *h* is given by:

$$A_{ih} = A_{hi} = 100 \times \frac{\text{Number of roll calls with } i \text{ and } h}{\text{Number of roll calls with } i \text{ and } h \text{ both voting}}$$

These scores range from 0 to 100. In the dynamic scalings, an agreement score is computed for every pair of legislators with a common period of service. This produces a symmetric *p*-by-*p* matrix of scores.

It is tempting to interpret the scores as inverse distances—that is, the higher the score, the closer the ideal points of the two legislators are in the underlying policy space. Morrison (1972), however, showed that such an interpretation is incorrect. The reason is that the agreement scores depend on the distribution of roll calls and on the location of legislators. Suppose, for example, that most votes had cutting lines that divided moderate conservatives from extreme conservatives. In that case, a moderately conservative legislator could have a higher agreement score with an extreme liberal than with another conservative slightly to the legislator's right. Thus the inverse-distance interpretation should be looked on as only approximately correct. Fortunately, the approximation leads to good starts for D-NOMINATE.

The first step in applying metric-similarities scaling to the agreement scores is to transform them into distances by applying the transformation:

$$d_{ih}^* = \left[\frac{100 - A_{ih}}{50} \right]$$

This transformation produces distances on a zero-to-two scale.

The next step is to double-center the matrix of squared distances. For every element of the matrix, double-centering consists of subtracting the corresponding row and column mean distances, adding the matrix mean distance, and dividing by -2. This transformation removes the squared terms from the expansion of the d^{*2}'s, thereby producing a cross-product matrix. Specifically:

$$\mathbf{Y} = -\tfrac{1}{2}[\mathbf{D}^* - \mathbf{r}\mathbf{J}' - \mathbf{J}\mathbf{c}' + \mathbf{J}\mathbf{J}'m] = \mathbf{X}\mathbf{X}' + \mathbf{E} \tag{A11}$$

where $\mathbf{D}^*$ is the *p*-by-*p* matrix of d^{*2}'s; $\mathbf{r}$ and $\mathbf{c}$ are the *p*-length vectors of row and column means; $\mathbf{J}$ is a *p*-length vector of ones; m is the mean of the matrix; $\mathbf{X}$ is the *p*-by-*s* matrix of legislators' ideal coordinates on the *s* policy dimensions; and $\mathbf{E}$ is a *p*-by-*p* matrix of unknown errors. (Note that, because $\mathbf{D}^*$ is symmetric, $\mathbf{r} = \mathbf{c}$—we retain the distinction here for discussion purposes.)

Because the cross-product matrix, $\mathbf{Y}$, is symmetric, it can be written as the product of a single *p*-by-*p* matrix of eigenvectors, $\mathbf{U}$, and a *p*-by-*p* diagonal matrix of eigenvalues, Λ; that is,

$$\mathbf{Y} = \mathbf{X}\mathbf{X}' + \mathbf{E} = \mathbf{U}\Lambda\mathbf{U}' \tag{A12}$$

where

$$\mathbf{U}\mathbf{U}' = \mathbf{U}'\mathbf{U} = \mathbf{I}_p$$

and $\mathbf{I}_p$ is a *p*-by-*p* identity matrix.

To obtain starting estimates in *s* dimensions for the metric scaling procedure, we use a standard result in matrix-decomposition theory (Eckart and Young, 1936). To find the best least-squares approximation of **Y** in s dimensions, simply set at zero the $p - s$ smallest eigenvalues in Λ—let the result be the matrix $\tilde{\Lambda}$—and substitute $\tilde{\Lambda}$ for the Λ in equation (A12). This is equivalent to discarding the $p - s$ eigenvectors; specifically,

$$\hat{\mathbf{Y}} = \mathbf{U}_s \tilde{\Lambda}_s \mathbf{U}'_s \tag{A13}$$

where $\mathbf{U}_s$ is the p-by-s matrix, consisting of the s eigenvectors of **U** corresponding to the s largest eigenvalues; and where Λ_s is the s-by-s diagonal submatrix of Λ, containing the s largest eigenvalues. The starting estimates for the metric scaling are, therefore,

$$\hat{\mathbf{X}}_0 = \mathbf{U}_s \left[\tilde{\Lambda}_s \right]^{1/2} \tag{A14}$$

The discussion above assumes that there is no missing data—that is, that all p legislators overlap one another so that an agreement score can be calculated. In practice, however, the longer the time series being analyzed, the larger the number of missing entries in **D***. For example, 9,759 individuals served in the House from 1789 to 1985.[4] The 9,759-by-9,759 agreement-score matrix has about a 70 percent missing-entries rate. To overcome this problem, we inserted the matrix mean, $\mathfrak{m}$, into the missing entries in **D***. When the number of missing entries is small, this ad hoc solution works very well. When the number of missing entries is large, the starting coordinates for the metric scaling procedure are not very reliable. However, the metric scaling procedure is very robust in one dimension, to starting coordinates (Poole, 1990); and in two or more dimensions, long experience with similar scaling procedures has proven them to be reasonably reliable in cases of poor starting coordinates (Kruskal and Wish, 1978).

The metric scaling procedure estimates legislator coordinates that minimize the standard squared error loss function:

$$\mu = \sum_{i=1}^{p} \sum_{h=1}^{p} \left[d_{ih}^* - \hat{d}_{ih} \right]^2 \tag{A15}$$

where

$$\hat{d}_{ih} = \left[\sum_{k=1}^{s} (\hat{x}_{ik} - \hat{x}_{gk})^2 \right]^{1/2}$$

Estimating the $\hat{x}$'s is a well-known psychometric problem. A simple geometric explanation of a very efficient method of estimation is given in Poole (1984). The estimated $\hat{\mathbf{X}}$ matrix is used to provide legislator starts for D-NOMINATE.

For the most part, the approach detailed above works well in practice. However, when the membership of either the House or the Senate shifts very rapidly—so that there is very little membership overlap across a short sequence of Congresses—the resultant starting coordinates for the second and higher dimensions were often unreliable.

Our solution for this problem was to produce and study animated videos of the scaling results. When rapid movement induced a "twist" in the position of legislators, we investigated the possibility of multiplying the second-dimension starting coordinates by -1, thus "flipping" them over. We then reran the entire scaling with these corrected starts. This always improved the overall log-likelihood and substantially reduced the magnitudes of the estimated legislator trend parameters ($\mathbf{x}_{i1}$ in equation [A5]).

In essence, when there is little overlap to tie the space together, it is difficult to identify the parameters of spatial movement. The results we report in this book reflect the best log-likelihoods we have been able to achieve; and they also have lower trend coefficients than solutions with slightly worse log-likelihoods.

Roll Call Starts. As we explained above, starting values for the z_{mj} and d_j are needed only for the first dimension. The starting estimate of a z_{mj} is simply the cutting point that best classifies the roll call. The starting estimate of a d_j is approximately ½. For dimensions two and above, the starting values for the roll call parameters are always at zero.

Starting Value for β. Finally, as we explained earlier, because we use a scaling constant of ⅕, we have found empirically that a starting value of 15 for β works very well.

Constraints on the Estimated Parameter Values

Even when the underlying model developed above accurately represents behavior, estimated values of the x_i, z_{mj}, and d_j can be unreasonable. Roll call parameters can take on unreasonable values if the voting is "perfect" or if it is very lopsided.

A perfect roll call is one in which the cutting line perfectly classifies the observed choices. Note that such perfect roll calls are expected to arise—with a small probability—even in our stochastic model. The random realizations of the errors could lead to an empirically perfect pattern. An example of such a pattern is:

$$YYYYYYYYYYYYYYYYYYYYYYYYYYYYY \mid NNNNNNNNNNNNNNNNNNNN$$

where the cutting point is between the two legislators denoted with the vertical line. As argued earlier, the cutting point is obviously precisely estimated, but d_j is not. From the viewpoint of optimal classification, any pair of outcome coordinates equidistant from the cutting point are consistent with the pattern of voting. We are in the ironic position of needing voting errors to pin down the locations of the outcome coordinates. Because we use a quasi-concave (normal-distribution-like) deterministic utility function (u), d_j will not "explode." (As $d_{jk} \to \infty$; $P_{ijy} \to$ ½.) However, for some perfect roll calls, d_j does take on a value that places the outcome coordinates outside the space spanned by the legislators. The magnitude of d_j in a perfect roll call is a function of the percentage of the legislators in the majority. We should reiterate, however, that the midpoint is always identified and is reliably estimated.

When a roll call vote is very lopsided, it is difficult to estimate the roll call parameters. We included all roll calls with 2.5 percent of the legislators, or more, in the minority. Although such roll calls tend to be very noisy, they provide information that helps to differentiate legislators at the extremes of the space. The 2.5 percent rule represents a trade-off between introducing noisy roll calls that are, on average, not reliably estimated and a gain in the accuracy of the estimation of extremist legislators. We settled on the 2.5 percent rule after extensive experimentation with one-dimensional estimation on the 1979–80 Senate.

For a typically noisy but very lopsided vote (for example, 95 percent to 5 percent), the log-likelihood will be maximized by placing the cutting line so that all legislators are predicted to vote with the majority; this will cause the cutting line (and at least one outcome coordinate) to drift outside the space spanned by the legislators. In this case, we constrain the midpoint to be equal to the location of the most extreme legislator for the dimension being estimated, and we set d_{jk} at 0.5.

We also have an identification problem with perfect-voting extremist legislators who either always vote as a conservative or always vote as a liberal. For example, in one dimension, let C denote the policy outcome to the right of the cutting point, and let L denote the policy outcome to left of the cutting point. The voting pattern for a legislator near the center of the space might look like this:

$$LLLLLLLLLLLLLLLLLLLLLLLLLLLLLLLL \mid CCCCCCCCCCCCCCCCCCCCCCCC$$

where the L's and C's represent how a legislator located at the vertical line voted. This pattern is an example of the voting of a perfect nonextremist legislator. Note that, like the cutting line in a perfect roll call, perfect nonextremist legislators are identified.

Now, suppose a legislator always votes for the policy outcome to the right of the midpoint. This produces the following voting pattern:

$$CCCCCCCCCCCCCCCCCCCCCCCCCCCCCCCCCCCCCCCCCCCCCCC$$

Any ideal point to the right of the rightmost midpoint is consistent with this pattern of voting. To deal with this identification problem, constraints are imposed. After unconstrained estimates of $\mathbf{x}_{i0}$ to $\mathbf{x}_{im}$ are made on the k-th dimension, the maximum and minimum coordinates for each Congress are used to define constraint coordinates:

$$\tilde{x}_{tk} = \left[\frac{\left[\max_i x_{itk} \right]^2 + \left[\min_i x_{itk} \right]^2}{2} \right]^{1/2} \tag{A16}$$

For each legislator, we define a constraining ellipse by computing, for $k = 1, \ldots, s$:

$$\tilde{x}_{ik} = \frac{1}{\mathcal{T}_i} \sum_{t=1}^{\mathcal{T}_i} \tilde{x}_{tk}$$

with the $\tilde{x}_{ik}$ and the origin defining the ellipse. We then compute the average coordinate for a legislator over the $\mathcal{T}_i$ Congresses in which the legislator served—specifically,

$$\bar{x}_{ik} = \frac{1}{\mathcal{T}_i} \sum_{t=1}^{\mathcal{T}_i} x_{itk}$$

If $\bar{x}_{ik}$ is in the interior of the ellipse, defined by the origin and $\tilde{x}_{ik}$, then the legislator's coordinates are unconstrained. Otherwise, the coefficients of the legislator's time polynomial above the constant are set at zero for the current dimension, $x_{i1k} = x_{i2k} = \ldots = x_{imk} = 0$; and x_{i0k} is constrained to keep the legislator inside the ellipse—that is, $x_{i0k}^2 = \tilde{x}_{ik}^2$.

Far fewer legislators are constrained than roll calls. For example, 4.2 percent of the legislators and 14.1 percent of the roll calls were constrained for the two-dimensional, linear House estimation. The constraints are most often invoked for lopsided roll calls. Constraints are needed on more than half of the most lopsided votes (10 percent of legislators or less in the minority). In contrast, constraints are invoked in under 1 percent of the very close roll calls (45 percent or more in the minority), and only 3 percent of those roll calls with 35 percent or more in the minority were constrained. Consequently, almost all roll calls that are of interest to scholars are unconstrained.[5]

Statistical Issues

The use of constraints and of the dimension-by-dimension, three-step structure of our algorithm means that conventional procedures for computing the standard errors of our model will not apply. When the BHHH gradient method is employed, at convergence the standard errors are obtained by taking the square root of the diagonal elements of ∇^{-1} (see equation [A8]). In our case, we only have standard errors for subsets of parameters, given that all other parameters remain fixed. The appropriate procedure would be to compute—when the overall algorithm has converged for all subsets of parameters—the ∇ matrix for all the parameters and invert it, thereby obtaining the correct standard errors. However, the ∇ matrix would be greater than 100,000 by 100,000, and it simply is not practical to invert a matrix of that size. As a consequence, the standard errors produced by the D-NOMINATE algorithm must be viewed as heuristic descriptive statistics.[6]

To get a handle on the reliability of the standard errors produced by D-NOMINATE, we applied Efron's (1979) bootstrap method to one-dimensional legislator coordinates of the 94th Senate ($s = 1$, with, of course, no time coefficients). We took the 1,311 actual roll calls and then drew, with replacement, 50 samples of size 1,311. Consequently, some actual roll calls will not appear while others will appear more than once in each sample. We then ran D-NOMINATE for each of the 50 samples and computed the standard deviation of the 50 estimates for each senator. The results appear in table A.1.

Table A.1   Distribution of Bootstrap Standard Errors for Senators, 94th Senate

	D-NOMINATE[a]	W-NOMINATE[b]	
Range of Bootstrap Standard Errors	No. of Senators	No. of Senators, 1st Dimension	No. of Senators, 2nd Dimension
0.00–0.01	0	0	0
0.01–0.02	11	15	0
0.02–0.03	62	52	3
0.03–0.04	21	19	6
0.04–0.05	5	11	13
0.05–0.06	1	3	25
0.06–0.07	0	0	26
0.07–0.08	0	0	13
0.08–0.09	0	0	7
0.09–0.10	0	0	3
0.10–0.11	0	0	2
0.11–0.12	0	0	1
0.12–0.13	0	0	1
0.13–0.14	0	0	0
0.14–0.15	0	0	0
Total	100	100	100

Note: 50 samples in both experiments.

[a] One-dimensional model.

[b] Two-dimensional model.

The largest bootstrap standard error is 0.051, and 73 of 100 senators have bootstrap standard errors that are under 0.03. Since the space has a range of approximately two units, the senators' locations are precisely estimated. We did not apply the bootstrap method to our dynamic estimation because of computer-time limitations. Clearly, however, at least in one dimension, the dynamic model will be precisely estimated because, typically, three or more Congresses, rather than one, will be used to estimate the location of a legislator.

In addition to the problem of standard errors, we have an additional problem, which reflects the fact that every legislator and every roll call has a specific set of parameters. Therefore, we always have additional parameters to estimate as we add observations. This is known as the incidental-parameters problem.[7] Consequently, the standard proof of the consistency of maximum likelihood does not apply. That is, even with infinitely many observations, maximum-likelihood estimates cannot be guaranteed to converge to the true values of the parameters.

As a practical matter, this is not an important problem because the amount of data grows at a much faster rate than the number of parameters. For example, consider the two-dimensional linear model for the Senate, and assume that we add a new Senate with 15 freshman senators and 500 roll calls. This would add 60 parameters for the senators (assuming they all acquired trend terms), and 2,000 parameters for the roll calls. To estimate these 2,060 new parameters, we would have 50,000 (100×500) new observations for a ratio of data to parameters of 25 to 1. For the House of Representatives, a similar ratio would be over 100 to 1.

Haberman (1977) obtained analytical results on consistency for a problem closely related to ours. He treated the Rasch model from the educational-testing literature. In place of p legislators voting on q roll calls, p subjects take q tests. Each subject has an "ability" parameter and each test has a "difficulty" parameter; the roles of Yea and Nay votes are played by "correct" and "incorrect" answers. A version of the Rasch model analyzed by Lord (1975) is in fact isomorphic with a one-dimensional Euclidean model of roll call voting developed by Ladha (1991).

Haberman considered increasing sequences of integers $\{q_n\}$ and $\{p_n\}$, for which $q_n \geq p_n$. In other words, the number of roll calls always exceeds the number of legislators. In addition, he makes the (innocuous) technical assumption that $\log(q_n)/p_n \to \infty$. Under these conditions, Haberman establishes consistency for the Rasch model.

Few actual processes, including that of Congress, can be thought of as satisfying Haberman's stringent requirement that both p and q grow as n grows. But Haberman cites Monte Carlo studies by Wright and Douglas (1976), which show excellent recovery for conventional maximum-likelihood estimators for p between 20 and 80 and for q of 500. In D-NOMINATE, the effective p is 100 in the modern Senate and 435 in the modern House. The effective q is about 900. Similar Monte Carlo evidence is contained in Lord (1975).

Monte Carlo Tests of D-NOMINATE

The D-NOMINATE model differs from the Rasch model in that the former's utility is a nonlinear function of the parameters. Although Haberman's theoretical results and the previous Monte Carlo results are suggestive, there is no substitute for direct Monte Carlo tests of our algorithm.

In Poole and Rosenthal (1987a), we reported on extensive Monte Carlo studies of our earlier one-dimensional NOMINATE algorithm. As true locations, we used the estimated senator coordinates from a scaling of 297 roll calls that took place in 1979. We used a wide variety of alternative sets of true roll call coordinates and alternative true values of β between 7.5 and 22.5. Over all the runs, the squared correlations between the recovered legislator coordinates and the true coordinates exceeded 0.98. The standard error of recovery of individual coordinates (the variability across Monte Carlo runs) was on the order of 0.05 relative to a space of 2.0 units. Recovered β's are slightly higher than the true value. Recovery came closer to the true value of β as the number of observations was increased.

The recovery of the midpoints is about as accurate as the recovery of the legislators. This result is a consequence of the fact that, as we illustrated above, legislators and midpoints are two sides of the same coin in our model. However, for reasons we discussed earlier, the recovery of the outcome coordinates (that is, the $\mathbf{d}_j$) is not as good as the recovery of the legislators and midpoints—specifically, the outcome coordinates are sensitive to the level of noise in the roll call. In Poole and Rosenthal (1991a), we reported on an extensive set of Monte Carlo studies of the two-dimensional D-NOMINATE algorithm. These studies included tests of how robust our algorithm was to a violation of the constant β assumption. (The constant β assumption is equivalent to assuming that the noise is constant across roll calls.) The testing was done using a hypothetical Senate of a single Congress. We did not pursue simulations of the dynamic model because such simulations are too costly in terms of computer time.

To simulate a Senate, we had 101 senators vote on 420 roll calls. The $\mathbf{x}$'s and $\mathbf{z}_{mj}$'s were drawn for each dimension from a uniform distribution over $[-1, +1]$. We used a 2×2 design to study roll call voting. In one contrast, we used a constant β condition, where β was set at 15.75 to match typical estimates from actual data; and we compared it to a variable β condition, where the noise level of each roll call was randomly determined. In the other contrast, we varied the $\mathbf{d}_j$'s to produce low and high noise levels. The low rate corresponded to an error rate of about 14 percent of the artificial choices, which was about the level of classification error attained by D-NOMINATE with the congressional data. The high rate was set about 30 percent, which was above that for the worst fitting Congresses in our scaling.[8]

We ran 25 simulations at each combination of β condition and error level for a total of 100 simulations. We found the recovery of the senators to be highly robust to whether the true world has a fixed β across roll calls or a β in which each roll call "rolls" its own β. In addition, the recovery was highly successful in matching the predicted choices from the recovered coordinates to the true choices that the senators would have made if they had chosen without error. For both β conditions, the percentage agreement was over 94 percent at the low error level and remained over 88 percent at the high error level.

Similar studies of the one-dimensional D-NOMINATE algorithm and studies of the stability, in one and two dimensions, of the algorithm to random starting coordinates are presented in Poole and Rosenthal (1991a). In sum, the weight of the Monte Carlo evidence from these various studies supports the conclusion that the D-NOMINATE algorithm is reliable and highly accurate.

Static Weighted Nominal Three-Step Estimation (W-NOMINATE)

W-NOMINATE is a static version of D-NOMINATE, with a number of improvements being designed to increase the efficiency of the algorithm so that it can be run on a desktop personal computer. To this end, W-NOMINATE differs from D-NOMINATE in two ways: It uses a slightly different deterministic utility function; and, because it is a static algorithm, it constrains the legislators and roll call midpoints to lie within an s-dimensional hypersphere of radius one (in contrast to the rather flexible constraint structure necessitated by the dynamic model).

The W-NOMINATE Weighted Deterministic Utility Function

The deterministic utility function for W-NOMINATE is:

$$u_{ijy} = \beta \exp\left[-\frac{\sum_{k=1}^{s} w_k^2 d_{ijyk}^2}{2} \right] \tag{A17}$$

where the w_k's are weighting factors common to all individuals. As we noted in our discussion of equation (A2), we found, from extensive experimentation in our very early work with a one-dimensional model, that β and w were highly collinear. Consequently, in D-NOMINATE, $w = \frac{1}{2}$. In one dimension, because of the collinearity of β and w, D-NOMINATE and W-NOMINATE are essentially identical. The only difference is that in W-NOMINATE, w_1 is adjusted to offset a linear transformation of the legislator and roll call coordinates, which is applied to keep the maximum and minimum legislators at +1 and –1, respectively.

In more than one dimension, the two treat β and the w_k's differently. In D-NOMINATE, the w_k's were all set at $\frac{1}{2}$, and β was reestimated each time a dimension was added to the model. Because β had to be estimated in the third step (see figure A.3), the previous dimension's value of β affected the initial estimates of the current dimension's values for the outcome and legislator coordinates. In addition, since β is a signal-to-noise ratio, simply adding more dimensions must increase the value of β.

In the W-NOMINATE algorithm, β is only estimated for the first dimension and is thereafter kept constant. For dimension 2, and higher dimensions, the corresponding w_k is estimated. In each dimension, the starting value of w_k is set at $\frac{1}{2}$. In comparison with D-NOMINATE being applied to a single Congress, this has the effect of speeding up convergence for the coordinates on the second and higher dimensions. The two procedures produce virtually the same legislator coordinates. The Pearson R²'s between the corresponding first-dimension and second-dimension coordinates are almost always above 0.95.[9]

Constraints on the Estimated Parameter Values in W-NOMINATE

W-NOMINATE handles the identification problem of perfect and near-perfect conservative/liberal legislators (discussed above) somewhat differently than does D-NOMINATE. In D-

NOMINATE, this is much less of a problem because there are usually so many roll calls that the legislator's position can be pinned down without too many problems. With just one Congress, however, more stringent constraints must be placed on the estimate of legislator coordinates.

The starting estimates of the legislator coordinates for the first dimension that are obtained from the decomposition method (detailed above) are adjusted so that they range from -1 to $+1$. Subsequently, if the furthest left/right legislator's coordinate "blows up," as a result of perfect or near-perfect liberal or conservative voting, and is 0.1 units or more away from the nearest legislator, then the legislator's coordinate is constrained in that it is not estimated during the next iteration. As a practical matter, this sets the coordinate at either -1 or $+1$. For example, suppose legislator A has an estimated coordinate of -1.2; legislator B has an estimated coordinate of -1.0; legislator C has a coordinate of $+1.1$; and legislator D has a coordinate of $+1.05$. The transformation into a -1 to $+1$ scale is:

$$\frac{-1.2 - (-.05)}{1.15} = -1.0 \quad \text{and} \quad \frac{+1.1 - (-.05)}{1.15} = +1.0$$

where

$$-.05 = \frac{-1.2 + 1.1}{2} \quad \text{and} \quad 1.15 = 1.1 - (-.05)$$

Legislator A is now constrained and his coordinate is no longer estimated, but the rest of the legislators—B, C, and D—are unconstrained.

This same linear transformation is then applied to the roll call outcome midpoints; that is,

$$z_{mj}^{(new)} = \frac{z_{mj} - (-.05)}{1.15}$$

and the exponent of the utility function is adjusted so that the log-likelihood is unaffected by the linear transformation—namely

$$u_{ijy}^{(new)} = \beta \exp\left[-\frac{(1.15)^2 w_1^2 d_{ijy}^2}{2}\right] = \beta \exp\left[-\frac{w_1^{*2} d_{ijy}^2}{2}\right]$$

where $w_1 = .5$, and $w_1^* = .575$ is the adjusted w_1. This adjustment of w is performed only for the first dimension. For $k = 2, \ldots, s$, β remains fixed and w_k is estimated.

In W-NOMINATE, all legislators and roll call midpoints are constrained to lie within a unit hypersphere. If a legislator's current-dimension coordinate is such that he is estimated outside the unit hypersphere—that is, if $\sum_{k=1}^{s'} x_{ik}^2 > 1$ (where s' is the current number of dimensions)—then a simple grid search is performed on the surface of the unit hypersphere near the point on the hypersphere's surface where the vector, x_i, exits the hypersphere. For example, in two dimensions, if a legislator's coordinate for the second dimension results in the legislator's point being outside the unit circle, then a grid search is performed around that point on the unit circle where the vector, x_i, passes through the unit circle. A similar grid search is performed for a roll call midpoint if $\sum_{k=1}^{s'} z_{mjk}^2 > 1$.

Monte Carlo Tests of W-NOMINATE

Table A.1 shows the results of a bootstrap experiment identical to that described earlier in this appendix, except that W-NOMINATE is discussed here, rather than D-NOMINATE. The first-dimension bootstrap standard errors for W-NOMINATE are better than those for D-NOMINATE; the largest bootstrap standard error for W-NOMINATE is 0.050, with the bulk of the standard errors being under 0.04. The results for the second dimension are not as precise, because the second dimension is much less important than the first dimension in the 94th Senate. The second dimension only adds about 4 percent to the classifications; nevertheless, the largest standard error is only 0.125, with the bulk of the second-dimension standard errors being below 0.08. Given that the diameter of the space is two units (a circle of radius one), the senators are precisely estimated. (See chapters 3 and 4 for an extensive discussion of the dimensionality of congressional voting.)

In order to test the accuracy of the recovery of coordinates by W-NOMINATE, we performed tests similar to those described earlier for D-NOMINATE. We used the coordinates from one of the bootstrap estimations of the 94th Senate to create artificial roll call matrices. There were 100 senators and 1,146 roll calls with estimated coordinates from the bootstrap estimation (there were a total of 1,311 roll calls, but only 1,146 had 2.5 percent in the minority or more). We assumed that the W-NOMINATE coordinates from the bootstrap run were true, and we created the deterministic portions of the utility functions from these coordinates and the converged values for β, w_1, and w_2. The stochastic portions were generated by random draws from the log of the inverse exponential (or logit) distribution. The average level of classification errors produced by this Monte Carlo procedure (15.5 percent) matched almost exactly the observed level in the actual roll call data for the 94th Senate.

We applied W-NOMINATE to 50 artificial roll call matrices and calculated the Pearson R^2 for the true and the reproduced coordinates. The average R^2 for the 100 senators was 0.99 on the first dimension and 0.98 on the second dimension. Because any pair of outcome points parallel to, and equidistant from, the true cutting line will reproduce the same roll call splits, we used two statistics to evaluate the roll call estimates. In the first, we compared the true angle of the cutting line with the reproduced angle. In the second, we compared the classifications of the reproduced outcome coordinates with the true outcome coordinates. If a senator is predicted to vote Yea in both sets of coordinates, or Nay in both, we counted that as a success.

The average R^2 between the true cutting-line angle and the reproduced angle for unconstrained roll calls was 0.86. The R^2 for the roll calls is lower than that for the senators because the number of senators that can pin down the roll call cutting line is 100, as opposed to the much larger figure of 1,146 roll calls that pins down a senator's coordinates. We excluded constrained roll calls—those where the cutting line predicts unanimity—because all cutting lines at the edge of the circle are identical. Typically, about 970 of the 1,146 roll calls were unconstrained.

In the classification analysis, the average agreement between the predictions of the reproduced coordinates and those of the true coordinates was 95.1 percent. On average, there were approximately 97,000 choices (970 roll calls times 100 senators). Of these 97,000 choices, on average, 92,247 were correctly predicted by the reproduced coordinates.

In conclusion, the W-NOMINATE algorithm differs from the D-NOMINATE algorithm (outlined in figure A.3) only in its treatment of the second and higher dimensions. In sum:

First dimension:

Step 1: Estimate the z_{mj1} and the d_{j1}.
Step 2: Estimate the x_{i1}.
Step 3: Estimate β and adjust w_1

Second and higher dimensions:

Step 1: Estimate the z_{mjk} and the d_{jk}.
Step 2: Estimate the x_{ik}.
Step 3: Estimate w_k.

Appendix B: The Dimensionality of Spatial Voting

How Many Dimensions Are There?

Is there any objective way of determining the dimensionality of roll call voting? The answer is a qualified yes, if roll call voting is in accord with the model of perfect spatial voting (no errors) that we outlined in chapter 2. Technically, in this case, the votes can be broken down into subsets that form perfect Guttman scales (a two-point model, as it is termed in chapters 6 and 7). If the scales are orthogonal, then a principal-components analysis of the Yule's Q matrix will reveal the exact dimensionality underlying the voting. If the scales are correlated, the *approximate* dimensionality will be shown (Weisberg, 1968, pp. 151–161).[1]

Figure B.1 shows the percentage of variation explained by the first three eigenvalues of the Yule's Q matrix, computed for each House and Senate.[2] All roll calls with at least 10 percent in the minority were used.[3] Three dimensions account for almost all the variation in most of the Houses, and two dimensions account for over 90 percent in 91 of the 100 Congresses. The patterns for the Senate are not as high as for the House because of much smaller memberships in the Senates, making the Yule's Q matrix noisier in the Senate than in the House. Nevertheless, two dimensions account for over 80 percent of the variation in 83 of the 100 Congresses and in all twentieth-century Congresses.

The explained-variation pattern of the Yule's Q eigenvalues closely matches the pattern of correct classifications from D-NOMINATE that is shown in figure 3.1. Again, the worst-fitting Congresses are found during the Era of Good Feelings and the early 1850s. The correlation between the classifications in figure 3.1 and the percentage of two-dimensional explained variation in figure B.1 is 0.79 for the House and 0.92 for the Senate.

Figure B.2 shows more evidence on dimensionality. In this instance, we computed the legislator-by-legislator covariance matrices and extracted the eigenvalues.[4] Figure B.2 displays the percentage of variance explained by the first three eigenvalues.[5] The correlation between the two-dimensional explained variation in figure B.1 and the two-dimensional explained variance of figure B.2 is 0.92 for the House and 0.90 for the Senate.

With the exception of the brief periods discussed earlier, the number of dimensions for roll call voting is, at most, two. In most Congresses, the second dimension is very weak. The structure of the covariance matrix has been largely accounted for by the first eigenvalue, with the second eigenvalue playing an important role only on occasion.

Finally, figure B.3 shows, for the House of Representatives, the correlations between the D-NOMINATE coordinates and both the coordinates computed from our version of the Heckman-Snyder (H-S) procedure (Heckman and Snyder, 1995; see also note 4) and those computed by the metric scaling procedure represented by equation (A15), in appendix A. The

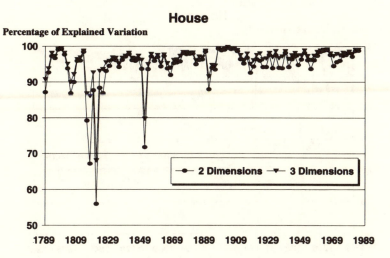

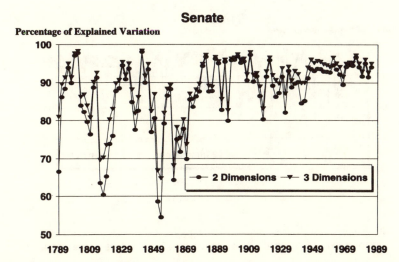

Figure B.1. Cumulative percentage of variation in Yule's Q roll-call-by-roll-call matrix explained by second and third eigenvalues. The results strongly support the conclusion that roll call voting is, at most, two-dimensional. The most important additions from the third eigenvalue occur in the two antebellum "chaos" periods that preceded and followed the Democratic/Whig party system.

correlations between the D-NOMINATE first dimension and the other two methods are all very high—above 0.95 for 83 of the 100 Houses. Note that the H-S and metric procedures are computed *separately* for each House. If the correlations are based on the static W-NOMINATE coordinates (that is, coordinates estimated separately for each House), then *all* the pairwise correlations (including those between the H-S and the metric procedure) are above 0.92,

House

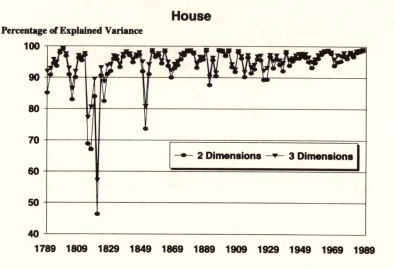

Senate

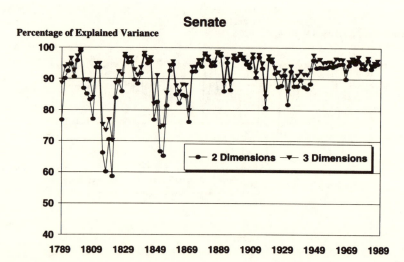

Figure B.2. Cumulative percentage of variation in the legislator-by-legislator covariance matrix explained by second and third eigenvalues. The results are highly similar to those of figure B.1.

and for only three Houses are the correlations between W-NOMINATE and the other two below 0.95.

Consistent with our discussion in chapter 3, the various correlations for the second dimension are much lower. Note that the two periods when the second-dimension correlations are stable and high in figure B.3 are the Whig-Democratic period after the Era of Good Feelings, and the period after the late 1930s, during the three-party era.

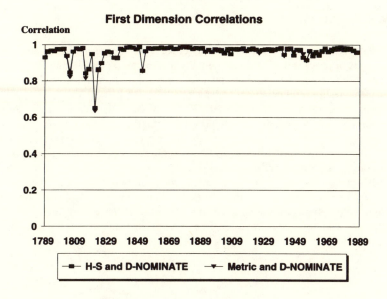

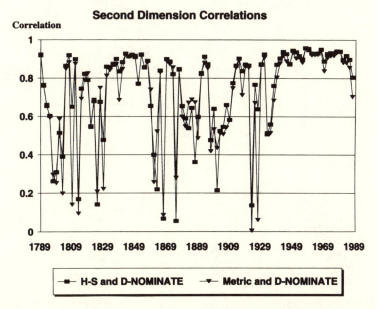

Figure B.3. Correlations of legislator coordinates from D-NOMINATE with coordinates from Heckman-Snyder scaling and from metric unfolding of legislator-agreement scores, House of Representatives (1789–1988). The top part shows the first-dimension correlations. These are uniformly high, except for the two "chaos" periods before and after the emergence of the Whig/Democratic system. The bottom part shows the second-dimension correlations. Although these are generally much weaker than the first-dimension correlations, they are high in the Whig/Democratic and three-party eras, the two occasions when a second dimension has importance.

How Well Should One Dimension Classify?

Koford (1989) observed that a useful null model for evaluating estimated spatial models assumes that the true space is of high dimensionality with perfect spatial voting. The projection of this perfect voting onto a lower-dimensional space, equal to the number of dimensions being estimated, provides a useful comparative benchmark. Poole, Sowell, and Spear (1992) solved this problem for a projection onto one dimension. In particular, they assumed a uniform distribution of voters within an s-dimensional hypersphere of radius one, with perfect spatial voting. For a fixed proportion of minority voters, m, the alternatives are drawn from a uniform distribution over the hypersphere (this is equivalent to the cutting plane being randomly rotated around the origin of the hypersphere).

Figure B.4 shows several examples of perfect voting in two dimensions, with 50–50 votes ($m = 0.5$). One line through each circle is the perpendicular bisector of the line joining the two policy alternatives—the cutting line. Note that the angle of the cutting line determines how noisy the projection is onto one dimension. In part A of figure B.4, the cutting line is perpendic-

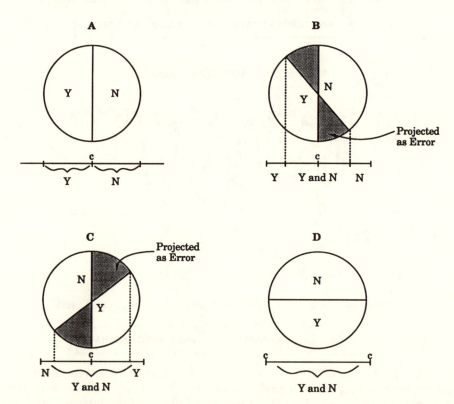

Figure B.4. Vote classification with one dimension with perfect spatial voting. In each part of the figure, voters are uniformly distributed over the circle, and the cutting lines are chosen such that all votes are 50–50. Point c denotes optimal classification cutpoints when the ideal points are projected onto the line below. In part A, the two-dimensional cutting line is vertical; projection of ideal points maintains perfect classification. In part B, the cutting line has an angle of 135° (or – 45°); projection results in correct classifications of only 75 percent. Similarly, classification is 75 percent in part C, where the cutting-line angle is 45°. In part D, the cutting line is horizontal; only 50 percent are correctly classified.

ular to the projection dimension so that the cutting point, c, perfectly divides the Yeas from the Nays—the percentage of the individual votes correctly classified would be 100 percent. In part B of figure B.4, the angle of the cutting line is 45°, and in part C, it is −45°. These two projections produce the same cutting point as in part A, but the percentage correctly classified falls to 75 percent. To see this, note that the shaded regions are areas of the plane that will be incorrectly classified when projected onto the single dimension. The shaded portions make up 25 percent of the area of the circles. Finally, in part D of figure B.4, the cutting line is parallel to the projection dimension so that only 50 percent—which is simply equal to the marginals of the vote—is correctly projected; the cutting point can be at either end of the projection dimension.

Poole, Sowell, and Spear (1992) use this model to derive the probability-density function of the classification error on the projection dimension, for all minority proportions, *m,* and for all dimensions, *s.* Hence, given a set of classification errors and minority proportions from some set of roll calls scaled in one dimension, the likelihood that the observed set of roll calls is a projection of perfect voting in a voting space of *s* dimensions can be calculated for each *s.*

Using these results to calculate the likelihood that we would observe the combination of margins (which are given in the real-world data) and classification percentages from our D-NOMINATE one-dimensional scaling,[6] we can calculate likelihoods for two through seven dimensions. Confining our attention to the House of Representatives because the accuracy of the Poole, Sowell, and Spear results increases with the number of voters, figure B.5 graphs the mean likelihood (that is, the log-likelihood divided by the number of votes and exponentiated) for two- and three-dimensional perfect-voting projections for all 100 Houses. (We calculated the likelihoods for up to seven dimensions, but we show them for only two and three dimensions in order to reduce clutter in the figure.)

The striking fact about figure B.5 is the clear dominance of two dimensions. For every House since the 32nd, the likelihood function peaks at two dimensions. The likelihood of three dimensions becomes closer to the two-dimensional likelihood after World War I (during the 66th House) and almost surpasses it for the 85th House. In line with our findings for the later

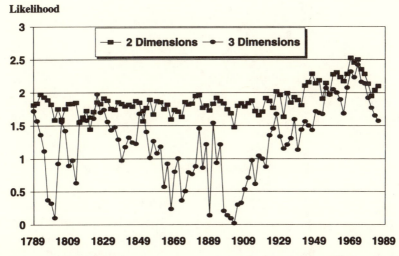

Figure B.5. Mean likelihoods for two and three dimensions for the first 100 Houses. The likelihood that the roll calls are a projection of perfect voting in an *s*-dimensional voting space is computed using the classification errors from the one-dimensional D-NOMINATE estimation and the observed majority-minority split. If perfect voting were occurring, it would most likely be two dimensional.

Houses, before the 32nd House, two dimensions predominate, except for the Era of Good Feelings. Indeed, the likelihood peaks at four or five dimensions in the 17th, 19th, and 32nd Houses.

Poole, Sowell, and Spear (1992) also performed a simple Guttman scaling of each matrix of House roll call votes in order to obtain—for the same set of roll call margins—another set of classification percentages as a check on the results given above. The percentage of classification errors, by roll call, obtained from the Guttman scalings will tend to be smaller than that from one-dimensional D-NOMINATE because Guttman scaling minimizes classification errors and because each House was scaled separately. Hence the likelihoods computed using the classification percentages from D-NOMINATE should be biased upward (because D-NOMINATE does not minimize classification errors), relative to the Guttman scaling likelihoods. Nevertheless, the results are almost identical (Poole, Sowell, and Spear, 1992, p. 94, figure 5). The order of the likelihoods does differ in the predicted direction for some of the Houses during the Era of Good Feelings. For example, the order of the likelihoods for the 17th House was 5–4–3–2 when we used the D-NOMINATE classification percentages; with the Guttman scaling classification percentages, the order was 3–4–2–5.

Appendix C: Roll Call Coding Categories

Coding Schemes

Below, we detail the three coding schemes we used to classify all the roll call votes in the first 100 Houses and Senates. For the Clausen (1973) and Peltzman (1984) schemes, we list some issue areas that fall within each category; our own specific issue codes comprise the third scheme.

Each roll call received, at most, one specific issue code, exactly one Clausen code, and one or two Peltzman codes. Our codings of the individual roll calls can be obtained by purchasing the VOTEVIEW (for DOS or Windows) package from Richard Schaeffer, financial officer at the Graduate School of Administration, Carnegie Mellon University, Pittsburgh, PA 15213.

Our specific issue codes are not exhaustive. Some historical topics were not covered. Researchers interested in other topics can find them quickly by using the keyword search structure of VOTEVIEW for Windows.

Clausen Categories

1. Government management: environmental control; government regulation of business; natural-resource management; government ownership of business; government control of the economy; budget balancing; tax policy; interest rates; management of the bureaucracy.

2. Social welfare: social security; public housing; urban renewal; labor regulation; education; urban affairs; employment opportunities and rewards; welfare; Medicare; unemployment; minimum wage; legal services.

3. Agriculture: price supports and subsidies; commodity control; acreage limitations.

4. Civil liberties: civil rights; equality; criminal procedure; privacy; guarantees of the Bill of Rights; slavery; Hatch Act.

5. Foreign and defense policy: international policy; foreign aid; aid to international organizations; armament policy; defense procurement; international trade; military pensions.

6. Miscellaneous policy: unclassifiable or unidentifiable votes; all votes concerned with the internal organization of Congress; procedural motions.

Peltzman Categories

1. Budget—general interest: debt limit; budget targets; revenue sharing; unemployment insurance; tax rates; continuing appropriations.

2. Budget—special interest: authorization/appropriations for agencies, departments; public works; subsidized housing; NSF; parks; food stamps.

3. Regulation—general interest: general tariffs; minimum wage; gasoline rationing; auto emissions; water pollution.

4. Regulation—special interests: union regulations; coal-mine regulations; export/import controls; fish and wildlife.

5. Domestic social policy: abortion; school prayer; busing; criminal code and federal courts; immigration; gun control; Hatch Act; veterans' preferences; Legal Services Corporation; voting rights; slavery.

61. Defense-policy budget: authorization/appropriations for the military; military pensions.

71. Defense-policy resolutions: number of Army divisions; duties of officers.

62. Foreign-policy budget: authorization/appropriations for State Department and international organizations.

72. Foreign-policy resolutions: condemn/thank foreign nations; U.S.-Taiwanese relations; disapproval of apartheid.

8. Government organization: setting up new agencies/bureaus/commissions; civil-service regulations; government reorganization; Federal Election Commission; constitutional amendments; admission of states; census.

9. Internal organization: election of House Speaker; party ratios on committees; creating committees; procedural rules; disputed elections; congressional pay.

10. Indian affairs: Indian treaties; appropriations for the Indian Department; Indian lands and reservations.

11. D.C.: all votes dealing with the District of Columbia.

Specific Issue Codes
1. Abortion/care of deformed newborns
2. Agriculture
3. Airlines/airports/airline industry
4. Alien and Sedition Acts
5. Amnesty (all wars)
6. Arms control
7. B-1 Bomber
8. Banking and finance
9. Breeder reactor
10. Budget resolution
11. CIA/spying/intelligence
12. Campaign contributions/House ethics/lobbying/campaign laws
13. Central America
14. Children (aid, infant mortality, etc.)
15. Civil rights/desegregation/busing/affirmative action
16. Civil service and patronage
17. Coal-mining regulation/strip mining/black lung
18. Communists/Communism/un-American activities
19. Congressional pay and benefits
20. Constitutional amendments
21. Consumer Protection Agency/consumer protection
22. Debt ceilings
23. Disputed elections to Congress
24. Education
25. Election of House officers
26. Election of the Speaker of the House
27. Electoral votes
28. Emergency fuel assistance
29. Energy

30. Exchange rates
31. Firearms
32. Fish and wildlife
33. Food stamps/food programs
34. Gasoline rationing/allocation
35. Handicapped
36. Homosexuality
37. Housing/housing programs/rent control
38. Human rights
39. Humanitarian assistance (foreign)
40. Immigration/naturalization
41. Impeachment of the president
42. Impeachments and investigations
43. Interstate commerce/antitrust/restraint of commerce
44. Iran
45. Judiciary
46. Korean War
47. MX Missile
48. Mediterranean pirates
49. Military pensions/veterans' benefits
50. Minimum wage
51. Minorities (nonblack)
52. Narcotics
53. National bank
54. Neutron bomb
55. Nuclear power
56. Nuclear weapons
57. Nullification/secession/reconstruction
58. OSHA
59. Panama Canal
60. Parks and conservation
61. Peace movements/pacifism/antimilitary activities
62. Pollution and environmental protection
63. Impeachment of officials other than the President
64. Price controls
65. Public health
66. Public lands
67. Public safety
68. Public works
69. Radio/television/motion pictures/telecommunications
70. Railroads
71. Ratio of representatives to population
72. Religion
73. Supersonic transport
74. School prayer
75. Science and technology
76. Selective service (the draft)
77. Shipping/maritime
78. Slavery
79. Social Security
80. South Africa/Rhodesia

81. Space exploration/NASA
82. States' rights versus federal government
83. Supreme Court
84. Taiwan (1979–80)
85. Tariffs
86. Tax rates
87. Temperance and liquor
88. Treaties
89. United Nations
90. U.S. currency
91. Unemployment/jobs
92. Union regulation/Davis-Bacon/Common Situs Picketing Bill
93. Vietnam War
94. Voting rights
95. World War I
96. Welfare
97. Whiskey Rebellion
98. Women's equality
99. Workplace conditions/eight-hour day

Notes

Chapter 1

1. The viewpoint that, due to the reelection motive, local constituency interests are the dominant influence in the choices made by members of Congress is so widespread that a complete set of references would be a very lengthy one. Among the more prominent works are Mayhew (1974); Fiorina (1974, 1989); and Cain, Ferejohn, and Fiorina (1987).

2. Among the numerous case studies of the legislative process, Bailey (1950) and Redman (1973) are two excellent examples.

3. The "chaos" school is represented by Riker (1980).

4. For evidence that diversity has increased in the House of Commons, see Gaines and Garrett (1992).

5. A discussion of responsiveness is found in Ansolebhere et al. (1992) and Fiorina (1989). That nonresponsiveness in regard to national interests is the norm is suggested by John F. Kennedy's characterizing those whose votes reflect the national interest as representing *Profiles in Courage* (1955).

6. Two studies of economic interests are Kalt and Zupan (1984); and Gilligan, Marshall, and Weingast, (1989). See chapter 6 for further references.

7. *Congressional Record,* December 19, 1884, p. 368.

8. To be precise, our estimation centers on a dynamic analysis that covers all roll call voting between 1789 and 1985. This analysis was conducted at the John Von Neumann National Supercomputing Center at Princeton University. Subsequently, we added separate analyses for 1986–88. We also conducted separate analyses for 1989–95. The work for 1989–90 (the 101st Congress) is used briefly in chapters 2 and 5.

9. See Cox and McCubbins (1993), for example, on how the House Democratic caucus constrained the behavior of conservative Democrats.

10. See Groseclose (1994a).

11. More detailed rejoinders can be found in Poole and Rosenthal (1991c, 1994b) and Rosenthal (1992).

Chapter 2

1. See Converse (1964).

2. Indeed, on 520 of 638 roll calls (83.1%) cast in the 101st Senate (1989–90), the voting of Kerry, Gore, Nunn, Dole, and Helms was consistent with their left-right ordering.

3. Ordeshook (1976); Hinich and Pollard (1981); Enelow and Hinich (1984).

4. Indifference is an empirical knife edge and need not be discussed.

5. Nunn's ideal point is the median of the five ideal points. Our example illustrates the median-voter theorem (Black, 1958).

6. The theoretical implications of "open"-versus-"closed" rules are analyzed in Denzau and Mackay (1983). The importance of the status quo is analyzed by Romer and Rosenthal (1978; 1979).

7. We do not consider here whether such a trade could survive as a stable outcome in a world of vote trading. For further discussion of vote trading, see Ordeshook (1986, pp. 89–94).

8. This example is one of those discussed by Enelow and Koehler (1980) and is also discussed, at length, by Ordeshook (1986, pp. 289–90). The votes discussed occurred on March 23 and are numbers 82 and 83 in VOTEVIEW.

9. More generally, if legislators have complete information about each other's preferences, any strategic pairwise vote in a binary-amendment tree can be represented as a sincere vote that involves two of the true alternatives (Ordeshook, 1986, pp. 271–74.) Therefore, methods of roll call analysis developed for the analysis of sincere voting can be directly applied to this form of strategic voting.

10. The Voting Rights Act was originally passed in 1965 and was primarily aimed at ensuring that blacks could vote in the southern states.

11. When we did our supercomputer work in 1986–88, data for the 100th Congress (1987–88) were not available. Consequently, our dynamic model, D-NOMINATE, was applied only to the first 99 Congresses. We scaled the 100th Congress separately and transformed the coordinates so that they could best fit the previous Congresses. Almost all of the analysis in this book pertains to these first 100 Congresses.

12. There is no guarantee that the alternating procedure we have described will find the globally best ordering or that the same ordering will be produced from different starting configurations. But extensive use of actual roll call data leads us to conclude that, although there may be slight differences, final configurations are very highly robust to the choice of starts.

13. If there is strategic voting with some errors, we can recover the correct roll call outcomes.

14. See appendix A for a further discussion and a qualification of this point.

15. There is some bias in the estimate of roll call outcome coordinates. As the bias decreases rapidly with the sample size, bias should not be a major problem for any House or Senate with more than 50 members. See Poole and Rosenthal (1985b) for a more detailed discussion of bias.

Chapter 3

1. In many of the graphs in this chapter, we show the 100th House and Senate. As noted previously, the 100th-Congress data were unavailable when we did our initial supercomputer work

in 1986–88. Consequently, we scaled the 100th Congress separately and transformed the coordinates so that they could best fit the previous Congresses.

2. Pairs and announced votes were treated as actual votes.

3. A correct classification is, as in chapter 2, one for which the legislator's ideal point is on the "correct" side of the estimated roll call cut—that is, the D-NOMINATE model assigns a probability greater than ½ to the actual choice (Yea or Nay). For the probability model, see appendix A.

4. See Costner (1965) and Hildebrand et al. (1977) for a discussion of the use of *PRE* measures in evaluating the fit of models.

5. Since the denominator in the equation above is constant for all entries for a house of Congress in table 3.1, the entries in the *APRE* part of the table are simply linear transformations of the corresponding classification entries.

6. In this book, we rely mainly on substantive relevance and less often on tests of statistical significance (or on standard errors). Previously (Poole and Rosenthal, 1991a), we presented various tests of significance. The standard tests presented there typically supported our substantive statements at truly infinitesimal p values (see chapter 9 for a discussion of p values). The luxury of 11,000,000 observations allows us to focus on the big picture and not to be preoccupied with whether a tree belongs in the forest. For example, given our sample size, adding dimensions or time-polynomial terms always yields statistically significant increments in the log-likelihood, without really adding to our ability to understand roll call voting behavior. For a discussion of standard errors, see appendix A.

7. To derive the theoretical distribution of errors, we computed the probabilities for each legislator on every roll call, using the estimated coordinates and β value (see appendix A for details). The smaller of the Yea probability and the Nay probability is the probability of an error. The "theoretical" line shown in figure 3.2 is the average of these error probabilities, broken down by distance from the cutting line.

8. Recall that our dynamic estimation included all nonunanimous roll calls from 1789 through 1985 (the year of the first session of the 99th Congress).

9. About 15 percent of all roll calls are constrained, but constraints are most often invoked for lopsided roll calls. Constraints are invoked for less than 1 percent of the roll call votes that are closer than 55–45. Almost all roll calls of interest to scholars are unconstrained. In contrast, constraints are needed on more than half of the most lopsided votes—those with a minority percentage of less than 10 percent. See Poole and Rosenthal (1991a) and appendix A for more detail.

10. We used Kenneth Martis's (1989) *The Historical Atlas of Political Parties in the United States Congress: 1789–1989* to determine the majority and minority parties for each House and Senate.

11. Indeed, in the presidential election of 1812, Madison and the Jeffersonians became identified as the "war party," and Madison won reelection with the solid backing of the South and the West. De Witt Clinton, the Federalist candidate, carried every northern state except Pennsylvania and Vermont. For a good summary of the War of 1812, see Hofstadter, Miller, and Aaron (1959, vol. 1, pp. 332–47). For its effect on the Federalist party, see Hofstadter (1969, chap. 5).

12. Throughout this book, the South is defined as the 11 states of the Confederacy, plus Oklahoma and Kentucky.

13. We defined a North-versus-South vote as one where at least one political party was divided along regional lines, with a majority of southern members opposing a majority of

northern members on the roll call. We then examined a histogram for just these roll calls; the "N. vs. S." in figures 3.3 and 3.4 indicates where the bulk of these roll call cutting lines fell.

14. We argue in chapter 5 that a realignment, in congressional voting, must be a structural change in the basic dimensions of voting. No such change occurred in the 1890s or the 1930s, when the realignments of the mass electorate were marked by a wholesale replacement of members of Congress. However, the replacement did not affect the basic structure of congressional voting, as it did in the 1850s.

15. See Poole and Rosenthal (1994a) for details.

16. Because of our stringent definition of a party-line roll call, the number of roll calls that met the definition was quite small in some Houses and Senates. In 15 Senates and 8 Houses, the number of party-line votes dropped below five. Not surprisingly, these were concentrated in the Era of Good Feelings (during Congresses 15 to 18, [1817–24]), when there was, as a practical matter, no minority party.

17. The other main culprits were John Blaine of Wisconsin; Robert Howell of Nebraska; William McMaster of South Dakota; Lynn Frazier of North Dakota; and Smith Brookhart of Iowa. In addition, William Borah of Idaho; Peter Norbeck of South Dakota; and Gerald Nye of North Dakota were located at the right edge of the Democrats on the first dimension and above most of the Democrats on the second dimension.

18. The midwestern Republicans in the House during this same period were more moderate than their northeastern counterparts. They were located at the left edge of the party and somewhat above the northeasterners on the second dimension. Unlike their senatorial counterparts, however, they were much closer to their fellow Republicans than to the Democrats.

19. Not every roll call received a specific issue code. Our 99 issue categories were designed to pick up the most important policy issues, not all issues (see appendix C).

20. The accuracy of our coding depends on the accuracy of the descriptions of the roll call votes in the ICPSR codebooks. The codebook descriptions sometimes do not reflect the true character of the roll calls. For example, a critical vote on the Wilmot Proviso (August 8, 1846), concerning slavery, was, formally speaking, a vote on foreign-affairs appropriations—the codebook description does not mention the Wilmot Proviso. Whenever, from other sources, we know of such instances we have coded the roll calls and corrected the codebooks appropriately. (We are thankful to Barry Weingast for alerting us to this example.)

21. The first presidential candidates to identify themselves as Whigs were William H. Harrison, Hugh L. White, and Daniel Webster, all of whom received electoral votes in 1836. For the Jacksonian period (1823–37), Martis (1989) codes members of Congress as being either "Jacksons" or varieties of "Anti-Jacksons." We use Martis's codings throughout this book and follow his classifications.

22. We recognize that slavery, before the Civil War, was an economic issue as well as a race issue. Indeed, as Fogel (1989) argues, the abolitionists were not very successful in their fight against slavery until they were able to cast it as an economic issue ("Free soil, free speech, free labor, and free men"). We maintain this distinction for clarity.

23. We also chose the 85th House because it was studied, with other methods, by Weisberg (1968). Weisberg analyzed roll calls for sets of issue areas, such as foreign policy, within the 85th. He found very high dimensionality. Our results indicate that his methods were inappropriate.

24. Weighting the dimensions causes the indifference curves shown in figure 2.4 to become ellipses. Some legislators could have ellipses elongated on the vertical dimension; others, on

the horizontal. An even more general, and still less parsimonious, model would allow for a variation in the angle of rotation—with respect to the basic space—of the axes of the ellipses. See Enelow and Hinich (1984) for technical details.

25. It is difficult to pin these lower correlations on a specific item. In the 95th Congress, foreign- and defense-policy votes included 14 on the CIA, spying, or intelligence; 11 on South Africa or Rhodesia; 8 on military pensions or veterans' benefits; 7 on the Panama Canal; 7 on the B-1 Bomber; 5 on arms control; and 5 on the United Nations.

26. Fits were not as good for the 49 votes in the agriculture category, with correct classifications of 75 percent in one dimension and 80 percent in two. Because of the small number of votes, agriculture had to be placed in the residual category.

27. The original gatekeeping model was presented by Denzau and Mackay (1983), who adapted the agenda-control model in Romer and Rosenthal (1978, 1979) to a legislative setting.

28. If ρ_a is the proportion of roll calls in category a, the index H is given by H = $\sum_a \rho_a^2$. H equals 1.0 if all the votes are in one category. For the Clausen categories, H would reach a minimum of $\frac{1}{6}$ if the roll calls were split evenly among the six categories.

Chapter 4

1. The R^2 values for the regressions described above using the chamber means on the second dimension, are 0.03 for both the post-Reconstruction period and the twentieth century.

2. Note that during this period, the dispersion of the Senate on the second dimension was very low. Consequently, even though the bulk of the Republican senators were located at the center of the second dimension, only a few Republicans with substantial second-dimension coordinates were necessary to get the mean above the Democrats.

3. There is an extensive literature on the emergence of the first political-party system. See Martis (1989, pp. 27–28), and the literature cited therein. We follow Martis's party designations, so that for Houses 1–3, we use *proadministration* and *antiadministration* for the two "parties." Subsequent to the 3rd House, these groups become the Federalists and Republicans, respectively. (For Houses 1–3, in figure 4.6, we use *Federalist* and *Republican* to identify these earlier blocs.)

4. Martis (1989, pp. 30–31) codes the two parties as "Adams" and "Jackson" during the administration of John Quincy Adams (1825–29). He then changes these codes to "Anti-Jackson" and "Jackson," respectively, for the period of Andrew Jackson's presidency (1829–37). Thereafter, he codes them as "Whig" and "Democrat."

5. The Martis (1989) codes for the 18th Congress (1823–25) include factions for Adams, Jackson, William H. Crawford, and Henry Clay.

6. See Alesina and Rosenthal (1995, chap. 2), for a review of the literature on the theory of political polarization.

7. See Alesina and Rosenthal (1995, pp. 127–36).

8. If only one outcome is inside the space, it is almost always the winning outcome.

9. Poole and Rosenthal (1987b) discuss results with similar substantive implications in cases where the data are not filtered. Similar results also obtain when one considers only close votes. The measure we use underestimates the change, because the excluded roll calls have extreme outcomes.

10. The fact that the response is to both seat share and control supports the checks-and-balances model of Alesina and Rosenthal (1995, chap. 3).

11. Both in the research reported below and in our dynamic-model estimation, where time is kept constant for each Congress, we do not deal with shifts in preferences within a given Congress. This is an important topic for future research.

12. There are obviously no members common to the 1st and 100th Congresses and to many other pairs.

13. This table differs somewhat from table 5 of Poole and Rosenthal (1991a) because we used W-NOMINATE to estimate the legislator coordinates in the static scalings for this book. The differences are not very great, however (see the discussion of W-NOMINATE in appendix A).

14. We calculated these correlations between the absolute value of a member's coordinate for each Congress and the length of service, including the current Congress. The number of observations for the House was 31,306 and for the Senate, 7,618 (Congresses 1–99). The correlation between the absolute value of a member's *last coordinate* in his or her career and his or her total length of service was only −0.04 for the House and −0.10 for the Senate (10,898 and 1,829 observations, respectively). For just the twentieth century, the correlations corresponding to the two definitions given above were −0.07 and −0.07 for the House (18,556 and 4,567 observations), and −0.13 and −0.12 for the Senate (4,299 and 875 observations).

15. Recall that the space has a diameter of 2 units. In turn, figure 4.7 shows postwar per-Congress movement to be between 0.02 and 0.03 units.

16. The correlation for all 99 Congresses is 0.72.

17. Poole and Romer (1993) regressed the one-dimensional static coordinates, for each House, on the corresponding one-dimensional dynamic coordinates. That is, they estimated: $x_i^{(d)} = \beta_0 + \beta_1 x_i^{(s)} + e$, where $x_i^{(d)}$ and $x_i^{(s)}$ are the dynamic and static coordinates, in one dimension, for the i-th representative. The estimated coefficients were used to transform the static coordinates; that is: $\tilde{x}_i^{(s)} = \hat{\beta}_0 + \hat{\beta}_1 x_i^{(s)}$, where $\tilde{x}_i^{(s)}$ is simply a linear transformation of the original static coordinates. This has the effect of putting each pair of Houses in the same metric. See Loomis (1995) and Poole and Romer (1993) for further detail.

18. The exit coding was done by Loomis (1995).

19. An F test on the 18 fixed-effect variables indicates that they are jointly significant (F = 36.82). An F test on the 8 other variables indicates that they, too, are jointly significant (F = 4.16).

20. If a representative died in office, *NOTVOTE* is the fraction of roll calls the representative would have been eligible for but did not vote in (that is, roll calls taken after the representative died are not used in the computation).

21. That is, illness may have prevented a member from voting for some period before his death.

22. Lott and Bronars (1993), using interest-group ratings, show that there is little change in the voting behavior of members of Congress in their last Congress.

23. More elaborate specifications failed to find any further meaningful structure. For example, we tried to incorporate measures of moderation by using the number of congressional districts in the state, which we interacted (in various combinations) with a representative's party and with how extreme the representative was in the House (on the theory that the representative, if extreme, must become more moderate to represent a large state in the Senate). Some coefficients in some of the various multivariate specifications were statistically significant, but

never was the magnitude of the effect substantively meaningful. Hence we opt for reporting simple Pearson (R) correlations.

24. Also, see Hibbing (1993) for a discussion of, and references to, this sizable literature.

25. See the caption to figure 4.10 for the missing values.

26. For more details on the adjustment of southern Democrats, see Poole and Rosenthal (1991a, pp. 258–64).

27. Technically, this is

$$\left\{ \frac{\sum_{i=1}^{m} \sum_{j=1}^{n} \sum_{k=1}^{s} \left(x_{ik} - x_{jk} \right)^2}{mn} \right\}^{\frac{1}{2}}$$

where *m* and *n* are the numbers of legislators in the two parties, and *s* is the number of dimensions, with $s = 2$.

28. Technically, this is

$$\left\{ \frac{\sum_{i=1}^{m-1} \sum_{j=i+1}^{m} \sum_{k=1}^{s} \left(x_{ik} - x_{jk} \right)^2}{m(m-1)/2} \right\}^{\frac{1}{2}}$$

where *m* is the number of members of the political party, and *s* is the number of dimensions, with $s = 2$.

29. Numerous studies by political scientists, using a variety of techniques, have shown that members of Congress vote consistently over time on issues and are very sensitive to their voting history (Clausen, 1973; Fiorina, 1974; Clausen and Van Horn, 1977; Asher and Weisberg, 1978; Stone, 1980; Bullock, 1981; Smith, 1981).

Chapter 5

1. See Burnham (1970); Ginsberg (1972, 1976); Sinclair (1977, 1981); Brady (1979, 1982); and Sundquist (1983).

2. Following most authors, we do not treat the long transition from the collapse of the Federalist party until the emergence of the Whig and Democratic parties, in the late 1820s and early 1830s, as a realignment. Before 1824, election statistics are not reliable, and turnout was low. In 1824 the legislatures of 6 states were still choosing their presidential electors. By 1828, 20 of the 22 states were choosing electors by popular election (the holdouts were Delaware and South Carolina). Consequently, there are no reliable mass-voting data, before 1828, to analyze.

3. See also Aldrich (1983).

4. Consequently, it might be preferable to focus on changes in probabilities rather than on classifications (Poole and Rosenthal, 1991a). But because the results are similar, we develop the discussion in terms of the more easily interpretable *PRE* measure.

5. These totals are for the first 39 Congresses—that is, for those until the end of the Civil War.

6. See Rosenthal (1995) for a more detailed discussion of Missouri Compromise votes.

7. It is the second worst-fitting House in American history. (The worst occurred in the 17th Congress, when the Federalists collapsed.) Joel Silbey (1967) in his analysis of voting in the 32nd Congress in *The Shrine of Party* writes: "The most significant fact in the legislative voting in 1851 and 1852 was that large-scale cohesive forces no longer influenced Congressional behavior to the degree they once had. . . . Congressional voting had broken down . . . into a multiplicity of factional groupings, behavioral factors, and individual decision-making, with only occasional alignments of these patterns into large-scale partisan or sectional groupings" (p. 135).

8. Douglas's motives in pushing the Kansas-Nebraska Act have generated a very large literature. An excellent discussion and summary of the various points of view on this debate is given in Nevins (1947, chap. 3). An interesting account of the opposition to Douglas is given in Donald (1960, pp. 249–259).

9. This vote is VOTEVIEW number 71 in the 32nd House. The division on the vote was 119 Yeas to 74 Nays. There were 35 classification errors.

10. The overlap is in fact understated to the extent that the linear adjustment in positions used by D-NOMINATE prohibits rapid changes of member positions during a spatial collapse.

11. This vote is VOTEVIEW number 309 in the 33rd Congress. The division on the roll call was 113 Yeas to 100 Nays. D-NOMINATE correctly classified 204 of 213 votes.

12. The destabilization of the existing political parties is precisely what many opponents of slavery wanted and set out to achieve. See the discussion by Riker (1982, chap. 9).

13. See Unger (1964, chaps. 2 and 3) for a detailed discussion of the various "soft money" proposals made during the 1865–70 period.

14. These are VOTEVIEW number 126 in the 43rd House and number 119 in the 43rd Senate, respectively. In the House, the division on the roll call was 140 Yeas to 102 Nays. With pairs, the vote was 150 Yeas to 111 Nays. D-NOMINATE correctly classified 196 of 261 representatives (75.1 percent, 0.41 *PRE*). (*There were thus 10 paired Yeas and 9 paired Nays. That the numbers don't balance reflects the original data. This is true of other imbalances throughout this book.*) In the Senate, the division on the roll call was 29 Yeas to 24 Nays. With pairs, the vote was 36 Yeas to 31 Nays. D-NOMINATE correctly classified 61 of 67 senators (91.0 percent; *PRE* =0.81).

15. These are VOTEVIEW number 93 in the 45th House and number 153 in the 45th Senate. The vote to override in the House was 196 Yeas to 73 Nays. With pairs, the vote was 203 Yeas to 78 Nays. D-NOMINATE correctly classified 249 of 269 representatives (92.6 percent; 0.74 *PRE*). The vote to override in the Senate was 46 Yeas and 19 Nays. With pairs, the vote was 51 Yeas and 21 Nays. D-NOMINATE correctly classified 66 of 72 senators (91.7 percent; 0.71 *PRE*).

16. See Stewart and Weingast (1992) for an extensive discussion of the admission of new states during this period.

17. These are VOTEVIEW number 60 in the 53rd House and number 80 in the 53rd Senate. The vote to repeal in the House was 194 Yeas to 94 Nays. With pairs, the vote was 198 Yeas and 97 Nays. D-NOMINATE correctly classified 260 of 295 representatives (88.1 percent; 0.64 *PRE*). In the Senate the vote to repeal was 43 Yeas to 32 Nays. With pairs, the vote was 47 to 36. D-NOMINATE correctly classified 78 of 83 senators (94.0 percent; 0.86 *PRE*).

18. The Civil War Congresses—37, 38, 39, and 40—were lopsidedly Republican, but the Democrats managed to hang onto about 20 percent of the seats, even with the 11 states of the Confederacy absent. The imbalance in favor of the Republicans peaked in the 40th Congress at 80.3 percent of the total seats, but three states (Texas, Mississippi, and Virginia) were not yet back in the Union.

19. See chapter 6 for a more detailed discussion of civil-rights voting in the 48th Congress.

20. For an account of the fights over voting rights, see Young (1956, pp. 82–89). For the origins of the conservative coalition, see Brady and Bullock (1980).

21. Sinclair (1977, p. 948) argues that "Southerners feared that a nationwide minimum wage would nullify their region's advantage in attracting industry." Sinclair also argues that the North-South split on the minimum wage was also due in part to the fact that it was a permanent measure, as opposed to temporary measures such as work relief. "A positive vote on them does imply a commitment to continued government activism in the social welfare area. It is on such programs that the North-South split in the Democratic party begins to appear" (1977, p. 949).

Chapter 6

1. See Bloch (1980); Krehbiel and Rivers (1988); Silberman and Durden (1976).

2. Other important early work that finds that economic variables have modest explanatory power, in comparison to an ideological variable, is represented by several studies of Senate roll call voting: Kau and Rubin (1979); Kalt (1981); and Kau, Keenan, and Rubin (1982). Bernstein and Horn (1981) find that ratings of the Americans for Democratic Action (ADA) have more explanatory power than measures of oil and gas interests in House voting on energy policy. For alternative analyses that mix ideological and economic measures, see Jackson and King (1989) and Jackson and Kingdon (1992).

3. The measurement problem has two sources. First, the data that measure the underlying variables may be missing or very noisy. For example, in the case of strip mining, how does one measure the value constituents place on reclaimed land? Second, even if one has relevant variables, how does one relate the variables to the political process? (See Fiorina, 1974.) For example, does Jesse Helms respond to the median-income voter in North Carolina, the median-income voter among Republican-primary voters, or the median-income campaign contributor? For an excellent, more technical discussion of measurement issues, see Jackson and Kingdon (1992).

4. See the various examples of killer amendments that are discussed in Riker (1982) and our analyses in chapter 7 of these examples.

5. Levitt (1994) attempts to disentangle the influence of party ideology, voter preferences, and personal ideology of senators in the composite represented by one-dimensional ideological scores, both in W-NOMINATE and in the ratings of the Americans for Democratic Action. He concludes that personal ideology is by far the greatest determinant of the score. See chapter 8 for the relationship of ADA ratings to W-NOMINATE scores.

6. We are indebted to Charles Brown for suggesting this test at a National Bureau of Economic Research conference in 1990. Krehbiel (1993) performs a similar test for the 101st Congress. He calls this test a "match rate."

7. More precisely, he estimated the correlation in the errors in the utility function (equation A2 in appendix A).

8. Margins cited in the text refer to those actually voting. The statistical analysis presented in the tables treats actual voters, plus pairs and announced voters, as voting.

9. Although simple to interpret, the linear-probability model has statistical problems, including producing estimated probabilities below 0 or above 1. For example, a representative with a 0 D-NOMINATE score on the first dimension and a + 1 score on the second is seen as voting for Reagan with a probability of $0.502 + 0.980 = 1.482$. This problem vanishes with the use of a logit model. Logit estimates can be found in Poole and Rosenthal (1993b). The substantive implications are similar to those developed on the basis of the linear-probability model.

10. Using the D-NOMINATE utilities for the two outcomes as regressors gives similar results.

11. For more detailed discussion of these variables, see Gilligan et al. (1989) and Poole and Rosenthal (1993b). For a much more detailed discussion of voting on railroad regulation, see Poole and Rosenthal (1994a).

12. Although the second-dimension coefficient is slightly larger than the first's coefficient, the first dimension has more influence because variation in first-dimension scores is about twice that of the second dimension.

13. In the 49th Congress, 176 roll calls occurred before the Cullom bill was brought to the floor. Of these, we retained (for the estimation) 161 in which over 2.5 percent of those voting voted for the minority position. On these roll calls, 323 representatives voted 25 times or more and were retained for our analysis.

14. For other examples of party being insignificant after one controls for ideology, see Poole and Romer's (1993) discussion of Richardson and Munger's (1990) work on the Social Security Act and Poole and Rosenthal's (1993b) discussion of the study by Gilligan et al. (1989) of the Interstate Commerce Act.

15. We used a standard modification to cope with the problem of state delegations that had 0 PROs or 0 CONs. See Pindyck and Rubinfeld (1981, p. 252). In both 1964 and 1967, a Yea vote was in favor of food stamps.

16. Krehbiel and Rivers were mainly interested in a method for estimating ideal points on minimum wages as a function of constituency characteristics. The usefulness of their technique depends, however, on the quality of the underlying model. This chapter argues that simple economic models are routinely of poor quality.

17. Again, these results, mirroring our results cited above for railroads, are not sensitive to the sample used to construct the D-NOMINATE variables. Roll calls preceding all minimum-wage voting in 1977 or roll calls in 1975–76 give similar results to the estimates taken from our two-dimensional dynamic model. We also do better than Krehbiel and Rivers with a one-dimensional model. In the cases where the legislator coordinates have been estimated from prior votes, the one-dimensional model is a model with just one independent variable, whereas Krehbiel and Rivers used 6 to 8 independent variables. See Poole and Rosenthal (1991b, table 7.2, p. 227) for details.

18. Our data are for 1975 and are from *Statistical Abstract of the United States, 1988,* p. 415.

19. Garn's votes in 1977 are even more puzzling when one observes that he was a stalwart opponent of minimum-wage increases in 1988.

20. The bill passed by the House went to the Senate and to conference. After the House accepted the conference report, the bill was vetoed by President Nixon.

21. See Snyder (1990) for a formal model and an empirical analysis that differentiates local from national contributors in House races.

22. Our discussion of Kalt and Zupan draws heavily on Poole and Romer (1983, 1993). See also Poole and Rosenthal (1985a, pp. 52–56).

23. See Kalt and Zupan (1984) for a list of the roll calls.

24. For more details on the variables, see Kalt and Zupan (1984). The Herfindahl indices are defined similarly to the definition for roll calls given in note 28, chapter 3.

25. Again, see Kalt and Zupan (1984) for details. See also chapter 8, where W-NOMINATE is used to estimate the position of the LCV.

26. This represents all roll calls with less than 2.5 percent on the minority side. Peltzman (1984) used a 25 percent cutoff.

27. The results are consistent with those obtained—using a different methodology—by Levitt (1994). (See note 5 above.)

28. Significance tests are based on chi-square probabilities from the likelihood contribution for each roll call. See Poole and Rosenthal (1985a) for further details on the testing and model comparisons.

29. The OSHA votes were originally discussed by Romer and Rosenthal (1985).

30. The t statistic for the null hypothesis of equality is 8.6.

31. The t statistic for equality is 2.07. Since we hypothesize that classifications improve as new issues result in permanent legislation, a one-tailed test is appropriate, with $p = 0.02$.

32. This regression provides a better description than does the use of a pre–World War II dummy variable.

33. *New York Times,* December 14, 1937.

Chapter 7

1. With pairs and announced voters, the two votes were 249 to 179 and 207 to 220, respectively. The pairs and announced voters are shown with the actual voters in figure 7.3. There were 47 errors on the Sarasin amendment and 52 errors on the final-passage vote. This produced *PRE*s of 0.74 and 0.75, respectively.

2. There were two Panama Canal treaties—one provided for the permanent neutrality of the canal, after its transfer to Panama; and the other covered the actual transfer.

3. The roll calls are numbers 673 and 702 in VOTEVIEW.

4. Mathias was elected to the Senate in 1968.

5. These votes all took place on August 9, 1966. They are vote numbers 289, 292, and 293 in VOTEVIEW.

6. The splits for those actually voting on the Mathias amendment: NDs, 150 to 33; SDs, 19 to 74; Rs, 68 to 69. On the Moore motion to recommit: NDs, 24 to 160; SDs, 80 to 12; Rs, 86 to 50. On final passage: NDs, 169 to 17; SDs, 14 to 79; Rs, 76 to 61. With pairs and announced, the votes were 241 to 180, 198 to 231, and 265 to 162, respectively.

7. These are vote numbers 122 and 124 in VOTEVIEW. There were 5 pairs on both votes.

8. This is vote number 456 in VOTEVIEW.

9. Indeed, the Sutherland amendment struck the following sentence: "The times, places, and manner of holding elections for Senators shall be prescribed by the legislatures thereof." Clearly, if the southerners controlled who could vote for senator, blacks would not be permitted to vote. See the discussion in Riker (1982, pp. 193–94).

10. These are vote numbers 244 and 248 in VOTEVIEW. With pairs, the vote totals were 51 to 39 for the Sutherland amendment, and 55 to 34 for final passage. There were 3 errors on the Sutherland amendment and 20 errors on the final-passage vote.

11. Voting on interstate-commerce regulation was covered in chapter 6. See Poole and Rosenthal (1994a) for a lengthy development of the voting on racial discrimination.

Chapter 8

1. See chapter 10 for a fuller discussion of the theory of rational abstention.

2. "Wilson backs state abortion funding," Ken Chavez, *San Francisco Examiner,* August 8, 1995, p. A-7.

3. Fowler (1982), in her interviews with staff members of the interest groups, found that the staffers were skeptical of the way academics used their ratings. In the view of the staffers, the ratings had "their greatest impact on the distribution of campaign funds, because they provide a simple test of support or opposition" (p. 403).

4. Some groups count absences as "incorrect" votes, and other groups weight votes in their ratings.

5. We used the 96th Congress because it was the latest Congress in the data set used by Poole and Daniels (1985).

6. The correlations were computed between the D-NOMINATE estimates for the 96th House and Senate and the corresponding ratings. We recalculated the ratings using all the votes chosen by each group for the entire 96th Congress. The correlations would be lower if we, like many authors of applied papers, had used annual ratings rather than the two-year ratings. Thus, this chapter conservatively understates the problems of using interest-group evaluations as direct measures of ideology.

7. See Peltzman (1984), who uses the ADA ratings in a broad-based analysis of roll call voting; Kalt and Zupan (1984), who use the LCV ratings in an analysis of strip-mine legislation; or Weingast and Moran (1983), who use ADA ratings in a study of legislation affecting the Federal Trade Commission. In chapter 9 we discuss essays that use interest-group ratings to measure preferences of members of committees.

8. These data were originally compiled by Keith Poole and have been used by Poole and Daniels (1985) and by Snyder (1992a).

9. The geometric mean probability for the scaling was 0.66, with 80.3 percent of the votes being classified correctly. For the roll calls, 928 out of 1,054 had margins of at least 2.5 percent in the minority and were scalable.

10. The 2.5 percent criterion is discussed in chapter 2.

11. The geometric mean probability for two dimensions was 0.69, with 82.7 percent of the votes being classified correctly.

12. Standard errors are discussed in appendix A.

13. We conducted a simulation study in which we created 8 additional "interest groups" by duplicating the records of Senators Lloyd Bentsen (D-TX), Quentin Burdick (D-ND), Robert Byrd (D-WV), Howard Cannon (D-NV), Frank Church (D-ID), Barry Goldwater (R-AZ), Daniel Inouye (D-HI), and Henry Jackson (D-WA) (the first 8 senators in the VOTEVIEW data). We then randomly drew 50 roll calls from the total of 1,054, to simulate the effect of adding the 8 interest groups to the 101-senator roll call matrix. (The total number of scalable roll calls for each of the 8 simulated interest groups varies from 40 to 50 because the random draw will include varying numbers of nonscalable roll calls.) This approach allows us to compare the recovery of the simulated interest group with the senator from which it was created.

We performed ten experiments and found that the average absolute difference between the 8 senators and their clones was 0.065 on the first dimension and 0.063 on the second dimension. On average, the positions of the simulated interest groups that had only a small number of votes were more toward the periphery of the space than their corresponding senators were. Thus, small sample sizes lead to some bias toward peripheral positions. But the small absolute average deviations show that the bias is quite small, certainly much too small to account for the systematically extreme positions of the real interest groups. The standard errors for the simulated groups were 4 to 5 times the size of those for their corresponding senators. But the standard errors for the simulated interest groups are smaller than those for the actual groups because the actual groups are near the rim of the space and, as a consequence, will have larger standard errors.

14. Technically, the ratings are converted to distances by the linear transformation $d_{ij}^* = (100 - \delta_{ij})/50 = d_{ij} + e_{ij}$, where δ_{ij} is the rating issued by the jth interest group of the ith legislator, and d_{ij} is the corresponding Euclidean distance. (The division by 50 is an arbitrary normalization that has no effect on the analysis.) The following loss function is minimized:

$$\sum_i \sum_j e_{ij}^2 = \sum_i \sum_j \left\{ d_{ij}^* - \left[\sum_{k=1}^{s} (x_{ik} - z_{jk})^2 \right] \right\}$$

where s is the number of dimensions, and x_{ij} and z_{jk} are the legislator and interest-group coordinates on the kth dimension.

In one dimension, the loss function reduces to a combinatorial problem; in more than one dimension, standard gradient techniques can be used. Unfortunately, the statistical properties of this loss function are not known. Rivers (1987) has shown that, under certain conditions in one dimension, the estimates are not consistent. Brady (1989), using the generalized-method-of-moments (GMM) approach, argues that the loss function above is inappropriate. However, Monte Carlo work reported by Poole (1984, 1990) shows that the estimation method is highly accurate. Finally, Poole and Spear (1992) show that, for the unidimensional problem, under restricted conditions, the correct ordering of the points will be estimated.

The fact that the methods are indeed accurate vitiates the criticisms. Indeed, the accuracy of the methods is consistent with more than 30 years of experience with multidimensional scaling techniques pioneered by Shepard (1962) and Kruskal (1964a, 1964b). A close variant of the loss function shown above is used in one form or another in all these techniques.

15. The interest-group ratings were computed from the roll calls each interest group chose for 1979 and 1980.

16. There were 101 senators, 439 representatives, 28 interest groups, and President Carter, for a total of 569 "legislators." (Senators total more than 100 and representatives total more than 435 because of within-Congress replacements.) We used all 28 groups rather than the 8 used in the Senate analysis because combining the House and Senate ratings typically doubled

the number of roll calls per interest group, leading to sample sizes generally sufficient for analysis. Of the 1,276 roll calls cast in the House, 1,067 had at least 2.5 percent in the minority and were scalable. The corresponding figures for the Senate were 1,054 and 928, respectively. In the combined scaling, there were a total of 1,987 roll calls (1,067 + 928 − 8). In one dimension, the geometric mean probability was 0.696, with 83.6 percent being correctly classified. The corresponding numbers for two dimensions were 0.717 and 83.9 percent, respectively.

17. We performed simple difference-of-means tests between the House and Senate data on the coordinates of northern Democrats, southern Democrats, and Republicans, and none was significantly different. In fact, the largest t value in the six comparisons was less than 0.2.

18. The increase in correct classification and *PRE* for 2 of the 8 roll calls is not unexpected for two reasons: first, maximizing likelihood is not the same as maximizing classification; second, W-NOMINATE is maximizing likelihood across all roll calls. Repositioning the legislators can improve overall classification, even if classification falls on a few roll calls.

Chapter 9

1. See also Krehbiel (1992).

2. Cox and McCubbins (1993, p. 200) define committees with widespread impact as "uniform externality committees." The committees of this type are Science, Post Office, Veterans' Affairs, Public Works, Appropriations, Rules, Ways and Means, Commerce, Government Operations, and House Administration.

3. Some authors have compared means rather than medians.

4. Maltzman (1994) takes a somewhat different approach. He uses issue dimensions defined by a cluster analysis of Yule's Q's, computed between jurisdiction-specific roll calls.

5. The results we develop below concern party contingents on a committee and the committee as a whole. As we discussed in chapter 8, within a party, positions on the first and second dimensions in the two-dimensional model, after World War II, are highly correlated because the Democrats and Republicans lie in ellipses roughly at 45°angles (see figure 3.3, for example). Consequently, the results for the second dimension for the party contingents will be almost the same as for the first dimension. We checked the overall committee results—that is, when both parties are included—on the second dimension, and there were no substantial differences from those we found using the first dimension.

6. See chapter 8 for a further discussion of this point.

7. When the relevant number of legislators is even, we compute the median as the average of the two D-NOMINATE scores in the center of the distribution.

8. This topic is the focus of Shepsle (1978).

9. The 22 distributions of scores for committee *chairs* should be identical, except for sampling variations. Indeed, the empirical distribution of D-NOMINATE scores could be directly used for a test. If, for example, 4 percent of the actual Democrats had a D-NOMINATE score farther from the party median than the actual chair had, the *p* value would be 0.04. Nevertheless, it should be recognized that the results of the 22 tests are not independent. If, for example, an archconservative heads one committee, that person cannot head another committee.

10. There is no formula for the *M*'s because of the dependency imposed by the row and column sums. In the example given in the text, there are $\binom{16}{3}$ ways to assign seats to the member represented by the first row. If the first member draws all 3 of her assignments from committees

with only one three-assignment member, then 0's have to be placed elsewhere in these 3 committees' columns to satisfy the marginals. Consequently, there would be $\binom{13}{3}$ ways to assign the member represented by the second row. Note that, at a minimum, the last row of the matrix will always be determined by the assignments above it.

11. To see why, consider the following. Divide the committees into two sets: the Agriculture Committee and all other committees. Because sampling without replacements is being used, if the Agriculture Committee members are drawn first, then the results for the Agriculture Committee, based on either the *STRU* model or the *FULL* model, will be identical except for sampling variations. This is so because in both instances the constraints embedded in the two models are invoked for the set of all other committees—but *not* for the Agriculture Committee.

12. The Senate did not have many committees until the 14th Senate (Nelson, 1994). The plots for figures 9.1 to 9.4 are based on Monte Carlo analyses with sample sizes of 100, rather than 1,000. We found that a sample size of 100 gave essentially the same results, so we used the smaller sample sizes for these large analyses.

13. Note that the overall committee comparison would not be informative because changes in party control would result in an underestimation of the level of consistent bias.

14. These classification results are from our two-dimensional dynamic scaling.

15. The party-cohesion score is simply an aggregate party-support score. For each roll call, we determine which way a majority of the party voted and then calculate the proportion supporting the party position across all roll calls. In symbols, let $C_{ij} = 1$ if the ith party member voted with the party majority on the jth roll call; let $\delta_{ij} = 1$ if the ith party member voted on the jth roll call; then

$$\text{Party cohesion} = \frac{\sum_i \sum_j C_{ij}}{\sum_i \sum_j \delta_{ij}}$$

Chapter 10

1. The theory of rational abstention was initially developed in a decision-theoretic framework by Downs (1957) and was formalized by Riker and Ordeshook (1968). Ledyard (1981, 1984) integrated the decision-theoretic model into an equilibrium game-theoretic, incomplete-information model that encompassed both choice, in two alternative votes, and abstention. Palfrey and Rosenthal (1983, 1985) developed the game-theoretic model for complete information and characterized the incomplete-information equilibrium for large voting populations. This chapter's focus comes from these theoretical developments.

2. Note that the spatial utilities themselves are unlikely to contain a substantial level of bias, even though we have ignored abstention in D-NOMINATE. As long as members on opposite sides of the true cutting line are, if they vote at all, more likely to vote Yea than to vote Nay, we will—depending on the legislator coordinates—obtain *accurate* estimates of the roll call cutting lines. Similarly, depending on the roll call coordinates, we will obtain accurate estimates of the legislator coordinates. The estimates could be improved by using abstentions. If, for example, abstentions tended to occur among legislators close to the cutting line, the pattern of abstentions on a roll call would provide additional information about the cutting line. The gain from this information would not be substantial, given the large number of observations available to us for estimating both the roll call coordinates and the legislator positions.

3. In applying the model to elections, one is often concerned with what happens if the election ends in a tie. In the case of Congress, ties are broken in the House by the Speaker and in the Senate by the vice president. We assume that the Speaker and the vice president always vote in such cases, and that their preferences are common knowledge. This assumption implies that a decisive voter will always change the outcome completely rather than, in the standard electoral model, creating or breaking a tie. Thus, *B* is appropriately defined. In measuring *B,* we ignore the measurement error induced by the fact that our values of the legislators' ideal points and outcome coordinates are estimates. We also ignore the measurement error introduced by our excluding the stochastic portion of utility.

4. This approach was followed by Cohen and Noll (1991).

5. We approximated distance to Washington using the software we had developed for VOTEVIEW. The U.S. maps of congressional districts prepared by Martis (1989) were digitized into a Euclidean coordinate system. For each congressional district, we had, for display purposes, placed a center-dot coordinate at roughly the geographical center of the district. *LNDIS* was based on the Euclidean distance between the center dot and the coordinates representing Washington, D.C. Usual problems such as the curvature of the earth and rail lines not following the minimum distance apply. These should be minor inaccuracies in relation to the disparities in distance between, say, Virginia and Montana.

6. Cohen and Noll (1991) analyzed the abstentions on 8 roll calls on the Clinch River Breeder Reactor Project that took place between 1975 and 1982. They used each member's participation rate (one minus the abstention rate) for the year as an independent variable. The smallest t statistic on this variable, in any of their three specifications, was -11.0. The largest t statistic (in magnitude) of any of 15 other variables in any specification was 3.57. These results attest to the importance, in any analysis of specific roll calls, of controlling for the legislator's overall propensity to vote. As against using the participation rate for an entire year, our *ABSAVG* and *ABSPREV* variables have the slight advantage of being predetermined.

7. We note that the problem we have in applying the classical decision-theoretic model to roll calls also pertains to mass elections where voters have more than one decision to make, such as when they simultaneously vote for president and representative. Typically, the problem is handled in empirical work by adding independent variables. For example, equations for turnout in the races for Senate seats might include an independent variable for presidential years and another variable for the presence of a gubernatorial race. The joint turnout decision is rarely modeled explicitly.

8. Shirking was first discussed, and the literature on it cited, in chapter 4.

9. Cohen and Noll (1991) also make this prediction, but with a different motivation. They hypothesize that legislators are more likely to abstain on bills that are less salient to their constituents. They also hypothesize that constituents are more sensitive to being on the losing side of an issue than to being on the winning side. As a result, a vote for the winning side is less salient than a vote for the losing side. Hence, it is less costly for a legislator to abstain if the legislator's constituents support the winning side.

10. United States, *Constitution* Art. 1, sec. 5, par. 1.

11. Note that being present but abstaining does not prevent a quorum from being reached.

12. Cohen and Noll (1991, p. 99). Of course, virtually certain outcomes would be consistent with instrumental voting if most legislators had negative net voting costs, *c.*

13. We did exclude the votes that were plurality votes among multiple candidates for congressional offices.

14. Recall that, throughout this book, legislators voting fewer than 25 times in a given Congress are excluded for that Congress.

15. Of course, the logit technique does not permit the computation of estimates for roll calls for which perfect classification is possible. We exclude such votes from the computations of all figures in this chapter. As these roll calls typically provide an excellent fit for our models of turnout and voting, omitting these roll calls only introduces a conservative bias.

16. The discussion of travel times is based on maps presented by Chandler (1977, pp. 84–85.)

17. The percentage, like others in this section, was computed by averaging the turnout rates for the 100 Congresses. All mean differences are significant from 0, at the 0.05 level or better, by conventional t tests.

Appendix A

1. See the discussion of lopsided roll calls later in this appendix.

2. For those legislators who had discontinuous periods of service, we used t to index the actual Congresses in which they served. Thus, time "stopped" when these legislators were not in Congress.

3. More than one cutting point may minimize classification errors. If so, we use the point closest to zero as a starting point.

4. They voted on at least 25 roll calls in at least one Congress.

5. See Poole and Rosenthal (1991a, table A-1), for further details on constrained roll calls.

6. The use of constraints is another source of caution. It implies that some estimated parameters do not represent—even with the condition that other parameters remain constant—maximum-likelihood estimates.

7. See, for example, Chamberlain (1980).

8. For further details on the simulations, see the appendix to Poole and Rosenthal (1991a).

9. We say "almost always" because W-NOMINATE uses a different constraint structure than the one used by D-NOMINATE—which was designed for dynamic estimation of multiple Congresses. In particular, near-perfect extremist legislators would produce a "sag" problem in D-NOMINATE. For example, in the 91st House, Schmitz (R-CA), a near-perfect conservative extremist, was estimated to be at 3.845, by D-NOMINATE, with the next closest representative being estimated at 1.354. This "sag" produced an R^2 of 0.857 between the D-NOMINATE and W-NOMINATE estimates for the first dimension. Removing Schmitz from the calculation raises the R^2 to 0.992.

Appendix B

1. Yule's Q is a measure of the degree of association in voting on two roll calls. Let YY (and NN) be the number of legislators voting Yea (or Nay) on both roll calls; let YN be the number voting Yea on the first and Nay on the second, and NY be the number voting Nay on the first and Yea on the second. (Disregard those voting on only one of the two roll calls). Yule's Q is defined as:

$$Q = (YY \times NN - YN \times NY)/(YY \times NN + YN \times NY)$$

Note that Yule's Q is 1.0 whenever YN = 0 or NY = 0. That is, whenever all legislators who voted Nay on roll call i were also Nay on roll call j, or whenever all who voted Yea on i were also Yea on j, Q is 1.0. In the case of negative association, Q is − 1.0 whenever YY = 0 or NN = 0. Yule's Q = 0 whenever the numerator is zero—that is, whenever the data show the pattern that would be expected were votes on one roll call statistically independent from the votes on the other roll call. For a *PRE* interpretation of Q, see Hildebrand et al. (1977).

2. Technically, we use the percentage of variation rather than variance because the sum of the squared eigenvalues of a symmetric matrix is equal to the sum of the squared elements of the matrix.

3. The Cray XMP/48 at the Pitt/CMU national supercomputer center was used to perform the decompositions. Because of memory limitations entailed by the program we used, the size of the Yule's Q matrices used had to be limited to a maximum of 1,000 by 1,000. This maximum was reached only in the 94th Senate, where 1,027 roll calls met the 10 percent minority criteria; we used the first 1,000 of the 1,027 roll calls.

4. We used the Heckman and Snyder (1995) method to compute the covariance matrices. First, we transformed the roll call matrix by computing the Yea mean for each roll call (the number of Yeas, paired Yeas, and announced Yeas was divided by the total number of legislators voting on that roll call); the Yea mean for each legislator; and the overall Yea mean for the entire matrix. We then subtracted from each entry of the matrix both the roll call mean and the legislator mean, and added the overall Yea mean. (Note that this is double-centering (Torgerson, 1958), in that we are subtracting the row and column means and adding the matrix mean.) If there was a missing entry, we inserted the matrix mean and performed the above subtractions and addition (this is equivalent to inserting the negative of the sum of the row and column means into the missing entries of the double-centered matrix). Let $\mathbf{X}$ be the legislator-by-roll-call, double-centered matrix; the covariance matrix is then simply $\mathbf{X'X}$.

5. In this instance, because the entries of the covariance matrix sum to zero, the sum of the squared eigenvalues is equal to the variance of the matrix.

6. Technically, since D-NOMINATE maximizes a likelihood function and not the classification error, it is possible for the classification error to be greater than the margin, *m*. In those cases, we make the classification error equal to the margin.

References

Aldrich, John (1983). "A Spatial Model with Party Activists: Implications for Electoral Dynamics." *Public Choice,* 41:63–100.

Alesina, Alberto, and Howard Rosenthal (1995). *Partisan Politics, Divided Government, and the Economy.* New York: Cambridge University Press.

Alford, John R., and David W. Brady (1993). "Personal and Partisan Advantage in U.S. Congressional Elections, 1846–1990." In Lawrence C. Dodd and Bruce Oppenheimer, eds., *Congress Reconsidered.* Washington, D.C.: Congressional Quarterly Press.

Ansolebhere, Stephen, David W. Brady, and Morris Fiorina (1992). "The Marginals Never Vanished?" *British Journal of Political Science,* 22:21–38.

Asher, Herbert B., and Herbert F. Weisberg (1978). "Voting Change in Congress: Some Dynamic Perspectives on an Evolutionary Process." *American Journal of Political Science,* 22:391–425.

Bailey, Stephen K. (1950). *Congress Makes a Law.* New York: Columbia University Press.

Bell, Daniel (1961). *The End of Ideology.* New York: Collier.

Berndt, E. K., Bronwyn H. Hall, Robert E. Hall, and Jerry Hausman (1974). "Estimation and Inference in Nonlinear Structural Models." *Annals of Economic and Social Measurement,* 3/4:653–66.

Bernhardt, M. Daniel, and Daniel Ingberman (1985). "Candidate Reputations and the 'Incumbency Effect.' " *Journal of Public Economics,* 27:47–67.

Bernstein, Robert A., and Stephen R. Horn (1981). "Explaining House Voting on Energy Policy: Ideology and the Conditional Effects of Party and District Economic Interests." *Western Political Quarterly,* 34:235–45.

Black, Duncan (1958). *The Theory of Committees and Elections.* Cambridge, Eng.: Cambridge University Press.

Bloch, Farrell (1980). "Political Support for Minimum Wage Legislation." *Journal of Labor Research,* 1:245–53.

Brady, David W. (1979). "Critical Elections, Congressional Parties and Clusters of Policy Changes." *British Journal of Political Science,* 8:79–99.

Brady, David W. (1982). "Congressional Party Realignment and Transformations of Public Policy." *American Journal of Political Science,* 26:333–60.

Brady, David W., and Charles S. Bullock III (1980). "Is there a Conservative Coalition in the House?" *Journal of Politics,* 42:549–59.

Brady, Henry (1989). "Multidimensional Scaling in Political Science." Working paper, Department of Political Science, University of Chicago.

Bullock, Charles S., III (1981). "Congressional Voting and the 1982 Congressional Elections." *Journal of Politics,* 45:767–70.

Burnham, Walter D. (1970). *Critical Elections and the Mainsprings of American Politics.* New York: Norton.

Cain, Bruce, John Ferejohn, and Morris P. Fiorina (1987). *The Personal Vote: Constituency Service and Electoral Independence.* Cambridge: Harvard University Press.

Chamberlain, Gary (1980). "Analysis of Covariance With Qualitative Data." *Review of Economic Studies,* 47:225–38.

Chandler, Alfred D., Jr. (1977). *The Visible Hand.* Cambridge: Harvard University Press.

Clausen, Aage (1973). *How Congressmen Decide: A Policy Focus.* New York: St. Martin's Press.

Clausen, Aage, and C. Van Horn (1977). "The Congressional Response to a Decade of Change: 1963–1972." *Journal of Politics,* 39:624–66.

Cohen, Linda, and Roger Noll (1991). "How to Vote, Whether to Vote: Decisions About Voting and Abstaining on Congressional Roll Calls." *Political Behavior,* 13:97–127.

Converse, Philip E. (1964). "The Nature of Belief Systems in Mass Publics." In David E. Apter, ed., *Ideology and Discontent.* New York: Free Press, 206–61.

Coombs, Clyde (1964). *A Theory of Data.* New York: John Wiley.

Cooper, Joseph, and David W. Brady (1981). "Institutional Context and Leadership Style: The House from Cannon to Rayburn." *American Political Science Review,* 75: 411–25.

Costner, Herbert L. (1965). "Criteria for Measures of Association." *American Sociological Review,* 30:341–53.

Cox, Gary W., and Mathew D. McCubbins (1993). *Legislative Leviathan: Party Government in the House.* Berkeley: University of California Press.

DeBrock, Lawrence, and Wallace Hendricks (1996). "Roll Call Voting in the NCAA." *Journal of Law, Economics and Organization,* vol. 12, forthcoming.

Denzau, Arthur, and Robert Mackay (1983). "Gatekeeping and Monopoly Power of Committees." *American Journal of Political Science,* 27:740–61.

Donald, David Herbert (1960). *Charles Sumner and the Coming of the Civil War.* New York: Fawcett Columbine.

Downs, Anthony (1957). *An Economic Theory of Democracy.* New York: Harper.

Eckart, Carl, and Gale Young (1936). "The Approximation of One Matrix by Another of Lower Rank." *Psychometrika,* 11:211–18.

Efron, Bradley (1979). "Bootstrap Methods: Another Look at the Jackknife." *Annals of Statistics,* 7:1–26.

Enelow, James (1981). "Saving Amendments, Killer Amendments, and an Expected Utility Theory of Sophisticated Voting." *Journal of Politics,* 43:1062–89.

Enelow, James, and Melvin Hinich (1984). *The Spatial Theory of Voting.* New York: Cambridge University Press.

Enelow, James, and David H. Koehler (1980). "The Amendment in Legislative Strategy: Sophisticated Voting in the U.S. Congress." *Journal of Politics,* 42:396–413.

Fenno, Richard F., Jr. (1973). *Congressmen in Committees.* Boston: Little, Brown.

Fenno, Richard F., Jr. (1978). *Home Style: House Members in Their Districts.* Boston: Little, Brown.

Ferejohn, John (1986). "Logrolling in an Institutional Context: The Case of Food Stamps." In Leroy Resielbach et al., eds., *Congress and Policy Change.* New York: Agathon Press, 232–53.

Fiorina, Morris P. (1974). *Representatives, Roll Calls, and Constituencies.* Lexington, Mass.: Heath.

Fiorina, Morris P. (1989). *Congress: Keystone of the Washington Establishment,* 2nd ed. New Haven: Yale University Press.

Fiorina, Morris P. (1992). *Divided Government.* New York: Macmillan.

Fogel, Robert W. (1989). *Without Consent or Contract: The Rise and Fall of American Slavery*. New York: Norton.

Fogel, Robert W. (1990). "Modeling Complex Dynamic Interactions: The Role of Intergenerational, Cohort, and Period Processes and of Conditional Events in the Political Realignment of the 1850s." National Bureau of Economic Research, Working Paper Series on Historical Factors in Long-Run Growth, no. 12.

Fogel, Robert W., and Stanley L. Engerman (1974). *Time on the Cross*. Boston: Little, Brown.

Fort, Rodney, William Hallagan, Cyril Morong, and Tesa Stegner (1993). "The Ideological Component of Senate Voting: Different Principles or Different Principals?" *Public Choice,* 76:39–57.

Fowler, Linda L. (1982). "How Interest Groups Select Issues for Rating Voting Records of Members of the U.S. Congress." *Legislative Studies Quarterly,* 7:401–13.

Freehling, William W. (1990). *The Road to Disunion: Secessionists at Bay 1776–1854*. New York: Oxford University Press.

Friedman, Milton, and Anna Schwartz (1971). *A Monetary History of the United States*. Princeton, N.J.: Princeton University Press.

Gaines, Brian, and Geoffrey Garrett (1992). "The Calculus of Dissent: Party Discipline in the British Labour Government, 1974–79." Mimeographed. Stanford University.

Gilligan, Thomas W., and Keith Krehbiel (1990). "Organization of Informative Committees by a Rational Legislature." *American Journal of Political Science,* 34:531–64.

Gilligan, Thomas W., William Marshall, and Barry R. Weingast (1989). "Regulation and the Theory of Legislative Choice: The Interstate Commerce Act of 1887." *Journal of Law and Economics,* 32:35–61.

Ginsberg, Benjamin (1972). "Critical Elections and the Substance of Party Conflict: 1844–1968." *Midwest Journal of Political Science,* 16:603–25.

Ginsberg, Benjamin (1976). "Elections and Public Policy." *American Political Science Review,* 70:41–49.

Groseclose, Tim (1994a). "A Model and Test of Blame-Game Politics." Mimeographed. Carnegie Mellon University.

Groseclose, Tim (1994b). "Testing Committee Composition Hypotheses for the U.S. Congress." *Journal of Politics,* 56:440–58.

Haberman, Shelby J. (1977). "Maximum Likelihood Estimation in Exponential Response Models." *Annals of Statistics,* 5:815–41.

Hall, Richard L., and Bernard Grofman (1990). "The Committee Assignment Process and the Conditional Nature of Committee Bias." *American Political Science Review,* 84:1149–66.

Heckman, James N., and James M. Snyder, Jr. (1995). "A Linear Latent Factor Model of Roll Call Voting." Mimeographed. University of Chicago.

Hibbing, John R. (1993). "Careerism in Congress: For Better or For Worse." In Lawrence C. Dodd and Bruce I. Oppenheimer, eds., *Congress Reconsidered.* Washington, D.C.: Congressional Quarterly Press, 67–88.

Hildebrand, David K., James D. Laing, and Howard Rosenthal (1977). *Prediction Analysis of Cross Classifications*. New York: Wiley.

Hinich, Melvin, and Peter C. Ordeshook (1969). "Abstentions and Equilibrium in the Electoral Process." *Public Choice,* 7:81–106.

Hinich, Melvin, and Walker Pollard (1981). "A New Approach to the Spatial Theory of Electoral Competition." *American Journal of Political Science,* 25:323–41.

Hinich, Melvin, and Richard Roll (1981). "Measuring Nonstationarity in the Parameters of the Market Model." *Research in Finance,* 3:1–51.

Hofstadter, Richard (1969). *The Idea of a Party System: The Rise of Legitimate Opposition in the United States, 1780–1840*. Berkeley: University of California Press.

Hofstadter, Richard, William Miller, and Daniel Aaron (1959). *The American Republic* (2 vols.). Englewood Cliffs, N.J.: Prentice Hall.

Jackson, John, and David C. King (1989). "Public Goods, Private Interests, and Representatives." *American Political Science Review,* 83:1143–64.

Jackson, John, and John W. Kingdon (1992). "Ideology, Interest Group Scores, and Legislative Votes." *American Journal of Political Science,* 36:805–23.

Kalt, Joseph P. (1981). *The Economics and Politics of Oil Price Regulation.* Cambridge: MIT Press.

Kalt, Joseph P., and Mark A. Zupan (1984). "Capture and Ideology in the Economic Theory of Politics." *American Economic Review,* 74:279–300.

Kau, James B., and Paul H. Rubin (1979). "Self-Interest, Ideology, and Logrolling in Congressional Voting." *Journal of Law and Economics,* 21:365–84.

Kau, James B., Donald Keenan, and Paul H. Rubin (1982). "A General Equilibrium Model of Congressional Voting." *Quarterly Journal of Economics,* 93:271–93.

Kennedy, John F. (1955). *Profiles in Courage.* New York: Harper and Row.

Kiewiet, D. Roderick, and Mathew D. McCubbins (1991). *The Logic of Delegation: Congressional Parties and the Logic of Delegation.* Chicago: University of Chicago Press.

Kirkpatrick, Jeanne (1976). *The New Presidential Elite.* New York: Russell Sage Foundation.

Koford, Kenneth (1989). "Dimensions in Congressional Voting." *American Political Science Review,* 83:949–62.

Koford, Kenneth (1991). "On Dimensionalizing Roll Call Votes in the U.S. Congress (Controversy with Keith T. Poole and Howard Rosenthal)." *American Political Science Review,* 85:955–75.

Koford, Kenneth (1994). "What Can We Learn about Congressional Politics from Dimensional Studies of Roll Call Voting?" *Economics and Politics,* 6:173–86.

Krehbiel, Keith (1990). "Are Congressional Committees Composed of Preference Outliers?" *American Political Science Review,* 84:149–63.

Krehbiel, Keith (1992). *Information and Legislative Organization.* Ann Arbor: University of Michigan Press.

Krehbiel, Keith (1993). "Constituency Characteristics and Legislative Preferences." *Public Choice,* 76:21–38.

Krehbiel, Keith, and Douglas Rivers (1988). "The Analysis of Committee Power: An Application to Senate Voting on the Minimum Wage." *American Journal of Political Science,* 32:1151–74.

Kruskal, Joseph B. (1964a). "Multidimensional Scaling by Optimizing Goodness of Fit to a Nonmetric Hypothesis." *Psychometrika,* 29:1–28.

Kruskal, Joseph B. (1964b). "Nonmetric Multidimensional Scaling: A Numerical Method." *Psychometrika,* 29:115–30.

Kruskal, Joseph B., and Myron Wish (1978). *Multidimensional Scaling.* Beverly Hills, Calif.: Sage Publications.

Ladha, Krishna K. (1991). "A Spatial Model of Legislative Voting with Perceptual Error." *Public Choice,* 68:151–74.

Ladha, Krishna K. (1994). "Coalitions in Congressional Voting." *Public Choice,* 78:43–64.

Ledyard, John O. (1981). "The Paradox of Voting and Candidate Competition: A General Equilibrium Analysis." In G. Horwich and J. Quirk, eds., *Essays in Contemporary Fields of Economics.* West Lafayette, Ind.: Purdue University Press.

Ledyard, John O. (1984). "The Pure Theory of Large Two-Candidate Elections." *Public Choice,* 44:7–41.

Levitt, Steven (1994). "How Do Senators Vote? Disentangling the Role of Party Affiliations, Voter Preferences, and Senator Ideology." Mimeographed. Massachusetts Institute of Technology.

Londregan, John, and James M. Snyder, Jr. (1994). "Comparing Committee and Floor Preferences." *Legislative Studies Quarterly,* 19:233–66.

Loomis, Michael (1995). "Constituent Influences Outside the Spatial Structure of Legislative Voting." Doctoral dissertation, Carnegie Mellon University.

Lord, F. M. (1975). *Evaluation with Artificial Data of a Procedure for Estimating Ability and Item-Characteristic Curve Parameters.* Princeton, N.J.: Educational Testing Service.

Lott, John R., Jr., and Stephen G. Bronars (1993). "Time Series Evidence on Shirking in the U.S. House of Representatives." *Public Choice,* 76:125–50.

Macdonald, Stuart E., and George Rabinowitz (1987). "The Dynamics of Structural Realignment." *American Political Science Review,* 81:775–96.

MacRae, Duncan, Jr. (1958). *Dimensions of Congressional Voting.* Berkeley: University of California Press.

MacRae, Duncan, Jr. (1970). *Issues and Parties In Legislative Voting.* New York: Harper and Row.

Maltzman, Forrest (1994). "Meeting Competing Demands: Committee Performance in the Post-Reform House." Mimeographed. George Washington University.

Maltzman, Forrest, and Steven S. Smith (1994). "Principals, Goals, Dimensionality, and Congressional Committees." *Legislative Studies Quarterly,* 19:457–76.

Martis, Kenneth (1989). *The Historical Atlas of Political Parties in the United States Congress: 1789–1989.* New York: Macmillan.

Mayhew, David R. (1974). *Congress: The Electoral Connection.* New Haven: Yale University Press.

McCarty, Nolan, and Keith T. Poole (1995). "An Empirical Spatial Model of Congressional Campaigns." Mimeographed. Carnegie Mellon University.

McCarty, Nolan, Keith T. Poole, and Howard Rosenthal (1996). "The Realignment of American Politics: From Goldwater to Gingrich." Mimeographed. Carnegie Mellon University.

McCloskey, Herbert, P. J. Hoffman, and Rosemary O'Hara. (1960). "Issue Conflict and Consensus among Party Leaders and Followers." *American Political Science Review,* 54:406–27.

Morrison, Richard J. (1972). "A Statistical Model for Legislative Roll Call Analysis." *Journal of Mathematical Sociology,* 2:235–47.

Myagkov, Mikhail, and D. Roderick Kiewiet (1996). "Czar Rule in the Russian Congress of People's Deputies?" *Legislative Studies Quarterly,* 21:5–40.

Nelson, Garrison (1994). *Committees in the U.S. Congress.* Washington, D.C.: CQ Press.

Nevins, Allan (1947). *Ordeal of the Union: A House Dividing, 1852–1857.* New York: Charles Scribners.

Niskanen, William A. (1971). *Bureaucracy and Representative Government.* Chicago: Aldine-Atherton.

Ordeshook, Peter C. (1976). "The Spatial Theory of Elections: A Review and a Critique." In Ian Budge, Ivor Crewe, and Dennis Farlie, eds., *Party Identification and Beyond.* New York: Wiley.

Ordeshook, Peter C. (1986). *Game Theory and Political Theory.* New York: Cambridge University Press.

Palfrey, Thomas R., and Howard Rosenthal (1983). "A Strategic Calculus of Voting." *Public Choice,* 41:7–53.

Palfrey, Thomas R., and Howard Rosenthal (1985). "Voter Participation and Strategic Uncertainty." *American Political Science Review,* 79:62–78.

Peltzman, Sam (1984). "Constituent Interest and Congressional Voting." *Journal of Law and Economics,* 27:181–210.

Peltzman, Sam (1985). "An Economic Interpretation of the History of Congressional Voting in the Twentieth Century." *American Economic Review,* 75:656–75.

Pindyck, Robert S., and Daniel L. Rubinfeld (1981). *Econometric Models and Economic Forecasts,* 2nd ed. New York: McGraw-Hill.

Polsby, Nelson (1968). "Institutionalization in the U.S. House of Representatives." *American Political Science Review,* 62:144–168.

Poole, Keith T. (1981). "Dimensions of Interest Group Evaluation of the U.S. Senate, 1969–1978." *American Journal of Political Science,* 25:49–67.

Poole, Keith T. (1984). "Least Squares Metric, Unidimensional Unfolding." *Psychometrika,* 49:311–23.

Poole, Keith T. (1988). "Recent Developments in Analytical Models of Voting in the U.S. Congress." *Legislative Studies Quarterly,* 13:117–33.

Poole, Keith T. (1990). "Least Squares Metric, Unidimensional Scaling of Multivariate Linear Models." *Psychometrika,* 55:123–49.

Poole, Keith T., and R. Steven Daniels (1985). "Ideology, Party, and Voting in the U.S. Congress, 1959–80." *American Political Science Review,* 79:373–99.

Poole, Keith T., and Thomas Romer (1983). "Economic Versus Ideological Factors in Congressional Voting." Mimeographed. Carnegie Mellon University.

Poole, Keith T., and Thomas Romer (1985). "Patterns of Political Action Committee Campaign Contributions to the 1980 Campaigns for the U.S. House of Representatives." *Public Choice,* 47:63–111.

Poole, Keith T., and Thomas Romer (1993). "Ideology, Shirking and Representation." *Public Choice,* 77:185–96.

Poole, Keith T., Thomas Romer, and Howard Rosenthal (1987). "The Revealed Preferences of Political Action Committees." *American Economic Review,* 77:298–302.

Poole, Keith T., and Howard Rosenthal (1983). "A Spatial Model for Legislative Roll Call Analysis." Graduate School of Industrial Administration Working Paper no. 5-83-84, Carnegie Mellon University.

Poole, Keith T., and Howard Rosenthal (1984). "The Polarization of American Politics." *Journal of Politics,* 46:1061–79.

Poole, Keith T., and Howard Rosenthal (1985a). "The Political Economy of Roll Call Voting in the 'Multi-Party' Congress of the United States." *European Journal of Political Economy,* 1:45–58.

Poole, Keith T., and Howard Rosenthal (1985b). "A Spatial Model for Legislative Roll Call Analysis." *American Journal of Political Science,* 29:357–84.

Poole, Keith T., and Howard Rosenthal (1986). "The Dynamics of Interest Group Evaluations of Congress." Graduate School of Industrial Administration Working Paper no. 3-86-87, Carnegie Mellon University.

Poole, Keith T., and Howard Rosenthal (1987a). "Analysis of Congressional Coalition Patterns: A Unidimensional Spatial Model." *Legislative Studies Quarterly,* 12:55–75.

Poole, Keith T., and Howard Rosenthal (1987b). "The Unidimensional Congress, 1919–84." Graduate School of Industrial Administration, Working Paper no. 44-84-85 (revised 1987), Carnegie Mellon University.

Poole, Keith T., and Howard Rosenthal (1991a). "Patterns of Congressional Voting." *American Journal of Political Science,* 35:228–78.

Poole, Keith T., and Howard Rosenthal (1991b). "The Spatial Mapping of Minimum Wage Legislation." In Alberto Alesina and Geoffrey Carliner, eds., *Politics and Economics in the 1980s.* Chicago: University of Chicago Press, 215–46.

Poole, Keith T., and Howard Rosenthal (1991c). "On Dimensionalizing Roll Call Votes in the U.S. Congress (Controversy with Kenneth Koford)." *American Political Science Review,* 85:955–75.

Poole, Keith T., and Howard Rosenthal (1993a). "Spatial Realignment and the Mapping of Issues in American History: The Evidence from Roll Call Voting." In William H. Riker, ed., *Agenda Formation.* Ann Arbor: University of Michigan Press, 13–39.

Poole, Keith T., and Howard Rosenthal (1993b). "The Enduring Nineteenth Century Battle for Economic Regulation: The Interstate Commerce Act Revisited." *Journal of Law and Economics,* 36:837–60.

Poole, Keith T., and Howard Rosenthal (1994a). "Congress and Railroad Regulation: 1874–1887." In Claudia Goldin and Gary Libecapp, eds., *The Regulated Economy.* Chicago: University of Chicago Press, 81–120.

Poole, Keith T., and Howard Rosenthal (1994b). "Dimensional Simplification and Economic Theories of Legislative Behavior." *Economics and Politics,* 6:163–72.

Poole, Keith T., Fallaw B. Sowell, and Stephen Spear (1992). "Evaluating Dimensionality in Spatial Voting Models." *Mathematical and Computer Modeling,* 16:85–101.

Poole, Keith T., and Stephen Spear (1992). "Statistical Properties of Metric Multidimensional Scaling." Mimeographed. Carnegie Mellon University.

Poole, Keith T., and L. Harmon Zeigler (1985). *Women, Public Opinion, and Politics.* New York: Longman.

Redman, Eric (1973). *The Dance of Legislation.* New York: Simon and Schuster.

Richardson, L.E., Jr., and Michael Munger (1990). "Shirking, Representation, and Congressional Behavior: Voting on the 1983 Amendments to the Social Security Act." *Public Choice,* 67:11–33.

Riker, William H. (1962). *The Theory of Political Coalitions.* New Haven: Yale University Press.

Riker, William H. (1980). "Implications from the Disequilibrium of Majority Rule for the Study of Institutions." *American Political Science Review,* 74: 432–46.

Riker, William H. (1982). *Liberalism against Populism.* San Francisco: W. H. Freeman.

Riker, William, and Peter C. Ordeshook (1968). "A Theory of the Calculus of Voting." *American Political Science Review,* 52:25–42.

Rivers, Douglas (1987). "Inconsistency of Least Squares Unfolding." Paper presented at the Political Methodology Meetings, Durham, N.C.

Romer, Thomas, and Howard Rosenthal (1978). "Political Resource Allocation, Controlled Agendas, and the Status Quo." *Public Choice,* 33:27–43.

Romer, Thomas, and Howard Rosenthal (1979). "Bureaucrats vs. Voters: On the Political Economy of Resource Allocation by Direct Democracy." *Quarterly Journal of Economics,* 93:563–87.

Romer, Thomas, and Howard Rosenthal (1985). "Modern Political Economy and the Study of Regulation." In Elizabeth E. Bailey, ed., *Public Regulation: New Perspectives on Institutions and Politics.* Cambridge: MIT Press, 73–116.

Romer, Thomas, and Barry R. Weingast (1991). "Political Foundations of the Thrift Debacle." In Alberto Alesina and Geoffrey Carliner, ed., *Politics and Economics in the 1980s.* Chicago: University of Chicago Press, 175–209.

Rosenthal, Howard (1992). "The Unidimensional Congress is Not the Result of Selective Gatekeeping." *American Journal of Political Science,* 36:31–35.

Rosenthal, Howard (1995). "Incumbents and New Entrants in the Expansion of the United States." Paper presented at the CEPR/ECARE/Yrjö Jahnsson Foundation Workshop, The EU Post 96: Incumbents vs. New Entrants, Brussels.

Rosenthal, Howard, and Subrata Sen (1973). "Electoral Participation in the Fifth French Republic." *American Political Science Review,* 67:29–54.

Rothenberg, Lawrence S. (1994). *Regulation, Organizations, and Politics.* Ann Arbor: University of Michigan Press.

Schattschneider, E. E. (1942). *Party Government.* New York: Holt, Rinehart and Winston.

Shepard, Roger N. (1962). "The Analysis of Proximities: Multidimensional Scaling with an Unknown Distance Function." *Psychometrika,* 27:125–39, 219–46.

Shepsle, Kenneth A. (1978). *The Giant Jigsaw Puzzle.* Chicago: University of Chicago Press.

Shepsle, Kenneth A., and Barry R. Weingast (1994). "Positive Theories of Congressional Institutions." *Legislative Studies Quarterly,* 19:149–80.

Silberman, Jonathon, and Gary Durden (1976). "Determining Legislative Preferences on the Minimum Wage: An Econometric Approach." *Journal of Political Economy,* 84:317–29.

Silbey, Joel (1967). *The Shrine of Party.* Pittsburgh: University of Pittsburgh Press.

Sinclair, Barbara (1977). "Party Realignment and the Transformation of the Political Agenda: The House of Representatives, 1925–1938." *American Political Science Review,* 71:940–53.

Sinclair, Barbara (1981). "Agenda and Alignment Change: The House of Representatives, 1925–1978." In Lawrence C. Dodd and Bruce I. Oppenheimer, eds., *Congress Reconsidered.* Washington, D.C.: Congressional Quarterly Press, 237–57.

Smith, Steven S. (1981). "The Consistency and Ideological Structure of U.S. Senate Voting Alignments, 1957–1976." *American Journal of Political Science,* 25: 780–95.

Snyder, James M., Jr. (1990). "Campaign Contributions as Investments: The U.S. House of Representatives, 1980–1986." *Journal of Political Economy,* 98:1195–1227.

Snyder, James M., Jr. (1992a). "Artificial Extremism in Interest Group Ratings." *Legislative Studies Quarterly,* 17:319–45.

Snyder, James M., Jr. (1992b). "Committee Power, Structure-Induced Equilibria, and Roll Call Votes." *American Journal of Political Science,* 36:1–30.

Stewart, Charles III, and Barry R. Weingast (1992). "Stacking the Senate, Changing the Nation: Republican Rotten Boroughs, Statehood Politics, and American Political Development." *Studies in American Political Development,* 6:223–71.

Stone, Walter J. (1980). "The Dynamics of Constituency: Electoral Control of the House." *American Politics Quarterly,* 8:399–424.

Sundquist, James L. (1983). *Dynamics of the Party System.* Washington, D.C.: Brookings Institution.

Torgerson, Warren S. (1958). *Theory and Methods of Scaling.* New York: Wiley.

Tversky, Amos, and Daniel Kahneman (1974). "Judgement Under Uncertainty: Heuristics and Biases." *Science,* 125:1124–31.

Unger, Irwin (1964). *The Greenback Era.* Princeton, N.J.: Princeton University Press.

Van Doren, Peter (1990). "Can We Learn the Causes of Congressional Decisions from Roll Call Data?" *Legislative Studies Quarterly,* 15:311–40.

Weingast, Barry R. (1991). "Political Economy of Slavery: Credible Commitments and the Preservation of the Union, 1800–1860." Paper presented at the Seventh International Symposium in Economic Theory and Econometrics, St. Louis.

Weingast, Barry R., and Mark Moran (1983). "Bureaucratic Discretion or Congressional Control? Regulatory Policymaking by the Federal Trade Commission." *Journal of Political Economy,* 91:775–800.

Weisberg, Herbert F. (1968). *Dimensional Analysis of Legislative Roll Calls.* Doctoral dissertation, University of Michigan.

Weiss, Roger (1970). "The Issue of Paper Money in the American Colonies, 1720–1774." *Journal of Economic History,* 30:770–84.

White, Halbert (1980). "A Heteroskedasticity-Consistent Covariance Matrix Estimator and a Direct Test for Heteroskedasticity." *Econometrica* 48:817–38.

Wilson, James Q. (1980). *The Politics of Regulation.* New York: Basic Books.

Wright, B. D., and G. A. Douglas (1976). "Better Procedures for Sample-Free Item Analysis." Research Memorandum no. 20, Statistical Laboratory, Department of Education, University of Chicago.

Young, Roland (1956). *Congressional Politics in the Second World War.* New York: Columbia University Press.

Index

Aaron, Daniel, 105, 265 n. 11
abortion, 112–13
abstention, 10, 217–26, 229
   and close votes, 219, 222
   due to indifference, 222–23
   and exit from House, 74–76, 220–21
   and exit from Senate, 220–21
   by majority side on issue, 223–25
   and size of chamber, 225–26
   theory of, 210–17, 277 n. 1
   and travel costs, 212, 217–20
Adams, John Quincy, 267 nn. 4–5
agenda and dimensionality, 56–57
Aldrich, John, 269 n. 3
Alesina, Alberto, 208, 267 nn. 6–7, 268 n. 10
Alford, John R., 205
Allen, James, 152, 155
amendment voting. See sophisticated voting
Ansolebhere, Stephen, 263 n. 5
APRE, 30
Asher, Herbert B., 269 n. 29
Atkins, Chester, 190

Bailey, Stephen K., 263 n. 2
Bartlett, Dewey F., 129–30, 138
basic space. See ideology
belief system. See ideology
Bell, Daniel, 229
Berndt, E. K., 238
Bernhardt, M. Daniel, 85
Bernstein, Robert A., 271 n. 2
Black, Duncan, 264 n. 5
black caucus, 231
Blaine, John, 266 n. 17
Bland-Allison Act, 103
Bloch, Farrell, 129, 132, 271 n. 1
Borah, William, 266 n. 17

Bork, Robert, 5, 138, 227
Brady, David W., 59, 205, 263 n. 5, 269
   n. 1, 271 n. 20
Brady, Henry, 275 n. 14
British parliamentary model, 34
Brookart, Smith, 266 n. 17
Bronars, Stephen G., 268 n. 22
Brown, Charles, 271 n. 6
Bullock, Charles S., III, 269 n. 29, 271 n. 20
Burnham, Walter D., 269 n. 1
Bush, George H., 6, 111, 139

Cain, Bruce, 205, 229, 263 n. 1
Camden, Johnson, 144–45
Carter, James E. , 69, 139, 167, 179, 275
   n. 16
Case, Clifford, 138–39
Chamberlain, Gary, 279 n. 7
Chamber of Commerce of the United States,
   166–67, 174–175, 180
Chandler, Alfred D., Jr., 279 n. 16
Church, Frank, 152
civil rights
   and 1966 Open Housing Bill, 153–55
   and three-party system, 5, 44, 64, 82,
   109–12
   See also race
classification error, 7, 20
   distribution of, 31–34
   minimizing in one dimension, 22–23, 264
   n. 12
   and perfect spatial voting in many
   dimensions, 256–58
   See also spatial model
Clausen, Aage, 54–55, 259, 269 n. 29
   category scalings, 55
Clay, Henry, 267 n. 6

Clinton, De Witt, 265 n. 11
Clinton, William J., 165
closed rule, 14
    See also gatekeeping
coalitions, 4–6, 116, 144–45, 164, 227
    See also logrolling
Cohen, Linda, 214–15, 278 nn. 4, 6, 9, 12
committees, 3, 9–10
    assignment of members to, 184, 186–88,
        190, 200
    and common interests of members, 204–8
    as information-gathering bodies, 184,
        208–9
    measuring the representativeness of,
        186–200
    and party control, 185, 208–9
    and preference outliers, 184–86, 200–204,
        208
Common Situs Picketing bill, 16, 19, 150–51
Compromise of 1850, 97–98
constituents, 3, 4, 9, 116, 118, 208–9, 212
    and purely economic theories of voting,
        118–21
constraint, 11, 14, 111
    and logrolling, 35
    and sophisticated voting, 15–16
    See also ideology
Converse, Philip E., 4, 111
Coombs, Clyde, 176
Cooper, Joseph, 59
Costner, Herbert L., 265 n. 4
Cox, Gary W., 185, 204, 208–9, 263 n. 9, 276
    n. 2
Crawford, William H., 267 n. 5
Cullom, Shelby M., 122–24, 216, 272 n. 13
Curtis, Carl, 138–39

Danforth, John C., 131
Daniels, R. Steven, 136, 176, 274 nn. 5, 8
Denzau, Arthur, 264 n. 6, 267 n. 27
DePew, Chauncey, 160–64
Dies, Martin, 142
dimensionality of roll call voting, 27–31,
    51–57, 252–55
direct election of senators, 160–62, 225–26
D-NOMINATE, 233–49
    comparison to other scaling methods,
        252–55, 257–58
    cutting-line angles, 18–19, 117, 137–45
    data used in estimation, 263 n. 8, 264 n. 11
    dynamic model, 25–26, 229

fit to roll call data, 8, 27–34
    legislator coordinates, 5, 25
    outcome coordinates, 5, 24
    outline of, 23–26, 242
    statistical issues, 246–49, 264 nn. 14–15,
        265 nn. 6–7, 269 nn. 27–28, 275 n. 13,
        277 n. 2, 279 nn. 6–9, 280 n. 6
    utility function, 24, 234
    See also spatial model
Dole, Robert, 12, 165
Douglas, G. A., 248
Douglas, Stephen A., 95–96, 270 n. 8
Downs, Anthony, 211, 277 n. 1
Durden, Gary, 129, 132–33, 271 n. 1

Eckart, Carl, 243
Eckhardt, Bob, 182
economic conservative, 17
economic interests, 9, 115–18
    measurement issues, 271 n. 3
    and spatial voting, 118–21, 228
    See also interest groups
economic versus ideological models, 118–37
Edmunds, George, 144–45
Enelow, James, 150, 152–53, 155, 157, 264
    nn. 3, 8, 267 n. 24
Engerman, Stanley L., 35
Era of Good Feelings
    fit of spatial model, 31, 38–39, 52–53
    relation to Missouri Compromise, 93–94
Erlenborn, John N., 132–33, 138, 149
error. *See* classification error

Fair Labor Standards Act. *See* minimum
    wage
farming interests, 116, 125, 166
Fenno, Richard F., Jr., 184
Ferejohn, John, 115–16, 124, 205, 229, 263
    n. 1
Fiorina, Morris P., 184, 205, 208, 229, 263
    n. 1, 269 n. 29, 271 n. 3
first dimension
    correlation of House and Senate means,
        59–64
    and the 1850s, 95–100
    Era of Good Feelings, 71, 93–95
    and first dimension from interest-group
        unfolding, 177–79
    and interest-group ratings, 167–69
    and party-line voting, 46–48, 115–16,
        125–26

and race in the 1990s, 230–32
and realignment of the 1850s, 97–99
and realignment of the 1890s, 106
and realignment of the 1930s, 106–9
  stability of, 7–8, 71–73, 228
  stability of legislators on, 7–8, 73–77, 227–28
  See also second dimension
Fogel, Robert W., 35, 100, 266 n. 22
food stamps, 115, 124–29, 143–44, 181
Fowler, Linda L., 274 n. 3
Frazier, Lynn, 266 n. 17
Freehling, William W., 92
Friedman, Milton, 100, 105

Gaines, Brian, 263 n. 4
Garn, Jake, 131, 272 n. 19
Garrett, Geoffrey, 263 n. 4
gatekeeping, 56
  See also closed rule
geometric mean probability (GMP), 31
Gilligan, Thomas W., 115–16, 122–23, 184, 208–9, 272 nn. 11, 14
Gingrich, Newt, 64
Ginsberg, Benjamin, 106, 269 n. 1
Gore, Albert, Jr., 12
Gramm, Phil, 227
Grant, Ulysses S., 102
Great Depression, 68, 106
Great Society, 68
greenbackism, 101–2
Grofman, Bernard, 185–86
Groseclose, Tim, 185, 263 n. 10

Haberman, Shelby J., 247–48
Hall, Bronwyn H., 238
Hall, Richard L., 185–86
Hall, Robert E., 238
Hamilton, Alexander, 37, 66
Harrison, William H., 266 n. 21
Hatch, Orrin, 131
Hatfield, Mark, 139, 227–28
Hausman, Jerry, 238
Hayes, Rutherford B., 103
Heckman, James N., 252–53, 280 n. 4
Heinz, John, 139
Helms, Jesse, 12, 111, 147, 227–28
Hewitt, Abram S., 4, 116
Hibbing, John R., 269 n. 24
Hildebrand, David K., 265 n. 4, 280 n. 1
Hinich, Melvin, 223, 236, 264 n. 3, 267 n. 24

Hoffman, P. J., 165
Hofstadter, Richard, 65, 95, 105, 265 n. 11
Horn, Stephen R., 271 n. 2
House spatial maps
  5th, 40
  16th, 94
  25th, 96
  27th, 41
  28th, 97
  29th, 161
  32nd, 98
  33rd, 98
  35th, 42, 99
  43rd, 102
  45th, 104
  53rd, 43
  71st, 107
  73rd, 107
  80th, 44
  84th, 159
  88th, 143
  89th, 154–55
  90th, 143
  93rd, 130–31
  95th, 151
  96th, 182
  99th, 45
Howell, Robert, 266 n. 17

ideology
  versus economic models of voting, 122–37
  and liberalism/conservatism, 4–5
  and mapping of issues, 5, 118, 137–45
  predictability of issue positions, 4, 11
  and voting along party lines, 126
  See also constraint
Inflation Bill of 1874, 101–2
Ingberman, Daniel, 85
interest groups, 228
  campaign contributions, 132, 183, 274 n. 3
  exterior to legislators, 170, 174–76
  and joint House-Senate scaling, 179–82
  polarizing role, 165
  ratings, 9, 166–73
  and unfolding, 170–71, 176–79
  and vote trades, 146
Interstate Commerce Act, 115, 122–24
  and cutting-line angles, 138, 144–145
issues
  change, 112–14

issues (*continued*)
　　correlation between, 55–56
　　selection in roll call voting, 56–57

Jackson, Andrew, 67, 267 nn. 4–5
Jackson, John, 271 n. 3
Jefferson, Thomas, 35, 66
Johnson, Lyndon B., 69, 111

Kahneman, Daniel, 212
Kalt, Joseph P., 115–16, 133–35, 271 n. 2,
　　273 nn. 23–25, 274 n. 7
Kansas-Nebraska Act, 95–96, 99, 270 n. 8
Kau, James B., 271 n. 2
Keenan, Donald, 271 n. 2
Kennedy, John F., 263 n. 5
Kerry, John, 12
Kiewiet, D. Roderick, 170, 186
King, David C., 271 n. 2
Kingdon, John W., 271 n. 2
Kirkpatrick, Jeanne, 165
Koehler, David H., 150, 152, 264 n. 8
Koford, Kenneth, 8, 53–54, 256
Krehbiel, Keith, 129–32, 138, 184–86,
　　208–9, 271nn. 1, 6, 272 nn. 16–17, 276
　　n. 1
Kruskal, Joseph B., 275 n. 14

Ladha, Krishna K., 150, 247
La Follette, Robert M., Jr., 48
La Follette, Robert M., Sr., 48
Laing, James D., 265 n. 4, 280 n. 1
lame-duck sessions, 213, 220–21
League of Conservation Voters, 115, 134–35,
　　166, 175–76
Ledyard, John O., 277 n. 1
Legislative Reform Act of 1946, 185, 200,
　　208
Leland, Mickey, 182
Levitt, Steven, 271 n. 5, 273 n. 27
logrolling, 6, 9
　　and issues, 56, 115, 138, 146
　　and political parties, 35, 116–17
Londregan, John, 185–87
Loomis, Michael, 121, 145, 268 n. 18
Lord, F. M., 247–48
Lott, John R., Jr., 268 n. 22
Lugar, Richard, 139

Macdonald, Stuart E., 56
Mackay, Robert, 264 n. 6, 267 n. 27

MacRae, Duncan, Jr., 26
Madison, James, 265 n. 11
Maltzman, Forest, 185, 276 n. 4
Marshall, William, 115–16, 122–23, 272
　　nn. 11, 14
Martis, Kenneth, 265 n. 10, 266 n. 21, 267
　　nn. 4–5, 278 n. 5
Mathias, Charles, 153–55, 164, 273 n. 4
Mayhew, David R., 184, 263 n. 1
McCarty, Nolan, 46, 132, 183
McCloskey, Herbert, 165
McCubbins, Matthew D., 170, 185–86, 204,
　　208–9, 263 n. 9, 276 n. 2
McCulloch, Hugh, 100
McMaster, William, 266 n. 17
Miller, William, 105, 265 n. 11
minimum wage, 9, 14–15, 112, 115, 117–18,
　　129–33, 137–38, 149–50, 271 n. 21
　　and cutting-line angles, 139–42
　　and race, 110–11, 142
Missouri Compromise, 94–95
Mitchell, George, 6
monetary policy, 100–106
Monroe, James, 31, 39
Moore, Arch, 154–55
Moran, Mark, 274 n. 7
Munger, Michael, 272 n. 14

Nader, Ralph, 175–76
National Rifle Association, 165
National Science Foundation, 20–21
Nelson, Garrison, 277 n. 12
Nevins, Allan, 270 n. 8
New Deal. *See* party realignment
1956 school aid bill, 157–59, 164
Niskanen, William A., 184
Nixon, Richard M., 68–69, 272 n. 20
Noll, Roger, 214–15, 278 nn. 4, 6, 9, 12
NOMINATE. *See* D-NOMINATE
Norbeck, Peter, 266 n. 17
Norris, George, 48
Nunn, Sam, 12
Nye, Gerald, 266 n. 17

Occupational Safety and Health Administra-
　　tion (OSHA), 9, 13–14, 115, 138–39,
　　149–50
O'Hara, John, 162
O'Hara, Rosemary, 165
O'Neill, Thomas (Tip), 3
open rule. *See* closed rule

Ordeshook, Peter C., 211, 223, 264 n. 3, 277 n. 1

Packwood, Bob, 111, 139
Palfrey, Thomas R., 213–14, 277 n. 1
Panama Canal Treaty, 20–21, 152–53, 180–81
party loyalty, 6
party polarization, 8, 67–70, 80–85, 228–32
  and interest groups, 9, 165
party realignment, 86–88, 227
  of the 1850s, 41–42, 91–100
  of the 1890s, 42–43, 100–106
  of the 1930s, 106–9
  number of, 9
  spatial theory of, 88–90
  three-party system, 3, 109–11
party systems
  Democrat/Republican, 42–43, 46, 62–64
  Federalist/Republican, 36–38, 65–66
  mean spatial positions, 58–67
  three-party system, 44–45, 109–11
  Whig/Democrat, 40–41, 66–67
Peltzman, Sam, 115, 118, 120, 136–37 , 259, 273 n. 26, 274 n. 7
perfect spatial voting in many dimensions
  and classification, 256–58
Pindyck, Robert S., 272 n. 15
polarization. *See* party polarization
policy swings, 58, 67–70, 228
Polk, James K., 160
Pollard, Walker, 264 n. 3
Polsby, Nelson, 78
Poole, Keith T., 46, 74, 112, 117, 129, 132, 135–36, 138, 149, 176–77, 183, 213, 229, 231, 235, 243–44, 248–49, 256–58, 263 n. 11, 264 n. 15, 265 nn. 6, 9, 266 n. 15, 267 n. 9, 268 nn. 13, 17, 269 nn. 4, 26, 272 nn. 9, 14, 17, 273 nn. 22, 28, 274 nn. 5, 8, 11, 275 n. 14, 279 nn. 5, 8
Powell, Adam Clayton, Jr., 157–59, 164
PRE, 29–30
predictive dimension, 12
  See also ideology
prohibition, 113–14

quorum, 214

Rabinowitz, George, 56
race, 227
  and direct election of senators, 160–63

and Interstate Commerce Act, 117, 138
  and minimum wage, 142
  and redistribution, 232
  and three-party system, 44–45, 109–11, 230–32
  See also civil rights; slavery
railroads. *See* Interstate Commerce Act
Rasch model, 247–48
Reagan, John H., 122–24, 138, 144, 162, 216
Reagan, Ronald R., 3, 69
realignment. *See* party realignment
redistricting, 74–76
Redman, Eric, 263
replacement of members, 58, 77–80
reputation and stability of legislators, 84
Richardson, L. E., Jr., 272 n. 14
Riker, William H., 109, 157–62, 164, 211, 263 n. 3, 270 n. 12, 271 n. 4, 274 n. 9, 277 n. 1
Rivers, Douglas, 129–32, 138, 271 n. 1, 272 nn. 16–17, 275 n. 14
Roll, Richard, 236
roll call
  coding categories, 48, 54–55, 57, 259–62, 266 n. 20
  cutting lines and points, 24
  and liberal/conservative continuum, 4
  outcome coordinates, 24
  See also dimensionality of roll call voting
Romer, Thomas, 74, 132, 135, 149, 264 n. 6, 267 n. 27, 268 n. 17, 272 n. 14, 273 n. 29
Rosenthal, Howard, 46, 112, 117, 129, 132, 138, 149, 176–77, 208, 213–14, 223, 229, 235, 248–49, 263 n. 11, 264 nn. 6, 15, 265 nn. 4, 6, 9, 266 n. 15, 267, nn. 6–7, 9, 27, 268 n. 13, 269 nn. 4, 26, 270 n. 6, 272 nn. 9, 14, 17, 273 nn. 22, 28, 274 n. 11, 277 n. 1, 279 nn. 5, 8, 280, n. 1
Rubin, Paul, 271 n. 2
Rubinfeld, Daniel L., 272 n. 15

Sarasin, Ronald A., 150–51, 155, 273 n. 1
Scalia, Antonin, 5, 138
Schattschneider, E. E., 87
Schmitz, John G., 279 n. 9
Schwartz, Anna, 100, 105
second dimension
  content of, 48–51

second dimension (*continued*)
  correlation of House and Senate means,
    59–64
  disappearance of, 230–32
  of the 1850s, 97–99
  and interest-group ratings, 167–69
  need for, 5, 17–19, 227
  and race and slavery, 51, 67, 91–95,
    109–11, 230–32
  and region, 64, 67
  relative importance of, 53–54, 111
  and second dimension from interest-group
    unfolding, 177–79
  See also first dimension
Sen, Subrata, 223
Senate spatial maps
  7th, 36
  30th, 37
  35th, 38
  43rd, 102
  45th, 104
  62nd, 163
  83rd, 39
  95th, 21, 153
  96th, 174–75, 182
  97th, 21
  101st, 112
Shepard, Roger N., 275 n. 14
Shepsle, Kenneth A., 56, 184, 186, 200, 208,
    276 n. 8
Sherman Silver Purchase Act, 103–5
shirking, 74–75, 213, 220–21
Silberman, Jonathon, 129, 132–33, 271 n. 1
Silbey, Joel, 270 n. 7
sincere voting, 14
  See also sophisticated voting
Sinclair, Barbara, 106, 269 n. 1, 271 n. 21
slavery
  as economic issue, 266 n. 22
  in the 1830s and 1840s, 4–5
  and Era of Good Feelings, 93
  and Missouri Compromise, 94–95
  and realignment of the 1850s, 5, 95–100
  roll call votes on, 91
Smith, Steven S., 185, 269 n. 29
Snyder, James M., Jr., 8, 56, 170–71, 185–87,
    252–53, 274 n. 8, 280 n. 4
social conservative, 17
sophisticated voting, 146–47, 228
  and both ends against the middle, 155–56
  killer amendments, 152–55, 157–63

  in one dimension, 6–7, 15–17, 155–56
  saving amendments, 147–49, 153–55
  in two dimensions, 19, 157–63
Sowell, Fallaw B., 256–58
spatial model
  estimation, 22–23
  probabilistic, 20–21
  symmetric preferences, 13, 18–19
  and three-party model, 129
  utility function, 24
  with weighted dimensions, 54, 266 n. 24
  See also D-NOMINATE
Spear, Stephen, 256–58, 275 n. 14
Specter, Arlen, 227
stability of legislator positions. *See* first
    dimension
Stewart, Charles, III, 59, 270 n. 16
Stone, Walter J., 269 n. 29
Stowe, Harriet Beecher, 95
strategic voting. *See* sophisticated voting
strip mining, 115, 133–35
Sundquist, James L., 87–88, 100, 269 n. 1
Supreme Court nominations, 5
Surface Mining Control and Reclamation
    Act. *See* strip mining
Sutherland, George, 162, 274 nn. 9–10

Taft-Hartley Act, 140
three-party system. *See* party systems
Torgerson, W. S., 243, 280 n. 4
Tower, John, 12, 129–30, 138
Truman, Harry S., 140
turnout. *See* abstention
Tversky, Amos, 212

unfolding, 170–71, 176–79
Unger, Irwin, 101

Van Doren, Peter, 8, 56
Van Horn, C., 269 n. 29
vetoes, 3, 103, 111, 140, 179–81, 272 n. 20
vote buying. *See* logrolling

War of 1812, 38
Watergate, 68
Webster, Daniel, 266 n. 21
Weingast, Barry R., 59, 93–94, 96, 100,
    115–16, 122–23, 186, 208, 266 n. 20,
    270 n. 16, 272 nn. 11–14, 274 n. 7
Weisberg, Herbert F., 252, 266 n. 23, 269 n. 29
Weiss, Roger, 100

White, Halbert, 122
White, Hugh L., 266 n. 21
Williams, Harrison, 139
Wilmot, David, 160–61, 164, 266 n. 20
Wilson, Pete, 165–66
W-NOMINATE, 26, 249–51
    fit in 15 dimensions, 52
    and interest-group scalings, 177–82
    See also D-NOMINATE

women in Congress, 231–32
Wright, B. D., 248

Young, Gale, 236
Young, Roland, 271 n. 20

Zeigler, L. Harmon, 231
Zupan, Mark A., 115–16, 133–35, 233, 273
    nn. 23, 25, 274 n. 7